Green & Sustainable Finance
From vision to market practice

綠色及可持續金融
從願景到市場實踐

VOLUME 1

上冊

Edited by HKEX

香港交易所　主編

商務印書館
THE COMMERCIAL PRESS

Green & Sustainable Finance: From vision to market practice (Volume 1)

Executive editor: Chris CHEUNG

Publisher: The Commercial Press (H.K) Ltd.,
                    8/F, Eastern Central Plaza, 3 Yiu Hing Road,
                    Shau Kei Wan, Hong Kong

Distributor: The SUP Publishing Logistics (H.K.) Ltd.,
                    16/F, Tsuen Wan Industrial Building,
                    220-248 Texaco Road, Tsuen Wan, New Territories, Hong Kong

Printer: Elegance Printing and Book Binding Co. Ltd.
                    Block A, 4th Floor, Hoi Bun Building
                    6 Wing Yip Street, Kwun Tong, Kowloon, Hong Kong

© 2022 Hong Kong Exchanges and Clearing Limited
First edition, First printing, February 2022

ISBN: 978 962 07 6678 7
Printed in Hong Kong

綠色及可持續金融：從願景到市場實踐（上冊）

責任編輯：張宇程

出　　版：商務印書館（香港）有限公司
　　　　　香港筲箕灣耀興道 3 號東滙廣場 8 樓
　　　　　http://www.commercialpress.com.hk

發　　行：香港聯合書刊物流有限公司
　　　　　香港新界荃灣德士古道 220-248 號荃灣工業中心 16 樓

印　　刷：美雅印刷製本有限公司
　　　　　九龍觀塘榮業街 6 號海濱工業大廈 4 樓 A 室

版　　次：2022 年 2 月第 1 版第 1 次印刷
　　　　　© 2022 香港交易及結算所有限公司

　　　　　ISBN 978 962 07 6678 7
　　　　　香港印刷

Contents

Volume 1

1   Current landscape and prospects: Global, Asia and China

目錄

2   Market practice and infrastructure

2　市場實踐與基礎設施

Risk statements and disclaimer

Risks of securities trading

Trading in securities carries risks. The prices of securities fluctuate, sometimes dramatically. The price of a security may move up or down, and may become valueless. It is as likely that losses will be incurred rather than profit made as a result of buying and selling securities.

Risks of trading futures and options

Futures and options involve a high degree of risk. Losses from futures and options trading can exceed initial margin funds and investors may be required to pay additional margin funds on short notice. Failure to do so may result in the position being liquidated and the investor being liable for any resulting deficit. Investors must therefore understand the risks of trading in futures and options and should assess whether they are suitable for them. Investors are encouraged to consult a broker or financial adviser on their suitability for futures and options trading in light of their financial position and investment objectives before trading.

Disclaimer

All information and views contained in this book are for informational purposes only and do not constitute an offer, solicitation, invitation or recommendation to buy or sell any securities, futures contracts or other products or to provide any advice or service of any kind. The views expressed in this book do not necessarily represent the position of Hong Kong Exchanges and Clearing Limited ("HKEX") or the other institutions to which the authors of this book belong ("Relevant Institutions"). Nothing in this book constitutes or should be regarded as investment or professional advice. While information contained in this book is obtained or compiled from sources believed to be reliable, the authors of this book, HKEX, the Relevant Institutions or any of HKEX's or the Relevant Institutions' subsidiaries, directors or employees will neither guarantee its accuracy, timeliness or completeness for any particular purpose, nor be responsible for any loss or damage arising from the use of, or reliance upon, any information contained in this book.

風險與免責聲明

買賣證券的風險

證券買賣涉及風險。證券價格有時可能會非常波動。證券價格可升可跌，甚至變成毫無價值。買賣證券未必一定能夠賺取利潤，反而可能會招致損失。

買賣期貨及期權的風險

期貨及期權涉及高風險，買賣期貨及期權所招致的損失有可能超過開倉時繳付的按金，令投資者或須在短時間內繳付額外按金。若未能繳付，投資者的持倉或須平倉，任何虧損概要自行承擔。因此，投資者務須清楚明白買賣期貨及期權的風險，並衡量是否適合自己。投資者進行交易前，宜根據本身財務狀況及投資目標，向經紀或財務顧問查詢是否適合買賣期貨及期權合約。

免責聲明

本書所載資料及分析只屬資訊性質，概不構成要約、招攬、邀請或推薦買賣任何證券、期貨合約或其他產品，亦不構成提供任何形式的建議或服務。書中表達的意見不一定代表香港交易及結算所有限公司（「香港交易所」）或本書其他作者所屬的機構（「有關機構」）的立場。書中內容概不構成亦不得被視為投資或專業建議。儘管本書所載資料均取自認為是可靠的來源或按當中內容編備而成，但本書各作者、香港交易所和有關機構及其各自的附屬公司、董事及僱員概不就有關資料（就任何特定目的而言）的準確性、適時性或完整性作任何保證。本書各作者、香港交易所和有關機構及其各自的附屬公司、董事及僱員對使用或依賴本書所載的任何資料而引致任何損失或損害概不負責。

Green and sustainable finance: Evolving and mainstreaming

Hurricanes, floods, droughts, bushfires… the increasing frequency of extreme weather events around the world points to the devastating effects of the climate crisis and the need for immediate global action.

In recent years, global and regional leaders have made commitments to tackle climate change. Asia's three biggest economies, China, Japan and Korea, which together emit around one third of all global carbon emissions (according to 2018 data compiled by the International Energy Agency), have made some brave carbon neutrality commitments. In late 2020, Chinese President Xi Jinping said the country aims to peak carbon emissions before 2030 and achieve carbon neutrality before 2060. The Hong Kong Special Administrative Region (HKSAR) government has also committed to carbon neutrality by 2050. And many other nations, though not all, have made similar pledges.

As the global community works towards achieving the goals set out in the Paris Agreement and the United Nations Sustainable Development Goals, capital markets have a key role to play in the smooth transition to a low-carbon, climate resilient economy.

Such a transition requires huge investment — USD 90 trillion by 2030 according to the United Nations. It also requires an ever-innovative financial system, a robust ecosystem of Green and Sustainable Finance (GSF) products and services, and a supportive regulatory environment.

The business case for sustainable business practices, and sustainable finance, is becoming stronger day by day. Today, an increasing number of investors are factoring in environment, social and governance (ESG) considerations, driving the growth of ESG investment and providing funds for sustainable development. The number of signatories to the United Nations-supported Principles for Responsible Investment (PRI) increased from 1,295 institutions in 2016 to 3,513 institutions in 2020, while assets under management increased from USD 86.3 trillion to USD 103.4 trillion.

Many sustainable and green investments have a long-term horizon, and their objectives and revenue structures may be different from those in the traditional economy. To facilitate the growth of GSF we need to promote knowledge sharing, develop a robust product ecosystem, and establish frameworks and standards for market practices.

As the locus of financial market infrastructure, exchanges play an important role in supporting the formation and development of GSF. Hong Kong Exchanges and Clearing Limited (HKEX) functions to promote product innovation, information disclosure, and market liquidity, as well as connecting companies with investors and other stakeholders.

The development of GSF and ESG investment is uneven across global markets. Demand for sustainable investment is skewed, with Europe accounting for 34%-53% of the global total during 2016 to 2020, according to the Global Sustainable Investment Alliance. The world's first green bond was issued in Europe in 2007, but there was not a comprehensive policy framework for green bonds until 2019.

In Asia, the sustainable finance journey is still in its early days. Countries such as China have been driving regional change with strong commitments and innovative solutions. The People's Bank of China estimated that the infrastructure investment required could reach RMB 100 trillion to RMB 200 trillion by 2060. To support these targets, China adopted a top-down approach and was the first economy in the world to develop a comprehensive policy framework for green finance, launched in 2016.

Turning to Hong Kong as an example: As one of the world's leading international financial centres, Hong Kong is strongly positioned to lead Asia's sustainable finance transition. Hong Kong is now the largest asset management market in the region, the largest offshore liquidity pool for Renminbi in the world, and one of the largest capital raising centres in the world. With its world-class business infrastructure, sound regulatory environment, diversified pools of capital, liquidity, investors, financial products, and professional expertise, the Hong Kong market's role as a super-connector between China and the rest of the world will allow it to play a leading role in Asia's, and the globe's, green finance transition.

Following the announcement by the HKSAR government of its carbon-neutrality target, the Cross-Agency Steering Group for Green and Sustainable Finance was established to support these developments. The government had also previously announced a HKD 100 billion green bond programme in 2019, one of the world's largest government issuance schemes.

Looking more broadly, sustainable finance is a key strategic priority in the Guangdong-Hong Kong-Macao Greater Bay Area (GBA), with Hong Kong functioning as its international green finance hub. With a population of 86 million, the GBA region represents a new economic powerhouse with a key role to play in GSF. In September 2020, the HKSAR government joined forces with other GBA governments to form the Guangdong-Hong Kong-Macao Greater Bay Area Green Finance Alliance, with the aim to promote research and incubate green investments that will benefit the region.

As a regulator, market operator, and a corporate, HKEX has a critical role to play in the global sustainability journey. The HKEX Group's responsibility as a regional change agent is notable: providing the framework, guidance, transparency and access to resources for the long-term development of a robust sustainable finance ecosystem.

As a regulator with oversight for over 2,500 listed issuers, HKEX supports a framework and guidance for ESG disclosure, application and implementation, through listing rules and market education. As a market operator, the organisation promotes transparency, access to resources, and growth opportunities for issuers and investors, and supports a range of sustainable finance products. HKEX is also a passionate global advocate for GSF, driving market dialogue and policy change to position Hong Kong as a sustainability leader.

As a listed company, HKEX is committed to leading by example as a corporate champion in sustainability. As part of our commitment to accelerating the transition to a net-zero global economy, HKEX has recently joined the Glasgow Financial Alliance for Net Zero (GFANZ) and the Net Zero Financial Service Provider Alliance.

The development of global green finance has come a long way, but there is still much work to be done. Current challenges include the lack of universal classification standards; the availability and quality of ESG data; the diverse business practices of product labelling and potential misconduct such as greenwashing; and the limited spectrum of ESG investment products and risk management tools. HKEX encourages all stakeholders to work together to resolve these challenges for the development of GSF and ESG in the long run.

HKEX has prepared this book to bring together some of the world's leading institutions and experts in the field of GSF, and to introduce a selection of the latest market innovations and practices. We hope that this book will help all market participants, including issuers and investors, to better understand GSF and ESG investment, and implement them more extensively.

BA Shusong
Chief China Economist
Hong Kong Exchanges and Clearing Limited

November 2021

綠色及可持續金融：
不斷演變、漸成主流

颶風、洪水、旱災、山火等極端天氣事件頻頻在全球各地發生，氣候危機的破壞性影響有目共睹，全球採取應對行動實在刻不容緩。

近年來，全球及區內領導人紛紛就應對氣候變化作出承諾。亞洲三大經濟體 —— 中國、日本及韓國 —— 均已果斷作出多項致力達致碳中和的承諾（根據國際能源署編製的 2018 年數據，三國合共佔全球碳排放總量約三分之一）。於 2020 年年底，中國國家主席習近平表示，中國將力爭於 2030 年前實現碳達峰，於 2060 年前實現碳中和。香港特別行政區（香港特區）政府亦承諾於 2050 年前實現碳中和。許多其他（雖非所有）國家亦先後響應支持，相繼作出類似承諾。

隨着全球各國均致力實現《巴黎協定》所訂的目標及《聯合國可持續發展目標》，資本市場對促進經濟順利向低碳、靈活應對氣候變化的模式轉型，亦扮演着重要角色。

這個經濟轉型需要巨額投資 —— 根據聯合國資料，於 2030 年前這方面須耗資 90 萬億美元。這轉型亦需要一個不斷創新的金融體系、蓬勃的綠色及可持續金融產品及服務生態圈，以及相關監管環境的推動支持。

同時，可持續營商實踐與可持續金融對企業的發展亦越見重要。如今，越來越多投資者在作出投資決定前都會考慮環境、社會及管治（Environment、Social、Governance，簡稱 ESG）方面的因素，推動了 ESG 投資的增長，並為可持續發展提供了資金。聯合國支持的《責任投資原則》的簽署機構數目已由 2016 年的 1,295 家增加至 2020 年的 3,513 家，而其管理的資產總值亦由 86.3 萬億美元增加至 103.4 萬億美元。

許多可持續及綠色投資都具有長遠視野，其目標及收益結構可能有別於傳統經濟。為促進綠色及可持續金融的發展，我們需要推廣知識共享、建立強大的產品生態圈，以及制定有關市場常規的框架及標準。

作為金融市場基建的核心，一眾交易所在支持綠色及可持續金融的創設與發展方面發揮着重要作用。香港交易及結算所有限公司（「香港交易所」）亦一直致力促進產品創新、提升信息披露及市場流動性，並充當上市公司與投資者及其他持份者之間的橋樑。

環顧全球，國際市場在發展綠色及可持續金融與 ESG 投資方面的步伐並不一致，各國對可持續投資的需求各有不同。根據全球可持續投資聯盟的數據，歐洲於 2016 年至 2020 年期間佔全球可持續投資總值的 34% 至 53%；2007 年全球首隻綠色債券亦是於歐洲發行，但直至 2019 年才見其有針對綠色債券的全面政策框架。

在亞洲，可持續金融仍處於初步發展階段。包括中國在內等多個國家一直透過堅定承諾及創新解決方案推動區內變革。據中國人民銀行估計，到 2060 年，可持續金融所需投入的基建投資將會達人民幣 100 萬億元至 200 萬億元。中國採取了自上而下的方式實踐可持續發展的目標，於 2016 年推出全面的綠色金融政策框架，亦成為了全球首個制定相關政策框架的經濟體。

以香港為例：香港作為全球領先的國際金融中心之一，在引領亞洲進行可持續金融轉型負起舉足輕重的責任。香港現為區內最大的資產管理市場、擁有全球最大的離岸人民幣資金池，以及是全球最大的集資中心之一。憑藉其世界一流的商業基礎設施、完善的監管環境、多元化的資本供應、流動性、投資者、金融產品及專業人才，香港市場能作為超級連繫人，緊密連接中國與世界各地，帶領亞洲以至全球進行綠色金融轉型。

在香港特區政府公佈其碳中和目標後，「綠色和可持續金融跨機構督導小組」正式成立，以支持相關發展。香港特區政府早於 2019 年已公佈一項涉及 1,000 億港元的綠色債券計劃，是全球最大的政府發行計劃之一。

宏觀來看，可持續金融是粵港澳大灣區的關鍵戰略重點，當中香港肩負國際綠色金融樞紐的角色。粵港澳大灣區人口達 8,600 萬，具備龐大的經濟發展潛力，並有能力在推動綠色及可持續金融發展方面發揮重要角色。2020 年 9 月，香港特區政府與其他大灣區政府攜手成立「粵港澳大灣區綠色金融聯盟」，旨在推動研究及培育有利區內發展的綠色投資。

作為同時是監管者及市場營運機構的一家企業，香港交易所在全球可持續發展進程中任重道遠。香港交易所集團對推動區內變革也起着顯著作用：為長遠發展穩健的可持續金融生態圈提供框架、指引、透明度及資源渠道。

作為逾 2,500 家上市發行人的前線監管者，香港交易所一直透過《上市規則》及市場教育，為 ESG 的信息披露、應用及實施提供框架及指引。作為市場營運機構，香港交易所為發行人及投資者提供透明度、資源渠道及增長機會，並支持推出一系列可持續金融產品。除此之外，香港交易所亦積極向全球推廣綠色及可持續金融，推動市場對話及政策改變，將香港定位為可持續發展的領導者。

作為上市公司，香港交易所致力以身作則，作為可持續發展的企業模範。為表我們對推動全球向淨零經濟轉型的決心，我們最近更加入了「格拉斯哥淨零金融聯盟」（Glasgow Financial Alliance for Net Zero）及「淨零金融服務提供者聯盟」（Net Zero Financial Services Provider Alliance）。

全球綠色金融發展雖有長足進展，但仍要在多方面繼續努力，凝聚更多力量以取得成績。當前的挑戰包括缺乏統一分類標準；ESG 數據不齊備及質量參差；產品標籤的商業常規迥異及潛在不當行為（如漂綠）；ESG 投資產品以及風險管理工具不夠多元廣泛。香港交易所鼓勵所有持份者共同努力，齊心克服這些挑戰，令綠色及可持續金融與 ESG 的發展走得更前、走得更遠。

本書由香港交易所編製，集合綠色及可持續金融領域內的一些全球領先機構與專家的真知灼見，同時介紹了一些最新的市場創新及慣例。希望本書能有助所有市場參與者，包括發行人和投資者，更深入了解並全面實踐綠色及可持續金融與 ESG 投資。

巴曙松
香港交易所　首席中國經濟學家

2021 年 11 月

1

Current landscape and prospects: Global, Asia and China

當前格局與前景：
全球、亞洲與中國

Chapter 1

The sustainable finance and investment ecosystem

Vivek PATHAK
Director, Climate Business,
International Finance Corporation

Summary

At the time of writing, the COVID-19 pandemic continues to proliferate, with devastating consequences on people, businesses, and markets, especially in the poorest countries. While unprecedented interventions and stimulus packages have been deployed to stem the worst effects of the pandemic, we cannot ignore the looming catastrophe that demands a more aggressive and collaborative global response: climate change. A crisis with multi-trillion-dollar consequences, climate change is a systemic risk that is impacting the finance industry, as it is for all sectors of the global economy. Financial institutions have to manage the physical and transitional risks that stem from our changing climate. These risks will impact the real economy and asset value, creating financial instability unless investors and financial institutions manage these risks by shifting their portfolios to a low-carbon path. Unlike COVID-19, there is no vaccine for climate change. The world needs to act by rebuilding economies, particularly those in emerging markets, to be more sustainable and resilient and by putting green and sustainable finance at the heart of the response.

To build a safer, more equitable low-carbon future, investors and companies need to allocate proceeds into assets and activities that deliver sustainable and measurable outcomes. Banks and financial institutions must allocate capital and direct financial flows towards low carbon, climate resilient investments and to create tools to put climate change risk into the heart of global markets. Governments and regulators need to implement frameworks, taxonomies, and policies that provide green and sustainable finance with longevity, transparency, and certainty. For emerging markets, that will experience widely divergent recovery paths in the wake of COVID-19, green and sustainable finance can play a critical role in prioritising large-scale public investment in green sectors and promoting private sector investment through supportive policies. This first chapter examines the nascent and ever-evolving global sustainable finance development ecosystem and what financial institutions, governments and regulators can do to help investors and companies transition to a more sustainable future. It examines the forces driving the green and sustainable finance market, the key components required for sustainable finance to grow and thrive, and the role that key market participants play. It concludes with an assessment of green and sustainable market practices in Asia and what is needed to further scale up investments there.

The big picture: What are the forces driving green and sustainable finance?

In 2015, in a ground-breaking speech to Lloyd's of London[1], Mark Carney, the then Governor of the Bank of England warned that climate change presented a major risk to the global economy and global financial stability, and that businesses and regulators needed to act immediately to stem the potential economic damage. Calling it the "tragedy of the horizon", Carney cautioned that climate change would lead to catastrophic financial crises and falling living standards unless the world's leading countries did more to ensure that their companies rectified current and future carbon emissions. This warning from one of the world's most powerful central bankers, landing with force in boardrooms around the globe, was indicative of how the discussion of climate change within the financial world had moved beyond the theoretical to the specific. "…Once climate change becomes a defining issue for financial stability," Carney said, "it may already be too late."

In the nearly six years since Carney issued this stark warning, green and sustainable finance (GSF) has become more prominent in the global policy agenda. Spurred by the Paris Agreement, a number of regions and countries around the world, including China, Europe, Canada, South Africa, Colombia and Chile, have introduced regulatory sustainable finance frameworks, taxonomies, and action plans. Taking a page out of Carney's book, other financial titans have broken their silence to publicly voice their concerns about the threat of climate change to financial stability. In 2020, Laurence D. Fink, chief executive officer of BlackRock, arguably the world's most powerful investor, issued a letter[2] warning that the world is "on the edge of a fundamental reshaping of finance", and that climate change would be a defining factor in the long-term prospects of companies around the globe. That same year, in its 15th Global Risks Report[3], the World Economic Forum (WEF) declared that for the first time in the report's history, all of the top long-term risks were related to the environment.

Since the first green bond was issued by the World Bank in November 2008, followed by the emergence of the first benchmark sized green bonds issued by the International

---

1   "Breaking the tragedy of the horizon — climate change and financial stability — speech by Mark Carney", speech given at Lloyd's of London, published on the website of Bank of England, 29 September 2015.
2   "A fundamental reshaping of finance", Larry Fink's 2020 letter to CEOs, published on the website of BlackRock, 14 January 2020.
3   World Economic Forum, *The Global Risks Report 2020*, published on WEF's website, 15 January 2020.

Finance Corporation (IFC) in 2013, GSF has accelerated exponentially. The introduction of the Green Bond Principles by the International Capital Market Association (ICMA) in 2014 — a set of guidelines for the issuance and reporting of green bonds globally — have helped boost the integrity, credibility, and growth of the market. A game changer instrument in green finance, green bonds have mainstreamed the market and dramatically increased the flow of capital to green projects. Green bonds continue to be the instrument of choice for lenders with eligible green projects to seek financing through both domestic and offshore investors. For issuers, distributing a green bond sends an honourable signal and may attract a wider pool of lenders than regular bonds as they lead to improved company-level environmental footprints and financial performance. Green bonds have undeniably shaped investor behaviour, evolving capital markets from ones where investors knew little about what their investments were supporting to new markets where purpose and conscience matters more than ever. In 2020, despite the turbulence and disruption of COVID-19, green bond issuance rebounded in the second half of the year to reach a record-breaking US$269.5 billion[4]. Emerging market countries have also seen a steady rise in green bond issuance — from US$1 billion in 2012 to US$52 billion in 2019[5]. With a sixty-percent average annual growth since 2015, the green bond market surpassed a cumulative US$1 trillion milestone at the end of 2020, cementing the instrument as the dominant driving force of the GSF market[6].

Additional forces shaping the GSF market include a series of frameworks calling for greater transparency about how companies manage their risk and adapt to the future. These proposals and initiatives by investors, governments and regulators are helping businesses to "future proof" their bottom line and prepare for climate risks that may "strand" high-emitting assets such as coal, oil and gas reserves in the ground that will remain unrecoverable. Leading this regulatory push is the Task Force on Climate-Related Financial Disclosures (TCFD), established in 2015 by the Financial Stability Board (FSB) and Mark Carney, just weeks after he delivered his "tragedy of the horizons" speech. The TCFD structures its recommendations around four thematic areas under which companies operate: governance, strategy, risk management, and metrics and targets. It requires companies to undergo "scenario analysis", in which material climate risks are analysed. TCFD reporting aims to help investors better understand the climate risk in their

---

4   Source: "Record $269.5bn green issuance for 2020: Late surge sees pandemic year pip 2019 total by $3bn", published on the website of Climate Bonds Initiative (CBI), 24 January 2021.

5   Source: Cashion, P. and P. Stein (IFC), "Debt capital markets: Helping lenders scale climate finance in emerging markets", published on CBI's website.

6   Source: "Record $269.5bn green issuance for 2020: Late surge sees pandemic year pip 2019 total by $3bn", published on CBI's website, 24 January 2021.

portfolios and to help move money from high-carbon investments to more climate-resilient companies that are transitioning to a net-zero (emissions) path.

The influence of the TCFD has been far reaching in a short period of time. In February 2019, the United Nations (UN)-supported Principles for Responsible Investment (PRI), announced that it was requiring its entire base of 2,250 signatories — including asset owners, investment managers and service providers who collectively represent approximately US$100 trillion in assets[7] — to report against TCFD indicators about climate change risks in their portfolios. The European Union (EU) non-financial reporting directive, which lays down the rules on the disclosure of non-financial and diversity information by large companies, is also closely modelled on the TCFD. In March 2021, the main financial regulator in the United States (US), the Securities and Exchange Commission, took a leaf out of the TCFD handbook by announcing the establishment of its own task force to examine environmental, social and governance (ESG) issues, and to examine more closely climate-related disclosures for listed firms[8]. Regulators in Britain, New Zealand and Switzerland have also announced their intention to implement mandatory climate risk reporting in line with the TCFD recommendations.

The Network for Greening the Financial System (NGFS), a group of 54 central banks and supervisors, collates guidelines and recommendations for regulators and disseminates scenarios to help analyse potential losses to the financial system[9]. The People's Bank of China (PBOC), China's central bank, and the Monetary Authority of Singapore (MAS) were both instrumental in helping establish the NGFS. In October 2019, the NGFS issued guidance for central banks on how to integrate sustainability factors into the management of their own portfolios[10]. The NGFS has recommended the establishment of an agreed environmental taxonomy for financial assets, where internationally accepted standards would rate how environmentally friendly or not various assets were.

The Climate Action 100+ is a group of institutional investors, including BlackRock, with over US$54 trillion in assets[11] who agree to set emissions-reduction targets and to push

---

7   Source: "TCFD-based reporting to become mandatory for PRI signatories in 2020", press release on the *PRI* website, 18 February 2019.

8   Source: "Regulators want firms to own up to climate risks", *The Economist*, 13 March 2021.

9   Source: "Green initiative: Network for greening the financial system", published on the website of the Central Banking Institute, 4 February 2020.

10 Source: *A Sustainable and Responsible Investment Guide for Central Banks' Portfolio Management*, published on the NGFS website, October 2019.

11 Source: "Climate Action 100+ issues its first-ever net zero company benchmark of the world's largest corporate emitters", press release on the *Climate Action 100+* website, 22 March 2021.

for greater disclosure on climate risks. In March 2021, the group released a benchmark analysis which assesses the performance of focus companies against the benchmark's three goals: emissions reduction, governance, and disclosure[12]. The benchmark evaluates corporate ambition and action and may be the first step to increase capital cost for carbon intensive companies if they fail to decarbonise. The Transition Pathway Initiative (TPI), a global, asset-owner led initiative, uses company-disclosed data to provide a sector-level analysis of companies' management of their carbon emissions and alignment with the Paris Agreement. In addition, net-zero commitments by investors, cities, and regions as part of the Race to Zero Dialogues, a global campaign mobilising a coalition of leading "real economy" actors, now covers more than half of the world's gross domestic product (GDP).

Sustainable finance is the future of finance

While green bonds sparked the growth of the green finance ecosystem and remain the markets' most mature instruments, there is more to sustainable finance than just green bonds. In recent years, a wide range of innovative financial solutions have rapidly developed, broadening the understanding of GSF. They include, among others, green loans, sustainability bonds, social bonds and, more recently, sustainability-linked bonds and loans. This diverse toolbox of new instruments is testament to the vast increase in market demand for sustainable finance. As companies increasingly look to align their funding strategies with their climate and sustainability targets, these instruments share the common goal to attract investors, balance credibility and avoid greenwashing.

In 2017, the Dutch bank ING issued an €1 billion loan to the health technology company Philips, the world's first ever loan tied to a company's sustainability performance and rating[13]. A landmark facility, the transaction inspired the creation of the *Sustainability-Linked Loan Principles* issued by the Loan Market Association (LMA). The sustainability-linked bond, a sibling to sustainability-linked loans, is one of the more sophisticated new structures in this group of new financial instruments. Unlike the green bond, these general-purpose bonds tie interest payments to the achievement of a target, holding the issuer responsible to its promised performance. In 2019, the Italian electricity giant, Enel issued a US$1.5 billion sustainability-linked bond linked to an increasing share of

---

12 Ditto.
13 Source: "ING and Philips collaborate on sustainable loan", press release on the ING's website, 19 April 2017.

renewables in its generation capacity[14]. It reflects an increasing awareness of issuer's overall sustainability strategy and performance, and the fact that investors are not only looking for green or sustainable projects — they are increasingly looking for sustainable companies.

Despite the success of these new financial instruments in redirecting capital to sustainable projects and companies, green finance alone will not help us reach the targets of the Paris Agreement. More is needed, especially to help carbon-intensive industries such as the cement, chemicals, steel, and heavy transport sectors to reach net-zero targets. That is why increasing focus is turning to "climate transition finance" to implement corporate decarbonisation strategies and/or use of proceeds to finance projects that help the issuer reduce its carbon footprint. Investments include greenfield gas power plants displacing coal, cogeneration plants, carbon capture and storage, waste-to-energy, gas-powered shipping, alternative fuels for aircraft, and energy efficiency investments. For carbon-intensive companies, a failure to meet future carbon requirements will likely increase their operating and financial costs, have a negative impact on their bottom line and, in the worst case, cancel their licence to operate.

Although global issuances still remain very small, climate transition bonds are generating excitement for those ambitious enough to "walk the extra mile" towards decarbonisation. Climate transition finance — which requires issuers to commit to a net-zero pathway in line with the goals of the Paris Agreement — help fills a critical market gap for companies who are hesitant about the perceived reputational risk of issuing green bonds to a not-so-green market participant. Expanding the market will take time but recent advancements and frameworks suggest that climate transition bonds may play a pivotal role in the green finance mainstream for companies and asset managers alike. In December 2020, the ICMA published guidance for issuers seeking to utilise green bonds, sustainability bonds or sustainability-linked bonds towards their climate transition strategy. This *Climate Transition Finance Handbook* sets the standard for use-of-proceeds products (i.e. products where the proceeds are designated to be used for green and sustainability development) which can opt for an add-on "transition" label[15]. Such climate transition labels apply to use-of-proceeds finance like green loans and bonds and to sustainability-linked finance, and can help reallocate investment to green projects and to decarbonisation strategies. Long-term institutional investors can use the Climate Transition strategy to rebalance their

---

14 Source: "Enel ditches green bonds for controversial new format", *Reuters*, 4 October 2019.
15 Source: "ICMA publishes transition bond guidelines", published on the website of Nordic Sustainable Investments, 17 December 2020.

portfolios and to redistribute capital to decarbonisation investments. In January 2021, the Hong Kong branch of the Bank of China issued the world's first ever transition bond raised under the guidelines in the ICMA *Climate Transition Finance Handbook*[16]. While the proceeds of the bond will be used to finance eligible transition projects, some experts have questioned the credibility and ambition of the transaction noting that gas projects have been included in the offering.

While there is no one clear solution for companies who wish to identify a decarbonisation transition pathway, the *Climate Transition Finance Handbook* recommends that issuers follow appropriate benchmark and sector-specific decarbonisation trajectories as part of a credible transition process. It further recommends that issuers align their business plans to a Paris Agreement-aligned trajectory. In addition, there are some market initiatives including free-to-use and commercially available tools to make it easier for issuers to explore climate scenario analysis. Among them, the Paris Agreement Capital Transition Assessment (PACTA) tool aims to develop pathways for industries at the company level, using asset-level data to provide portfolio-level analysis of transition risk in public equities and corporate bonds. In October 2020, the Science Based Targets initiative (SBTi), a joint initiative between Carbon Disclosure Project (CDP), the UN Global Compact (UNGC), the World Resources Institute (WRI) and the World Wide Fund for Nature (WWF), launched a new framework to allow financial institutions — including banks, investors, insurance companies, pension funds and others — to set science-based targets to align their lending and investment activities with the Paris Agreement.

What more can be done to help the GSF ecosystem grow?

Across the GSF ecosystem, participants — investors, companies, issuers, regulators, system operators, intermediaries, and service providers — play diverse, competing and, at times, complementary roles. While GSF remains a nascent space, it is fast-changing and dynamic, requiring nimble and flexible approaches from those within the ecosystem in order for it to succeed. But while investor and customer demand remain a key driver of change in the GSF space, more regulatory initiatives are needed to help investors,

---

16 Source: "Bank of China plans to announce its first transitions bonds transaction in offshore market", press release published on the Bank of China's website, 6 January 2021.

companies and financial institutions transition to net-zero targets, particularly in terms of enhanced frameworks, disclosure, transparency, and reporting. So is building market capacity by enabling issuers to become more ambitious in their sustainable commitments, and by encouraging investors to push issuers into more robust decarbonisation trajectories if they believe they are not ambitious enough. Such momentum will undoubtedly drive the direction of the GSF ecosystem into a more committed net-zero path; holding companies and issuers alike accountable to their new trajectories and making it harder for them to return to the market with a non-sustainable bond.

Around the world, governments have a critical role to play in nudging the global economy in the right direction through green finance incentives, strategies, and regulations. The Grantham Research Institute at the London School of Economics has, by early 2021, tallied over 2,200 pieces of climate policies and legislation around the world, with almost two-thirds passed in the last ten years alone[17]. In order to usher the world towards a net-zero financial trajectory, government direction is key. As we have already seen through initiatives like the TCFD, regulatory guidance and frameworks help the broader financial system understand the issues that matter to governments, which is then reflected in private sector policy and investment decisions. Multi-lateral development banks have seen this scenario play out across emerging markets where the private sector, in particular financial institutions, listen very carefully to what regulators are looking for. Certain initiatives, such as the Sustainable Banking Network (SBN) — a unique, voluntary community of financial sector regulatory agencies and banking associations from emerging markets committed to advancing sustainable finance in line with international good practice — are advancing regulatory green finance best practice in markets where it is needed most. Of 11 low-income countries (IDA-eligible countries[18]) within the network, four — namely, Bangladesh, Kenya, Mongolia and Nigeria — are in the advanced stage of their sustainable finance journeys having introduced national policies or industry frameworks to promote sustainable finance and to encourage behaviour change by financial institutions[19].

Although governments are there to prod the economy in the right direction, they must also provide the private and financial sectors with the right green finance tools. One of the biggest hurdles to wider growth has been the lack of a consistent approach to defining what constitutes "green". Issuers and investors must rely on definitions that are robust and

---

17 Source: "Climate change laws of the world", webpage on the website of the Grantham Research Institute on Climate Change and the Environment, viewed on 13 May 2021.

18 International Development Association (IDA)-eligible countries are those with low per capita incomes that lack the financial ability to borrow from the International Bank for Reconstruction and Development (IBRD).

19 Source: SBN, "Overview May 2021", published on the IFC's website, May 2021.

practical, and that is where taxonomies can fill the void. Taxonomies are critical guidance "cheat sheets" to help issuers, investors and financial institutions understand exactly what it is they are trying to achieve in the green finance space. They provide market clarity on eligible green assets and their metrics and thresholds, and provide confidence and assurance to investors. A number of jurisdictions around the world have implemented legislation to create official definitions of sustainable finance. In China, the China Banking and Insurance Regulatory Commission (CBIRC) has been guiding Chinese banks for over a decade in the development of green financial instruments and unified definitions of green assets. In May 2020, the PBOC, the National Development and Reform Commission and the Mainland securities watchdog jointly issued for consultation a draft new version of the *Green Bonds Endorsed Project Catalogue* to move China one step closer to a single green finance taxonomy, the final version of which was released in April 2021. Although there were previously different sets of taxonomies in China's green bond market, the new guidelines stipulate that from now on there will only be one official green bond taxonomy. In addition, the new list of eligible investments no longer includes the financing of clean coal projects, a new bar reflecting the influence of other global regulators.

While appropriately designed green finance taxonomies can bring benefits, their success hinges on the existence and quality of robust sustainable finance standards, reporting, transparency, and disclosure. In developing countries, capital market development, the momentum generated by existing green bond issuance, and political stability are critical elements too. Investors and issuers can strengthen the integrity of GSF by adhering to the various standards on the market. *Green Loan Principles* issued by the LMA, of which IFC is a signatory, provides a high-level framework of market standards, guidelines, and a consistent methodology for use across the green loan market. The *Green Bond Principles*, issued by the ICMA, act as a guide to issuers of the key components for specific environmentally sustainable activities.

Prioritising disclosure to validate the quality of labelled green finance, to build market credibility and integrity, and to enable resource reallocation — a key objective of the TCFD — is essential to driving GSF growth. So is ensuring transparency and credibility, as is the role of accredited and approved third-party verifiers who can ensure that green finance investments are of the highest certification and standards. As sustainable investors become more sophisticated, and as investment models change, the need for transparency will also evolve to avoid "greenwashing" and to improve impact. Without better transparency, savvy investors could demand a higher interest rate or refuse to fund an investment entirely. Helping financial institutions and lenders to forensically examine and understand the projects in their business and climate portfolios, and to acquire the necessary expertise to identify, manage and report on their climate lending, is also critical. If banks and businesses cannot report credibly on their climate lending or investments, the sustainability of the green finance market will be in jeopardy. To date, the limited availability and quality of information related to the measurement and reporting on GSF has been a significant challenge. Realistic, clear targets — and the appropriate tools to track them — will allow investors and lenders to trust the reporting of green investments. This is harder to achieve in emerging markets, where environmental disclosures remain limited and where the positive impact from any one borrower is difficult to determine. Here, multilateral development banks have a role to play in working with the public and private sectors to provide technical assistance and also tracking tools. IFC, through the Green Bond-Technical Assistance Program (GB-TAP), is developing the *Green Finance Review Protocol* (GFRP) to help investors and other market participants perform proper analysis and decision making. This voluntary protocol provides a mechanism to make green loan information comparable and agreeable so it can be used by lenders and other market participants regardless of the particular nuances and approaches used in the green finance process. In addition, IFC's *Climate Assessment for Financial Institutions* helps banks in developing markets understand what investments constitute climate at the project level, and helps monitor the impact and volume of their climate portfolio.

Bolstering and clarifying "nationally determined contributions" (NDCs) — the decarbonisation plans that countries agree to follow under the Paris Agreement — will enable investors and businesses to understand the priorities and future of the market, including how to define a carbon transition pathway for net-zero. NDCs provide the broad roadmap for regulators, helping governments direct the real economy in making the transition to a net-zero future. They also enable investors and companies to determine the best decarbonisation strategy or trajectory to pursue. Implementing each country's NDCs requires a unique approach but one that should be underpinned by a strong regulatory framework. Many NDCs include carbon pricing, a key action that governments can take to slow global warming. Pricing carbon creates a market signal that helps reduce emissions by driving investments in clean, more efficient technologies. Analysis by the Carbon Pricing Leadership Coalition showed that putting a price on carbon neither limits economic and industrial growth, nor encourages big polluters to flee to other jurisdictions, proving that there is a way to put a price on carbon and preserve competition in the marketplace[20].

---

20 Source: Philippe Le Houérou (chief executive of IFC), "Imposing a price on carbon sends a financial signal to investors that low-carbon investments are valuable today and will be even more valuable in the future", *Thomson Reuters Foundation News*, 20 February 2020.

While investor demand is picking up and the appetite for GSF shows no sign of slowing, more is needed to help investors and companies, especially amidst heightened concerns and scrutiny about greenwashing. Given the prevailing high level of liquidity in the green market, there is a stronger demand for risk mitigation and longer-term funding, as most climate-related loans, especially in sectors like infrastructure, require longer maturities than is typically offered. As a result, access to the right tenor of financing and capital is critical. So is reducing the cost of capital by providing low-cost debt in the form of concessional and blended finance through multilateral development banks. Institutions like IFC and other development banks can provide debt at lower interest rates over a longer term and provide technical assistance. Long-term institutional investors can foster growth by protecting the value of investments, rebalancing and redistributing climate-related risks, and ensuring financial stability. Investors and companies with strong sustainability standards who exhibit good disclosure and transparency practices, are proven to significantly outperform their counterparts[21].

Green and sustainable finance in Asia: Now and the future

With many low-lying coastal cities home to tens of millions of people, many Asian societies and economies face extreme exposure to the physical risks of climate change, including typhoons, hurricanes, floods, drought, extreme precipitation, and changes to water supply. In April 2021, the global insurance giant Swiss Re issued a report stating that the effects of climate change could be expected to shave up to 14% off global economic output by 2050[22]. Economies in Asia would be hardest hit, with China at risk of losing nearly 24% of its GDP in a severe scenario. For many Asian emerging markets, already vulnerable following the economic shocks of the COVID-19 crisis and to rising global temperatures, the consequences would be far greater. If the increase in global temperature is held to two degrees Celsius (°C) — despite current trajectories that they are set to increase to 2.6°C by 2050 — Malaysia, the Philippines and Thailand would experience economic growth 20% below what they could otherwise expect by 2050, according to Swiss Re. Worst case projections modelling a 3.2°C rise by 2050, would see levels of wealth in those same countries dropping almost by half.

---

21 Source: Morningstar, *Sustainable Funds U.S. Landscape Report,* February 2021.
22 Source: "Climate change could cut world economy by $23 trillion in 2050, insurance giant warns", *The New York Times,* 22 April 2021.

Yet, a recent report by IFC analysing the economic and climate benefits of a post-COVID green recovery showed that investments in 10 key sectors across 21 emerging markets has the potential to generate US$10.2 trillion in investment opportunity, create 213 million new jobs, and reduce greenhouse gas emissions by 4 billion tonnes by 2030[23].

While Asia remains one of the most vulnerable regions to climate change, several regional economies have emerged as leaders in sustainable finance. As IFC's above report shows, some countries including China, India, Indonesia, Nigeria, and South Africa have already incorporated green measures into their COVID-19 stimulus packages, albeit a small portion of the total funding[24]. China dominates as the world's largest green finance economy with US$1.8 trillion (RMB 11 trillion) in green credit across 21 domestic banks and US$190 billion (RMB 1 trillion) in green bonds by 2020[25]. Other major green bond issuers in Asia are Hong Kong, India, Japan, and South Korea[26]. China, the leading global issuer of green bonds since 2016, recently announced plans to be carbon-neutral by 2060[27] — a policy shift that will require a tectonic transformation of the Chinese economy. South Korea's new green deal — part of a post COVID-19 recovery push — will see the close of 30 of the country's coal plants by 2034[28]. While outside of China, many Asian sustainable market economies are in their infancy, there is enormous potential to scale up green finance across the region. Critical to this growth is the need to meet developing Asia's surging energy demand which is expected to comprise two-thirds of global energy-demand growth by 2040[29].

While sustainable finance in Asia differs across the region's economic landscape, regulation has been a key driver in its success. China has been a leader in regulation by setting consecutive green financial standards and guidelines, taxonomies, incentives, and environmental information disclosure requirements. The country operates two sector-based taxonomy frameworks — the *Green Bonds Endorsed Project Catalogue* and the *Green Industries Guidance Catalogue.* In October 2020, backed by five government

23 Source: "Supporting a green post-COVID recovery can generate over $10 trillion in investment opportunities in emerging markets, says new IFC report", published on the IFC's website, 13 January 2021.
24 Source: IFC report, "Ctrl-Alt-Delete: A green reboot for emerging markets", published on IFC's website, 17 January 2021.
25 Source: "China must boost green finance to achieve carbon neutrality by 2060", published on the website of *China Dialogue*, 17 November 2020.
26 Based on data provided by the Climate Business Department of IFC, April 2021.
27 Source: "China's pledge to be carbon neutral by 2060: What it means", *New York Times,* 4 December 2020.
28 Source: "Moon vows to shut down 30 more coal plants to bring cleaner air and battle climate change", *The Korea Herald,* 8 September 2020.
29 Source: Azhgaliyeva, D. and B. Liddle. (2020) "Introduction to the special issue: Scaling up green finance in Asia", *Journal of Sustainable Finance & Investment*, Volume 10, Issue 2, pp.89-91.

agencies, China announced ambitious new investment and financing guidelines that will work to improve financial regulation to support and incentivise banks and financial institutions to develop green finance products[30]. While China has set the tone on regulation in the Mainland, other Asian markets are following suit. In May 2019, the Hong Kong Monetary Authority (HKMA) introduced three key measures to support and promote the development of green finance in Hong Kong[31]. A year later, the HKMA published a White Paper on green and sustainable financing which sets out a clear regulatory roadmap and nine guiding principles to help financial institutions implement a framework for managing the risks and opportunities brought by climate change[32]. In January 2021, the MAS, through their Green Finance Industry Taskforce (GFIT), issued a proposed taxonomy for Singapore-based financial institutions to identify activities that can be considered green or transitioning towards green[33]. The GFIT also issued a handbook on how to implement environmental risk management for asset managers, banks, and insurers[34]. In late 2020, Malaysia's central bank, Bank Negara Malaysia, circulated a discussion paper, *Climate Change and Principle-based Taxonomy,* to introduce a national taxonomy in the country in 2021[35].

While China and other developed economies across Asia have signalled to financiers the importance of integrating climate risk into the banking sector, many banks in emerging markets in the region are still not aware of the potential financial disruption caused by climate change. Given its geographical location and the probability of extreme weather events and heatwaves, Asia stands out as being potentially more exposed to physical climate risks than other parts of the world. The complexity of these climate scenarios combined with insufficient methodologies and tracking tools, make it difficult for financial institutions in emerging markets in Asia to understand climate opportunities and risks and to mainstream them into their businesses. Due to this lack of knowledge, most banks lack a strategic vision on climate business and the capacity to plan and execute a climate risk management strategy. Although many banks in Asian emerging markets are open to exploring climate finance opportunities, few are able to transform their institutions into

---

30 Source: "China outlines ambitious plan on climate investment and finance", *Regulation Asia,* 28 October 2020.
31 Source: "HKMA introduces key measures on sustainable banking and green finance", press release on the HKMA's website, 7 May 2019.
32 Source: "Cross-Agency Steering Group launches its strategic plan to strengthen Hong Kong's financial ecosystem to support a greener and more sustainable future", press release on the HKMA's website, 17 December 2020.
33 Source: "Industry taskforce proposes taxonomy and launches environmental risk management handbook to support green finance", media release on the MAS' website, 28 January 2021.
34 *Handbook on Implementing Environmental Risk Management for Asset Managers, Banks and Insurers,* published on the website of the Association of Banks in Singapore, 28 January 2021.
35 Bank Negara Malaysia (BNM), *Discussion Paper on Climate Change and Principle-based Taxonomy,* published on the BNM's website, 27 December 2019.

green banks in line with the TCFD recommendations. As the main facilitators of capital allocation in emerging markets, banks play a critical role in closing the climate finance gap. Measuring and managing their exposure to climate risks and opportunities requires best-in-class quantitative and qualitative methods and a robust strategy and governance structure. These methods also help banks move towards full disclosure.

Multilateral development banks can help bridge the gap across the financial sector in emerging markets in Asia by helping develop the methodologies, criteria, and climate risk assessment to help companies and banks assess whether their financing can be considered green. In 2020, the HKMA joined the Alliance for Green Commercial Banks, an initiative created by IFC to encourage banks across Asia to adopt strategies and targets to become greener. The alliance will bring together financial institutions, banking industry associations, research institutions, and technology providers across Asia to develop, build, and boost the capacity for green finance and promote climate investments. In April 2021, the World Bank Group (WBG) presented to their board the key elements of a Climate Change Action Plan (CCAP) to help client countries and companies integrate climate and development, maximise climate finance impact and to make progress on adaptation and mitigation[36]. To achieve these ambitious goals, the WBG will align its financing flows with the Paris Agreement goals, assessing investments in financial institutions and funds through a newly created Paris Agreement alignment methodology. To directly address the knowledge gap on climate risk and opportunities, IFC will roll out the GB-TAP in the banking sector of several emerging markets in Asia. The pilot programme aims to build and improve the capacity of client banks in climate opportunities, risk assessment and management through one-on-one advisory activities and to produce a climate risk management toolkit for financial institutions.

While overall GSF is on the rise across Asia, there are key drivers that can help scale up investment including adaptation finance, which continues to lag far behind mitigation finance. Adaptation financing, which reduces vulnerability to existing impact, is all the more critical given Asia's vulnerability to the physical risks of global warming. For financial institutions, integrating climate adaptation consideration into every project, and pricing the benefit, constitutes a major gap. Across Asia, private sector adaptation funding is low, but innovative risk management and insurance mechanisms and cost-benefit analysis can

---

36 Source: "World Bank Group president's statement on Climate Change Action Plan", statement on the World Bank's website, 2 April 2021.

scale up adaptation investments and profitability. A recent joint WBG report[37] proposes a blueprint for action to develop, finance, and implement priority adaptation and resilience investments — one driven by countries' goals and national investment plans — that can help accelerate and scale up investment to address the needs of the world's most climate vulnerable communities and economies. The public sector plays a critical role in mobilising private investment while the multilateral development banks fill an important gap as conveners and facilitators for this approach to take root.

While issuers, investors and regulators play a role in driving adaptation finance, so can companies specialising in sub-sectors such as technology providers. While some major economies in the region are leading the global markets in technologies, from electric vehicles to renewable energy, companies or private equity funds that drive technology cost solutions may play a more prominent role in the future. Take for example, the Lightsmith Group, a private equity firm that invests in technology-enabled companies that are providing climate-resilience solutions in focus areas such as water, agriculture, food, and energy. Partnering with the Asian Infrastructure Investment Bank (AIIB), the Lightsmith Group will invest in companies across Asia specialising in software, data and analytics, technology-enabled products, and technology-enabled services. Enabling financial institutions to find private companies and capital to produce and scale up the technological tools and solutions to address the risks of climate change represents an enormous growth opportunity.

Conclusion

As climate change continues unabated, and the economic impacts of global warming grow, a "business as usual" approach by financial institutions and private sector players is no longer tenable. But thanks to an increased focus on regulatory reform, enhanced transparency and disclosure, and the motivation for investors to seek out more sustainable investments, the green and sustainable finance ecosystem continues to grow and thrive. Traditional lending that targets climate-smart businesses, technologies, and financing specific climate-related improvements remains critical. Given the increasing importance of global trade flows, trade finance instruments will play a key role in the overall greening

---

37 WBG and the Global Facility for Disaster Reduction and Recovery (GFDRR), *Enabling Private Investment in Climate Adaptation and Resilience: Current Status, Barriers to Investment and Blueprint for Action*, published on the WBG's website, 4 March 2021.

needed. Governments' enabling policies, regulations, and financial support will play a key role in helping build a pipeline of investable and bankable green asset classes. Financial policies and regulations that require climate risk disclosures for banks and investors can accelerate the rebalancing of financial portfolios away from high-emitting sectors towards low-carbon assets.

As the world struggles to stem the economic devastation of the coronavirus pandemic, green finance will be critical to fuel a post-COVID green recovery. Green financial products and instruments — green bonds, green loans, municipal resilience bonds, sustainability-linked bonds, and loans that offer variable interest rates based on achieving quantifiable climate results — will help power this growth. Emerging market economies can take the lead in advancing financial market reforms and creating new markets to encourage green finance, and a number of them are already doing so. Most of the growth in these emerging markets can be found in greening existing and future energy infrastructure, building climate-smart cities, and helping speed the transition of key industries to green production practices. Concerted, committed and sincere actions by public and private players across these areas can deliver economic recovery in the short term and deliver long-term sustainable and low-carbon growth.

The human health and economic costs of the COVID-19 pandemic continue to be tragically high. But the crisis has also provided an unprecedented opportunity to change course and to nurture a GSF ecosystem that is more resilient in the face of future shocks such as climate change. More than ever, investors, banks and financial institutions must be encouraged to place sustainability at the heart of their investment and business strategies and to avoid the pitfalls of a well-trodden high-carbon path. It is a financial plan that is not only positive for the environment, but also good for people and profitability too.

第1章

可持續發展金融
和投資生態系統

維維克・帕塔克
國際金融公司　氣候業務總監

摘要

截至撰寫本文時，新冠肺炎疫情還在持續蔓延，給人們、企業和市場造成毀滅性影響，尤其是在極其貧窮的國家。儘管已採取了前所未有的干預措施、實施了前所未有的刺激方案，以遏制疫情造成的負面影響，但我們依然面臨着迫在眉睫的災難—氣候變化，這個災難需要全世界的人們更加積極團結應對。氣候變化可能給人類造成數萬億美元的損失，目前它正令金融行業以及全球經濟的各個領域面對系統性風險。金融機構須管理氣候變化帶來的自然風險和轉型風險。除非投資者和金融機構通過將其投資組合轉向低碳路徑來管理這些風險，否則這些風險將給實體經濟和資產價值帶來嚴重影響，造成金融不穩定。與新冠肺炎不同，氣候變化沒有疫苗。整個世界需要行動起來，重建經濟，特別是新興市場的經濟，將綠色及可持續發展金融作為核心應對措施，讓經濟更加可持續、更具韌性。

為了構建一個更安全、更公平的低碳未來，投資者和企業需要將資金分配到能夠帶來可持續和可衡量結果的資產和活動中。銀行和金融機構須將資本分配到、並引導資金投入到低碳和應對氣候變化的投資中，創建工具，將氣候變化風險置於全球市場的核心。政府和監管機構需要長期、透明、明確地落實相關框架、分類標準和政策，以提供綠色及可持續發展金融。對於在新冠疫情後復甦路徑各異的新興市場而言，綠色及可持續發展金融對綠色領域的大規模公共投資項目進行優先排序和通過支持性政策促進私營部門投資至關重要。本書的第一章探討了新興的、不斷演進的全球可持續金融發展生態系統，以及金融機構、政府和監管機構在幫助投資者和企業向更加可持續的未來轉型方面可以做的工作；具體研究了推動綠色及可持續發展金融市場的力量，促進可持續發展金融的發展和增長的關鍵因素，以及關鍵市場參與者所扮演的角色。最後對亞洲在綠色及可持續發展的市場實踐方面進行了評估，並提出進一步擴大對亞洲相關投資所需做的工作。

整體情況：推動綠色及可持續發展金融的力量有哪些？

2015 年，在對倫敦勞合社的開創性演講中 [1]，英格蘭銀行時任行長馬克·卡尼（Mark Carney）警告道，氣候變化嚴重威脅着全球經濟和全球金融穩定性，企業和監管機構需要立即行動起來，遏制氣候變化可能帶來的經濟損失。卡尼稱氣候變化為「地平線悲劇」（"tragedy of the horizon"），他警告，除非世界主要國家採取更多措施，確保其企業糾正當前和未來的碳排放，否則氣候變化會導致災難性的金融危機，人們的生活水平會嚴重下降。這位全球最有權力的央行官員之一所作出的警告，震撼了全球各地的決策者，這表明了金融界對氣候變化的討論已經從理論走向具體實踐。卡尼表示：「一旦氣候變化成為金融穩定的決定性因素，就為時已晚了。」

自卡尼發出此嚴厲警告以來的近 6 年裏，綠色及可持續發展金融（green and sustainable finance，簡稱 GSF）在全球政策議程中變得更加突出。在《巴黎協定》的推動下，包括中國、歐洲、加拿大、南非、哥倫比亞和智利在內的世界上許多地區和國家，已經推出了可持續發展金融的監管框架、分類標準和行動計劃。仿效卡尼的做法，其他金融界領軍人物也紛紛打破沉默，表示他們也很擔心氣候變化會威脅到金融的穩定。2020 年，可能是全球最具影響力的投資企業貝萊德的首席執行官勞倫斯·D·芬克（Laurence D. Fink）發佈了一封信 [2]，信中警告道：世界「金融業正處於根本重塑的邊緣」，以及氣候變化將是全球企業長期發展的一個決定性因素。同年，世界經濟論壇（World Economic Forum）在其第 15 期全球風險報告中 [3] 首次宣佈，所有首要的長期風險都與環境有關。

世界銀行於 2008 年 11 月發行首隻綠色債券，隨後國際金融公司（International Finance Corporation，簡稱 IFC）於 2013 年發行首隻基準規模的綠色債券。自此，GSF 市場呈幾何級增長。國際資本市場協會（International Capital Market Association，簡稱 ICMA）於 2014 年推出的《綠色債券原則》，是一套全球綠色債券發行和匯報的指南，極大地促進市場的誠信、信譽和增長。綠色債券改變了綠色金融的遊戲規則，並成為市場融資的主要工具，大幅增加了流向綠色項目的資本。對於那些手持合格綠色項目的貸款機構來說，綠色債券一直是他們通過國內外投資者尋求融資的可選工具。對債券發行人來說，發行綠色債券是件體面的事情，可能比發行普通債券吸引廣泛的貸款者，因為綠色債券能幫助他們改善公司層面的環境足跡和財務表現。無可否認，綠色債券塑造了投資者的行為，過去的

1　〈打破地平線悲劇 —— 環境變化和金融穩定 —— 馬克·卡尼（Mark Carney）演講〉（"Breaking the tragedy of the horizon — climate change and financial stability — speech by Mark Carney"），演講地點：倫敦勞合社，載於英格蘭銀行的網站，2015年9月29日。

2　〈金融業的根本重塑〉（"A fundamental reshaping of finance"），拉里·芬克（Larry Fink）在2020年致首席執行官的信，載於貝萊德的網站，2020年1月14日。

3　世界經濟論壇《2020年全球風險報告》（The Global Risks Report 2020），載於世界經濟論壇的網站，2020年1月15日。

資本市場中，投資者對自己投資資金的去向知之甚少，現在的資本市場中，投資資金的用途以及用途的正當性對投資者來說比以往任何時候都更重要。儘管新冠肺炎疫情帶來了很大的負面影響，但 2020 年下半年綠色債券發行量反彈，達到 2,695 億美元，創造了債券發行量的新記錄 [4]。新興市場國家的綠色債券發行量穩步增長 —— 從 2012 年的 10 億美元上升至 2019 年的 520 億美元 [5]。2015 年以來，綠色債券市場年均增長 60%，截至 2020 年年底，債券累計發行量超過 1 萬億美元，鞏固了債券作為 GSF 市場主導力量的地位 [6]。

塑造 GSF 市場的力量還有一系列框架，這些框架要求企業提高透明度，揭示其如何運作風險管理和適應未來。這些由投資者、政府和監管機構提出的提案和倡議，正在幫助企業「向未來證明」自己的底線，並為氣候風險做好準備，這些風險可能會把煤炭、石油和天然氣等高排放資源「留」在地下，使其無法繼續開採。領導此項監管工作的是「氣候相關財務信息披露工作組」(Task Force on Climate-Related Financial Disclosures，簡稱 TCFD)，該小組由金融穩定委員會 (Financial Stability Board，簡稱 FSB) 和馬克‧卡尼於其在 2015 年發表「地平線悲劇」的演講後幾週內共同成立。TCFD 圍繞企業運營的四個主題領域制定建議：治理、戰略、風險管理，以及指標和目標。它要求企業進行「場景分析」，分析重大氣候風險。TCFD 報告旨在幫助投資者更好地了解其投資組合中的氣候風險，並幫助將資金從高碳投資轉移到氣候適應性更強、正在向淨零（排放）路徑轉型的公司。

TCFD 在很短時間內產生了深遠的影響。2019 年 2 月，聯合國支持的《責任投資原則組織》(Principles for Responsible Investment，簡稱 PRI) 宣佈，正在要求該組織的 2,250 個簽署國（包括資產總額約為 100 萬億美元的資產所有者、投資經理和服務供應商）[7] 根據 TCFD 指標匯報其投資組合中的氣候變化風險。歐盟的非財務報告指令，在極大程度上仿效了 TCFD，規定了大型企業非財務信息和多樣性信息披露規則。2021 年 3 月，美國的主要金融監管機構 —— 美國證券交易委員會 —— 仿效 TCFD 手冊，宣佈成立本身的工作組來研究環境、社會和治理 (environmental, social and governance，簡稱 ESG) 問題，更加密切地研究上市公司披露的氣候相關信息 [8]。英國、紐西蘭和瑞士的監管機構也宣告按照 TCFD 的建議實施強制性氣候風險匯報的意向。

---

4 資料來源：〈2020年綠色債券發行量達到創紀錄的2,695億美元：後期激增使2020年債券發行量比2019年高出30億美元〉("Record $269.5bn green issuance for 2020: Late surge sees pandemic year pip 2019 total by $3bn")，載於氣候債券倡議組織(Climate Bonds Initiative，簡稱CBI)的網站，2021年1月24日。

5 資料來源：P. Cashion 與 P. Stein (IFC)〈債務資本市場：幫助貸款機構擴大在新興市場上的氣候融資規模〉("Debt capital markets: Helping lenders scale climate finance in emerging markets")，載於CBI的網站。

6 資料來源：〈2020年綠色債券發行量達到創紀錄的2,695億美元：後期激增使2020年債券發行量總額比2019年高出30億美元〉("Record $269.5bn green issuance for 2020: Late surge sees pandemic year pip 2019 total by $3bn")，載於CBI的網站，2021年1月24日。

7 資料來源：〈2020年，基於TCFD的建議進行匯報將成為對PRI簽署國的強制性要求〉("TCFD-based reporting to become mandatory for PRI signatories in 2020")，《PRI》網站上的新聞稿，2019年2月18日。

8 資料來源：〈監管機構希望企業坦白其投資組合中的氣候風險〉("Regulators want firms to own up to climate risks")，載於《經濟學人》，2021年3月13日。

由 54 家央行和監管機構組成的「綠色金融體系網絡」（Network for Greening the Financial System，簡稱 NGFS）負責為監管機構整理指引和建議，並發佈各種情景，幫助分析金融體系可能遭受的損失 [9]。中國人民銀行（中國的中央銀行）和新加坡金融管理局（簡稱「新加坡金管局」）都在幫助建立 NGFS 方面發揮了重要作用。2019 年 10 月，NGFS 發佈了關於中央銀行如何將可持續發展因素納入其投資組合的指南 [10]。NGFS 建議為金融資產建立一個公認的環境分類體系，用國際公認的標準來評定各種資產的環境友好程度。

「氣候行動 100+」是個機構投資者羣體，成員包括資產超過 54 萬億美元的貝萊德 [11]，貝萊德同意設置減排目標，並加大氣候風險相關信息的披露力度。2021 年 3 月，該羣體發佈了一項基準分析，根據基準的三個目標：減排、治理和披露，評估重點企業的表現 [12]。該基準對企業的目標和行動進行評估，如果碳密集型企業不能成功脫碳，該基準將成為令這些企業增加其資本成本的第一步。資產所有者領頭發起的全球性「轉型路徑倡議」（Transition Pathway Initiative，簡稱 TPI），利用企業披露的數據提供行業層面的企業碳排放管理分析，並與《巴黎協定》保持一致。此外，作為「零競爭對話」（Race to Zero Dialogues）的一部分，投資者、城市和地區的淨零承諾涵蓋了全球一半以上的國內生產總值。「零競爭對話」是一項全球性運動，旨在動員主要「實體經濟」參與者組成聯盟。

可持續發展金融是金融業的未來

雖然綠色債券刺激了綠色金融生態系統的發展，而且綠色債券仍然是市場上最成熟的工具，但可持續發展金融卻不僅限於綠色債券。近年來，湧現了一大批創新性的金融解決方案，拓寬了人們對 GSF 的理解。這包括綠色貸款、可持續發展債券、社會債券以及最近新出現的可持續發展掛鈎債券和貸款等。這個有多種不同新工具的工具箱説明市場對可持續發展融資的需求大幅增長。隨着企業越來越注重將其融資戰略與氣候和可持續發展的目標保持一致，這些工具都有共同目標，就是吸引投資者、平衡信譽以及避免漂綠。

9　資料來源：〈綠色倡議：綠色金融體系網路〉（"Green initiative: Network for greening the financial system"），載於 Central Banking Institute 的網站，2020年2月4日。

10　資料來源：《央行投資組合管理的可持續和責任投資指南》（*A Sustainable and Responsible Investment Guide for Central Banks' Portfolio Management*），載於 NGFS的網站，2019年10月。

11　資料來源：〈氣候行動100+發佈了其首個全球最大企業排放者的淨零公司基準〉（"Climate Action 100+ issues its first-ever net zero company benchmark of the world's largest corporate emitters"），氣候行動100+網站上的新聞稿，2021年3月22日。

12　同上。

2017 年，荷蘭銀行荷蘭國際集團（ING）向醫療科技公司飛利浦發放了 10 億歐元的貸款，這是全球首筆與公司可持續發展表現和評級掛鈎的貸款[13]。這是一項具有里程碑意義的交易，啟發了貸款市場協會（Loan Market Association，簡稱 LMA）發佈《可持續發展掛鈎貸款原則》。可持續發展掛鈎債券，與可持續發展掛鈎貸款相似，是這些新金融工具中較為複雜的一個新工具。與綠色債券不同，這些「普通用途」債券將利息支付與目標的實現掛鈎，讓債券發行人對其承諾的表現負責。2019 年，意大利電力巨頭意大利國家電力公司發行了一隻與可再生能源發電在其發電能力中所佔比重的上升情況有連繫的 15 億美元可持續發展關聯債券[14]。這隻債券反映了債券發行人對可持續發展戰略和表現的整體意識正在提高，以及投資者不僅在尋找綠色或可持續項目，還在尋找可持續發展的公司。

儘管這些新的金融工具在將資本引入可持續發展項目和企業方面取得了成功，但僅綠色金融無法幫助我們實現《巴黎協定》的目標。需要做的工作還有很多，特別是在幫助水泥、化工、鋼鐵和重型運輸等碳密集領域實現淨零排放目標方面。因此，越來越多的注意力轉向了「氣候轉型融資」，以實施企業脫碳戰略，和／或將所得資金用於幫助發行者減少碳足跡的項目。投資標的包括取代煤炭的綠地天然氣發電廠、熱電聯產廠、碳捕獲和儲存、廢物轉化能源、天然氣動力航運、飛機替代燃料，以及能源效率投資。對於碳密集型企業來說，若無法達到未來的碳排放要求，會使其營運和財務成本增加，對它們的收支平衡產生負面影響；最糟糕的情況下，它們的營運牌照會被吊銷。

儘管氣候轉型債券的全球發行規模依然很小，但這種債券正讓那些雄心勃勃、願意向脫碳「多走一英里」的人興奮不已。氣候轉型金融要求發行人根據《巴黎協定》的目標對自己的淨零排放路徑作出承諾，對那些因為向「不甚綠色」的市場參與者發行綠色債券所帶來的聲譽風險感到憂慮的企業來說，關鍵性地填補了市場的不足。擴大市場是需要時間的，但最近的進展和框架的推出則顯示，氣候轉型債券可能在企業和資產管理公司的綠色金融主流化中發揮關鍵作用。2020 年 12 月，ICMA 發佈了一套指引，指導發行人在其氣候轉型戰略中使用綠色債券、可持續發展債券或可持續發展掛鈎債券。這本《氣候轉型融資手冊》為哪些特定收益用途產品（即其收益指定作為綠色及可持續發展資金）可以使用「轉型」標籤設定了標準[15]。這些氣候轉型標籤適用於特定收益用途為綠色及可持續發展的金融工具，如綠色貸款、綠色債券、可持續發展掛鈎金融工具，並且可以幫助將資金再分配給綠色項目和脫碳戰略。長期機構投資者可以利用氣候轉型戰略，重新平衡其投資組合，重新分配資本，用於脫碳投資。2021 年 1 月，中國銀行香港分行發行了全球首隻根據 ICMA《氣候轉型融資手冊》中的指引發行的轉型債券[16]。儘管這隻債券的收益將用於為合格的轉型項目

---

13 資料來源：〈荷蘭國際集團與飛利浦就可持續發展貸款展開合作〉（"ING and Philips collaborate on sustainable loan"），荷蘭國際集團網站上的新聞稿，2017年4月19日。

14 資料來源：〈意大利國家電力公司放棄綠色債券，轉而尋求有爭議的新形式〉（"Enel ditches green bonds for controversial new format"），載於《路透社》，2019年10月4日。

15 資料來源：〈ICMA發佈了轉型債券指引〉（"ICMA publishes transition bond guidelines"），載於北歐可持續發展投資（Nordic Sustainable Investments）的網站，2020年12月17日。

16 資料來源：〈中國銀行計劃在境外市場公佈第一筆轉型債券交易〉，中國銀行網站上的新聞稿，2021年1月6日。

提供資金，但一些專家對該債券的可信度和宏偉目標提出了質疑，指出天然氣項目仍包括在此次發行中。

雖然對於希望確定脫碳轉型路徑的企業來說沒有明確的解決方案，但《氣候轉型融資手冊》建議發行人在遵循適當的基準和特定領域的脫碳路線，以實行一個可靠的轉型過程。該手冊還建議發行人按照《巴黎協定》的目標制定其業務計劃。此外，還有一些包括免費的商用工具在內的市場舉措，讓發行人更容易探索氣候情景分析。其中，《巴黎協定資本轉型評估》（Paris Agreement Capital Transition Assessment，簡稱 PACTA）工具的目的是為各行業在企業層面開發路徑，利用資產層面的數據對公共股權和公司債券的轉型風險進行投資組合層面的分析。2020 年 10 月，由碳信息披露項目（Carbon Disclosure Project，簡稱 CDP）、聯合國全球契約組織（UN Global Compact，簡稱 UNGC）、世界資源研究所（World Resources Institute，簡稱 WRI）和世界自然基金會（World Wide Fund for Nature，簡稱 WWF）成立的《科學基礎減碳目標倡議組織》（Science Based Targets initiative，簡稱 SBTi）發佈了一個新框架，讓金融機構（包括銀行、投資者、保險公司、養老金投資機構等）設定基於科學的目標，使其放貸和投資活動與《巴黎協定》的目標保持一致。

我們還能做甚麼來幫助 GSF 生態系統發展？

在 GSF 生態系統中，各個參與者（投資者、企業、發行人、監管機構、系統營運商、仲介機構和服務供應商）扮演着不同的角色，有時相互競爭，有時又互為補充。雖然 GSF 仍是個新領域，但它瞬息萬變，充滿活力，生態系統內的參與者要迅速、靈活地採取相關措施才能成功運用 GSF。雖然投資者和客戶的需求依然是驅動 GSF 領域發展的關鍵因素，但要幫助投資者、企業和金融機構向淨零目標轉型，特別是框架鞏固、信息披露、透明度和匯報方面，還需要更多的監管措施。此外，還須擴大市場容量，這需要讓發行人在許下可持續發展的承諾方面變得更有決心，並鼓勵投資者促使發行人採用更穩健的脫碳路線（如果投資者認為發行人決心不足的話）。這種勢頭無疑將推動 GSF 生態系統更加堅定地走向其淨零路徑；讓企業和發行人對他們的新發展路線負責，讓他們難以再於市場上發行不可持續發展的債券。

全球各國政府通過綠色金融激勵措施、各種戰略和監管規定，在推動全球經濟沿着正確的方向發展方面發揮着關鍵作用。倫敦政治經濟學院格蘭瑟姆研究所統計了截至 2021 年初的資料，發現全球有 2,200 多項氣候政策和立法，其中近三分之二是在過去十年內通過的 [17]。為了讓世界走上淨零的金融軌道，政府的工作方向是關鍵。正如我們從 TCFD 等舉措

17　資料來源：〈全球氣候變化規律〉（"Climate change laws of the world"），格蘭瑟姆氣候變化與環境研究所網站上的網頁，
　　於2021年5月13日閱覽。

看到的那樣，監管指引和各種框架可以幫助更廣闊範疇的金融系統理解那些對政府來說非常重要的問題，然後將其反映在私營部門的政策和投資決策中。多邊開發銀行注意到這種情況在新興市場已非常普遍，新興市場中的私營部門（尤其是金融機構）極其關注監管機構的監管目標。某些舉措，如可持續銀行網絡（Sustainable Banking Network，簡稱 SBN，是一個獨特的新興市場金融業監管機構和銀行業協會志願團體，致力於按照國際良好做法推進可持續發展金融），正在於最需要綠色金融監管的市場中推行綠色金融監管的最佳實踐。該網絡的 11 個低收入國家（符合國際開發協會資格的國家 [18]）中，有 4 個國家（孟加拉、肯尼亞、蒙古和尼日利亞）的可持續發展金融路程目前處於先進的階段，它們出台了國家政策或行業框架來推動可持續發展金融，鼓勵金融機構改變行為 [19]。

雖然政府負責推動經濟沿着正確的方向發展，但政府還必須向私營部門和金融領域提供可用的綠色金融工具。實現更全面增長的最大障礙之一，是缺乏對「綠色」進行統一定義，而發行人和投資者必須依賴健全和實用的定義，這方面的不足正是分類標準可以彌補的。分類標準是一套重要的指導性「文件」，幫助發行人、投資者和金融機構明確制定他們在綠色金融領域的目標。分類標準說明了市場對合格的綠色資產及其衡量標準和門檻的要求，而且還幫助投資者建立信心，為投資者提供保證。世界各地的一些司法權區已通過立法對可持續發展金融進行官方定義。在中國，中國銀行保險監督管理委員會十多年來一直在指導中國的銀行業發展綠色金融工具和統一綠色資產的定義。2020 年 5 月，中國人民銀行、國家發展和改革委員會和內地的證券監管機構聯合發佈了新版《綠色債券支持項目目錄》草案徵求意見，讓中國向單一綠色金融分類標準邁進了一步，最終版於 2021 年 4 月發佈。雖然之前中國的綠色債券市場有多種不同的分類標準，但新指引規定，從今以後只有一套官方的綠色債券分類標準。此外，新的合格投資項目名單不再包括對清潔煤炭項目的投資，這也是受其他全球監管機構影響的結果。

雖然設計合理的綠色金融分類標準可以帶來好處，但分類標準的成功實施則取決於有否一個完善的可持續發展金融標準、匯報、透明度和披露機制。在發展中國家，資本市場的發展情況、現有綠色債券發行所產生的勢頭，以及政治穩定也是關鍵因素。投資者和發行人可以通過遵守市場上的各種標準來提高 GSF 的誠信度。LMA 發佈的《綠色貸款原則》（IFC 也簽署了這個《原則》）為整個綠色貸款市場提供了一個高水平的框架，涵蓋市場標準、指引和一致的方法。ICMA 發佈的《綠色債券原則》為發行人提供了一套指引，列出具體可持續環境發展活動的重要元素。

將信息披露視作優先，以此驗證已打上綠色標籤的金融工具的質量、建立市場信譽和誠信，並實現資源的重新分配（TCFD 的一個關鍵目標），對推動 GSF 發展至關重要。此外，確

18　符合國際開發協會（International Development Association，簡稱IDA）資格的國家是指人均收入低、缺乏從國際復興開發銀行（International Bank for Reconstruction and Development，簡稱IBRD）借款能力的國家。

19　資料來源：SBN（2021年5月概述），載於IFC的網站，2021年5月。

保透明度和可信度，以及經認可和批准的第三方驗證機構的作用也至關重要，這些機構可以確保綠色金融投資達到最高認證標準。隨着可持續發展投資者和投資模式越來越成熟，對透明度的需求也將越來越高，以避免「漂綠」，並改善投資效果。如果不提高透明度，唯利是圖的投資者可能會要求更高的利率，或完全拒絕為一個投資項目提供資金。幫助金融機構和貸款機構仔細研究和了解其業務和氣候貸款組合中的各個項目，獲得所需的專業知識來識別、管理和匯報其氣候貸款也至關重要。如果銀行和企業不能可靠地匯報其氣候貸款或投資，綠色金融市場的可持續性將受危害。迄今為止，用來對 GSF 作衡量和匯報的有關信息相當有限，質量亦然，故這方面一直是一項重大挑戰。切實、明確的目標，以及對這些目標進行追蹤的適當工具，將可讓投資者和貸款機構對綠色投資的匯報建立信任。這在新興市場較難實現，因為在新興市場，所披露的環境信息依然非常有限，而且很難確定任何一個借款人會帶來甚麼積極影響。在這方面，多邊開發銀行可以在與公共和私營部門合作、提供技術援助和跟蹤工具方面發揮作用。IFC 正在通過《綠色債券技術援助計劃》（Green Bond — Technical Assistance Program）制定《綠色金融審查議定書》（Green Finance Review Protocol），以幫助投資者和其他市場參與者進行適當的分析和決策。這個自發制定的議定書提供一個對比和綜合綠色貸款信息的機制，這樣不管綠色資助過程中存在何種細微差別，或使用的方法有何不同，貸款機構和其他市場參與者都能夠使用這些信息。此外，IFC 的《金融機構氣候評估》（Climate Assessment for Financial Institutions）還能幫助發展中國家的銀行從項目層面了解哪些投資屬於氣候投資，並幫助監測其氣候投資組合的影響和規模。

「國家自主貢獻」（nationally determined contributions，簡稱 NDC）是各國在《巴黎協定》下根據自身情況確定的脫碳計劃。鼓勵各國制定及明確説明其 NDC，將可讓投資者和企業了解當前市場的優先事項和市場的未來，包括如何確定實現淨零碳排放的轉型路徑。NDC 為監管機構提供了廣闊的路線圖，説明政府指導實體經濟向淨零碳排放轉型。NDC 還幫助投資者和企業制定最佳的脫碳戰略，或實現淨零碳排放的路線圖。每個國家在實現其 NDC 上有其所需的獨特方法，但每一種方法都應以強而有力的監管框架為基礎。許多 NDC 都包括碳定價，這是各國政府可以採取的、用於減緩全球暖化速度的關鍵行動。為碳定價會發出一個市場信號，推動對清潔、高效技術的投資來幫助減少碳排放。「碳定價領導聯盟」的分析顯示，為碳定價既不會限制經濟和工業增長，也不會鼓勵大型污染製造者轉移到其他司法權區，這説明是有辦法為碳作出定價並保持市場競爭 [20]。

儘管投資者的需求正在回升，對 GSF 的胃納也沒有放緩的跡象，但要幫助投資者和企業，需要做的工作還有很多，尤其是在對「漂綠」的擔憂和審查加劇的情況下。鑒於目前綠色

20　資料來源：Philippe Le Houérou（IFC的首席執行官）〈對碳定價向投資者發出了一個金融信號，即低碳投資是今天價值所在，而未來價值會更高〉（"Imposing a price on carbon sends a financial signal to investors that low-carbon investments are valuable today and will be even more valuable in the future"），載於《湯森路透基金會新聞》，2020年2月20日。

市場的流動性水平較高，對降低風險和長期供資的需求更大，因為大多數與氣候有關的貸款（特別是基礎設施等領域）需要的貸款期限比一般貸款的期限更長。因此，獲得適當期限的融資和資本至關重要。此外，通過多邊開發銀行以優惠和混合融資的形式提供低成本貸款來降低資本成本也相當重要。IFC 等機構和其他開發銀行可以以較低的利率提供長期貸款，並提供技術援助。長期機構投資者可以通過保護投資價值、重新平衡和重新分配氣候相關風險，以及確保金融穩定等來促進市場的增長。事實證明，擁抱強大的可持續發展標準、在信息披露和透明度實踐方面表現良好的投資者和企業，其表現明顯優於同行 [21]。

亞洲綠色及可持續發展金融的現在和未來

許多亞洲社會和經濟體有不少地勢低窪的沿海城市居住着數千萬人，他們都面臨着氣候變化帶來的巨大自然風險，包括颱風、颶風、洪水、乾旱、極端降水和供水變化。2021 年 4 月，全球保險業巨頭瑞士再保險公司發佈了一份報告，稱預計到 2050 年，氣候變化的影響將使全球經濟產出減少 14%[22]。亞洲的經濟體受到衝擊將會最嚴重，在嚴重情況下，中國有可能損失近 24% 的國內生產總值。許多亞洲新興市場在受到新冠肺炎疫情帶來的經濟衝擊和全球氣溫上升的影響後已經很脆弱，對它們來説，這種氣候變化的衝擊將會更嚴重。瑞士再保險公司表示，如果全球氣溫上升保持在攝氏 2 度（℃）（儘管目前的趨勢是到 2050 年將上升到 2.6℃），馬來西亞、菲律賓和泰國到 2050 年的經濟增長率將比預期低 20%。最壞的情景模擬是到 2050 年全球氣溫上升 3.2℃，在這種情況下，這些國家的財富水平將下降近一半。

然而，IFC 最近一份報告，分析關於新冠肺炎疫情後期綠色復甦的經濟和氣候效益，結果表明在 21 個新興市場的 10 個關鍵領域的投資可能會產生 10.2 萬億美元的投資機會，創造 2.13 億個新的就業機會，使溫室氣體排放量到 2030 年減少 40 億公噸 [23]。

雖然亞洲仍然是最容易受到氣候變化影響的地區之一，但亞洲幾個地區經濟體已經成為可持續發展金融領域的先導者。如上述的 IFC 報告顯示，包括中國、印度、印尼、尼日利亞和南非在內的一些國家已將綠色措施納入其新冠肺炎疫情刺激方案，儘管只佔總資金的一小部分 [24]。截至 2020 年，中國已成為全球最大的綠色金融經濟體，21 家國內銀行的綠色信

---

21 資料來源：晨星《美國可持續發展類基金概況報告》（*Sustainable Funds U.S. Landscape Report*），2021年2月。

22 資料來源：〈保險業巨頭警告，到2050年，氣候變化可能使全球經濟損失23萬億美元〉（"Climate change could cut world economy by \$23 trillion in 2050, insurance giant warns"），載於《紐約時報》，2021年4月22日。

23 資料來源：〈IFC的新報告稱，支持新冠肺炎疫情後的綠色復甦可以在新興市場產生10萬億美元的投資機會〉（"Supporting a green post-COVID recovery can generate over \$10 trillion in investment opportunities in emerging markets, says new IFC report"），載於 IFC 的網站，2021年1月13日。

24 資料來源：IFC報告〈Ctrl-Alt-Delete：新興的市場綠色重啟〉（"Ctrl-Alt-Delete: A green reboot for emerging markets"），載於IFC的網站，2021年1月17日。

貸總額達 1.8 萬億美元（約合 11 萬億元人民幣），綠色債券總額達 1,900 億美元（約合 1 萬億元人民幣）[25]。亞洲其他主要的綠色債券發行地有香港、印度、日本和韓國[26]。自 2016 年以來，中國一直是全球領先的綠色債券發行國。最近，中國宣佈到 2060 年實現碳中和的計劃[27]，這一政策轉變需要中國經濟進行結構性轉型。韓國的綠色新政，作為新冠肺炎疫情後復甦工作的一部分，計劃到 2034 年關閉 30 家燃煤發電廠[28]。儘管在中國以外，許多亞洲可持續發展市場經濟體仍處於起步階段，但在亞洲地區擴大綠色金融的潛力相當巨大。實現這種增長的關鍵在於滿足亞洲發展中國家（地區）激增的能源需求，預計這些需求將佔到 2040 年全球能源需求增長量的三分之二[29]。

雖然亞洲各地的可持續發展金融因該地區的經濟格局而有所不同，但監管一直是其成功的關鍵驅動因素。中國通過制定連貫的綠色金融標準、指引、分類標準、激勵措施和環境信息披露要求等，在監管方面一直處於領先地位。中國有兩套以部門為基礎的分類標準框架，即《綠色債券支持項目目錄》和《綠色產業指導目錄》。2020 年 10 月，在五家政府機關的支持下，中國發佈了一份雄心勃勃的新投融資指引，旨在完善金融監管，以支持和激勵銀行和金融機構開發綠色金融產品[30]。隨着中國為內地的監管定下基調，其他亞洲市場紛紛仿效中國的做法。2019 年 5 月，香港金融管理局（簡稱「香港金管局」）推出三項主要措施，以支持和推動香港綠色金融的發展[31]。一年後，香港金管局發佈了《綠色及可持續銀行業白皮書》，當中列出了清晰的監管路線圖和九項指導性原則，幫助金融機構實施一套框架來管理氣候變化帶來的風險和機遇[32]。2021 年 1 月，新加坡金管局通過其綠色金融產業工作組，為新加坡金融機構發佈了一套分類標準，以確定哪些是綠色或向綠色轉型的活動[33]。該工作組還發佈了一本關於資產管理公司、銀行和保險公司如何落實環境風險管理的手冊[34]。2020 年年底，馬來西亞央行（即馬來西亞國家銀行）分發了一份討論文件《氣候變化和基

25　資料來源：〈實現碳中和，中國需力促綠色金融發展〉，載於《中外對話》網站，2020年11月17日。

26　基於IFC氣候業務部門提供的數據，2021年4月。

27　資料來源：〈中國承諾到2060年實現碳中和：這意味着甚麼？〉（"China's pledge to be carbon neutral by 2060: What it means"），載於《紐約時報》，2020年12月4日。

28　資料來源：〈為了讓空氣變得更清潔，同時也是為了應對氣候變化，文在寅誓言要關閉30多家燃煤電廠〉（"Moon vows to shut down 30 more coal plants to bring cleaner air and battle climate change"），載於《韓國先驅報》，2020年9月8日。

29　資料來源：D. Azhgaliyeva 與 B. Liddle（2020年）〈專題介紹：擴大亞洲的綠色金融〉（"Introduction to the special issue: Scaling up green finance in Asia"），載於《可持續發展金融與投資》（*Journal of Sustainable Finance & Investment*），第10期，第2卷，第89-91頁。

30　資料來源：〈中國制定了宏偉的氣候投融資計劃〉（"China outlines ambitious plan on climate investment and finance"），載於《Regulation Asia》，2020年10月28日。

31　資料來源：〈金管局公佈可持續銀行業及綠色金融的重要舉措〉，香港金管局網站上的新聞稿，2019年5月7日。

32　資料來源：〈綠色和可持續金融跨機構督導小組推出策略計劃　鞏固香港金融生態系統　共建更綠和更可持續未來〉，香港金管局網站上的新聞稿，2020年12月17日。

33　資料來源：〈行業特別工作小組提出分類標準並推出支援綠色金融的環境風險管理手冊〉，載於新加坡金管局的網站，2021年1月28日。

34　《資產管理公司、銀行和保險公司的環境風險管理實施手冊》（*Handbook on Implementing Environmental Risk Management for Asset Managers, Banks and Insurers*），載於 The Association of Banks in Singapore 的網站，2021年1月28日。

於原則的分類標準》（Climate Change and Principle-based Taxonomy），計劃於 2021 年在馬來西亞引入國家分類標準 [35]。

儘管中國和亞洲其他發達經濟體已向金融家發出了將氣候風險融入銀行業的重要信號，但亞洲各新興市場的許多銀行仍未意識到氣候變化可能導致金融震盪。考慮到亞洲的地理位置以及發生極端天氣事件和熱浪的可能性，亞洲可能比世界其他地區更容易受到自然氣候風險的影響。這些氣候情景的複雜性，加上方法和追蹤工具的不足，使得亞洲新興市場的金融機構難以理解氣候變化所帶來的機遇和風險，並將其納入他們的主流業務。由於這方面知識的缺乏，大多數銀行沒有關於氣候業務的戰略願景，以及規劃和執行氣候風險管理戰略的能力。儘管亞洲新興市場的許多銀行對探索氣候融資機會持開放態度，但很少有銀行能夠按照 TCFD 的建議將自己的機構轉變為綠色銀行。作為新興市場資本配置的主要推動者，銀行在彌補氣候融資不足方面發揮着關鍵作用。衡量他們在面對着多大的氣候風險和機遇中，管理該等氣候風險和機遇需要最好的定量和定性方法，以及穩健的戰略和治理結構。這些方法還可幫助銀行進行全面的信息披露。

多邊開發銀行可以通過幫助制定氣候風險評估的標準和方法，幫助企業和銀行評估其供資項目是否可以評為「綠色」，從而幫助彌補亞洲新興市場金融領域的不足。2020 年，香港金管局加入了「綠色商業銀行聯盟」。該聯盟由 IFC 創立，旨在鼓勵亞洲各地的銀行採取更加環保的戰略和目標。該聯盟將匯集亞洲各地的金融機構、銀行業協會、研究機構和技術供應商，共同開發、建設和提高綠色金融能力，並促進氣候投資。2021 年 4 月，世界銀行集團向其董事會介紹了《氣候變化行動計劃》（Climate Change Action Plan，簡稱 CCAP）的主要內容，以幫助借款國和企業將氣候與發展問題結合起來，最大化氣候融資的影響，以及適應和減緩氣候變化 [36]。為實現這些宏偉目標，世界銀行集團將根據《巴黎協定》的目標調整其供資流，通過新制定的《巴黎協定》調整方法評估對金融機構和資金的投資。為直接彌補氣候風險和機遇方面知識的不足，IFC 將在亞洲幾個新興市場的銀行業領域推出「綠色債券技術援助計劃」。該試點計劃旨在通過一對一的諮詢活動，建立和提高客戶銀行在氣候機遇、風險評估和管理方面的能力，並為金融機構提供氣候風險管理工具包。

正當整個亞洲的總體 GSF 都呈上升趨勢，有一些關鍵驅動因素可以幫助擴大投資，包括適應性金融，但適應性金融現仍遠遠落後於緩解性金融。鑒於亞洲對全球暖化帶來的自然風險的抵禦能力薄弱，能有助提高對現有氣候影響的抵禦能力的適應性供資就顯得更加重要。金融機構方面，它們在將氣候適應因素納入每個項目以及為收益定價方面還有很大的不足。縱觀亞洲，私營部門的適應性資金很低，但創新性風險管理和保險機制以及成本效

---

35 資料來源：馬來西亞國家銀行（BNM）《氣候變化和基於原則的分類標準討論稿》（*Discussion Paper on Climate Change and Principle-based Taxonomy*），載於BNM的網站，2019年12月27日。

36 資料來源：〈世界銀行集團行長關於氣候變化行動計劃的聲明〉（"World Bank Group president's statement on Climate Change Action Plan"），世界銀行網站上的聲明，2021年4月2日。

益分析可以提升適應性投資和盈利能力。世界銀行集團最近的一份聯合報告[37]提出了一個制定、資助和實施優先適應和復原力投資的行動藍圖。該藍圖是根據各個國家的目標和國家投資計劃制定的，可以幫助加速和擴大投資，以應對世界上最易受氣候變化影響的社區和經濟體的需要。公共部門在動員私人投資方面發揮着關鍵作用，而多邊開發銀行在這重要方面填補了空白，為此作為召集人和促進者。

雖然發行人、投資者和監管機構在推動適應性金融方面很重要，但專注於各個子行業的企業在這方面也十分重要，例如技術供應商。雖然該地區一些主要經濟體在技術方面（從電動汽車到可再生能源）領先全球市場，但致力於推動開發低成本技術解決方案的企業或私募股權基金在未來可能發揮更重要的作用。以私募股權公司 Lightsmith 集團為例，該公司主要投資那些在水、農業、食品和能源等重點領域提供氣候適應解決方案的技術支援公司。Lightsmith 集團將與亞洲基礎設施投資銀行合作，投資亞洲那些專注於軟件、數據和分析、技術支援產品和技術支援服務的公司。幫助金融機構找到私營企業和資本來生產和擴大應對氣候變化風險的技術工具和解決方案，是一個巨大的增長機會。

結語

隨着氣候變化持續、全球暖化對經濟的影響日益加劇，金融機構和私營部門參與者在業務上已經不能「一切照舊」了。但由於對監管改革的關注度日益提升，透明度日益提高，披露力度日益加大，加之投資者尋求可持續發展投資的動機越來越強，綠色及可持續發展金融生態系統得以持續發展壯大。向氣候智能企業、技術和資助改善具體氣候相關方面提供傳統貸款仍然相當重要。鑒於全球貿易流動的重要性日益凸顯，貿易融資工具將在總體綠化所需融資中發揮重要作用。各國政府的相關政策、法規和金融支持將在幫助建立各種可投融資的綠色資產類別輸送鏈這方面發揮重要作用。要求銀行和投資者披露氣候風險的金融政策和法規，可以加速金融投資組合的再平衡，使其投資資產從高碳排放領域轉向低碳排放領域。

在全球都在努力遏制新冠肺炎疫情對經濟造成的破壞之際，綠色金融對於推動後新冠肺炎疫情時代的綠色復甦至關重要。綠色金融產品和工具（綠色債券、綠色貸款、市政抗風險債券、可持續發展掛鈎債券，以及基於所實現的可量化氣候結果提供浮動利率的貸款）將幫助推動這種增長。新興市場經濟體可以帶頭推進金融市場改革，創造新市場以鼓勵綠色金融，其中一些經濟體已經在這麼做了。這些新興市場的增長主要體現在綠化現有和未來

37　世界銀行集團和全球減災與恢復基金（Global Facility for Disaster Reduction and Recovery，簡稱GFDRR），《促進氣候適應和恢復的私人投資：現狀、投資阻礙和行動藍圖》（*Enabling Private Investment in Climate Adaptation and Resilience: Current Status, Barriers to Investment and Blueprint for Action*），載於世界銀行集團的網站，2021年3月4日。

能源基礎設施，建設氣候智能城市，以及幫助加快主要產業向綠色生產實踐轉型。公共和私營部門在這些領域採取的一致、堅定和真誠的行動，可以在短期內實現經濟復甦，在長期內實現可持續和低碳增長。

新冠肺炎疫情對人類健康和經濟造成的嚴重影響將會持續。但是，這場危機也提供了一個前所未有的機會，去改變方向、培育一個更能抵禦氣候變化等未來衝擊的 GSF 生態系統。目前比以往任何時候都更重要的是，須鼓勵投資者、銀行和金融機構將可持續性放在其投資和業務戰略的核心位置，避免落入高碳路徑的陷阱。這個金融計劃不僅有利於保護環境，而且有利於保護人類，兼且有利於利潤回報。

註：本文原稿是英文，另以中文譯本出版。如本文的中文本的字義或詞義與英文本有所出入，概以英文本為準。

Chapter 2

Practice and prospect of green finance in China — Enhancing the green financial system to achieve carbon neutrality

MA Jun

Chairman of Green Finance Committee of
China Society for Finance and Banking

President of the Institute of Finance and Sustainability

Chairman and President of
Hong Kong Green Finance Association

Summary

Since seven Mainland ministries and commissions jointly issued the *Guidelines for Establishing the Green Financial System* in 2016, China has made impressive strides in green finance in terms of market scale and products, policy framework, product innovation, pilot zones establishment and international cooperation. The outstanding balance of green loans and green bonds currently rank first and second in the world respectively.

In September 2020, Chinese President XI Jinping solemnly announced to the world that China aims to achieve carbon neutrality before 2060. In order to achieve this goal, at the real economy level, large-scale and thorough de-carbonisation in the electricity, transportation, construction and industrial sectors must be expedited. At the same time, the financial sector must undergo the transition to zero-carbon operations as well, not only to cater to the huge demand for green and low-carbon investment involving hundreds of trillions in Renminbi for the next three decades, but also to mitigate the risks caused by the transition of high-carbon industries. At present, China's green financial system still falls short of the development required of financing its carbon neutrality goal in aspects such as policy framework, market supply and risk management.

Based on the analysis of international experience in low-carbon investment and financing, this chapter proposes that China's local and industry departments should accelerate the planning of roadmaps towards carbon neutrality and recommends a series of policies for enhancing the green financial system to achieve carbon neutrality. These recommendations include revising green finance standards with carbon neutrality as the goal, improving the climate-related information disclosure and risk analysis capabilities of financial institutions, enhancing policy incentives to encourage low-carbon investment, encouraging sovereign investment institutions to engage in environmental, social and corporate governance (referred to as ESG) investment, mitigating environmental and climate risks associated with foreign investment, as well as leveraging the role of the carbon market in resource allocation. In the last part, this chapter outlines the prospects and market opportunities for the development of green finance in the Guangdong-Hong Kong-Macao Greater Bay Area.

Progress of development of green finance in China

Green finance has seen rapid development in China in recent years. With regulators continuously improving the top-level design of the green finance framework, reforms and innovation in the underlying systems are underway to drive vigorous bottom-up development of green finance, which together have yielding notable result in areas including standards setting, incentive mechanisms, product innovation, local pilot projects, and international cooperation.

Remarkable progress has been made in the green financial market and product innovation. As at the end of 2020, the balance of green loans in China's major financial institutions has approached RMB 1.2 billion, ranking first in the world, and the balance of green bonds amounted to about RMB 1.2 trillion, ranking second in the world[1]. The overall quality of green financial assets is good, with the non-performing loan ratio of green loans being far lower than that of the commercial banks across the country, and no default cases recorded for green bonds so far. The market's recognition of the concepts of green investment and responsible investment have gradually converged, conducing to the proliferation of new financial products and modes of business such as green funds, green insurance and green trusts as well as the promotion of various stress testing methods and tools for environmental risk measurement.

Green finance has gradually demonstrated its environmental benefits. According to the environmental benefit calculation rules determined by the Green Credit Statistics System, as at the end of 2019, the energy conservation and environmental protection projects and service loans provided by 21 major banking institutions in China are estimated to contribute to the saving of 282 million tonnes of standard coal and reducing carbon dioxide emissions by 567 million tonnes each year. As at the end of 2020, projects financed by China's green bonds contributed to the saving of approximately 50 million tonnes of standard coal per year, which is equivalent to reducing carbon dioxide emissions by more than 100 million tonnes[2].

---

1   Source: Data disclosed by the People's Bank of China (PBOC).
2   Source: "China's green bonds achieved remarkable results with cumulative issuance of about 1.2 trillion yuan" (〈我國綠色債券成效顯著、累計發行約 1.2 萬億元〉), published by The State Council Information Office of the People's Republic of China, 2021.

The green finance policy framework is progressively improving. Through China's top-down oriented financial reform, China has become the first country in the world to establish a systematic green finance policy framework. With regards to system establishment, seven Mainland ministries and commissions including the People's Bank of China (PBOC), the Ministry of Finance, the National Development and Reform Commission (NDRC) and the Ministry of Environmental Protection issued the *Guidelines for Establishing the Green Financial System* in August 2016, representing the establishment of the top-level structure of China's green financial system, and rolled out 35 specific green policy measures, including requirements on environmental information disclosure and policy incentives. In 2019, various departments of the central government introduced nearly 20 green finance-related policies covering finance, industries, fiscal and the environment, effectively facilitating the innovative development of green finance. The statistical system for green finance is also being improved to better collect key statistical data in areas such as green loans and green bonds with significantly enhanced quality[3]. In respect of policy incentives, the PBOC has included eligible green loans in the scope of qualified collateral for monetary policy operations and takes the lead in implementing green loans performance evaluation on financial institutions, thereby guiding financial institutions to increase green asset allocation and strengthen risk management, allowing the monetary policy to combat looming climate change. Green bonds supervision has become more standardised and the issue of information asymmetry has also been alleviated. Both the central and local governments have also deployed various measures, such as guarantees, interest subsidies and industrial funds, to mobilise more social capital to flow into green investment[4].

Local green finance pilot projects have gained invaluable experience replicable to other regions. China has launched nine pilot zones for green finance reform and innovation in six provinces since the debut of the first zone in June 2017[5]. Through this, China has accumulated practical and innovative experience constructive for the development of green finance across the country. As at the end of 2020, the outstanding balance of green loans in the pilot zones amounted to RMB 236.83 billion, accounting for 15.1% of China's total green loan balance, and the outstanding balance of green bonds reached RMB 135.05 billion[6]. In order to strengthen the horizontal and vertical collaboration on and

---

3 Source: *China Green Finance Development Report* (《中國綠色金融發展報告》), published by the PBOC, 2019.
4 Source: *China Green Finance Development Report* (《中國綠色金融發展報告》), published by the PBOC, 2019.
5 Green finance reform and innovation pilot zones include Zhejiang Province, Guangdong Province, Xinjiang Uygur Autonomous Region, Guizhou Province, Jiangxi Province and Gansu Province. Among them, the Lanzhou New District in Gansu Province was approved as a national-level green finance reform and innovation pilot zone in November 2019.
6 Source: Data disclosed by the PBOC.

exploration of green finance and advance the establishment of the pilot zones, the PBOC has guided these pilot zones to establish a self-regulatory mechanism of green finance and a joint meeting mechanism for all green finance reform and innovation pilot zones. This will provide support and advice to regions which are applying for establishing pilot zones. The pilot zones also create an integrated information platform utilising financial technology to promote the exchange of information between banks and enterprises and the sharing of climate and environmental protection information, laying the foundation for policy and market decision-making. In addition, these zones have developed an interdepartmental mechanism for green finance and environmental information exchange and sharing and a blacklist system to punish environmentally unfriendly enterprises[7].

China actively promotes and participates in international cooperation in green finance. From 2016 to 2018, under the initiation by multiple parties including China and the United Kingdom (UK), the G20 discussed green finance/sustainable finance issues for three consecutive years, promoting the international community's consensus over the development of green finance. In December 2017, the Network for Greening the Financial System (NGFS) was jointly established by eight central banks and regulators including PBOC and the Central Bank of France to collaboratively conduct research on the impacts of climate change on financial stability, environmental risk analysis, climate information disclosure, and the feasibility of green finance, contributing to the reaching of a number of international consensuses. In November 2018, the Green Finance Committee of China Society for Finance and Banking and the City of London Corporation led the initiative to develop the Green Investment Principles for the "Belt and Road" to enhance green investment made by global investment institutions in emerging market countries. By 27 August 2021, 39 institutional signatories from 14 countries and regions have pledged to fully consider environmental factors in investment and financing activities under the "Belt and Road" Initiative and expand green investment. In October 2019, China supported the launch of the International Platform on Sustainable Finance (IPSF) and called for member states to engage in international cooperation on the convergence of green finance standards and further promote global green finance development. In addition, China actively shares its practical experience in green development with the international community. For example, Chinese institutions have contributed to the development of multiple documents including "Sustainable Stock Exchanges Principles", "Principles for Responsible Banking" and "Environmental Risk Management Initiative for China's Overseas Investment"[8].

---

7   Source: *China Green Finance Development Report* (《中國綠色金融發展報告》), published by the PBOC, 2019.
8   Source: *China Green Finance Development Report* (《中國綠色金融發展報告》), published by the PBOC, 2019.

Enhance the green financial system to achieve carbon neutrality

On 22 September 2020, Chinese President XI Jinping made the solemnly announcement to the world at the general debate of the United Nations General Assembly that China would strive to peak carbon dioxide emissions before 2030 and achieve carbon neutrality by 2060. China's commitment is a milestone in the global response to climate change in that it will not only accelerate China's green and low-carbon transition, but also incentivise other major countries to commit to the goal of carbon neutrality, thus making it likely the most important driving force for the actual implementation of the Paris Agreement globally. The carbon neutrality commitments from major countries such as China will substantially increase the possibility of reaching the goals outlined in the Paris Agreement, thereby avoiding the climate refugees crisis which may affect hundreds of millions of people. Therefore, such commitment will become one of the paramount elements in building a shared future for mankind.

The paths of transformation of the real economy in achieving carbon neutrality

Research results from climate change experts in China and abroad show that China possesses adequate capacities to achieve a carbon emissions peak by 2030 and carbon neutrality by 2060. Given the available mature or developing green low-carbon technologies and their respective commercial viability, experts predict that China can reduce carbon emissions by about 70% compared to the current level (in 2020) in 2050, attain carbon neutrality and realise net-zero carbon emissions by 2060, provided that China adopts vigorous carbon neutrality policies in a timely manner[9].

In order to achieve carbon neutrality by 2060, large-scale de-carbonisation at the real-economy level in the electricity, transportation, construction and industrial sectors need to be expedited. The majority of industrial enterprises should aim to realise near-zero emissions, whereas a small proportion of carbon emissions which can hardly be eliminated or reduced are to be absorbed by forestry carbon sink (carbon fixation).

---

9 Source: "Research on China's long-term low carbon development strategy and transition pathways" (〈中國長期低碳發展戰略與轉型路徑研究〉), published by the Center for Finance and Development, Tsinghua National Institute of Financial Research, 2020.

Electricity: De-carbonisation and acceleration of clean energy development

Coal accounts for 60% of China's primary energy consumption. Power generation through the combustion of coal is the largest source of carbon emissions in China, equivalent to about half of the total carbon emissions of the power sector[10]. To achieve carbon neutrality, the power system needs to be deeply de-carbonised so that by 2050 the sector can become net-zero carbon emissions and non-fossil energy power will account for more than 90% of the total power generation. To this end, the production and consumption of and investment in photovoltaics, wind energy, nuclear energy and green hydrogen energy need to increase at an unprecedentedly high speed. Research by Tsinghua University indicates that the goal of carbon neutrality will require non-fossil energy to make up for more than 70% of China's total primary energy consumption by 2050. State Grid Energy Research Institute, the Wind Power Association and other institutions estimate that during the "14th Five-Year Plan" period, the installed capacity of newly added wind and solar energy facilities will reach about 100 gigawatts (GW) on average per year, which is double the amount during the "13th Five-Year Plan" period. By 2050, the total capacity of these facilities should reach about 4,000GW, more than ten times higher than the level in 2020 (about 350GW), and constitute over 65% of China's power generation in 2050.

Carbon neutrality calls for a drastic reduction in the production, consumption and investment of coal-related industries as soon as possible. Traditional coal mining and coal power companies will inevitably be discontinued and the "clean coal utilisation" strategy, which was once the main line of practice, will soon be phased out. Unless carbon capture technology can become commercially viable at low costs in the foreseeable future, various coal utilisation methods (including coal power generation, coal-to-gas, coal-to-liquid and other major chemical processing technologies involving coal) will be inconsistent with the goal of carbon neutrality given the high carbon emissions intensity of such methods. According to research conducted by the International Energy Agency (IEA) and other institutions, in order to halt the increase in global temperature under 1.5°C as required by the Paris Agreement, countries around the world must set a total carbon emissions limit (also referred to as "carbon budget"), which implies that 80% of the world's existing coal reserves and 70% of oil reserves will remain unused[11]. China must also be prepared for this future.

---

10 Source: "Statistical Communiqué of the People's Republic of China on the 2019 national economic and social development", published by the National Bureau of Statistics of China, 2019.
11 There have been many research institutions in the world that have predicted the recommended percentage of coal, oil and natural gas reserves that should be left unused for achieving the global warming control target. The related reports include "Unburnable carbon" issued by the Carbon Tracker Initiative and "The geographical distribution of fossil fuels unused when limiting global warming to 2°C" issued by the Institute of Sustainable Resources of University College London. The IEA's "The oil and gas industry in energy transitions" stated that "if there is no reduction in the combustion of the existing fossil fuel reserves, carbon dioxide emissions will be three times higher than the estimated amount."

Transportation: Electrification

Energy (mainly fuel) used in the transportation sector (including roads, railways, shipping, and aviation) not only constitutes the main source of air pollution, but is also a major contributor to carbon emissions. Electric vehicles emit no pollutants, and, even under China's current power structure, generate less carbon emissions than petrol vehicles do. In the future when the power sector achieved a high proportion of clean energy with zero carbon emissions, full employment of electric vehicles and electric railway transportation will be able to eliminate the carbon emissions associated with roads and railways. Given the aforesaid, the key to realising carbon neutrality in the transportation sector is to ensure full electrification in conventional road and railway transport. More provinces and cities are suggested to follow suit Hainan Province which has announced the timetable for a complete shift to electric vehicles for all sales in the near future (such as by 2030) and for a complete phase-out of fossil fuel vehicles. China should aim to boost the proportion of electric vehicles in the total vehicle sales to 50% in the nationwide scale by 2035.

The construction of vehicle charging and hydrogenation infrastructure should be accelerated, and the use of hydrogen vehicles, especially among heavy transportation vehicles, should be vigorously promoted to scale up the number of hydrogen vehicles to 1 million by 2035. Moreover, the shipping and air transportation sectors should be encouraged to switch to clean energy such as natural gas and electricity to accelerate the phasing out of energy-intensive transportation facilities and technologies. The urbanisation process should also focus on the construction of green infrastructure and the investment in public transportation facilities such as rail and rapid transit, the development of green travel facilities and environment for urban cycling and walking, to scale down the demand of transport by private motor vehicles, thereby lowering transportation-related carbon emissions from the source while boosting the vigour of cities.

Construction: Promote zero-carbon construction

The energy consumption of the construction sector accounts for about 20% of China's total energy consumption, the majority of which is used for lighting, heating and cooling and home appliances, and is generated mainly from thermal power with high carbon emissions[12]. There are two key ways for the construction sector to achieve net-zero emissions — the energy conservation in the construction stage and the use of green electricity (clean energy such as photovoltaics).

---

12 Source: "Annual research report on the development of architecture and energy conservation in China", Building Energy Research Center, Tsinghua University, 2018.

Compared with the power and transportation sectors, the technologies used in the construction sector for achieving low or even zero carbon emissions are considered more mature. The construction sector has the potential to become the first sector in China to achieve zero carbon emissions if the relevant ministries and local governments assist in organising resources and scale up the efforts in promoting and coordinating the relevant work. In Europe, several zero-carbon demonstration parks have been set up, in which all buildings have achieved net-zero emissions without reliance on government subsidies. Some existing pilot projects in China have also proved the technical and economic feasibility of zero-carbon buildings.

The fundamental elements for achieving overall zero emissions in the construction sector are: raising energy conservation standards for new buildings, developing and implementing ultra-low energy consumption and zero-carbon building standards as soon as possible while strongly promoting the construction of zero-carbon buildings; encouraging energy-saving renovation and retrofitting of existing buildings; establishing zero-carbon demonstration parks and improving zero-carbon building technologies; increasing the electrification rate of the energy consumed in the construction operations, fully utilising distributed renewable energy (such as photovoltaics) and adjusting the sourcing structure of heating in the northern areas and enhancing heating sourcing efficiency; promoting energy-saving and intelligent energy-efficient products (such as household appliances) and facilities.

Industrials: Adjust the structure to improve energy efficiency and promote low-carbon technologies

The industrial sectors, among which the manufacturing sector in particular, possesses a higher degree of technical complexity compared with the power, transportation and construction sectors, and thus faces greater difficulties in attaining zero carbon emissions. Research by Tsinghua University shows that the carbon emissions of the industrial sectors in China can be lowered by 70% by 2050 compared to the current level, by vigorously promoting industrial structure upgrade, energy efficiency enhancement, electrification transformation and the substitution of high-carbon raw materials[13]. There are four core elements to achieve this goal. The first is upgrading the industrial structure. Drawing upon the experience from developed countries, the proportion of low value-added industries in the total value added of the industrial sectors will dwindle as the per capita

---

13　Source: "Research on China's long-term low carbon development strategy and transition pathways" (〈中國長期低碳發展戰略與轉型路徑研究〉), published by the Center for Finance and Development, Tsinghua National Institute of Financial Research, 2020.

income increases. It was estimated that by 2050, the proportion of the added value from China's high value-added industries to the total industrial output will rise from the current level of 35% to about 60%, and industrial energy consumption will consequently drop by about 60% from the current level. The second is to improve the energy and resource utilisation efficiency form the industrial system. Energy efficiency enhancement is the key to curbing carbon emissions in industrial sectors while the recycling of resources (such as plastics, steel, aluminium and other raw materials) is also conducive to minimising carbon emissions during the raw materials production process. Through large-scale employment of energy-efficient, low-emission or even zero-emission technologies, China's energy consumption per unit of industrial added value can be reduced by about 65% from the current level by 2050. The third element is the electrification of the industrial sectors and the promotion of the use of low-carbon fuels/raw materials. Coal-fired boilers remain in heavy use for coal combustion in the industrial sectors in China and the sectors' electrification rate is just around 26%. In the future, increased electrification rate (up to 70% by 2050) and green electricity utilisation will result in significant carbon emissions reduction[14]. The fourth is to substitute fossil raw materials with assorted new materials (such as using hydrogen energy to substitute coking coal as a reducing agent for steel production) to minimise carbon emissions in the production process.

Opportunities and challenges faced by the financial sector in achieving carbon neutrality

Against the backdrop of large-scale transformation of the real economy to low-carbon or zero-carbon, the financial sector must also follow suit in order to cater to the huge demand for green and low-carbon investment and financing arising from such economic transformation on the one hand, and to prevent financial risks induced by climate transition risks on the other hand. These financial risks include default risks and devaluation risks of the high-carbon industries and systemic financial risks faced by certain high-carbon regions.

Achieving carbon neutrality requires green investment in hundreds of trillions

Achieving carbon neutrality requires a large amount of green and low-carbon investment, a large majority of which needs to be satisfied by mobilising social capital through the

---

14 Source: China's State Grid Energy Research Institute, *China Energy & Electricity Outlook 2020*.

financial system. Many experts and institutions have made different estimates regarding the scale of green and low-carbon investment required for carbon neutrality. For example, the report "Research on China's long-term low carbon development strategy and transition pathways" (《中國長期低碳發展戰略與轉型路徑研究》) published by Tsinghua University puts forward four scenarios, and the transformation required under one of these scenarios for realising the goal of lowering the global temperature by 1.5°C will entail a cumulative additional investment of approximately RMB 138 trillion which accounts for over 2.5% of China's gross domestic product (GDP) per year. Another estimate is made in a project report "Chongqing Carbon Neutrality Target and Green Finance Roadmap" (《重慶碳中和目標和綠色金融路線圖》) led by Ma Jun which states that for Chongqing City (whose GDP accounts for about 1/40 of the China's GDP) to achieve carbon neutrality in the next 30 years, low-carbon investment of an aggregate sum of over RMB 8 trillion will be required (excluding green investment such as environmental protection that is not related to emissions reduction). In addition, the Investment Association of China and Rocky Mountain Institute estimate that RMB 70 trillion of investment needs to be mobilised in seven areas including renewable energy, energy efficiency, zero-carbon technology and energy storage to turn the vision of carbon neutrality into reality[15]. Based on the above estimates, it is expected that the scale of green and low-carbon investment required for China to attain carbon neutrality in the next three decades should be over RMB100 trillion or even several hundreds of trillions, implying enormous opportunities for the development of green finance.

Carbon neutrality creates opportunities for the financial sector

The substantial demand for green investment driven by the carbon neutrality goal will provide opportunities to well-prepared financial institutions for the rapid growth of their green finance businesses. Typical product areas include:

- **Banks:** Innovate products and services suitable for clean energy and green transportation projects; promote the development of pilot projects for the financing of green buildings and explore innovative labelled financial products in areas such as star-level buildings, large-scale applications of renewable energy and green construction materials; develop asset securitisation products of energy efficiency credit loans, green bonds and green loans; design products and models that serve small and micro enterprises, consumers and the greening of agriculture; design financial products and

---

15 Source: "Investment opportunities arising from the goal of carbon neutrality", jointly published by Rocky Mountain Institute and the Investment Association of China, 2020.

services, such as transition loans, that are required to facilitate the green and low-carbon transition of sectors including the energy and industrial sectors.

- **Green bonds:** Issue innovative green bond products such as government special green bonds, green bond collection of small and medium-sized enterprises (SMEs), climate bonds, blue bonds and transition bonds; improve the liquidity of the green bond market and attract overseas green investors to invest in and hold such bond products.

- **Green stock market:** Simplify the verification or filing procedures for initial public offerings of green enterprises, and explore the establishment of a green channel mechanism for green enterprises; support green enterprises with good operating conditions and developmental prospects to participate in pilot programmes to be prioritised for listing board transfer.

- **Environmental rights market and financing:** Develop environment rights and collateral financing, and explore carbon finance and carbon derivative products.

- **Green insurance:** Develop and promote innovative green financial products such as climate (catastrophe) insurance, green building insurance, renewable energy insurance and new energy vehicle insurance.

- **Green funds:** Encourage the establishment of green funds and transition funds, support equity investment in green and low-carbon industries to meet the financing demand of the energy and industrial sectors during the transition period.

- **Private equity:** Encourage venture capital funds to engage in incubating green and low-carbon technology enterprises, and support equity funds in the mergers and acquisitions and restructuring of green projects or enterprises; guide private equity funds to collaborate with regional equity rights markets to support the quotation and transfer of green assets (enterprises).

- **Carbon market:** Extend the scope of emissions control to include other major energy-intensive industrial sectors, transportation and construction sectors, and enlist agriculture and forestry sectors as key development areas of voluntary emissions reduction and carbon sink.

The financial sector needs to prevent and manage climate risks

As major countries in the world have announced their carbon neutrality targets and stepped up their efforts to implement the Paris Agreement, the transition risk of climate change will become increasingly conspicuous for many industries and financial institutions with climate risk exposure. Transition risk refers to the economic and financial risks faced by certain enterprises and industries that arise from the shift in policies, technologies, and market awareness during the transition process of the real economy to a green and low-carbon one. For example, as countries adopt policies and measures to promote the greening of energy systems, the demand for fossil energy industries such as coal and oil will plummet; prices in the carbon market in many countries will soar under the efforts of implementing the Paris Agreement, causing a steep increase in the expenditure on acquiring carbon allowances for a large number of high-carbon companies; due to technological advancement, the cost of clean energy such as photovoltaics and wind power will dwindle, catalysing the displacement of fossil energy and thus the continuous decrease in fossil energy price.

Under these transition scenarios, coal and oil industries, manufacturing industries, such as petrochemical, iron and steel, cement and aluminium that still utilise high-carbon technologies, as well as industries and projects that engage in deforestation and other damage to biodiversity, may face significantly higher costs, lower revenues, severe losses, and even business discontinuation. For financial institutions and investors, these risks will induce loan/bond defaults and investment losses. In geographical areas where high-carbon industries are concentrated (such as Shanxi, Shaanxi, Inner Mongolia), risks related to climate transition may evolve into regional and systemic financial risks as well as unemployment and other social risks caused by large-scale closedown of enterprises.

Towards the goal of carbon neutrality, the loan default rate of China's coal power generation enterprises may rise to more than 20% within a decade (see Box 1) while the loan default rate of other high-carbon industries may also rocket. The financial risks caused by climate transition may give rise to systemic financial risks. In the past few years, some foreign central banks and regulators (such as the Bank of England, the Bank of the Netherlands, the Bank of France, the European Central Bank), international organisations and cooperation mechanisms (such as the NGFS) have begun to emphasise the necessity for the financial sector to conduct environmental and climate risk analysis. However, most financial institutions in China have not yet fully recognise the risks associated with climate transition, and lack the forward-looking judgments on climate transition risks and the relevant risk prevention mechanisms.

Box 1. Climate risk analysis

The NGFS supervisory working group issued two important publications on environmental risk analysis in September 2020 — *Overview of Environmental Risk Analysis* and *Case Studies of Environmental Risk Analysis Methodologies*, summarising the various models and methods developed or deployed by global financial institutions (including banks, insurance and securities companies) to conduct environmental and climate risk analysis. These publications provide assistance for financial institutions to estimate the risks of the rising non-performing loan ratio and the decrease in investment valuations caused by climate and environmental transition factors.

At the macro level, some institutions and central banks have studied the impact of climate-related risks on financial stability and conducted quantitative analysis. According to estimates by the Economist Intelligence Unit, under extreme conditions, climate change will lead to asset loss of US$43 trillion[16]; the central bank of the Netherlands predicts that 11% of the country's bank assets will be exposed to relatively large climate risks[17]. At the industry level, the risk analysis and forecast of listed equities conducted by a British consulting agency, Vivid Economics, indicates that the coal sector's equity devaluation may reach 80% and the valuation of the oil and gas sector may fall by 50%[18]; and the 2ii Institute presents that in the 2DS temperature rise scenario[19], the value of coal power assets may be impaired by 80%, therefore triggering the bank default rate to jump fourfold[20].

---

16 Source: The Economist Intelligence Unit. "The cost of inaction", published on *The Economist* website, 24 July 2015.

17 Source: Schellekens, G. and J. van Toor. (2019) "Values at risk? Sustainability risks and goals in the Dutch financial sector", *De Nederlandsche Bank*.

18 Source: Vivid Economics and HSBC Global Asset Management. "Low-carbon transition scenarios: Exploring scenario analysis for equity valuations", October 2018.

19 Under the "too late too sudden" climate scenario used by 2ii Institute, with the goal of keeping the global average temperature in 2100 within about 2°C above the pre-industrial level (i.e. 2DS), the transition to a low-carbon economy and control of carbon emissions start relatively late, while quantitative restrictions on carbon-intensive energy and its use are imposed suddenly, causing higher overall transition costs amid increased frequency of the occurrence of natural disasters.

20 Source: Hayne, M., S. Ralife, J. Thomä and D. Koopman (2019) "Factoring transition risks into regulatory stress-tests", *ACRN Journal of Finance and Risk Perspectives*, Vol. 8, pp.206-222.

The team of the Research Center for Green Finance Development of Tsinghua University has developed a set of transition risk models to estimate the transition risks faced by loans of China's thermal power sector after taking into account the five major transition factors in the next decade. The five major transition factors considered in the model for thermal power companies include:

- **Demand reduction:** Due to the energy transition policy, the future demand for thermal power will decline, dealing a blow to the sales revenue of thermal power companies;

- **Reduced cost of renewable energy:** Due to technological advancement, the cost of electricity generated from new energy sources such as photovoltaics and wind energy may fall below 50% of the cost of thermal power in the next decade, and thermal power prices will be forced to drop in the process;

- **Carbon price increase:** To achieve the goal of carbon neutrality, carbon prices should rise ten times in the next decade, and thermal power companies that do not strive to curtail emissions will have to purchase carbon allowances at a higher price;

- **Rating deterioration:** The three factors above will lead to the deterioration of the financial conditions of thermal power companies, resulting in lower ratings by banks or lower credit ratings in the bond market, leading to an increase in financing costs which will further worsen their financial conditions;

- **Adjusting risk weights by banks:** In the future, banks or regulating institutions may consider adjusting the risk weights applicable to different assets by reducing the risk weights of green assets and raising the corresponding weights of brown/high-carbon assets. If the weights of brown assets increase in the future, the financing costs of thermal power companies will inevitably surge.

After incorporating these five major transition factors into the climate transition risk model and conducting the simulation analysis based on data of three large listed thermal power companies, the result shows that their default rates could climb within a short time horizon. The default rate of China's sample thermal power companies would soar from about 3% in 2020 to about 22% in 2030 in the next decade, if taking into account factors such as demand reduction, price competition and rising financing costs[21]. Therefore, financial institutions should refrain from investing in these companies from the perspective of financial returns and risks. In such regard, over 100 large financial institutions around the world have announced their agenda on the restrictions of investing in thermal power companies, with some institutions expressing that they will divest from coal now while others will gradually reduce or exit such investments within a certain period of time[22].

International financial industry experience in supporting carbon neutrality

Developed economies such as Europe and the UK are among the earliest in the past few years to announce their carbon neutrality goals. Their financial industries and regulatory bodies have since then accumulated plenty of experience in supporting low-carbon investment. Key areas from their experience for reference include the following:

1. **Formulate and improve green finance standards with "do no significant harm to other sustainable development goals" as the principle**

   From the green finance and climate-related standards introduced by non-official organisations years ago, to the official sustainable finance taxonomy developed by the European Union (EU) in more recent years, the key underlying principle is to combat climate change, while encompassing other green and sustainable development goals,

---

21 Source: Ma Jun and Sun Tianyin. (2020) "Analysis methods and applications of climate transition risks and physical risks — Taking thermal power and mortgage loans as examples" (〈氣候轉型風險和物理風險的分析方法和應用 —— 以煤電和按揭貸款為例〉), *Tsinghua Financial Review* (《清華金融評論》), Vol. 9, pp.16-35.

22 Source: "Over 100 global financial institutions are exiting coal, with more to come", published on the website of Institute for Energy Economics and Financial Analysis, 27 February 2019.

such as reducing pollution, protecting biodiversity and facilitating resource recycling. However, the EU emphasises in its latest taxonomy for sustainable activities that economic activities that comply with the standards must do no harm to other sustainable development goals, that is, one goal cannot be achieved through causing harm to other objectives. For example, clean coal utilisation projects can effectively reduce air pollution, but since they cause a substantial increase in carbon emissions, such projects do not meet the sustainable finance taxonomy.

2. **Strengthen climate-related financial information disclosure requirements for enterprises and financial institutions**

The Task Force on Climate-related Financial Disclosures (TCFD) initiated by the former governor of the Bank of England, Mark Carney, under the Financial Stability Board (FSB) has developed information disclosure standards and recommended companies and financial institutions to disclose climate-related financial information according to these standards. This initiative has been supported by hundreds of large companies and financial institutions around the world, and has been used for reference or adopted formally by regulatory bodies of some developed countries. For example, in November 2019, the EU laid down disclosure obligations of sustainability matters at both the entity and financial product levels, which have become effective since March 2021[23]. In December 2020, the UK announced that the majority of companies will be required to disclose information in accordance with TCFD by 2025[24]. In July 2020, Autorité des Marchés Financiers, the financial markets regulator in France, required institutional investors to disclose ESG-related information[25]. In addition, many European and British institutions have already disclosed the carbon footprint of their investment portfolios and their carbon emissions information.

3. **Many institutions in developed countries have conducted environmental and climate risk analysis**

The NGFS released two research reports in September 2020[26], covering environmental and climate risk analysis methods and tools developed by more than

---

23 *Sustainability-related Disclosures in the Financial Services Sector*, issued by the EU, 27 November 2019.

24 Source: HM Treasury, *A Roadmap Towards Mandatory Climate-related Disclosures,* November 2020.

25 Source: Autorité des Marchés Financiers. *Position-Recommendation 2020-03*, 27 July 2020.

26 These two reports are *Overview of Environmental Risk Analysis by Financial Institutions* and *Case Studies of Environmental Risk Analysis Methodologies*.

30 institutions worldwide, including analysis of transition risks and physical risks. Most of these institutions are domiciled in developed economies in Europe.

4. Innovate green and climate-related financial products

Developed markets such as Europe are in a leading position in ESG financial products, carbon markets and carbon finance. Products that provide good examples for reference include various types of credit loans, bonds and exchange-traded fund (ETF) products linked to sustainable development goals, transition bonds, green supply-chain financial products and green asset securitisation. Furthermore, the European Union Emissions Trading System (EU ETS) covers 45% of the entire EU economy's carbon emissions, and the related derivative products have offered effective enabler for price discovery and liquidity improvement in the carbon market[27].

The gap between the current green financial system and the carbon neutrality goal

Since the State Council of China first proposed the establishment of a green financial system in the *Integrated Reform Plan for Promoting Ecological Progress* in 2015, China has made impressive strides in green finance standards, incentive mechanisms, disclosure requirements, product systems, local pilot projects and international cooperation, with achievements in certain areas demonstrating remarkable global influence. However, China's current green financial system still faces a number of issues and challenges in several areas, limiting its potential to reach the carbon neutrality goal:

1. The current green finance standard system is not fully compatible with the carbon neutrality goal

For example, although the new version of the Green Bonds Endorsed Project Catalogue (2021 Edition) no longer include carbon-intensive projects that are related to fossil energy such as "clean coal technology", the criteria for defining green finance in application (including green loan standards, guiding catalogue for green industries) has not been adjusted accordingly. Some of the green projects defined in these standards do not fully meet the carbon neutrality requirements for achieving net-zero carbon emissions.

---

27 Source: EU ETS webpage on the website of the European Commission, viewed on 27 August 2021.

2. **The environmental information disclosure does not meet the requirements of carbon neutrality**

Sufficient disclosure of environmental information by enterprises and financial institutions serves as an important basis for the financial system to channel capital to green industries, whereas the carbon emissions information disclosed by investee companies and projects is a key foundation for low-carbon investment decision-making. China has not imposed mandatory disclosure requirements relating to carbon emissions and carbon footprint information on most companies. Although some financial institutions have begun to disclose information on green financing/investment, most of them have yet to disclose information relating to brown/high-carbon assets. Most institutions still lack the capability to collect, calculate and analyse carbon emissions and carbon footprint information. Failure for financial institutions to measure and disclose the environmental risk exposure and carbon footprint information of their investment/loan portfolios will impair their capability to manage climate-related risks or understand their potential contribution in supporting the reduction of carbon in the real economy, and therefore keep them ill-prepared to achieve the carbon neutrality goal.

3. **The green financial incentive mechanism has not yet placed sufficient emphasis on low-carbon development**

Certain policies issued by the financial regulatory authorities endorsed by local governments (including supporting green finance through re-lending and incentivising banks to increase green loans through macro-prudential assessment) and mechanisms, including interest subsidies and guarantees for green projects, have motivated social capitals to participate in green investment to a certain extent. However, the effectiveness and coverage of the incentives are still insufficient and there lacks special incentives targeting low-carbon and zero-carbon investments to green projects. The design of these incentive mechanisms also fails to use carbon footprint of the investments or assets as an evaluation criterion.

4. **Insufficient knowledge of and analytical capabilities in climate transition risks**

China's financial regulatory authorities have started to emphasise the importance of financial risks caused by climate change. However, they have yet to develop systematic analytical capabilities in assessing climate risks, nor have they issued specific requirements for financial institutions to engage in environmental and climate risk analysis. Except for a few leading institutions in green finance which have carried out environmental and climate stress testing, most financial institutions in China have not yet fully understood the risks associated with climate transition and the relevant analysis models and methodologies, whereas most small and medium-sized financial institutions are still in the dark about the concept of climate risk. Chinese financial institutions still lag much behind their European counterparts in terms of the understanding of the relevant risks and internal capabilities in managing such risks.

5. **Green financial products are not yet fully adapted to the needs of carbon neutrality**

China has made much headway in developing green products such as green credit loans and green bonds, but still lags much behind the developed markets in terms of providing ESG products for investors and the diversification and liquidity of such products. Many green financial products are not yet linked to carbon footprint, while the role of the carbon market and carbon financial products in reallocating financial resources is still very limited. The degree of openness of the carbon market is also relatively low.

Policy recommendations

The low-carbon transformation of the economy would not be accelerated and net-zero emissions of major industries would not be realised without substantial and large-scale reform measures to provide necessary implementation support following China's announcement of its carbon neutrality goal. Relevant quantitative analyses show that if the economic development proceeds in accordance with existing industrial policies and regional development plannings, China's carbon emissions will remain at a high level in the next 30 years, making net-zero emissions impossible and difficult for China to honour its commitment to the international community of reaching a carbon peak by 2030.

As with the current status of China's financial industry, although the framework of a green financial system has been established, other aspects including the green finance standards, information disclosure and incentive mechanisms still fall short of the requirements for carbon neutrality. The product system is not yet able to fully cater to the demand of low-carbon investment. In addition, financial institutions are not fully aware of the financial risks associated with climate transition, nor have they taken adequate measures to prevent and manage these risks.

To address these issues, the establishment of a policy system targeting the goals of carbon peaking and carbon neutrality should be expedited from two aspects. The first is to require all local and relevant ministries to hasten the formulation of roadmaps towards 2030 and 2060 and to roll out a series of policies to stimulate the low-carbon and zero-carbon transition, stepping up cross-sectoral coordination and cooperation among various ministries, local governments and financial institutions. The second is to systematically refine the relevant policies through the four dimensions of standards, disclosure, incentives and products, to build a green financial system that meets the requirements for achieving the carbon neutrality goal, ensuring the active participation of social capital in the construction of low-carbon and zero-carbon future and effectively preventing climate-related risks.

Local and industrial departments should design carbon neutrality roadmaps

First, the central government should specifically require the governments at local level to put forward plans and implementation roadmaps for achieving the carbon neutrality goal, and encourage regions that currently possessing the required conditions to become carbon neutral to do so as soon as possible. According to the information collected from several regions, many provinces and municipalities (including the main persons in charge) have very limited understanding of the implication, background and significance of carbon neutrality, and a large majority of local industrial departments have not yet understood the extensive transformation that industries including electricity, transportation, construction and industrial sectors will need to undergo in order to achieve the goal of carbon neutrality. They also fail to realise that the long-term vision proposed by XI Jinping, the General Secretary of the Chinese Communist Party, calls for immediate action, which otherwise would result in a higher carbon peak that may cause greater social and economic burdens. Some may still misunderstand that they are obliged to fully utilise coal as gifted by the province's natural resource and therefore continue to plan for coal power projects and projects that utilise traditional high-carbon technologies. Other regions which are willing to implement the carbon neutrality goal are reluctant to take the lead in launching the carbon neutrality roadmap due to resistance from some traditional high-carbon industries and the lack of clear guidance from the central government. In light of all these, it is suggested that the central government should issue clear guidelines for local governments, requiring all local governments to develop plans and implementation roadmaps towards the carbon neutrality goal without delay; encourage regions with bountiful renewable energy resources, large forest coverage, relatively developed service industries, low dominance of manufacturing industries and strong technological innovation capabilities to achieve net-zero or near-zero emissions as soon as possible (around 2050); and establish net-zero emissions demonstration parks and demonstration projects for other regions to use for reference and replication.

Second, the central government should specifically require the relevant ministries and commissions to develop zero-carbon development plans and carbon sink forestry development plans, and to incorporate specific targets into the "14th Five-Year Plan" of the relevant industries. Since the achievement of the carbon neutrality goal involves the transformation of all high-carbon industries, coordination of planning among these industries is crucial. Preliminary analysis reveals that these industries must undergo fundamental changes during the "14th Five-Year Plan" period and need to deem substantial emissions reduction as the prerequisite or even the primary task over the next five to ten years, rather than treating it as an "icing on the cake" in policy plannings. For example, the "14th Five-Year Plan" and the 10-year plan of the energy sector must order for halting the building of new coal power plants, and substantially raise the investment goals of photovoltaic, wind power, hydrogen energy, offshore wind power and energy storage technologies. The central government should consider supporting well-qualified regions to announce a timetable for stopping the sale of fossil fuel vehicles, and continue to provide subsidies and support for renewable energy vehicles while investing in and deploying the relevant infrastructure such as charging stations on a larger scale. Regarding green buildings, the ultra-low energy consumption building standards and the near-zero-emissions building standards should be widely adopted as early as possible and greater fiscal and financial support should be directed to zero-carbon buildings. For industrial sectors, advanced low-carbon and zero-carbon technologies should be introduced and large-scale and comprehensive energy-saving transformations should be carried out in various industrial manufacturing sectors. Efforts should also be put into actively preserving, restoring and practising sustainable management of the ecosystem as well as strengthening sustainable forest management and afforestation to improve regional carbon storage and sinking capacity.

Enhance the green financial system to achieve carbon neutrality

The financial industry should start planning a green finance roadmap for achieving the goal of carbon neutrality. Hundreds of billions in Renminbi of green and low-carbon investments may be needed in the next few decades to realise carbon neutrality across the country. Based on the experience of green finance development, around 90% of the financing must be mobilised and channelled by the financial system in order to meet such a huge demand for investment. Therefore, it is necessary for financial regulators and local governments to take the lead in exploring and planning a green finance development roadmap with carbon neutrality as the goal.

The roadmap should include three main aspects: the first is to formulate the medium-
to long-term green development plan and regional planning for the main industries, the
investment and financing planning for green industries and key projects, and a series of
specific action plans and measures which includes developing renewable energy and
green hydrogen energy, facilitating the low-carbon transition of the industrial sectors,
the zero-carbon transition of the construction sector, electrification of transportation,
and phasing out outdated coal power production capacity. The second is to establish a
coordination mechanism between the planning of green industries and of green financial
development; develop a system of standards for green and low-carbon industries,
products and green finance; establish a synergistic mechanism between green projects
and green financing channels, including a platform to match green projects with green
funds. The third is to improve the green financial system with carbon neutrality as the
goal, including revising green finance standards, imposing requirements of mandatory
environmental information disclosure, enhancing the incentive mechanisms for green and
low-carbon investment and financing, and promoting financial product innovations for low-
carbon investment and financing. The specific recommendations are as follows:

**First, green finance standards should be revised with achieving carbon neutrality as
the goal.** China's green finance standards have not yet completely excluded high-carbon
projects including fossil energy that do not fully meet the net-zero carbon emissions
required to achieve carbon neutrality. In the future, the standards for green loans and
green industries should also be revised to align with the goal of carbon neutrality and
the scope of green funds and green insurance should be well defined accordingly. At
the same time, projects that meet these green standards must be ensured to cause no
significant harm on other sustainable development goals.

**Second, the regulatory authorities should require financial institutions to calculate
and disclose their risk exposure to high-carbon assets and the carbon footprint
of their major assets (see Box 2).** The PBOC, the China Banking and Insurance
Regulatory Commission (CBIRC), the China Securities Regulatory Commission (CSRC)
and other financial regulators are recommended to issue requirements that oblige financial
institutions to disclose environmental and climate information, including information on
the green and brown assets held by financial institutions as well as the carbon footprint of
these assets and major assets. At the initial stage, financial institutions may be required to
disclose their risk exposure in assets associated with brown or high-carbon industries (such
as loans and investments in industries like coal mining, coal power, iron and steel, cement,
chemical, aluminium) and the carbon emissions and carbon footprints of the companies
accepting loans or investments. At the interim stage, financial institutions may be required

Box 2. Environmental information disclosure by financial institutions

The environmental-related information of financial institutions required by the regulatory authorities has had the focus mainly on the environmental contribution of green loans and corporate green investments, but the requirements for negative information such as carbon emissions are absent. In the future, financial institutions should be required to disclose carbon emissions information, including carbon emissions generated by projects financed by bank loans and equity investments. The information about carbon emissions and carbon footprint is crucial in achieving the goal of carbon neutrality. Therefore, carbon-related information should be regarded as the central component and its disclosure should be made compulsory in the future upgrading of environmental information disclosure requirements. Regulators are also recommended to require banks to disclose carbon emissions information on all assets (mainly the investment projects of corporate borrowers). Recognising the potential challenges such measures may bring, the requirement can be applicable to large enterprises in the initial stage and be gradually expanded to SMEs. Now, the carbon emissions information of large and key emission companies already exists for public access in the environmental protection system. It will therefore be important to ensure communication between the key market players from the environmental protection end and the finance-oriented end to avoid the excess cost of repeated data collection.

Some foreign financial institutions have established preliminary standards for disclosing carbon footprints through practice. For example, in the UK-China Climate and Environmental Information Disclosure Pilot Programme Working Group, Aviva Group disclosed the carbon footprint of its equity and credit assets in 2018 and 2019, which marked a downward trend. Such experience proves the technical feasibility for financial institutions to publish their carbon footprints. In addition, Aviva Group also made available the results of climate stress testing analysis, i.e. the financial risks due to climate physical risks and transition risks. Therefore, it is also feasible for financial institutions to implement and disclose their forward-looking stress testing or scenario analysis. In addition, HSBC and China Industrial Bank have also disclosed their risk exposure to high-carbon assets.

Currently, Chinese regulators only require banks to measure and partially disclose green loans, but issue no requirements on the disclosure of brown or high-carbon assets. Some financial institutions are willing to disclose information on green loans, but reluctant to reveal their risk exposure regarding brown assets. In fact, financial institutions benefit from the disclosure of brown asset information due to the fact that the market will consider those who fail to disclose brown asset exposure as being not fully aware of such risks and thus more vulnerable thereof. On the contrary, if the financial institutions have calculated and disclosed these risks, the market will likely to consider them well prepared to take proactive actions against the climate risks and hence install stronger confidence in them.

to disclose the carbon footprint of major loans/investments (or loans/investments provided to large and medium-sized enterprises). Regulators, industry associations (either at the national or regional level, such as the Green Finance Committee of China's Society for Finance and Banking) and international cooperation mechanisms (such as the UK-China Climate and Environmental Information Disclosure Pilot Programme Working Group) should arrange to provide capacity building assistance to financial institutions to disclose environmental information and promote the best practices of leading institutions.

Third, regulatory authorities should give clear guidance to encourage financial institutions to conduct environmental and climate risk analysis and strengthen capabilities. Only a few banks in China have conducted environmental and climate risk analysis and most large financial institutions that remain aware of such practice have not yet developed relevant analytical capabilities, whilst most small and medium-sized institutions still know little about the credit risks, market risks, and reputation risks induced by climate transition. The PBOC, the CBIRC, the CSRC and other financial regulators are recommended to explicitly guide Chinese financial institutions to refer to NGFS and other relevant practices to conduct forward-looking environmental and climate risk analysis, including stress testing and scenario analysis. Industry associations, research institutes, and education and training institutions should also engage experts to support financial

Box 3. Financial incentive measures for supporting carbon neutrality

First, set up a re-lending mechanism earmarked for funding green and low-carbon projects. Green project re-lending support has been a part of the overall re-lending mechanism, but no re-lending options specifically for low-carbon projects is available. Some recent re-lending arrangements have even imposed additional conditions or constraints — SME loans must account for more than 50% of all loans, such that the green re-lending loan will not be released if the bank could not find an adequate number of SMEs as borrowers. In the future, given the goal of carbon neutrality, the number of low-carbon projects is set to shoot up and this will make it necessary, with the required conditions satisfied, to establish a re-lending mechanism of a scale of hundreds of billions of yuan per year to dedicated funding of green and low-carbon projects.

Second, allow green assets with relatively low risk to be included in the scope of qualified collateral for commercial banks when borrowing from the central bank. Banks with these green collaterals can borrow from the central bank at low interest rates.

Third, incorporate banks' carbon footprints into the macro-prudential assessment regime or the PBOC's green bank assessment mechanism. If a bank's carbon footprint drops rapidly, which represents a competent level of the bank's green performance, the PBOC may provide it with more supportive policy tools, such as liquidity support at lower costs and preferential required reserve ratios.

Fourth, the central bank and the CBIRC should consider lowering the risk weight of a bank's green assets and increasing the risk weight of brown/high-carbon assets while keeping the overall risk weight of the bank unchanged. Currently, a bank's risk weight for corporate loans is 100%. There may be potential to reduce the risk weight of green loans to 75% and increase the risk weight of brown loans to a certain level so as to maintain the overall risk weight unchanged. From a macro perspective, such adjustment does not impact the bank's overall capital adequacy ratio, but it can effectively drive structural adjustment by trimming the financing cost of green loans and increasing the financing cost of brown credit, thereby accelerating the transition to a green investment structure and a green real economy. Owing to the lack of standards and data for domestic green and brown assets, other countries still have not implemented any reforms on the risk weights of green and brown assets despite that relevant discussions have gone on for several years. China has 7 years' green loan data and the default rate of green loans is only about 0.5%, which is far lower than the overall domestic loan default rate of about 2%[28]. These data demonstrate that increasing the risk weight of green assets and reducing the risk weight of brown assets can not only accelerate the greening of the investment structure, but can also mitigate the transition risks challenging the entire banking industry. China possesses these fundamental data to introduce policy reform in the adjustment of risk weights.

institutions in their capability building, propelling more in international exchanges in this area. The central bank and financial regulators should take a leading role in organising environmental and climate risk analysis at the macro-level, evaluating the impact of these risks on financial stability, and considering requiring large and medium-sized financial institutions to progressively disclose the results of their environmental and climate risk analysis.

Fourth, a stronger incentive mechanism of green finance should be built to realise the carbon neutrality goal (see Box 3). The PBOC is recommended to consider developing a relatively large-scale re-lending mechanism (with the approximate scale of hundreds of billions in Renminbi per year) to provide financing support for low-carbon projects; to allow commercial banks to use green assets with relatively low risk as qualified collateral for borrowing from the central bank; to incorporate the carbon footprint of banks' assets into the assessment mechanism of green banks, and link the carbon footprint of banks with the usage of the central bank's monetary policy tools; to consider lowering the risk weight of green assets and increasing the risk weight of brown/high-

---

28 Source: *China Green Finance Development Report* (《中國綠色金融發展報告》), published by the PBOC, 2019.

carbon assets while maintaining the overall risk weight of the bank's assets unchanged. Before launching the measures of adjusting the risk weights to the entire banking industry, the PBOC may facilitate qualified regions and financial institutions that possess certain required conditions to carry out pilot work.

Fifth, the State Administration of Foreign Exchange (SAFE) and sovereign funds should engage in ESG investment and promote green investment management institutions (see Box 4). Foreign exchange management departments and sovereign funds may refer to the recommendations of NGFS and proactively carry out sustainable investments to guide the participation of the private sector and social capital. It is recommended that foreign exchange management departments and sovereign funds should establish a screening mechanism for investment targets and fund managers in accordance with sustainable/ESG investment principles, build up their environmental and climate risk analysis capabilities, disclose ESG information, support the development of the green bond market and fulfil the role of being active shareholders to promote the ESG performance of invested companies.

Sixth, the regulatory authorities should issue mandatory requirements for financial institutions to conduct environmental impact assessments for their overseas investments (including investment projects in the "Belt and Road"). Continuing to invest in coal power and other high-carbon projects in the "Belt and Road" region will undermine the China's green "Belt and Road" Initiative, bringing reputational and financial risks to Chinese financial institutions. It is recommended that relevant departments should establish a mandatory environmental impact assessment mechanism for China's foreign investment without delay, and strictly restrict overseas investments in pollution and high-carbon projects. Chinese financial institutions are also encouraged to commit to substantially cutting down and stopping investments in, and guarantees for, new overseas coal power projects. International cooperation should be promoted to enable China joining hands with Japan and South Korea to reduce and stop coal power investment in third countries.

Box 4. How sovereign funds embark on ESG investments

SAFE, sovereign funds and government-managed pension funds, as asset owners, can exercise influence over the behaviour of a large number of asset managers, thereby promoting the greening of China's asset management industry. In the process of selecting asset managers, if SAFE, sovereign funds and pension funds impose additional conditions and require that more resources be allocated to ESG projects in accordance with the principles of sustainable investment, and provide funds only to asset managers that meet the standards and have ESG management capabilities, a large number of asset management companies will be incentivised to embark on ESG transition and subsequently making other funds managed by these asset management companies greener as well. This is expected to have far-reaching implications, reaching far beyond the direct benefits of green investment of SAFE, sovereign funds and pension funds.

NGFS has put forward many suggestions in the "SRI Investment Guide"[29] that can be used as references for the greening of foreign exchange, sovereign and pension investments. The first and foremost is to establish a screening mechanism for investment targets and fund manager selection. Qualified fund managers to be selected must satisfy the required ESG management standards. The second is to develop the ability of sovereign funds or central banks to analyse climate-related risks, and to identify high-risk areas to be avoided and areas that should be supported. The third is to disclose ESG information on foreign exchange, sovereign and pension fund investments to promote the transparency of the entire industry. The fourth is to offer specific support towards certain green industries and green financial sectors, such as through investing in the green bond market to lower the financing cost of green bonds. The fifth is to leverage, with reference to the practice of Norges Bank (the central bank of Norway), the active role

---

29 Source: NGFS, *A Sustainable and Responsible Investment Guide for Central Banks' Portfolio Management*, October 2019.

as shareholders and drive investee companies to improve their ESG performance through shareholder engagement. Norges Bank manages more than US$1 trillion in assets and is an international leader in green sovereign investment. Its investment covers not only companies with good ESG performance, but also those with fair ESG performance and urges the latter ones to improve their ESG performance thereafter. Norges Bank has played a proactive role of a sovereign investor to facilitate, the ESG performance improvement of more than 1,000 investee companies, providing a positive example for other banks to draw on[30].

Seventh, financial institutions should be encouraged to explore transition financing, including setting up transition funds and issuing transition bonds. To achieve carbon neutrality, support should not only be offered to pure green projects (such as clean energy, new green transportation and green building projects), but should also be oriented to help the clean energy transition of fossil energy companies, the green and low-carbon retrofitting of existing old buildings as well as energy saving, emissions reduction and carbon reduction projects of high-carbon industrial enterprises. The latter are generally referred to as transitional economic activities, which also require a large amount of financing and incentive mechanisms. Europe has established some transition funds to subsidise high-carbon companies' changeover to low-carbon operations while averting unemployment. It has also introduced some transition bonds to aid traditional energy companies to launch new energy projects and reconstruct the abandoned mines into ecological scenic spots. China can draw on these experiences and establish mechanisms to promote transition financing in the areas of standards definitions, disclosure requirements and incentive mechanisms, encouraging financial institutions to roll out targeted financial instruments like transition bonds, transition funds and transition insurance.

Eighth, the role of the carbon market in resource allocation should be strengthened. Among the companies covered by the carbon market with emissions control, carbon trading has demonstrated the effect in guiding resource allocation, directing highly efficient companies to undertake more carbon emissions reduction activities. However, apart from

---

30 Source: Norges Bank Investment Management, *Responsible Investment*, 2019.

controlling emissions of thousands of companies, a more important function of the carbon market should be to influence the behavioural changes of tens of millions of companies in China and encourage them to engage in more low-carbon investments and activities. For the carbon market to fully perform the function of reallocating resources across the entire economy, the effectiveness of carbon pricing needs to be ensured, and the basis of such effect is that the carbon market must have high liquidity. A large number of buyers and sellers of financial institutions as trading participants in the carbon market are needed to ensure market liquidity. In addition, the development of carbon-related derivative products such as carbon futures and options are needed for enhancing market liquidity and providing enterprises with risk management tools.

Green finance outlook in the Greater Bay Area

As one of China's most open and economically dynamic regions, the Greater Bay Area has an important strategic role in the overall development of the country. On 18 February 2019, the Central Committee of the Communist Party of China and the State Council issued the *Outline Development Plan for the Guangdong-Hong Kong-Macao Greater Bay Area*, which clearly states that green finance should be vigorously promoted in the Guangdong-Hong Kong-Macao Greater Bay Area (GBA). In May 2020, the PBOC, CBIRC, CSRC and SAFE jointly issued the *Opinions on Financial Support for the Construction of the Guangdong-Hong Kong-Macao Greater Bay Area* to further propose key issues for advancing cooperation in the GBA on green finance. Local governments subsequently issued policies to support the construction of the GBA, which include a number of targeted measures to facilitate the development and improvement of green finance.

Since seven Mainland ministries and commissions issued the *Guidelines for Establishing the Green Financial System* in 2016, local governments in Guangdong province, Guangzhou, Shenzhen and other cities in the GBA have responded positively and have introduced targeted green finance policies. In order to further the development and cooperation on green finance in the GBA, under the guidance of the Green Finance Committee of China Society for Finance and Banking, the Green Finance Alliance was set up in Guangzhou on 4 September 2020 jointly by the Hong Kong Green Finance Association (HKGFA), the Green Finance Committee of Guangdong Society for Finance and Banking (GDGFC), the Green Finance Committee of Financial Society of Shenzhen Special Economic Zone (SZGFC), and the Macau Association of Banks. This initiative has received strong support from the governments of the four regions. As the world's first and China's first regional green finance alliance, the alliance could leverage the advantages of the Mainland, Hong Kong and Macao in areas including industrial, technological and international aspects to integrate resources and help match domestic and foreign financial, technology and product needs. The alliance has set up five working groups and has engaged in research and preparation works for projects on topics such as the carbon market in the GBA, green supply-chain finance, solid waste disposal, green building and blockchain trading of green assets. Some of the results are expected to be implemented in the GBA and promoted to other parts of the country.

Looking into the future, the GBA can explore breakthroughs in multiple aspects and lead the development of green finance innovation. The first is to encourage more Mainland companies in the GBA to issue green bonds in Hong Kong, so as to take full advantage of the Hong Kong Special Administrative Region Government's preferential policies for green bond issuers. The second is to explore the setup of a unified carbon market covering the GBA and establish a cross-border trading mechanism for the carbon market (referred to as "Carbon Connect") to attract global investors to participate in China's carbon market and to include the power, transportation and construction industries and enterprises in Hong Kong gradually (see Appendix 1 for details). The third is to promote the development of cross-border green asset-backed securities (ABS) to help alleviate China's current problem of lacking liquidity for its large volume of green loans; and explore ways to package green loans into ABS and sell them to global investors. The fourth is to integrate green finance into supply-chain finance, for example, allowing SMEs in the supply chain of automobiles, home appliances and the construction sector to obtain cheaper financing through green certification. This would not only help lower green suppliers' financing costs and promote the green transition of supply-chain enterprises, but also reduce the financing costs of green SMEs.

Appendix 1

Vision of a carbon market in the GBA

On the backdrop of China's proposal to strengthen its nationally-determined contributions by striving to peak its carbon dioxide emissions by 2030 and become carbon neutral by 2060, Guangdong, Hong Kong and Macao, being among the most developed economic regions in China, should take the lead to actively combat climate change in accordance with the national strategy and regard the development of a carbon market as an important starting point for meeting the goal of carbon neutrality. Given the close cooperation between Guangdong, Hong Kong and Macao, it is recommended that Guangdong, Shenzhen, Hong Kong and Macao shall consider jointly building a unified carbon market covering the GBA, and making reference to the Stock Connect and Bond Connect schemes, build a "Cabon Connect" scheme to connect international investors with the domestic carbon market. The specific suggestions are as follows[31]:

The importance of Hong Kong's participation in the setup of a GBA carbon market

Carbon trading is the most important market mechanism to reduce carbon emissions and realise carbon neutrality. The development of carbon markets has become a global trend and Hong Kong is highly recommended to consider playing a part in the building of a unified carbon market in the GBA, which will be crucial in facilitating the materialisation of the vision of carbon neutrality in Hong Kong and solidify its position as a financial centre.

Firstly, collaborating with Guangdong and Macao is the best way for Hong Kong to participate in the establishment of a carbon market given the limited scale of the local market in Hong Kong for establishing its own carbon market with adequate liquidity. Since the carbon market in Guangdong has established strong international influence and an

---

31 The proposal for setting up a unified carbon market in the GBA and Carbon Connect is purely a personal suggestion made by the author of this article after his own research. The institutions or departments mentioned in the article did not participate in the making of such proposal. Nor does such proposal represent the position or viewpoint of any such institution or department. Government departments, regulatory bodies and market institutions have not been communicated or consulted on such personal recommendations, nor have they given any approval, consent or agreement to the recommendations.

adequate level of liquidity, Hong Kong can be involved in the building of a carbon market in the GBA with Guangdong as the market centre. The joint effort of the two places will play a leading role in combating climate change at a regional level, thereby serving the country and the region in meeting the goals of carbon peak and carbon neutrality.

Second, Hong Kong's involvement in the development of a carbon market will reinforce its position as an international financial centre and create a differentiated green finance international centre. Since Hong Kong constitutes an important part of the carbon market in the Greater Bay Area, the development and launch of relevant carbon allowances and financial derivatives can reinvigorate Hong Kong's green finance to reach a higher level. Furthermore, carbon allowances and their financial derivatives will serve as the new subject to connect the countries and regions under China's "Belt and Road" Initiative and to connect China with the EU. This will enhance the competitive edge and influence of China under the global paradigm of green development where Korea, Japan and Singapore have all started to launch their own carbon markets.

Third, Hong Kong's participation in the establishment of the carbon market will help reduce the cost of emissions reduction and promote the improvement of the local environment. The costs of reducing emissions by various sectors in Hong Kong through technological innovation are very high. The introduction of a carbon market will lower such costs for the entire society. Since the sources of carbon emissions are the same as many air pollutants, Hong Kong's participation in building a carbon market and in strengthening the control over carbon dioxide emissions will further enhance the quality of the local environment and facilitate the green transformation of the real economy.

Fourth, with the support of Hong Kong financial infrastructure platforms such as those of Hong Kong Exchanges and Clearing Limited (HKEX) in establishing the carbon market in the GBA, Hong Kong's experience and advantages in facilitating mutual market connectivity between Hong Kong and the Mainland could be leveraged to assist the opening-up of the Mainland's carbon markets, thereby enhancing the breadth and depth of Hong Kong's financial services.

Building a unified carbon market in the GBA

It is recommended to steadily advance the establishment of a unified carbon market in the GBA as follows:

First, collaborate with the Mainland entities to jointly establish the working mechanism for the GBA carbon market, and establish a working group with Guangdong Province, Shenzhen Municipality and Macao to jointly work on the design of the GBA carbon market; have the plan gradually extended to cover the major carbon-emitting companies in Guangdong (including Shenzhen), Hong Kong and Macao within some years.

Second, consolidate the carbon trading market in Guangdong and Shenzhen, and construct the carbon market infrastructure in the GBA founded on the consolidated Guangdong carbon market (including Shenzhen) by the joint effort of Guangdong, Shenzhen, Hong Kong and Macao.

Third, join the Guangdong Province's inclusive voluntary carbon emissions reduction mechanism (" 廣東省碳普惠自願減排機制 ") and include Hong Kong's emissions reduction projects in industries such as construction, transportation, forestry and new energy in Guangdong's carbon market as products for voluntary trading, so as to accumulate experience to get prepared for compulsory implementation.

Fourth, launch a carbon trading module in HKEX and connect it with the Mainland trading platforms to provide global investors with various derivative products (including carbon futures, carbon swaps) based on the spot products in the GBA carbon market.

Fifth, commence the legislation process for carbon emissions trading in the Hong Kong Special Administrative Region at the appropriate time; have the GBA Office of the State Council take the lead to formulate and release carbon dioxide emissions information reporting and verification guidelines applicable to entities bound by carbon emissions control in the GBA, allocate carbon emissions quota in the GBA, and progressively enhance the unified carbon market in the area.

Establish Carbon Connect on HKEX

The proposed Carbon Connect scheme allows global investors to invest in the carbon market of the GBA more conveniently. It is recommended to use Hong Kong as the channel and the HKEX's platforms as the vehicle. Drawing upon the experience of cross-border trading models such as Stock Connect, Bond Connect, and the cross-border Wealth Management Connect, select a suitable cross-border trading mechanism in consideration of the different characteristics of carbon spot and futures products. In the initial stage after launch, Carbon Connect can achieve connectivity between international investors and the carbon market in the GBA. After gaining more experience, it can move on to realise connectivity between international investors and carbon markets across China. Carbon Connect has the potential to further promote the opening-up of China's carbon market to the world, thereby expanding its global influence through the GBA carbon market.

Remarks:
(1) Part of the content of this article has been published on the WeChat public account platform of *China Financial Times*.
(2) This paper has been produced in the Chinese language, published with a separate English language translation. If there is any conflict in this paper between the meaning of English words or terms in the English language version and Chinese words in the Chinese language version, the meaning of the Chinese words shall prevail.

第2章

中國的綠色金融實踐與前瞻 —— 以碳中和為目標完善 綠色金融體系

馬駿
中國金融學會綠色金融專業委員會主任
北京綠色金融與可持續發展研究院院長
香港綠色金融協會主席兼會長

摘要

自 2016 年中國七部委發佈《關於構建綠色金融體系的指導意見》以來,中國綠色金融在市場規模與產品、政策框架、產品創新、試驗區建設與國際合作等方面取得了長足的進展。綠色信貸存量規模現居世界第一,綠色債券存量規模現居世界第二。

2020 年 9 月,中國國家主席習近平向全世界莊嚴宣佈了中國將在 2060 年前實現碳中和的目標。在碳中和目標下,在實體經濟層面必須加速推動電力、交通、建築和工業的大規模深度脫碳。與此同時,金融業也必須向零碳轉型,不但需要滿足未來 30 年內數百萬億元計的綠色低碳投資需求,還應防範高碳產業轉型所帶來的風險。目前中國綠色金融體系在政策框架、市場供給、風險管理等方面尚未充分反映碳中和的要求。

本章在分析低碳投融資的國際經驗的基礎上,提出了中國地方和產業部門應加快規劃碳中和路線圖,以及以圍繞碳中和目標完善綠色金融體系的一系列具體政策建議。這些建議包括:以碳中和為約束條件修訂綠色金融標準、提升金融機構的氣候信息披露和風險分析能力、強化對低碳投資的激勵政策、鼓勵主權投資機構開展環境、社會和公司治理(簡稱 ESG)投資、防範對外投資的環境與氣候風險、充分發揮碳市場在資源配置中的作用等。最後,文章簡要討論了粵港澳大灣區綠色金融發展的前景和市場機遇。

中國綠色金融的進展情況

近年來，綠色金融在中國得到了迅速的發展。監管部門不斷完善綠色金融頂層設計，自下而上地深入開展綠色金融改革創新基層實踐體系，支持綠色金融跨越式發展，在標準制定、激勵機制、產品創新、地方試點和國際合作等領域取得了一系列令人矚目的成績。

綠色金融市場和產品創新取得了積極的進展。截至 2020 年末，中國全國主要金融機構綠色貸款餘額存量規模近 12 億人民幣，居世界第一；綠色債券存量規模約 1.2 萬億人民幣，居世界第二[1]。綠色金融資產質量整體良好，綠色貸款不良率遠低於全國商業銀行不良貸款率，綠色債券尚無違約案例。綠色投資和責任投資理念逐漸成為共識，綠色基金、綠色保險、綠色信託等新金融產品及業態不斷湧現，環境風險壓力測試方法和工具開始得到推廣。

綠色金融所產生的環境效益逐步顯現。根據綠色信貸統計制度確定的環境效益測算規則，截至 2019 年末，中國 21 家主要銀行機構節能環保項目和服務貸款預計每年可節約標準煤 2.82 億噸，減排二氧化碳 5.67 億噸。截至 2020 年末，中國每年綠色債券募集資金支持的項目可節約標準煤 5,000 萬噸左右，相當於減排二氧化碳 1 億噸以上[2]。

綠色金融政策框架逐步完善。中國金融改革通過自上而下的頂層設計，使得中國成為全球首個建立了系統性綠色金融政策框架的國家。制度建設方面，2016 年 8 月，中國人民銀行（以下簡稱「人民銀行」）聯合財政部、國家發展和改革委員會、環境保護部等七部委共同出台了《關於構建綠色金融體系的指導意見》，確立了中國綠色金融體系建設的頂層架構，從環境信息披露要求、政策激勵等角度提出了 35 條具體措施。2019 年，中央各部門出台了金融、產業、財政、環境等綠色金融相關政策近 20 項，形成了對綠色金融創新發展的有效激勵。綠色金融統計制度逐步完善，綠色信貸、綠色債券等主要統計數據質量明顯提高[3]。激勵政策方面，人民銀行將符合條件的綠色貸款納入貨幣政策操作合格抵押品範圍；率先實踐金融機構綠色信貸業績評價，有效引導金融機構增加綠色資產配置、強化風險管理，也為貨幣政策應對氣候變化預留了空間。綠色金融債券存續期監管逐步規範，信息不對稱狀況得到改善。中央和地方政府以擔保、貼息、產業基金等多種手段撬動社會資本參與綠色投入[4]。

1　資料來源：中國人民銀行已公開數據。
2　資料來源：中華人民共和國國務院新聞辦公室〈我國綠色債券成效顯著　累計發行約1.2萬億元〉，2021年。
3　資料來源：人民銀行《中國綠色金融發展報告》，2019年。
4　資料來源：人民銀行《中國綠色金融發展報告》，2019年。

綠色金融地方試點取得可複製的寶貴經驗。自 2017 年 6 月設立綠色金融改革創新試驗區以來，中國已設立六省九地綠色金融改革創新試驗區[5]，為全國綠色金融發展積累了豐富的實踐創新經驗。截至 2020 年末，六省九地試驗區綠色貸款餘額 2,368.3 億元，佔中國全部綠色貸款餘額的 15.1%；綠色債券餘額 1,350.5 億元[6]。為加強綠色金融「上下聯動」與協同探索，保障試驗區建設高質量推進，人民銀行引導試驗區建立綠色金融行業自律機制、綠色金融改革創新試驗區聯席會議機制，為申請設立試驗區的地區提供支持建立輔導機制。其次，試驗區運用金融科技手段建立一體化信息平台，促進銀行與企業信息對接及氣候與環保信息共享，為政策與市場決策提供信息基礎。此外，試驗區還建立了綠色金融環境信息跨部門互通共享機制，建立環境失信企業「黑名單」懲罰機制[7]。

中國積極推動和參與綠色金融國際合作。2016 至 2018 年，在中、英等各方推動下，G20 連續 3 年討論綠色金融 / 可持續金融議題，推進國際社會對綠色金融的發展共識。2017 年 12 月，由人民銀行與法國中央銀行等 8 家央行和監管機構共同發起的央行與監管機構綠色金融網絡（Network for Greening the Financial System，簡稱 NGFS）成立，在氣候對金融穩定的影響、環境風險分析、氣候信息披露、綠色金融可得性等方面開展合作研究並形成多項國際共識。2018 年 11 月，中國金融學會綠色金融專業委員會與倫敦金融城牽頭發起《「一帶一路」綠色投資原則》，推動全球投資機構在新興市場國家開展綠色投資。截至 2021 年 8 月 27 日，全球已有來自 14 個國家和地區的 39 家機構簽署方，承諾將在「一帶一路」相關投融資活動中充分考慮環境因素，加大綠色投資力度。2019 年 10 月，中國參與發起可持續金融國際平台（International Platform on Sustainable Finance，簡稱 IPSF），倡導各成員國開展綠色金融標準趨同等國際合作，進一步推動全球綠色發展。此外，中國積極與國際社會分享綠色發展實踐經驗，比如，中國機構參與制定了《可持續交易所原則》、《負責任銀行原則》、《中國對外投資環境風險管理倡議》等文件[8]。

以碳中和為目標完善綠色金融體系

2020 年 9 月 22 日，國家主席習近平在聯合國大會一般性辯論中，向全世界莊嚴宣佈，中國將力爭於 2030 年前實現碳達峰，在 2060 年前實現碳中和。中國的此項承諾是全球應對氣候變化歷程中的里程碑事件，它不但會加速中國的綠色低碳轉型，也正在激勵其他主要國家作出碳中和的承諾，有望成為確保《巴黎協定》在全球實質性落地的最重要推動力。中

5　綠色金融改革創新試驗區包含浙江省、廣東省、新疆維吾爾自治區、貴州省、江西省、甘肅省。其中，甘肅省蘭州新區於2019年11月獲批成為國家級綠色金融改革創新試驗區。

6　資料來源：人民銀行已公開數據。

7　資料來源：人民銀行《中國綠色金融發展報告》，2019年。

8　資料來源：人民銀行《中國綠色金融發展報告》，2019年。

國等主要國家的碳中和承諾將大大提高《巴黎協定》目標得以實現的可能性，進而避免出現億萬氣候難民的危機，因此，將成為構建人類命運共同體的最重要內容之一。

碳中和目標下實體經濟的轉型軌跡

中國內外氣候變化專家的研究顯示，中國有條件在 2030 年之前實現碳達峰，在 2060 年之前實現碳中和。基於目前已經成熟和基本成熟的綠色低碳技術和商業化的可行性，專家們預測，如果中國及時採取有力的碳中和政策，就有望在 2050 年將碳排放從目前（2020 年）水平降低 70% 左右，到 2060 年之前實現碳中和，即實現淨零碳排放[9]。

如果要在 2060 年之前實現碳中和，在實體經濟層面必須加速推動電力、交通、建築和工業的大規模去碳化，爭取在大多數產業實現自身的近零排放，較小比例難以消除或降低的碳排放將由碳匯林業來吸收（固碳）。

電力：去煤炭、加速發展清潔能源

煤炭佔中國一次能源消費的 60% 左右，燃煤發電是中國碳排放的最大來源，電力行業總碳排放的一半左右[10]。在碳中和的路徑之下，電力系統需要深度脫碳，到 2050 年左右實現行業淨零排放，非化石能源電力將佔總電量的 90% 以上；因此，包括光伏、風電、核能和綠色氫能等的生產、消費和投資，將以比過去所有規劃更快的速度增長。清華大學研究顯示，碳中和目標需要 2050 年非化石能源在中國一次能源總消費中佔達到 70% 以上。國網研究院、風電協會等機構估計，「十四五」期間新增風光裝機容量將達到年均 100 吉瓦（GW）左右，比「十三五」時期增加約一倍。到 2050 年，風光的總裝機容量應該達到 4,000GW左右，比 2020 年的水平（約 350GW）提高 10 倍以上，佔 2050 年中國發電量的 65% 以上。

碳中和要求煤炭相關產業的生產、消費和投資必須儘快大幅下降，傳統的煤炭開採、煤電產業將難以為繼，曾經是主流觀點的「煤炭清潔利用」戰略也將被快速淘汰。除非碳捕捉技術能夠在可預見的將來成為商業可行，且成本低廉，各類煤炭的利用方式（煤發電、煤製氣、煤製油和其他主要煤化工技術）由於其高強度的碳排放，都是與碳中和的目標相矛盾的。根據國際能源署等機構的研究，要實現《巴黎協定》要求的控制全球氣溫上升不超過1.5°C 的目標，全球必須設定碳排放總量的限額（碳預算），因此全球現存煤炭儲量的 80%和石油儲量的 70% 可能將不會得到利用[11]。中國也必須接受這個現實。

9　資料來源：清華大學氣候變化與可持續發展研究院〈中國長期低碳發展戰略與轉型路徑研究〉，2020年。

10　資料來源：中國國家統計局〈中華人民共和國2019年國民經濟和社會發展統計公報〉，2019年。

11　國際上已有多個研究機構針對升溫控制目標下建議不使用煤炭、石油、天然氣儲量的佔比測算，相關報告包括Carbon Tracker Initiative發佈的〈Unburnable carbon〉、倫敦大學學院可持續資源研究所發佈的〈The geographical distribution of fossil fuels unused when limiting global warming to 2°C〉等。IEA發佈的〈能源轉型中的石油和天然氣〉（"The oil and gas industry in energy transitions"）中闡述了「不減量燃燒當今所有化石燃料儲量將導致二氧化碳排放量比剩餘二氧化碳排放預算高出三倍」。

交通：實現電動化

交通行業（包括公路、鐵路、船運和航空）用能源（主要是燃油）不僅是空氣污染的主要源頭，還可導致大量碳排放。電動車不僅污染排放為零，即使在目前中國電力結構下，碳排放也比燃油車低。未來，電力行業實現了高比例清潔能源、零碳排放的條件下，使用電動車、電氣鐵路運輸即可基本解決公路和鐵路的碳排放問題。因此，交通行業實現碳中和的轉型路徑主要應該是確保在常規公路、鐵路交通中實現完全電動化和電氣化。更多的省市需要像海南省一樣，宣佈在不久的將來（如 2030 年）實現新車上市全電動，制定燃油車淘汰時間表。在全國範圍，應該爭取到 2035 年，純電動汽車銷售佔汽車銷售的 50% 左右。

同時超前建設汽車充電和加氫基礎設施，大力推廣氫燃料電池汽車，尤其是重型運輸車輛，力爭到 2035 年，使氫燃料電池汽車保有量達到 100 萬輛。此外，還要鼓勵船舶和航空運輸業使用天然氣、電能等清潔能源，加速淘汰高耗能交通運輸設備和技術。城市化過程應注重綠色基礎設施的建設，大力投資軌道、快速公交等公共交通設施，建設城市騎行、步行等綠色出行設施和環境，減少私人機動車出行需求，從源頭減少與交通相關的碳排放，提升城市活力。

建築：大力推廣零碳建築

建築用能佔中國總能耗的 20% 左右，主要用於建築物的照明、供暖製冷、家電能耗等，而這些能源大部分來自高碳的火力發電[12]。建築業要想實現淨零排放，主要有兩個路徑：一是建築節能，二是使用綠電（光伏等清潔能源）。

與電力、交通行業相比，建築行業實現低碳甚至零碳的技術已經基本成熟，只要相關部門和地方政府組織資源，加大有關工作的推動和協調力度，有望成為中國最早實現零碳化的部門。在歐洲，已有若干零碳示範園區，園區中所有建築物已經實現淨零排放，且不需要政府補貼。中國的一些試點項目也證明了零碳建築在技術和經濟上的可行性。

實現建築部門總體零排放的基本要素是：提高新建建築物節能標準，儘早制定和實施超低能耗和零碳建築標準，大力推廣零碳建築；加大既有建築節能改造力度；建立零碳示範園區，完善零碳建築技術；提高建築用能電氣化率，充分使用分佈式可再生能源（如光伏），調整北方採暖地區供暖熱源結構和提升熱源效率；推廣節能和智能化高效用能的產品（如家電）、設施。

工業：調結構提能效、推廣低碳技術

與電力、交通和建築行業相比，工業尤其是製造業的技術複雜程度更高，要完全實現零碳

---

12 資料來源：清華大學建築節能研究中心〈中國建築節能年度發展研究報告〉，2018年。

的難度更大。清華大學的研究表明，大力推動產業結構升級、能效提升、電氣化改造和高碳原料的替代，到 2050 年，中國的工業碳排放水平有望比當前降低 70% 左右 [13]。實現這個目標的路徑主要有四個核心內容：一是工業產業結構的升級。根據發達國家的經驗，隨着人均收入的提高，低附加值產業佔工業增加值的比重會逐步下降。預計到 2050 年，中國高附加值行業增加值佔工業產出的比重將從目前的 35% 上升到 60% 左右，工業能耗會因此比目前水平下降 60% 左右。二是提高工業體系的能源和資源利用效率。能效提升是工業降低碳排放的重要路徑，各種資源（如塑料、鋼鐵、鋁等原材料）的循環利用也有助於降低在原料生產過程中的碳排放。通過大規模使用高效能、低排放甚至零碳技術，到 2050 年，中國單位工業增加值的能耗可能比目前水平下降 65% 左右。三是工業部門電氣化和推廣低碳燃料／原料的利用。目前，中國工業行業仍然大量使用燃煤鍋爐，電氣化率約為 26%，未來，可以通過提高電氣化率並使用綠電，來大幅降低碳排放，比如到 2050 年提升到 70% 左右 [14]。四是用各類新材料、新原料替代化石原料（如使用氫能替代焦煤作為鋼鐵生產的還原劑）來降低生產過程中的碳排放。

碳中和目標下金融業面臨的機遇和挑戰

金融業在實體經濟大規模向低碳、零碳轉型的過程中也必須轉型。金融業的轉型一方面要滿足實體經濟轉型帶來巨大的綠色低碳融資需求；另一方面也要防範由於轉型風險所帶來的各種金融風險，包括高碳產業的違約風險和減值風險以及某些高碳地區所面臨的系統性金融風險。

實現碳中和需要數百萬億元的綠色投資

實現碳中和需要大量的綠色、低碳投資，其中，絕大部分需要通過金融體系動員社會資本來實現。關於碳中和所需要的綠色低碳投資規模，許多專家和機構有不同的估算。比如，清華大學的《中國長期低碳發展戰略與轉型路徑研究》報告提出了四種情景構想，其中實現 1.5°C 目標導向轉型路徑，需累計新增投資約 138 萬億元人民幣（下同），超過每年中國國內生產總值的 2.5%。再如，馬駿牽頭的《重慶碳中和目標和綠色金融路線圖》課題報告估算，如果重慶市（其生產總值規模佔全國比重約 1/40）要在未來 30 年內實現碳中和，累計需要低碳投資（不包括與減排無關的環保類等綠色投資）超過 8 萬億元。此外，中國投資協會和落基山研究所估計，在碳中和願景下，中國在可再生能源、能效、零碳技術和儲能技術等 7 個領域需要投資 70 萬億元 [15]。基於這些估算，未來 30 年內，中國實現碳中和所需綠色低碳投資的規模應該在百萬億元以上，也可能達到數百萬億元，因此將為綠色金融帶來巨大的發展機遇。

13　資料來源：清華大學氣候變化與可持續發展研究院〈中國長期低碳發展戰略與轉型路徑研究〉，2020年。

14　資料來源：國網能源研究院《中國能源電力發展展望》，2020年。

15　資料來源：落基山研究所與中國投資協會（聯合發佈）〈以實現碳中和為目標的投資機遇〉，2020年。

碳中和為金融業帶來的機遇

為實現碳中和目標所產生的如此規模的綠色投資需求，將為有準備的金融機構提供綠色金融業務快速成長的機遇。其中，幾個典型的產品領域包括：

- **銀行**：創新適合於清潔能源和綠色交通項目的產品和服務；推動開展綠色建築融資創新試點，圍繞星級建築、可再生能源規模化應用、綠色建材等領域，探索貼標融資產品創新；積極發展能效信貸、綠色債券和綠色信貸資產證券化；探索服務小微企業、消費者和農業綠色化的產品和模式；探索支持能源和工業等行業綠色和低碳轉型所需的金融產品和服務，比如轉型貸款。

- **綠色債券**：發行政府綠色專項債、中小企業綠色集合債、氣候債券、藍色債券以及轉型債券等創新綠債產品；改善綠色債券市場流動性，吸引境外綠色投資者購買和持有相關債券產品。

- **綠色股票市場**：簡化綠色企業首次公開募股的審核或備案程序，探索建立綠色企業的綠色通道機制；對一些經營狀況和發展前景較好的綠色企業，支持優先參與轉板試點。

- **環境權益市場和融資**：開展環境權益抵質押融資，探索碳金融和碳衍生產品。

- **綠色保險**：大力開發和推廣氣候（巨災）保險、綠色建築保險、可再生能源保險、新能源汽車保險等創新型綠色金融產品。

- **綠色基金**：鼓勵設立綠色基金和轉型基金，支持綠色低碳產業的股權投資，滿足能源和工業行業的轉型融資需求。

- **私募股權投資**：鼓勵創投基金孵化綠色低碳科技企業，支持股權投資基金開展綠色項目或企業併購重組；引導私募股權投資基金與區域性股權市場合作，為綠色資產（企業）掛牌轉讓提供條件。

- **碳市場**：儘快將控排範圍擴展到其他主要高耗能工業行業，以及交通和建築領域等，同時將農林行業作為自願減排和碳匯開發的重點領域。

金融業需要防範和管理氣候風險

在全球主要國家紛紛宣佈碳中和目標、加大落實《巴黎協定》力度的背景下，由於應對氣候變化而帶來的轉型風險對許多產業和有氣候風險敞口的金融機構來說會越來越凸顯。轉型風險指的是在實體經濟向綠色低碳轉型的過程中，由於政策、技術和市場認知的變化，對某些企業、產業帶來的風險以及由此轉化而來的財務與金融風險。比如，在各國採取政策措施推動能源綠色化的過程中，煤炭、石油等化石能源產業的需求會大幅下降；為了落實《巴黎協定》，許多國家的碳市場價格將大幅上升，使得大量高碳企業必須支付更多的成本用於購買碳配額；由於技術進步，光伏、風電等清潔能源的成本快速下降，對化石能源會產生替代作用，並逼迫化石能源價格持續下降。

專欄 1：氣候風險分析

NGFS 監管工作組在 2020 年 9 月發佈了環境風險分析的兩份重要文件——《環境風險分析綜述》和《環境風險分析方法案例集》，總結了全球金融機構（包括銀行、保險、證券）中已經研發或使用的各類用於環境和氣候風險分析的模型方法，便於金融機構估算由於氣候和環境轉型因素導致的不良貸款比率上升和投資估值下降的風險。

在宏觀層面，一些機構和央行已經研究了氣候相關風險對金融穩定的影響，並進行量化測算。據經濟學人智庫（Economist Intelligence Unit）測算，在極端情況下，氣候變化會帶來 43 萬億美元資產的損失[16]；據荷蘭央行測算，該國 11% 的銀行資產將面臨較大的氣候風險[17]。在產業層面，根據英國諮詢機構生動經濟學（Vivid Economics）對於上市板塊的風險分析預測，結果顯示煤炭板塊股票減值幅度或將達到 80%，石油天然氣將下降 50%[18]；2ii 研究所認為，在 2DS[19] 溫升情況下，煤電資產或減值 80%，引發的銀行違約率或提高 4 倍[20]。

清華大學綠色金融研究中心的團隊開發了一套轉型風險模型，在考慮未來十年中的五大轉型因素後，對中國煤電領域貸款所面臨的轉型風險進行測算。模型中考慮對煤電企業的五大轉型因素包括：

1. **需求下降**：由於能源轉型政策，未來對煤電需求下降，導致煤電企業銷售收入下降；

2. **新能源成本下降**：由於技術進步，未來十年內，光伏、風能等新能源發電成本或將降至煤電成本的 50% 以下，在此過程中煤電價格將被迫下降；

3. **碳價格上升**：要落實碳中和的目標，未來十年內碳價格應當上升 10 倍，不努力減排的火電企業將以更高價格來購買碳配額；

16　資料來源：The Economist Intelligence Unit，"The cost of inaction"，載於《經濟學人》網站，2015年7月24日。

17　資料來源：G. Schellekens 與 J. van Toor〈Values at risk? Sustainability risks and goals in the Dutch financial sector〉，De Nederlandsche Bank，2019年。

18　資料來源：Vivid Economics與HSBC Global Asset Management〈Low-carbon transition scenarios: Exploring scenario analysis for equity valuations〉，2018年10月。

19　2ii研究所使用「太遲太突然」(too late too sudden)氣候情景，是指在2100年全球平均氣溫控制在相較工業化前水平上升大約2°C目標下(即2DS)，低碳經濟轉型及碳排放控制啟動較晚，對碳密集型能源及其使用突然實施數量限制，且自然災害的發生率已上升，導致總體轉型成本較高的氣候情景。

20　資料來源：M. Hayne、S. Ralire、J. Thomä 與 D. Koopman (2019年)〈Factoring transition risks into regulatory stress-tests〉，載於《ACRN Journal of Finance and Risk Perspectives》，第8期，206-222頁。

4. **評級下降**：以上三類因素將導致煤電企業財務狀況惡化，相關銀行評級或債券市場使用的信用評級下降，導致融資成本提高，使得其財務狀況進一步惡化；

5. **銀行改變風險權重**：未來，銀行或監管機構可能會考慮調整不同資產所適用的風險權重，降低綠色資產的風險權重，提高棕色／高碳資產的相應權重。如果未來棕色資產權重上升，煤電企業融資成本將面臨額外的上行壓力。

將這五大轉型因素放入氣候轉型風險模型，並以三個大型上市煤電公司數據為基礎進行模擬，結果是其違約率都將快速上升。未來十年，如果考慮需求下降、價格競爭、融資成本上升等因素，中國樣本煤電企業的違約概率將從2020年的約3%上升到2030年的約22%[21]。從金融或財務回報和風險的角度來看，金融機構就不應該再考慮此類投資標的。全球已有100家大型金融機構宣佈限制煤電投資，其中部分機構表示現在就不再投資，還有一些表示在一定期限內逐步減少和停止在該領域的投資[22]。

在這些轉型因素的推動下，煤炭、石油以及仍然使用高碳技術的石化、鋼鐵、水泥、鋁等製造業，涉及毀林和其他破壞生物多樣性的產業和項目都有可能出現嚴重成本上升、利潤下降、嚴重虧損，乃至倒閉。對金融機構和投資者來說，這些風險會體現為貸款／債券違約和投資損失。在某些高碳產業密集的地區（如山西、陝西、內蒙古等），此類與氣候轉型相關的風險可能會演化為區域性、系統性的金融風險，以及由於大規模企業倒閉所帶來的失業和其他社會風險。

在碳中和目標背景下，中國煤電企業貸款的違約率在10年內可能會上升到20%以上（見專欄1），其他高碳行業的貸款違約率也可能大幅上升。氣候轉型所帶來的金融風險可能成為系統性金融風險的來源。過去幾年，一些國外的央行和監管機構（如英格蘭銀行、荷蘭央行、法國央行、歐央行等）、國際組織和合作機制（如NGFS）已開始強調金融業開展環境和氣候風險分析的重要性。但是，中國的多數金融機構尚未充分理解氣候轉型的相關風險，普遍缺乏對氣候轉型風險的前瞻性判斷和風險防範機制。

---

21 資料來源：馬駿與孫天印（2020年）〈氣候轉型風險和物理風險的分析方法和應用 —— 以煤電和按揭貸款為例〉，載於《清華金融評論》，第9期，16-35頁。

22 資料來源：〈Over 100 global financial institutions are exiting coal, with more to come〉，載於 Institute for Energy Economics and Financial Analysis的網站，2019年2月27日。

金融業支持碳中和的國際經驗

歐洲、英國等發達經濟體在過去幾年中較早宣佈了碳中和的目標，其金融業和監管機構也在支持低碳投資方面有較多的經驗。至少有如下幾個方面值得借鑒：

1. **以「不損害其他可持續發展目標」為原則，制定和完善綠色金融標準**

   從多年前一些非官方機構所推出的綠色和氣候金融標準，到最近幾年歐盟正在制定的官方可持續金融標準，其主導原則是支持應對氣候變化，同時也覆蓋了其他綠色和可持續發展目標，如降低污染、保護生物多樣性、支持資源循環利用等。但歐盟在最新發佈的可持續金融標準中強調，符合其標準的經濟活動不得損害其他可持續發展目標，即不能因為實現了一個目標而損害了另一個目標。比如，煤炭清潔利用項目即使是可以有效降低空氣污染，但也由於大幅增加碳排放，不符合可持續金融標準。

2. **對企業和金融機構強化氣候相關的財務信息披露要求**

   英格蘭央行前行長馬克·卡尼（**Mark Carney**）在金融穩定委員會（**Financial Stability Board**，簡稱 **FSB**）下發起的氣候相關財務信息披露工作組（**Task Force on Climate-related Financial Disclosures**，簡稱 **TCFD**）制定了有關信息披露的標準，並建議企業和金融機構按此標準披露氣候相關的財務信息。該項倡議已得到全球數百家大型企業和金融機構的響應，也被一些發達國家的監管機構借鑒或採納。比如，歐盟在 2019 年 11 月發佈了金融機構和產品必須披露可持續發展相關信息的要求，並於 2021 年 3 月開始實施[23]。2020 年 12 月，英國宣佈要求幾乎所有公司在 2025 年按照 TCFD 開展信息披露[24]。2020 年 7 月，法國金融市場管理局要求機構投資者披露環境、社會和公司治理（ESG）相關信息[25]。此外，許多歐洲和英國機構已經披露了投資組合的碳足跡和機構自身運行的碳排放信息。

3. **不少發達國家的機構開展了環境和氣候風險分析**

   NGFS 在 2020 年 9 月發佈了兩份研究報告[26]，囊括了全球三十多個機構開發的環境和氣候風險分析的方法和工具，包括對轉型風險和物理風險的分析。這些機構中的大部分來自歐洲發達經濟體。

---

23 《金融服務業可持續性相關披露條例》（*Sustainability-related Disclosures in the Financial Services Sector*），歐盟發佈，2019年11月27日。

24 資料來源：英國財政部《A Roadmap Towards Mandatory Climate-related Disclosures》，2020年11月。

25 資料來源：法國金融市場管理局《Position-Recommendation 2020-03》，2020年7月27日。

26 兩份報告為《金融機構環境風險分析概述》（*Overview of Environmental Risk Analysis by Financial Institutions*）和《金融機構環境風險分析方法案例集》（*Case Studies of Environmental Risk Analysis Methodologies*）。

4. 創新的綠色和氣候金融產品

歐洲等發達市場在 ESG 金融產品和碳市場、碳金融方面處於明顯領先地位。值得借鑒的產品包括各類與可持續發展目標相關聯的信貸、債券和交易型開放式指數基金（exchange traded fund，簡稱 ETF）產品、轉型債券、綠色供應鏈金融產品、綠色資產證券化等。此外，歐盟碳排放交易體系（EU ETS）覆蓋了整個經濟體 45% 的碳排放，相關衍生品工具也為碳市場發現價格和改善流動性提供了較好的支持[27]。

目前綠色金融體系與碳中和目標的差距

自 2015 年中國國務院在《生態文明體制改革總體方案》中首次提出構建綠色金融體系以來，中國在綠色金融標準、激勵機制、披露要求、產品體系、地方試點和國際合作等方面取得了長足的進展，在部分領域的成就已經取得了重要的國際影響力。但是，與碳中和目標的要求相比，中國目前的綠色金融體系在幾個方面還面臨着一些問題和挑戰：

1. **目前的綠色金融標準體系與碳中和目標不完全匹配**

比如，雖然人民銀行主持修訂的新版《綠色債券支持項目目錄（2021 年版）》已經剔除了「清潔煤炭技術」等化石能源相關的高碳項目，但其他綠色金融的界定標準（包括綠色信貸標準、綠色產業目錄等）還沒有作相應的調整。這些標準中的部分綠色項目不完全符合碳中和對淨零碳排放的要求。

2. **環境信息披露的水平不符合碳中和的要求**

企業和金融機構開展充分的環境信息披露是金融體系引導資金投向綠色產業的重要基礎，被投資企業和項目的碳排放信息披露則是低碳投資決策的重要基礎。中國目前對大部分企業尚未強制要求披露碳排放和碳足跡信息，雖然部分金融機構已經開始披露綠色信貸／投資的信息，但多數還沒有對棕色／高碳資產的信息進行披露。多數機構也缺乏採集、計算和評估碳排放和碳足跡信息的能力。金融機構如果不計算和披露其投資／貸款組合的環境風險敞口和碳足跡信息，就無法管理氣候相關風險，不了解其支持實體經濟減碳的貢獻，也無法實現碳中和目標。

3. **綠色金融激勵機制尚未充分體現對低碳發展的足夠重視**

金融監管部門的一些政策（包括通過再貸款支持綠色金融和通過宏觀審慎評估體系考核激勵銀行增加綠色信貸等）和一些地方政府對綠色項目的貼息、擔保等機制在一定

---

27 資料來源：歐洲聯盟委員會的《EU Emissions Trading System》網頁，於2021年8月27日閱覽。

程度上調動了社會資本參與綠色投資的積極性，但激勵的力度和覆蓋範圍仍然不足，對綠色項目中的低碳、零碳投資缺乏特殊的激勵。這些激勵機制的設計也沒有以投資或資產的碳足跡作為評價標準。

4. **對氣候轉型風險的認知和分析能力不足**

中國的金融監管部門已經開始重視氣候變化所帶來的金融風險，但還未系統性地建立氣候風險分析的能力，也沒有出台對金融機構開展環境和氣候風險分析的具體要求。除了幾家在綠色金融方面領先的機構已經開展了環境、氣候壓力測試之外，中國多數金融機構尚未充分理解氣候轉型的相關風險及相關分析模型和方法，而多數中小型金融機構還從未接觸過氣候風險這個概念。在對相關風險的認識和內部能力方面，中國金融機構與歐洲機構相比還有較大差距。

5. **綠色金融產品還不完全適應碳中和的需要**

中國在綠色信貸、綠色債券等產品方面已經取得了長足的進展，但在面向投資者提供的 ESG 產品，以及產品的多樣化和流動性方面比發達市場還有較大的差距，許多綠色金融產品還沒有與碳足跡掛鈎，碳市場和碳金融產品在配置金融資源中的作用還十分有限，碳市場的對外開放度還很低。

政策建議

中國提出了碳中和的目標之後，如果沒有實質性的、大力度的改革舉措，經濟的低碳轉型並不會自動加速，主要行業的淨零排放也不會自動實現。相關數量分析表明，如果繼續按現有的產業政策和地區發展規劃來發展經濟，未來 30 年內中國的碳排放將持續保持高位，不可能達到淨零排放，也很難實現在 2030 年前達峰的國際承諾。

從中國金融業的現狀來看，雖然已經構建了綠色金融體系的基本框架，但綠色金融標準、信息披露水平和激勵機制尚未充分反映碳中和的要求，產品體系還沒有充分解決低碳投資所面臨的瓶頸，金融機構還沒有充分意識到氣候轉型所帶來的金融風險，也沒有採取充分的措施來防範和管理這些風險。

針對這些問題，應該從兩個方面加速構建落實碳達峰、碳中和目標的政策體系。一是要求各地方和有關部門加快制定 2030 年與 2060 年的路線圖，出台一系列強化低碳、零碳轉型的政策，強化各部門、地方政府和金融機構之間的協調配合。二是從標準、披露、激勵和產品四個維度系統性地調整相關政策，構建符合碳中和目標要求的綠色金融體系，保證社會資本充分參與低碳、零碳建設，有效防範氣候相關風險。

地方和產業部門應規劃碳中和路線圖

第一，中央應明確要求各地方政府拿出落實碳中和目標的規劃和實施路線圖，並鼓勵有條件的地區儘早實現碳中和。根據從若干地區了解的情況，許多省市（包括主要負責人）對碳中和的內涵、背景和意義的了解十分有限，絕大多數地方的產業部門也尚未理解碳中和目標意味着電力、交通、建築和工業等部門必須大幅度轉型，也沒有認識到習近平總書記提出的遠期願景需要現在就開始行動，否則會由於碳峰值過高帶來更大的社會和經濟負擔。一些地方仍然誤以為由於煤炭是本省的資源稟賦，必須充分利用，因此，還在繼續規劃煤電和依賴傳統高碳技術的項目。還有一些地方雖然有意願落實碳中和目標，但由於面臨部分傳統高碳行業的阻力，且中央沒有給出明確的指引，因此不願意率先推出碳中和路線圖。基於此，建議中央應該給予地方明確的指引，要求各地儘快制定落實碳中和目標的規劃和實施路線圖，並鼓勵可再生能源資源充裕、林木覆蓋率較高、服務業比較發達、製造業比重較低、科技創新能力較強的地區儘早（如在 2050 年前後）實現淨零或近零排放，建立淨零排放示範園區和示範項目，為其他地區提供可複製、可借鑒的樣板。

第二，中央應明確要求相關部委制定零碳發展規劃和碳匯林業發展規劃，並儘可能將具體目標納入相關行業的「十四五」規劃。碳中和目標的落實涉及所有高碳行業的轉型，因此互相協調的行業規劃十分重要。根據初步分析，這些行業規劃必須在「十四五」期間開始發生根本性的轉變，應該以大幅度減排作為未來五年、十年的約束性條件，乃至首要任務，而不是將低碳發展僅僅作為政策規劃中「錦上添花」式的點綴。比如，在能源行業的「十四五」和十年規劃中，必須明確提出停止新的煤電項目建設，大幅提高光伏、風電、氫能、海上風電和儲能技術的投資目標。應該考慮明確支持有條件的地方宣佈停止燃油車銷售的時間表，繼續保持對新能源汽車的補貼和支持力度，大規模進行充電樁等相關基礎設施的投資和部署。在綠色建築領域，應該儘快大規模實施超低能耗建築標準和近零排放建築標準，對零碳建築提供更大力度的財政和金融支持。在工業領域，應該大力引進國際上先進的低碳、零碳技術，對各類工業製造進行大規模的、全面的節能改造。積極開展生態系統保護、恢復和可持續管理，加強森林可持續經營與植樹造林以提升區域儲碳量與增匯能力。

以碳中和目標完善綠色金融體系

金融行業應該開始規劃支持碳中和目標的綠色金融路線圖。據估算，在未來幾十年內，在全國實現碳中和可能需要數百萬億元的綠色低碳投資。根據綠色金融發展的經驗，要滿足如此大規模的投資需求，90% 左右的資金必須依靠金融體系來動員和組織。因此，金融管理部門和各地方都有必要牽頭研究和規劃以實現碳中和為目標的綠色金融發展路線圖。

這個路線圖的主要內容應該包括三個方面的內容：一是目標落實到主要產業的中長期綠色發展規劃和區域佈局；編制綠色產業和重點項目投融資規劃；制定一系列具體的行動方案和措施，包括發展可再生能源和綠色氫能、工業低碳化、建築零碳化、交通電動化、煤電落後產能淘汰等。二是建立綠色產業規劃與綠色金融發展規劃之間的協調機制；制定一系列綠色低碳產業、產品和綠色金融標準體系；建立綠色項目與綠色融資渠道的協同機制，包括服務於綠色項目和綠色資金的對接平台。三是以碳中和為目標，完善綠色金融體系，包括修改綠色金融標準，建立強制性的環境信息披露要求，強化對綠色低碳投融資的激勵機制，支持低碳投融資的金融產品創新。具體建議如下：

一是以碳中和為約束條件，修訂綠色金融標準。中國綠色金融界定標準尚未完全剔除與化石能源相關的高碳項目等不完全符合碳中和對淨零碳排放要求的項目。未來，應該按照碳中和目標修訂綠色信貸、綠色產業標準，建立綠色基金、綠色保險的界定標準，同時保證符合這些綠色標準的項目不會對其他可持續發展目標產生重大的負面影響。

二是建議監管部門要求金融機構對高碳資產的敞口和主要資產的碳足跡進行計算和披露（見專欄 2）。建議人民銀行、中國銀行保險監督管理委員會（簡稱「銀保監會」）、中國證券監督管理委員會（簡稱「證監會」）等金融監管部門明確提出對金融機構開展環境和氣候信息披露的要求，其中，應該包括對金融機構持有的綠色、棕色資產的信息，也應該包括這些資產和主要資產的碳足跡。初期，可以要求金融機構披露其持有的棕色或高碳行業資產風險敞口（如煤炭採掘、煤電、鋼鐵、水泥、化工、鋁業等行業的貸款和投資），並計算和披露接受貸款和投資的企業碳排放和碳足跡。中期，可以要求金融機構披露主要貸款／投資的碳足跡（或向大中型企業提供的貸款／投資）。監管部門、行業協會（如全國性或地區性金融學會的綠色金融專業委員會，簡稱「綠金委」）和國際合作機制（如中英環境信息披露試點工作組）應組織金融機構開展環境信息披露方面的能力建設，推廣領先機構的最佳實踐。

三是監管機構應該明確鼓勵金融機構開展環境和氣候風險分析，強化能力建設。目前，中國只有數家銀行開展了環境和氣候風險分析，多數大型金融機構開始有所認知但尚未建立分析能力，多數中小機構還未意識到氣候轉型可能帶來的信用風險、市場風險和聲譽風險。建議人民銀行、銀保監會、證監會等金融監管部門明確指示中國金融機構參考 NGFS 等有關做法，開展前瞻性的環境和氣候風險分析，包括壓力測試和情景分析。行業協會、研究機構、教育培訓機構也應組織專家支持金融機構開展能力建設，並重點開展這個領域的國際交流。央行和金融監管部門應牽頭組織宏觀層面的環境和氣候風險分析，研判這些風險對金融穩定的影響，並考慮逐步要求大中型金融機構披露環境和氣候風險分析的結果。

四是圍繞碳中和目標，建立更加強而有力的綠色金融激勵機制（見專欄 3）。建議人民銀行考慮設立較大規模的再貸款機制（每年數千億元級別），專門用於支持低碳項目；將較低風險的綠色資產納入商業銀行向央行借款的合格抵押品範圍；將銀行資產的碳足跡納入綠色銀行的考核評估機制，並將銀行的碳足跡與央行貨幣政策工具的使用掛鉤；考慮在保持銀行總體資產風險權重不變的前提下，降低綠色資產的風險權重，提高棕色／高碳資產的風險權重。在對整個銀行業推出風險權重的調整辦法之前，可以支持有條件的地區和金融機構開展相關試點工作。

專欄 2：金融機構的環境信息披露

過去監管部門要求金融機構披露環境相關的信息，主要是披露綠色信貸、企業綠色投資對於環境的貢獻等，但對於碳排放等負面信息沒有披露要求。未來，應當要求金融機構披露碳排放信息，包括銀行貸款和股權投資的項目所產生的碳排放。只有知道碳排放和碳足跡，才有可能實現碳中和的目標。因此，未來在強化環境信息披露的過程中，要把碳相關的信息作為非常重要的內容，信息披露的要求也應該變成強制性要求。建議監管部門考慮要求銀行披露全部資產（主要是借款企業的投資項目）的碳排放的信息。雖然一步到位很難，但可以從大型企業開始做起，逐步擴展到中型和小型企業。大型、重點排放企業的碳排放信息是已經存在的，在環保系統裏面。環保口與金融口的信息溝通非常重要，能夠減少重複採集數據的成本。

國外一些金融機構已經初步建立起披露碳足跡的標準。比如，在中英環境信息披露試點小組內，英國英傑華集團（Aviva）就披露了 2018 年、2019 年所持有的股權資產和債權資產的碳足跡，該等數據顯示，其碳足跡正在逐年下降。此類案例表明，金融機構的碳足跡披露在技術上是可行的。此外，英傑華集團也披露了氣候壓力測試的結果，即機構面臨的由於物理風險和轉型風險而帶來的金融風險。因此，金融機構的前瞻性壓力測試或情景分析也是可行的、可披露的。此外，滙豐銀行（HSBC）、中國興業銀行等金融機構也就高碳資產的敞口進行了披露。

目前，國內監管機構只要求銀行統計和部分披露綠色信貸，沒有要求披露棕色或高碳資產。一些金融機構也只願意披露綠色貸款信息，不願意披露其在棕色領域的敞口和風險。其實，披露棕色資產信息對金融機構是好事：如果金融機構不分析、不披露其棕色資產的敞口和風險，市場會認為這些機構沒有充分了解相關風險，而不了解風險就可能出危險。金融機構在計算、披露了風險後，市場將會認為它們已經準備積極應對風險，市場對其認可度將隨之提高。

專欄 3：支持碳中和的金融激勵措施選項

一是專門設立支持綠色低碳項目的再貸款機制。之前支持綠色項目的再貸款是放在整體的再貸款機制中，沒有專門針對低碳項目的再貸款項目。最近一些再貸款的安排還有附加條件，如中小企業的貸款必須佔到 50% 以上，如果找不到足夠的中小企業就無法發放綠色再貸款，因此約束條件過多。未來，在碳中和的背景下，低碳項目數量將大幅增加，設立規模達每年數千億元的、專門支持綠色低碳項目的再貸款機制是有條件、有必要的。

二是將較低風險的綠色資產納入商業銀行向央行借款的合格抵押品範圍。擁有這些綠色抵押品的銀行就可以向央行借到便宜的資金。

三是將銀行的碳足跡納入宏觀審慎評估體系或者人民銀行的綠色銀行考核機制。如果某家銀行的貸款碳足跡下降得快，表明該銀行的綠色表現優異，人民銀行就可以對其多提供一些支持性政策工具，包括便宜的流動性、存款準備金率的優惠等。

四是央行和銀保監會應考慮降低銀行的綠色資產風險權重，提高棕色／高碳資產風險權重，同時保持整體風險權重不變。現在，銀行對企業貸款的風險權重是 100%，是否可以考慮把綠色貸款的風險權重降低至 75%，將棕色貸款的風險權重提高至某一水平，以保持總體風險權重不變。從宏觀意義上，這種安排對銀行的總體資本充足率沒有影響，但可以有效發揮結構調整的功能，即通過降低綠色信貸的融資成本、提高棕色信貸的融資成本，加快投資結構和實體經濟向綠色轉型的步伐。其他國家由於缺少國內綠色資產、棕色資產的標準和數據，所以討論了幾年綠色、棕色資產風險權重改革的議題，也還沒有實施。而中國有 7 年的綠色信貸數據，綠色貸款違約率只有 0.5% 左右，遠低於總體貸款的違約率 2% 左右的水平[28]。這些數據表明，提高綠色資產風險權重、降低棕色資產風險權重不但可以加速投資結構綠色化，也可能降低整個銀行業面臨的轉型風險。中國擁有這些數據方面的基礎條件，可以在風險權重調整方面引入改革政策。

28　資料來源：人民銀行《中國綠色金融發展報告》，2019年。

五是國家外匯管理局（簡稱「外管局」）和主權基金應開展 ESG 投資，培育綠色投資管理機構（見專欄 4）。外匯管理部門和主權基金可以參考 NGFS 的建議，主動開展可持續投資，以引領私營部門和社會資金的參與。建議外匯管理部門和主權基金按可持續／ESG 投資原則建立對投資標的和基金管理人的篩選機制，建立環境和氣候風險的分析能力，披露 ESG 信息，支持綠色債券市場的發展，積極發揮股東作用，推動被投資企業提升 ESG 表現。

六是監管部門應該強制要求金融機構在對外投資（包括對「一帶一路」投資項目）中開展環境影響評估。繼續在「一帶一路」地區投資煤電等高碳項目，有損中國「一帶一路」綠色化倡議的國際形象，也會對中國金融機構帶來聲譽風險和金融風險。建議有關部門儘快建立中國對外投資的強制性環境影響評估機制，嚴格限制對污染和高碳項目的海外投資；支持中國金融機構承諾大幅度減少和停止對海外新建煤電項目的投資和擔保。通過國際合作渠道，推動中、日、韓協同減少和停止對第三國的煤電投資。

七是鼓勵金融機構探索轉型融資，包括設立轉型基金和發行轉型債券。要實現碳中和，不僅要支持純綠的項目（如清潔能源、新建的綠色交通和綠色建築項目等），也要支持化石能源企業向清潔能源轉型、老舊建築的綠色低碳改造、高碳工業企業的節能減排和減碳項目等。後者一般被稱為轉型經濟活動，也需要大量融資和一定的激勵機制。歐洲已經建立了一些轉型基金，支持高碳企業向低碳轉型，同時避免失業；也推出了一些轉型債券，支持傳統能源企業引入新能源項目，將廢舊礦山改造為生態景區等。中國也應借鑒這些經驗，在認定標準、披露要求、激勵機制等方面探索建立支持轉型融資的機制，支持金融機構推出轉型債券、轉型基金、轉型保險等金融工具。

八是強化碳市場在配置資源中的作用。在被碳市場覆蓋的控排企業中，碳交易已經發揮了配置資源作用，引導高效企業承擔更多碳減排的活動。但是，除幾千家被納入碳市場的控排企業以外，碳市場的一個更加重要的功能應該是引導中國幾千萬家企業的行為變化，激勵它們更多地開展低碳的投資和其他活動。要讓碳市場在整個經濟發揮資源配置的作用，需要保證碳定價的有效性，而有效性的基礎是碳市場必須具有良好的流動性。要保證流動性，就需要大量金融機構的買家和賣家參與。同時，要開發碳期權、碳期貨等衍生產品，它們一方面是增加流動性的工具，另一方面是為企業提供的風險管理工具。

專欄 4：主權基金如何開展 ESG 投資

外管局、主權基金和政府管理的養老基金作為資產所有者可以影響一大批資產管理人的行為，從而推動中國基金業的綠色化。在選擇資產管理人時，外管局、主權基金和養老基金如果提出附加條件，要求按照可持續投資原則將更多的資源配置到 ESG 項目，並只向達到標準和有 ESG 管理能力的基金管理人提供資金，這將會帶動一大批資產管理公司向 ESG 轉型，同時把這些資管企業管理的其他資金也綠化。這個意義十分深遠，遠遠超出了外管局、主權基金和養老金資金的綠色投資的效益。

關於外匯、主權和養老投資的綠色化，NGFS 在《SRI 投資指南》[29] 中提出的許多建議可以作為參考：一是建立對投資標的和基金管理人的篩選機制，這是最重要的，選擇管理人需要滿足 ESG 要求，對達不到 ESG 管理水平的管理人不予通過遴選；二是建立主權基金或央行分析風險和氣候的能力，應識別須避免的高風險領域以及應該支持的領域；三是披露外匯、主權和養老基金投資的 ESG 信息，以帶動整個行業信息透明度提升；四是專門支持某些綠色產業和綠色金融板塊，如投資於綠色債券市場，以降低綠色債券的融資成本；五是參考挪威中央銀行（Norges Bank）的做法，發揮股東的積極作用，通過股東參與（engagement）推動被投資企業提升其 ESG 表現。Norges Bank 管理 1 萬多億美元資產，在綠色主權投資方面處於國際領先地位，該銀行不僅選擇 ESG 表現良好的公司，也選擇當前 ESG 表現一般的公司，在投資後推動被投資企業提升其 ESG 表現。Norges Bank 發揮主權投資者積極主動的作用，推動了 1,000 多家被投企業改善 ESG 的行動，這個經驗值得借鑒[30]。

29　資料來源：NGFS《A Sustainable and Responsible Investment Guide for Central Banks' Portfolio Management》，2019年10月。

30　資料來源：Norges Bank Investment Management《Responsible Investment》，2019年。

粵港澳大灣區綠色金融展望

粵港澳大灣區作為中國開放程度最高、經濟活力最強的區域之一，在國家發展大局中具有重要戰略地位。2019 年 2 月 18 日，中共中央、國務院印發了《粵港澳大灣區發展規劃綱要》，其中明確提出在粵港澳大灣區大力發展綠色金融。2020 年 5 月，中國人民銀行、銀保監會、證監會、外管局聯合發佈《關於金融支持粵港澳大灣區建設的意見》，進一步提出建立粵港澳大灣區綠色金融合作的重點事項。地方政府隨後出台支持粵港澳大灣區建設落地政策中，包含多條針對性舉措支持相關綠色金融的發展與完善。

自 2016 年中國七部委發佈《關於構建綠色金融體系的指導意見》以來，廣東、廣州、深圳和其他相關的大灣區內的地方政府積極響應，陸續出台針對性綠色金融政策。為支持大灣區綠色金融發展與合作，2020 年 9 月 4 日，在中國金融學會綠色金融專業委員會指導下，由香港綠色金融協會、廣東綠金委、深圳綠金委和澳門銀行業公會聯合發起的粵港澳大灣區綠色金融聯盟在廣州啟動，並得到了四地政府的大力支持。作為全球首個、全中國首個區域性綠色金融聯盟，該聯盟未來可發揮內地和港澳的產業、科技、國際優勢，整合資源並幫助匹配國內外金融、技術和產品需求。該聯盟現已設立五個工作組，正在開展大灣區碳市場、綠色供應鏈金融、固廢處理、綠色建築、區塊鏈交易綠色資產等項目的研究和籌備工作，部分成果有望落地並向大灣區和全國推廣。

展望未來，大灣區可探索多領域突破，以金融創新引領綠色金融發展。一是推動更多粵港澳大灣區的內地企業到香港發行綠色債券，讓內地企業充分利用香港特別行政區政府對綠債發行企業的優惠政策。二是研究覆蓋粵港澳大灣區的統一碳市場、和建立碳市場的跨境交易機制（也稱「碳市通」，Carbon Connect），吸引全球投資者參與中國碳市場；逐步將香港的電力、交通和建築業與企業納入大灣區的統一碳市場（詳見附件一）。三是推動綠色資產支持證券跨境業務的發展，改善中國綠色信貸規模大但缺乏流動性的困境，探索將綠色信貸打包成資產支持證券並向全球投資者銷售的路徑。四是將綠色金融融入供應鏈金融，例如，通過對汽車、家電、建築業供應鏈鏈條上的中小型企業進行綠色認證，使其通過綠色金融獲得更便宜的融資，在降低綠色供應商的融資成本的同時，推動供應鏈企業的綠色轉型，降低綠色中小型企業的融資成本。

附件一

對粵港澳大灣區統一碳市場的設想

在中國提出提高國家自主貢獻、力爭二氧化碳排放於 2030 年前達到峰值、努力爭取 2060 年前實現碳中和的目標背景下，作為中國國內最為發達的經濟區域之一，包括香港在內的粵港澳各地也應該以積極應對氣候變化的國家戰略為引領，將發展碳市場作為落實碳中和目標的重要抓手。在粵港澳緊密合作的大背景下，建議廣東、深圳、香港和澳門考慮聯合構建粵港澳大灣區統一碳市場，並以股票通、債券通等機制為借鑒建立連接國際投資者與國內碳市場的「碳市通」(Carbon Connect) 機制。具體建議如下 [31]：

香港參與粵港澳大灣區碳市場建設的重要意義

碳交易是實現碳減排和碳中和最為重要的市場化機制。目前，全球碳市場發展已成為主流，香港應該積極考慮參與建設粵港澳大灣區統一碳市場，這對香港落實碳中和願景和鞏固其金融中心地位至關重要。

首先，在香港本地市場規模過小、無法獨立建成有足夠流動性碳市場的情況下，與廣東、澳門共建統一碳市場是香港參與碳市場建設的最佳路徑。廣東碳市場已經具有較強國際影響力和流動性，香港投身以廣東為主體的粵港澳大灣區碳市場建設，可與廣東形成合力，使大灣區在全球氣候變化應對中發揮區域性引領作用，服務國家和地區的碳達峰和碳中和目標。

第二，香港發展碳市場有助鞏固其國際金融中心地位，打造差異化綠色金融國際中心。香港作為粵港澳大灣區碳市場的重要部分，與之相關的碳配額及其金融衍生產品開發上線可為香港綠色金融發展注入新活力，推動香港綠色金融更上台階。碳配額及其金融衍生產品更可成為聯通「一帶一路」國家和地區以及歐盟的標的物，在韓國、日本、新加坡紛紛推出碳市場的全球綠色發展格局中，佔據優勢地位和話語權。

第三，香港參與碳市場建設，有助於降低減排成本並推動本地環境改善。香港各部門通過技術革新進行減排的成本很高，實施碳市場有助於降低全社會減排成本。同時，由於碳排放與許多空氣污染物同源，香港參與碳市場建設，對二氧化碳排放加強控制，有利於進一步提升本地環境質量和實體經濟綠色轉型。

31　有關粵港澳大灣區統一碳市場與「碳市通」的建議純屬本文作者自行研究後提出的個人建議，　文中提及的任何機構或部門並未參與該等建議的提出，該等建議不代表文中提及的任何機構或部門立場或觀點。該等個人建議並未與任何政府機構、監管機構或市場機構進行溝通、諮詢，也未取得任何批准、同意或共識。

第四，依託香港交易所等香港金融基礎設施平台參與粵港澳大灣區碳市場建設，能繼續發揚其與內地金融「互聯互通」的經驗和優勢，幫助內地擴大碳市場的對外開放，提升香港金融服務輻射的深度和廣度。

循序漸進建設粵港澳大灣區統一碳市場

建議按如下步驟，穩步推進粵港澳大灣區統一市場的建設。

首先，與內地共同搭建粵港澳大灣區碳市場工作機制，與廣東省、深圳市和澳門共同組建粵港澳大灣區碳市場工作組，共同推動大灣區碳市場方案設計。該方案可在若干年內逐步覆蓋廣東（包括深圳）、香港和澳門的主要碳排放企業。

第二，整合目前廣東碳市場和深圳碳市場，以整合後的廣東（包括深圳）碳市場為基礎，由粵深港澳四地共同搭建大灣區碳市場基礎設施。

第三，加入廣東省碳普惠自願減排機制，將香港的建築、交通、林業、新能源等行業的減排項目作為產品納入廣東碳市場，進行自願交易，為下一步強制市場的實施積累經驗。

第四，香港交易所上線碳交易板塊，與內地的交易平台組合聯動，推出面向全球投資者的、以大灣區碳市場現貨產品為基礎的各類衍生產品，包括碳期貨、碳掉期等。

第五，適時啟動香港特別行政區碳排放權交易立法，由國務院灣區辦牽頭制定並發佈大灣區碳排放管控單位二氧化碳排放信息報告指南及核查規範，開展大灣區碳排放配額分配，逐步完善粵港澳大灣區統一碳市場。

在香港交易所建立「碳市通」機制

建議中的「碳市通」（Carbon Connect）機制，允許全球投資者通過該機制便利地參與粵港澳大灣區碳市場的投資。建議碳市通以香港為通道、香港交易所平台為載體。應研究借鑒目前股票通、債券通、「跨境理財通」等跨境交易模式經驗，根據碳現貨和碳期貨產品的不同特點，相應選擇合適的跨境交易方案。碳市通的第一階段可以實現國際投資者與大灣區碳市場的互聯互通，待取得較為成熟經驗之後，爭取實現國際投資者與全國碳市場的互通。通過「碳市通」，可推動中國碳市場對外開放，擴大大灣區碳市場的全球影響力。

註：本文的部分內容首於《中國金融時報》微信公眾號平台發表。

Chapter 3

Green and sustainable investment in Mainland China

Chenxi YU
Deputy Director of Strategy
Ping An Technology, OneConnect Financial Technology

Shiqing CUI
Senior Researcher of Investment
Ping An Technology, OneConnect Financial Technology

Summary

Under strong regulatory requirements for ESG disclosures and the broader guidance to build a "green financial system", Mainland China has witnessed rapid acceleration of the adoption of environment, social and governance (ESG) principles. Companies have improved in quantity and quality of disclosures and investors have seen growth in ESG-related investment products in the past few years. In this chapter, we provide an overview on main types of green and sustainable investment product in Mainland China and their latest development trend. We then provide a deep dive analysis into ESG indices and funds, the current landscape of sustainable investment data, and an outlook into future trends and recommendations.

Green and sustainable investment products in Mainland

Overview of current financial products

Green and sustainable investment has developed rapidly in China during the past few years. In 2016, seven ministries and regulators issued the *Guidelines for Establishing the Green Financial System,* which provided clear definition for green finance and green financial system. Green finance refers to "financial services provided for economic activities that are supportive of environment improvement, climate change mitigation and more efficient resource utilisation". The green financial system refers to the "institutional arrangement that utilises financial instruments such as green credit, green bonds, green stock indices and related products, green development funds, green insurance, and carbon finance, as well as relevant policy incentives to support the green transformation of the economy"[1].

Under the ambitious goals of achieving peak emissions before 2030 and carbon neutrality by 2060, green finance development is bound to further accelerate in Mainland China. A transition at this scale and speed requires massive investment. Green finance is a critical vehicle to facilitate and encourage more environmentally and socially responsible investment and to support growth of sectors that are net positive forces in the transition towards carbon neutrality. According to estimates from Tsinghua University, new investment of approximately RMB 138 trillion (US$20 trillion and over 2.5% of China's annual gross domestic product) is needed in the energy system alone before 2050 to achieve the target[2].

In terms of current financial products, on the financing end, green credit and green bonds are the two main instruments. On the investing end, ESG (Environmental, Social, and Governance) investment is driving more capital towards greener and more sustainable development areas.

---

1   Source: *Guidelines for Establishing the Green Financial System* (《關於構建綠色金融體系的指導意見》), issued by the State Council Information Office of the People's Republic of China, 31 August 2016.

2   Source: Institute of Climate Change and Sustainable Development at Tsinghua University, "China's long-term low-carbon development strategy and pathway" (〈中國長期低碳發展戰略與轉型路徑研究〉), published on *China Dialogue,* 12 October 2020.

Green credit

Green credit are loans banking financial institutions make to companies to encourage areas including environmental improvement, climate change mitigation and adaptation, resource utilisation, energy saving, clean energy, among others. Green credit policy is one of the earliest and the most important green finance policies in China. The *Green Credit Guidelines* issued by China Banking Regulatory Commission in 2012 is a founding policy document that clarified direction for China's green credit development, specifying requirements on banks' organisation and management, internal policy, lending procedures, internal management and information disclosure, and supervision towards green credit offering[3]. Additional regulatory guidelines further clarified data collection and monitoring requirements. Notably, the *Special Statistical Guidelines for Green Loans* issued by the People's Bank of China (PBOC) in 2018 requires banks to submit quarterly data on the amount of loan balance by purpose, industry and quality, as well as loans that have high environmental risks.

According to data from the PBOC and the China Banking and Insurance Regulatory Commission (CBIRC), as at the end of 2020, Mainland China's outstanding green loan balance reached nearly RMB 12 trillion (about US$1.84 trillion), which is the highest in the world (see Figure 1). Even though the amount of outstanding green loan balance has been growing consistently year over year, its relative size compared to the total amount of loan balance is still low, at 7.22% in the first quarter of 2021. This suggests that there is still ample room for growth. Among existing loans, the loan balance and growth rate of green transportation, renewable energy and energy conservation projects are among the top. The environmental benefits of green credit are gradually emerging. It was estimated that the 21 major banks' green credit can save more than 300 million tonnes of standard coal each year and reduce carbon dioxide emissions by more than 600 million tonnes[4].

---

3   Source: *Green Credit Guidelines* (《綠色信貸指引》), issued by China Banking Regulatory Commission, 24 February 2012.
4   Source: "At the end of 2020, the green loan balance of 21 major domestic banks exceeded RMB 11 trillion" (〈截至去年末國內 21 家主要銀行綠色信貸餘額超 11 萬億〉), *People's Daily,* 26 March 2021.

Figure 1. Balance of green loans of major financial institutions (in RMB and foreign currency) and its ratio to total loan balance (Dec 2018 – Mar 2021)

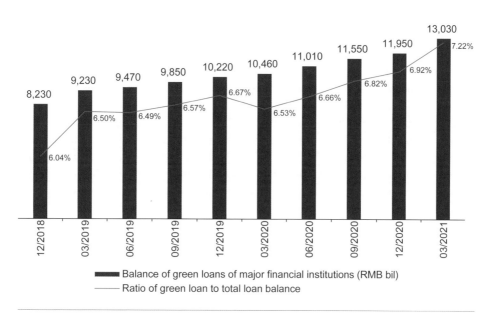

Source: Wind.

Green bonds

Green bonds are "marketable securities that use raised funds specifically to support green industries, green projects, or green economic activities that meet specified conditions". They include but are not limited to "green financial bonds, green corporate bonds, green enterprise bonds, green debt financing tools and green asset-backed securities (ABS)"[5]. Previously, different regulatory agencies in China had different definitions for what qualifies as green bonds. In 2021, the PBOC, the National Development and Reform Commission and the China Securities Regulatory Commission (CSRC) jointly developed the "Green Bonds Endorsed Project Catalogue (2021 Edition)", which provides an update to the 2020 version and most importantly, unified definitions and taxonomies. The new catalogue

---

5   Source: "Note on issuing the green bond endorsed projects catalogue (2021 edition)", published on the website of Climate Bonds Initiative, 2 April 2021.

specifies four levels of endorsed projects at varying levels of details. The first level covers projects across six major areas: energy saving and environmental protection, clean production, clean energy, ecology, green upgrading of infrastructure, and green services.

Despite the latest development to unify green bond guidelines, there are still discrepancies between China's guidelines and international ones. On project definitions, international guidelines emphasise more on climate change, while Chinese guidelines focus more on pollution reduction, resource conservation and ecological protection in addition to climate change mitigation and adaptation. Chinese guidelines also allow some use of proceeds for general corporate operating purposes. In 2019, Chinese green bonds that satisfy the Climate Bond Initiative (CBI)'s definition was the second highest in the world in terms of issuance amount, after the United States (see Figure 2). However, a significant amount of Chinese green bonds (44%) satisfies Chinese guidelines but not CBI definitions, highlighting the significant differences that still exist between international versus China's domestic guidelines[6].

Figure 2. Global green bond issuance —— Top 15 countries (2019)

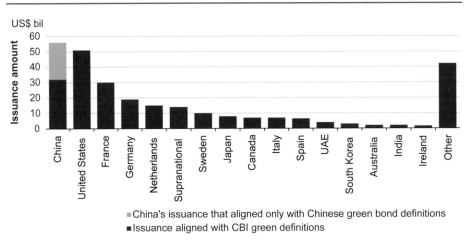

Source: CBI and CCDC Research Centre, "China green bond market: 2019 research report" (〈中國綠色債券市場 2019 研究報告〉), June 2020.

---

6   Source: CBI and China Central Depository and Clearing (CCDC) Research Centre, "China green bond market: 2019 research report" (〈中國綠色債券市場 2019 研究報告〉), June 2020.

In 2020, labelled green bonds issued in Mainland (excluding ABS) dropped by 19.6% from RMB 2,438.6 million to RMB 1,961.5 million, but the number of bonds issued increased by 17.8% from 163 to 192 (see Figure 3).   From 2016 to the end of 2020, cumulatively 618 labelled green bonds were issued, with the total issuance amount reaching RMB 1.035 trillion[7].   It is important to note that labelled green bonds is only part of the overall Chinese green bond market.   Unlabelled green bonds are also used to finance green industries but these are not labelled as "green" by the issuing entity.   It is estimated that in 2019, unlabelled green bonds' issuance amount was 2.3 times that of labelled green bonds[8].

Figure 3.   Issuance amount and number of labelled green bonds (not including ABS) (2016 – 2020)

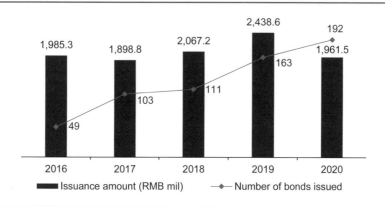

Source: International Institute of Green Finance, "Analysis of China green bond market (2020)" (〈中國綠色債券市場 2020 年度分析簡報〉), 20 January 2021.

Green bonds in the Mainland can be classified into financial bonds, corporate bonds, ABS, enterprise bonds, and other types.   These categories constituted 11.45%, 33.25%, 15.31%, 21.68%, and 18.3% respectively to the total issuance amount of green bonds in 2020, with corporate bonds having the highest share (see Figure 4).   According to analysis

---

7   Source: International Institute of Green Finance, "Analysis of China green bond market (2020)" (〈中國綠色債券市場 2020 年度分析簡報〉), 20 January 2021.

8   Source: International Institute of Green Finance, "Analysis of China's onshore unlabelled green bonds (2019)" (〈2019 年境內非貼標綠色債券發行情況分析〉), 1 September 2020.

from Ping An Securities, in 2016 the early development period of green bonds in the Mainland, financial bonds used to be the most dominant type[9].

Figure 4. Types of green bond issued in Mainland China and their percentage shares of issuance amount in 2020

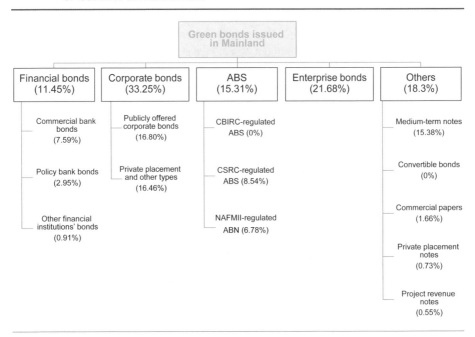

Note: (1) NAFMII is the National Association of Financial Market Institutional Investors. "ABN" are asset-backed notes.

(2) This classification is based on Wind financial database. There may be other ways of categorising different types of bonds.

(3) Percentages may not add up to the total or 100% due to rounding.

Source: Wind.

Motivated by the ambitious goal of reaching carbon neutrality by 2060, there have been increasing product innovation in the green bond market. On 8 February 2021, the country's first batch of six "carbon-neutral bonds" were successfully issued in the interbank

---

9   Source: Ping An Securities Research Institute, "Green Economy Report Series 3: Green bonds on the rise to assist development quality" (〈綠色經濟系列報告（三）：綠色債券方興未艾，助力提高發展質量〉), 5 May 2021.

bond market, with a total issuance size of RMB 6.4 billion. The issuers are 6 state-owned enterprises including Huaneng International, State Power Investment, and South China Power Grid. This is the world's first batch of labelled green bond products named "carbon-neutral". Carbon-neutral bonds are a subset of green bonds and focus more on low-carbon transition and emissions reduction areas. Such development indicates China's active efforts in the innovation of green financial products.

ESG investment

The issuance of ESG fund products underwent a booming period in 2020. As at the end of 2020, the Mainland market has 19 ESG indices that clearly use the constituent companies' ESG scores as the screening criteria in their index construction strategy, and 9 of them were released in 2020. However, there has been no clear definition of green funds in the market. We did a further screening on ESG-concept funds in Wind's database and estimated that there are more than 100 generic-ESG funds in the market, with a total size of about RMB 131 billion as at the end of 2020.

We provide a deeper dive into the development trends of ESG funds and indices in later sections of the chapter and for now, use the fund flows of ESG exchange traded funds (ETFs) to illustrate the growth of ESG investment products as they are an important and emerging vehicle to broaden market access for such products, especially among retail investors.

Globally, fund flows into ESG-themed ETFs reached a new high in 2019, tripling the amount in 2018. In Mainland China, ETF net fund flows had a year-on-year increase of 464% in 2019, on par with the US, and above other Asian regions such as Japan[10] (see Figure 5). However, the assets under management (AUM) of ESG-themed ETFs in Mainland China is still relatively small — below 1% of all ETFs compared to about 6% in Europe (see Table 1).

---

10 Other Asian regions excluding Japan have data levels too low to be reported.

Figure 5. Fund flows into ESG-themed ETFs by year and the invested region (2012 – 2019)

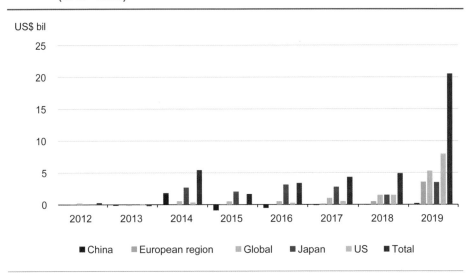

Table 1. Percentage increase in net fund flows into ESG-themed ETFs and AUM of ESG-themed ETFs as percentage of all ETFs (2019)

Region	Mainland China	European Region	Global	Japan	US	Total
Year-on-year percentage increase in ESG-themed ETF net fund flows	464%	639%	254%	132%	433%	305%
Year-end AUM of ESG-themed ETFs as a percentage of all ETFs	0.42%	5.99%	N.A.	5.34%	1.10%	1.25%

For fixed-income ESG investment products, due to the lack of established ratings and data, there are only a small number of fixed-income ESG products in the market, but they are gradually emerging. At the end of September 2020, China Central Depository & Clearing Co., Ltd. (CCDC) issued the China Bond-Huaxia Wealth ESG Preferred Bond Strategy Index. The index screened constituent bonds jointly according to Huaxia Wealth ESG and China Bond ESG Evaluation System, which was the first index product in China that explicitly used ESG scores to screen constituent bonds. From the point of fund products, there is no clear sign of bond funds using ESG scores as a standard for screening. In the market, there are only 2 bond funds of the environment theme.

From April 2019 to December 2020, domestic banks' wealth management subsidiaries have issued 29 ESG-themed wealth management products[11]. As of 13 October 2020, according to data from China Finance Network, among the 27 existing ESG-concept wealth management products, 16 are issued by Huaxia Bank and 6 are issued by Agricultural Bank of China. ESG wealth management products are mainly open-ended fixed-income products.

Trends and focus areas of ESG investment through an analysis of third-party research reports

The continuous opening of Mainland China's capital market drives more and more international capital with ESG investment philosophy into China, which promotes the recognition and acceptance of ESG and responsible investment principles. In recent years, ESG investment in the Mainland has developed rapidly.

The number and topical focus of ESG thematic research reports by securities companies are important indicators that reflect the market's level of attention and specific areas of focus. We collected a total of 103 ESG thematic research reports[12] with the earliest being released in 2017. Using Natural Language Processing (NLP) to analyse the reports' content, we generate and classify five distinct themes — "ESG concept introduction", "ESG in China"[13], "ESG rating system", "existing ESG products", and "ESG investment market performance". Through identifying keywords related to these topics, and calculating

---

11 Source: "Bank wealth management opens the path of ESG investment exploration" (〈銀行理財開啟 ESG 投資探索之 路〉), published on *Financial News,* 8 December 2020.

12 A total of 121 research reports with the title containing the keyword "ESG" were collected from Wind Database, and 103 ESG thematic research reports were selected by using text analysis technology.

13 "ESG in China" refers to the status quo and shortcomings of China's ESG development, relatively broad, not focusing on investment products and investment performance.

relative coverage of different topics in each report, we derive the yearly average coverage ratio of each topic since 2017.

Since 2017, the number of ESG thematic reports has been increasing rapidly year by year, from 1 in 2017 to 53 in 2020, indicating that the Mainland capital market has been paying more attention to ESG (see Figure 6). In terms of content focus, before 2018, the market focused more on "ESG concept introduction" and "ESG in China". After 2018, "ESG rating system", "existing ESG products" and "ESG investment market performance" began to become the market's focus. This is consistent with the logical arc of development for popularisation and gradual acceptance of the ESG concept by the investment market (see Figure 7).

The initial focus of the market is to conduct market education by clarifying a new concept, popularising it, and discussing the current situation and future demand of ESG development in Mainland China. After the initial market education phase, ESG rating system suitable for local market conditions need to be developed by drawing lessons from international rating providers. Having Mainland-specific ESG ratings and data is the foundation for developing ESG investment products in the Mainland. Subsequently, a series of ESG indices and investment strategies were launched in 2019 and 2020. With the increase in the number and scale of ESG fund products, the market performance and effectiveness of ESG investment are attracting more and more attention.

Figure 6. Number of ESG thematic reports in Mainland China by year (2017 – 2020)

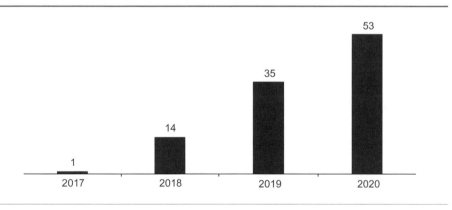

Note: Data up to10 September 2020.

Source: Analysis by Ping An Digital Economic Research Center based on data from Bloomberg.

Figure 7. Average coverage ratios of ESG research report topics in Mainland China by year (2017 – 2020)

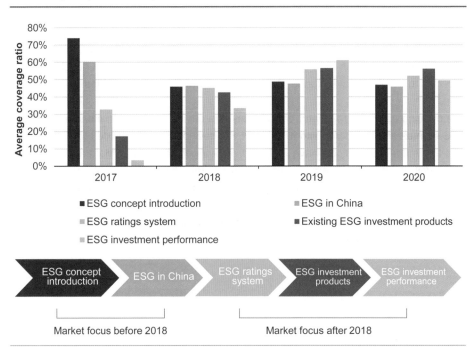

Notes: (1) In 2017, only China Industrial Securities published an ESG themed research report entitled "China Industrial Securities Research on Green Finance: ESG Disclosure, Evaluation and Application of Listed Companies". Here, the average coverage rate in 2017 only reflects the thematic coverage of this report.

(2) Average coverage ratio is not affected by the report collection time. However, since reports discussing ESG investment market performance are generally released at the end of each year, the coverage ratio on ESG investment market performance in 2020 may be affected.

(3) Data up to 19 October 2020.

Source: Analysis by Ping An Digital Economic Research Center based on data from Bloomberg.

Driving forces for the growth of ESG products

With stronger regulatory requirements for ESG disclosures and a broader guidance to build a "green financial system", Mainland China has witnessed an increase in the quantity and quality of disclosures, as well as rapid growth of ESG investment in recent years.

Related policy efforts are accelerating as President Xi announced China's goal to reach carbon neutrality by 2060 and carbon neutrality being officially included in the national

14th Five-Year Plan. The People's Bank of China announced that it will step up efforts to support green industries with innovative financial products and services to support the carbon neutrality goal. Local governments, such as the Shenzhen Municipal Government, have also announced and implemented green finance related policies to enforce disclosures, encourage development of financial products, as well as promote carbon trading markets. Under such policy backdrop, ESG and green finance development is expected to accelerate even further in the next few years in Mainland China.

The opening-up of the Mainland capital market is driving more international capital with ESG themes and mandates into it, driving ESG development alongside regulatory push. Globally influential indices have included or planned to include Mainland A-shares, which will attract a large amount of foreign capital. As international investors raise requirements for ESG and credit-rating agencies place more emphasis on ESG-related risks, international investors who invest in the Mainland will need to satisfy their domicile mandate when doing so. This is another driving force to push Chinese companies to achieve better ESG-related disclosures and better performance.

Latest development of ESG indices

The launch of "pure ESG" indices and ESG fixed-income indices

There are 19 "pure ESG" indices[14] in the Mainland market as at the end of 2020. Of these, only four were released before 2019, six in 2019, and nine in 2020, including five ESG equity indices launched by the China Securities Index Co., Ltd. (CSI) in late April 2020 (see Figure 8). With increasing interest on ESG in the Mainland's investment market, promotion of ESG data disclosure by regulatory authorities, and continuous improvement of ESG data, ESG indices has grown rapidly in China since 2019.

---

14 Pure ESG index has an index strategy in which a company's ESG score is explicitly used as a screening criterion. In this chapter, we do not include a generic-ESG index that only considers themes related to environmental protection, poverty alleviation or corporate governance, and does not explicitly include a company's ESG score in the selection criteria.

Figure 8. Issuance of "pure ESG" indices by year (2010 – 2020)

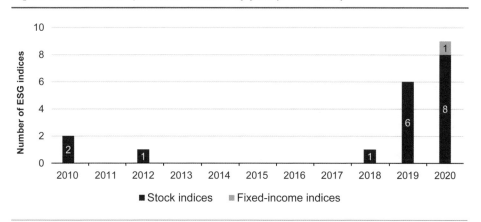

Source: Analysis by Ping An Digital Economic Research Center based on data from Wind.

Among the 19 pure ESG indices, there is only one fixed-income index named "China Bond-Huaxia Wealth Management ESG Preferred", which was released in September 2020. Since bond issuers are not subject to the information disclosure requirements of listed companies, it is difficult to obtain relevant ESG data on them. In establishment of corresponding ESG rating system for fixed-income products is often lagging behind that of equity products. In the future, with the establishment and development of ESG fixed-income rating system, we believe ESG fixed-income indices will develop further.

Investment strategies of "pure ESG" indices

Mainstream ESG investment methods in the market currently include: positive screening, negative screening, ESG factor integration, theme-specific sustainable development investment, and social impact investment. Since we only consider indices in the secondary market that explicitly consider ESG scores in the investment strategy, and do not consider specific topics (such as environmental protection, poverty alleviation, etc.) or private market conditions, we will focus on analysing two investment strategies: positive and negative screening, after further integration.

- **Positive screening:** Select highly ESG-rated companies from the stock pool based on companies' ESG scores.

- **Negative screening:** Remove low-ESG-rated companies from the stock pool based on the companies' ESG scores.

On the basis of positive and negative screening, further factor enhancement can be carried out. ESG scores are integrated with other fundamental factors, such as valuation and dividend ratio.

Of the 17 ESG indices with available information on investment strategy[15], only 4 adopts a negative screening strategy and 14 adopts a positive screening strategy ("China Securities ESG300" adopts a combination of positive and negative screening). Among them, only 9 had clear factor enhancement strategies on top of screening, and the main enhancement factors were valuation, quality, and dividend ratio. Positive screening and factor enhancement are the mainstream ESG index investment strategies in the market at present.

Before 2019, all pure ESG indices adopted positive screening without factor enhancement. All 9 indices released in 2020 include positive/negative screening with or without factor enhancement (see Table 2), and the factors are also more diverse. As ESG data and ratings continue to improve, ESG indices' strategies will be further enriched, giving investors more options for investment products. The development course of the types of ESG integration strategy is slightly different domestically compared to that globally. For ESG investment in developed markets, most of the early strategies were negative screening, eliminating "sin stocks"[16] such as weapons, tobacco, alcohol, and gambling. With the development of ESG data and rating systems, more comprehensive ESG integration strategies followed. In Mainland China, perhaps because the development of ESG investment can directly learn from most recent global trends, there is a positive selection strategy in practice from an early stage, rather than relying only on negative screening. (See Table 3 on the list of 17 ESG indices and their strategies.)

---

15 Data on the strategies of China Bond-Huaxia Wealth Management ESG Preferred and MSCI China A-share International Access ESG General are not available.

16 Source: Kelley, M. and C. Sardi. (2020) "ESG Investments – Part One: An Introduction to and History of ESG Investing", published on *ESL* website, 19 October 2020.

Table 2.　Number of "pure ESG" indices by investment strategy

Screening method	Factor enhancement	
	Yes	No
Positive screening	6	5
Negative screening	3[1]	3

Note: (1) China National Securities ESG300 (399378.SZ) combines positive selection strategy with negative screening, and is classified statistically as negative screening.

Source: Analysis by Ping An Digital Economic Research Center based on data from Wind.

Table 3.　Strategy classification of "pure ESG" indices

Index code	Index name	Strategy type	Factor enhancement	Enhancement factor	Sample scope (parent index)
399378.SZ	CNI ESG 300	Positive screening + negative screening	No	—	CNI 1000
000970.CSI	CSI ECPI ESG Sustainable Development 40	Positive screening	No	—	CSI 180
000846.CSI	CSI Caitong China Sustainable Development 100 (ECPI ESG)	Positive screening	No	—	CSI 300
931088.CSI	CSI 180 ESG	Negative screening	No	—	Shanghai Exchange listed companies
931148.CSI	CSI ECPI ESG 80	Negative screening	Yes	Volatility	CSI 300
931168.CSI	CSI CUFE SH-SZ 100 ESG Leading	Positive screening	No	—	CSI 300
931463.CSI	CSI 300 ESG Benchmark	Negative screening	No	—	CSI 300

(continued)

Index code	Index name	Strategy type	Factor enhancement	Enhancement factor	Sample scope (parent index)
931476.CSI	CSI ESG 120 Strategy	Negative screening	Yes	Valuation, dividend yield, quality and market factor score	CSI 300
931477.CSI	CSI Huaxia Bank ESG	Negative screening	Yes	Valuation, dividend yield, quality and market factor score	CSI 300
931465.CSI	CSI 300 ESG Leaders	Positive screening	No	—	CSI 300
931466.CSI	CSI 300 ESG Value	Positive screening	Yes	Valuation	CSI 300
931525.CSI	CSI CISC ESG Earnings 100	Positive screening	Yes	Return on equity	CSI 300
931565.CSI	CSI CMB Wealth Management Satellite Luminous ESG	Positive screening	Yes	Market capitalisation	CSI 300
995009.SSI	SSI Dividend & ESG	Positive screening	Yes	Continuous high dividend	Full market
980058.CNI	CACG Green Governance	Positive screening	No	—	Shenzhen Exchange listed companies
995002.SSI	SSI Value Delivery Sunshine 100	Positive screening	Yes	Liquidity, financial strength	A shares
995006.SSI	SSI High Dividend ESG Select total earning	Positive screening	Yes	Stable and high dividend yield, with a certain market cap and liquidity	A shares

Source: Analysis by Ping An Digital Economic Research Center based on data from Wind.

Latest development of ESG funds

Fund types and investment themes

As of 31 December 2020, there were 14 "pure ESG" funds[17], 50 environmental thematic funds, 9 corporate governance thematic funds and 36 Pan-ESG concept funds in the Mainland market (see Figure 9). From the perspective of investment asset class, they are mainly hybrid funds, including 71 hybrid funds and 34 equity funds. As of 31 December 2020, there were only two fixed-income funds which are environment-thematic funds, namely Fullgoal Green Pure Bond (005383.OF) and Industries Green Pure Bond One Year (009237.OF).

Figure 9. Distribution of ESG funds in number by theme and investment type (31 Dec 2020)

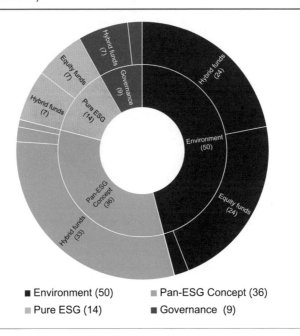

- ■ Environment (50)
- ■ Pure ESG (14)
- ■ Pan-ESG Concept (36)
- ■ Governance (9)

Source: Analysis by Ping An Digital Economic Research Center based on data from Wind.

17 "Pure ESG" funds refer to funds that consider at least two or more of the environmental, social and corporate governance dimensions. In addition to fund products that specifically integrate ESG scores, this category also includes funds that consider investment themes such as "sustainable development" or "social responsibility".

In terms of size, the total AUM of ESG funds was about RMB 130.3 billion as of 31 December 2020. Among them, 14 pure ESG funds had a total AUM of RMB 15 billion, accounting for 11.5% of the total size. Pan-ESG concept funds had the largest share, reaching RMB 52.1 billion, accounting for about 40% of the total size of the ESG fund market. In terms of investment asset class, hybrid funds have the largest scale, with the total AUM reaching RMB98.5 billion, accounting for more than 70% of the total. (See Figure 10.)

Figure 10. Distribution of ESG funds in size (AUM) by theme and investment type (31 Dec 2020)

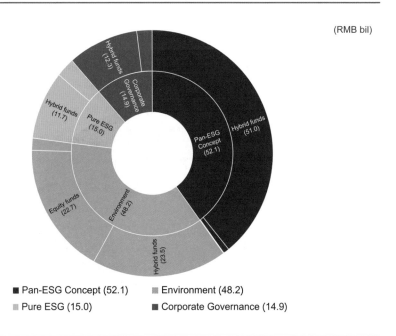

(RMB bil)

■ Pan-ESG Concept (52.1) ■ Environment (48.2)
■ Pure ESG (15.0) ■ Corporate Governance (14.9)

Source: Analysis by Ping An Digital Economic Research Center based on data from Wind.

Box 1. ESG thematic fund classification

In our tabulation, there are 109 ESG thematic funds in Mainland China in total. We classify them into four main categories: pure ESG Fund, environmental thematic fund, corporate governance thematic fund, and generic/pan-ESG concept fund according to their selection of investment targets.

- **Pure ESG funds:** Considers at two or more of the environmental, social, and corporate governance dimensions. In addition to fund products that specifically integrate ESG scores, this category also includes funds that consider investment themes such as "sustainable development" or "social responsibility".

  Note: Here, the screening criteria for pure ESG funds are relatively loose compared with pure ESG index, mainly considering that the number of pure ESG funds in the market is still small.

- **Environmental thematic funds:** Funds that mainly take environmental factors into account when formulating investment strategies and selecting investment targets. Keywords we chose include "environmental protection", "low-carbon", "beautiful China", "new energy", and "green energy".

  Note: Environmental thematic funds do not include "new energy vehicles" and other broader industry-specific thematic funds.

- **Corporate governance thematic funds:** Funds that highlights corporate governance capability when developing investment strategies and selecting investment targets.

- **Generic/Pan-ESG concept funds:** Other ESG concept funds included in the 109 ESG thematic funds but cannot be included in the above classification due to insufficient information.

The scope of ESG thematic funds is based on Wind ESG concept fund database. According to the definition by Wind, ESG concept funds are funds that include the following keywords in their product name / investment scope / investment objective / performance benchmark / investment philosophy:

"ESG", "social responsibility", "ethical responsibility", "green", "environmental protection", "low-carbon", "beautiful China", "corporate governance" or "sustainable development".

Then we removed different categories or grades of the same fund to avoid double counting, and the fund products that are in the fundraising period and have not yet been listed were screened out. In the end, a total of 109 fund products as of 31 December 2020 were analysed.

Issuance trend of ESG funds

The period 2014 to 2016 is the first booming period for ESG theme funds in Mainland China. In addition to market conditions, it is also closely related to the development of the Mainland's regulatory policies. The Environmental Protection Act was issued in 2014, which put forward specific provisions on environmental pollution information disclosure. The State Council in 2015 for the first time explicitly stated to "establish China's greenfinancial system", Seven ministries in 2016 published the *Guidance on Building Green Financial System.* These constitute the policy background for the first wave of launch of Chinese ESG funds. As a result, ESG thematic concept funds established during this period focused on environmental themes. The development of ESG concept started to accelerate in the Mainland in 2019, with ESG themed funds attract more and more market attention. More ESG funds have been established with varied types. New pure ESG fundincreased significantly, the market entered the second concentrated year of ESG funds establishment. (See Figure 11.)

Figure 11. Distribution of the number of ESG funds issuance by type (2003 – 2020)

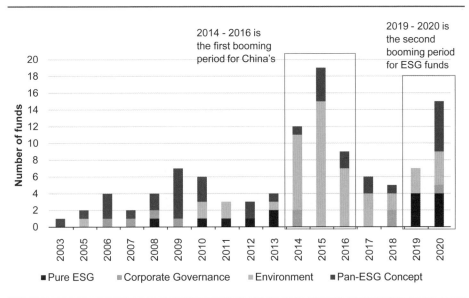

Source: Analysis by Ping An Digital Economic Research Center based on data from Wind.

In terms of issuance size, ESG thematic concept funds in general have been growing rapidly since 2018. The total issuance size of ESG thematic concept funds in 2020 increased by 37% compared with that in 2019, nearly double that in 2018. The main drivers of growth are still environmental themed funds and pan-ESG concept funds. The issuance amount of pure ESG funds increased significantly in 2019, while the issuance amount of corporate governance themed funds grew rapidly in 2020. (See Figure 12).

Figure 12. Distribution of the annual issuance size of ESG funds by theme (2015 – 2020)

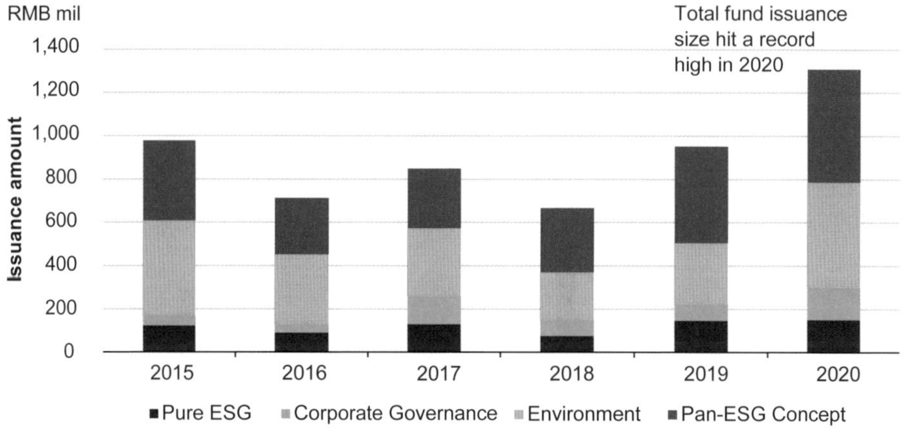

Source: Analysis by Ping An Digital Economic Research Center based on data from Wind.

Industry distribution of ESG funds

The number one heavy-weighed industries in ESG funds are the electrical equipment sectors. Environmental thematic funds prefer electrical equipment. This is mainly because many environmental theme funds limit their stock selection to environmental protection related industries, and there are a large number of electrical equipment companies in this industry. In pure ESG funds, the food and beverages industry has more weight. (See Figure 13.) Year reports of 2020 show that among the 28 industries, the electrical equipment, food and beverages sectors were also the top two most heavily weighted industries in the overall fund market. Electronics ranked third, pharma and biology ranked fourth. Industry distribution of ESG funds is basically consistent with the overall fund market. ESG factors have no obvious influence on the industry allocation. As observed, there have been few ESG-themed funds in China rigorously using ESG scores as a core evaluating criteria. The subjective opinion of fund managers is still the dominant determinant.

Figure 13. Number of funds in top three highest weighting industries of ESG funds by theme (as of 31 Dec 2020)

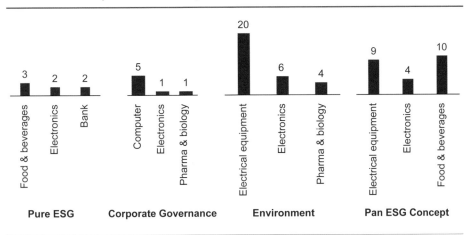

Source: Analysis by Ping An Digital Economic Research Center based on data from Wind.

Remaining gaps and opportunities in ESG investment products in Mainland China

The majority of ESG financial products in Mainland China are fixed-income products so far, with a focus on green bonds and loan products. The total issuance size of China's green bonds and loan products are relatively large, whereas the variety of products still lag behind developed markets. Some other sustainability-themed have also been gaining popularity, which presents future product opportunities. China's ESG bonds have been dominated by green bonds, while social bonds are also gaining popularity globally. Social bonds allow for proceeds to be used to fund projects that have a positive social impact, such as improving social welfare or serving disadvantaged groups.

In the loan market, China's ESG products also focus on green areas to finance specific green purposes. Other ESG loans like Sustainability-Linked Loan (SLL) is also gaining popularity across the globe. SLL are loans that encourage companies to achieve sustainable goals. If companies achieve certain sustainable targets successfully, such as carbon emissions reduction or energy efficiency improvement, the loan interest rate can be lowered. There is no limit to the scope of use of such loan funds. SLL have been issued in the US, Europe and Singapore.

Although some ESG ETFs have been issued in Mainland China, the total AUM is much smaller than that in the international market. As at the end of October 2020, the total AUM of ESG-themed passive funds, including environment-themed passive funds, in the Mainland market was only RMB 5.9 billion[18]. On 8 April 2021, BlackRock launched the largest ESG ETF ever in the world, the US Carbon Transition Readiness Fund. This fund alone has raised US$1.25 billion from institutional investors[19]. A sister fund that invests in non-US companies also launched on the same day and attracted US$475 million from investors[20].

In the private market, there is a wide gap between Mainland China and other major markets. Some Mainland private equity (PE) firms are embracing ESG proactively, for example, Envision Technology Group and Sequoia China who announced that they would jointly establish a carbon-neutral technology fund with a total size of RMB 10 billion[21]. However, there are very few PE firms that explicitly adopt ESG principles internally or within their portfolios in Mainland China. European PE firms lead the world in adopting ESG standards. *Financier Worldwide* states that, almost two thirds (63%) of UK PE firms now take ESG principles into account when making investments; 48% report in detail on the ESG impact of their investments; and 25% have a dedicated individual or team responsible for embedding ESG into the investment process[22].

Robust data: The pre-condition to further development of ESG investment

Overview of global and Mainland data providers

The foundation of ESG indices and associated financial products is robust ESG ratings and data. This is evident in the NLP analysis results above, where we see that ESG ratings and data are the foundation for further development of indices and fund products in the Mainland market. The landscape for ESG data and rating providers is a lot less concentrated than credit rating providers, with no clear market leaders. Globally, while there

---

18 Source: Ping An Digital Economic Research Center, "ESG Investment in China", November 2020.
19 Source: "BlackRock secures largest-ever ETF launch as green investing wave builds", *Financial Times,* 8 April 2021.
20 Ditto.
21 Source: "VC, PE companies expanding green efforts", *China Daily,* 6 May 2021.
22 Source: "From nice to have to mainstream: ESG in private equity", *Financier Worldwide,* February 2021.

are established players like MSCI and Sustainalytics, there are also a wide range of niche players that are gaining traction. For example, Trucost are known to have comprehensive environmental and climate related metrics. TruValue Labs and Owl Analytics are known for ESG alternative data, i.e. non-disclosure-based data. Interestingly, there have been a wave of acquisitions among ESG data companies (noted in Figure 14), especially by traditional financial data vendors to acquire niche players so that they can add ESG data to their offerings.

The nature of global versus Mainland ESG data landscape is vastly different. First, ESG data providers have a much longer history in the international market, where they first started emerging in the 1990s. In the Mainland, it is a much more recent phenomenon where ESG data and rating providers only started to emerge since 2015. However, the speed of development is impressive. During a span of merely five years, there are already eight providers in the Mainland market. Second, the type of provider is more diverse in the Mainland. Globally, 9 out of 15 providers are established data providers. Some of them are traditional financial data vendors such as FTSE Russell, Reuters, Refinitiv, and Bloomberg that have offered ESG data as part of their service. For example, Bloomberg hosts a wide range of ESG indicators and started to offer proprietary ESG ratings, starting from oil and gas sector in 2020. Others are ESG data providers that have had a long history of focusing on sustainability such as RobecoSAM, RepRisk, MSCI, and Sustainalytics. Since 2014, a wave of financial technology (fintech) companies has entered the market, with a focus on using alternative data such as news and social media to generate ESG signals. In Mainland China, however, the type of provider ranges from traditional index/data providers, fintech companies, asset managers, asset owners, academic/non-profit institutions, to consulting companies. We see a new wave of providers entering the market in 2020, motivated by stricter regulatory requirements and growing investor demand for sustainable finance products.

Figure 14. Landscape of ESG data and rating providers in the global and Mainland markets

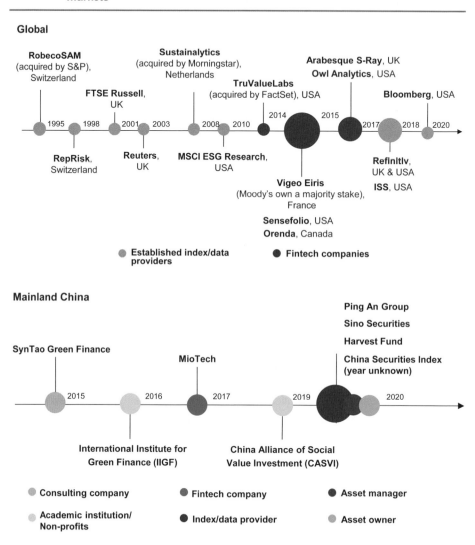

Source: Compiled by Ping An Digital Economic Research Center based on public information.

Supporting factors required

ESG ratings and data coverage in the Mainland market need to be further enhanced to improve alignment with the Mainland market to support the enrichment of ESG-themed investment products. The development of ESG rating and data in Mainland China is in its early stage, but the speed cannot be under-estimated. During the five years from 2015 to 2020, eight different types of data and rating provider have emerged. However, due to the relatively low availability of ESG data for China's A-shares, historical time series data of existing providers are insufficient with low coverage. This significantly limits the diversity of financial products and the verifiability of ESG factors' impact. Due to the lack of historical data, backtesting for strategy development is also restricted. There are already data providers that have started to cover all A shares with multiple years of data, such as Harvest Fund and Ping An's proprietary ESG data and rating system.

Establishment of ESG ratings and data for bonds and bond issuers is essential to accelerate the integration of ESG in to fixed-income investments. In addition to the equity market, improving coverage for fixed-income is another challenge. Bond issuers are not subject to the same requirement for information disclosure as listed companies, which makes it even more difficult to obtain ESG-related data for bonds and bond issuers. As a result, the corresponding ESG rating system for fixed-income significantly lags behind that of equity. The complex structure of fixed-income investment adds additional challenges. This, to a large extent, limits the development of ESG fixed-income products.

In addition to coverage, data and rating providers in the Mainland market should pay attention to the localisation of ESG concepts in Mainland China. Considering the different national conditions and development stages of Chinese companies, the Mainland's ESG rating system should also adjust the indicators and evaluation standards beyond integrating with international guidelines, so that the system can fully provide data in line with the Mainland's financial market. In this case, we should take advantage of the diversity of existing data and rating providers in Mainland China. Compared with the global market, the types of institution offering ESG data and rating services in Mainland China are more diversified, including academic institutions, non-profit organisations, financial institutions and consulting companies. Each type of institution has a different perspective. This kind of diversification can better stimulate market research and development of ESG standards more suitable for Mainland China's market conditions.

Recommendations

Regulators in Mainland China should develop unified guidelines and converge on a set of the most material indicators that companies must disclose. While different issuers would differ in their objectives and scope, there should be a subset of specific and material indicators that are mandatory. Mainland regulators and stock exchanges should make reference to guidelines and recommendations from international organisations such as Global Reporting Initiative (GRI) and United Nations-supported Principles for Responsible Investment (PRI), and integrate local market considerations specific to Chinese companies. They should also encourage companies to audit their ESG disclosures. ESG is an important complement to the governance of Chinese companies. Better ESG disclosures and performance can help improve the credibility and value of Chinese companies for global investors.

Companies should leverage technological solutions to collect, monitor, and learn from their ESG data. Instead of a manual process, it should be automated across departments. Instead of doing an annual exercise, it should be continuously monitored. Instead of having confusion around what indicators to disclose, there should be a customised list based on the preferred guidelines, reducing the resources required to respond to different requirements. Companies can leverage technology to streamline and simplify their ESG reporting process. Ping An Group's AI-ESG platform, for example, mapped more than 500 indicators from different regulatory agencies and helped automate data collection, monitor changes, and generate actionable insights through industry peer comparison.

Rating service providers should improve transparency on their methodologies and expand their ESG data sources to include alternative data that is not reliant on company disclosure, to improve objectivity and timeliness. Even though providers may not be able to disclose every detail of their methodologies due to intellectual property rights concerns, they could still be more transparent on their indicator scopes and scoring frameworks. MSCI, for example, has the most detailed documentation on its methodologies, which could provide industry standard. Providers should supplement the existing disclosure-based data with non-disclosure-based data, such as government announcements and news media reports, leveraging advanced analytical capabilities such as NLP and optical character recognition (OCR) to expand data coverage and improve timeliness. Providers should also focus on indicators that are material for investors, possibly by testing the impact of ESG indicators on medium- to long-term company valuations and reflecting that in their scoring models.

Investors should incorporate ESG information into their investment decisions, develop ESG investment tools, exert shareholder influence and encourage better ESG disclosures among Chinese companies. Even though ESG investing is still in its early stage in the Mainland, various investment managers, including China Asset Management, Harvest Fund, Ping An, Southern Asset Management, and E Fund, have all started expanding their ESG-themed research and financial products. We suggest that investors implement ESG investing in three stages:

- First, investment managers can start from simpler processes, such as negative and positive screening, by leveraging several mainstream ESG rating providers in the market.

- Second, deepen analysis and application of ESG indicators and ratings frameworks, analyse the impact of ESG indicators on investment decisions, and establish customised evaluation frameworks consistent with the investors' own investment styles.

- Third, fully integrate ESG factors into their own valuation models and develop targeted research on important ESG topics, such as climate change and demographic trends.

Asset owners can also include external managers' ESG practices as part of their manager selection criteria. During company engagement, investors should encourage companies to provide more specific and longer-timeline ESG data. Only with clear expectations from both investors and regulators will companies be more motivated to improve their disclosures.

Alternative data and technology can help investors distinguish between companies that are truly ESG compliant and well performing versus those who are not. As ESG continues to develop, investors have also become more conscious of the possibility of greenwashing, where companies' disclosures do not reflect their actual ESG performance. The definition of ESG products is also loose. For example, as we show in this chapter, funds and indices that explicitly use ESG scores for screening and those that only focus on a "green" theme are all considered in the ESG fund universe. This gives opportunities to wear a green hat but how green the underlying assets needs to be carefully examined. Tools will need to be developed to help better detect companies that show potential evidence of greenwashing. NLP-based transparency indicators could help distinguish "Brown" from "Green" firms and detect areas of under-reporting by "Brown" firms. ESG ratings could also be used to detect anomalies between companies who do disclose versus those who do not. These tools complement existing ESG ratings in the market to better distinguish truly well-performing firms.

Index providers and fund management companies should develop more diversified ESG products such as passive index funds, quantitative funds, and investment products for the primary market, providing more investment options for investor. Issuance of ESG indices and fund products exploded since 2019, and their investment strategies are also more diverse than prior to 2019. The five ESG indices released by CSI at the end of April 2020 used four different screening and factor enhancement strategies, which will provide more options of ESG products for investors in the future. In addition, only Sino-Securities Index's ESG stock pool covers all A-shares, while most other index products are still based on CSI 300 Index's stock pool. In the future, as more rating agencies cover the full A-share market, there would be more flexible choices for investors. Performance should also improve as a result.

In the fund market, there have been only a few passive ESG index funds, and the total size is far lower than that of active ESG funds of the same type. In the future, with the abundance of ESG indices and further popularisation of ESG investment philosophies, passive ESG fund products will develop further. We also notice that after the launch of the CX Quantitative Fund for Low-carbon and Environmental Protection Industry in 2017, another pure ESG quantitative fund was launched in 2020 — Morgan Stanley Huaxin ESG Quantitative First. The improvement and standardisation of ESG data will also provide new possibilities for quantitative ESG fund in the future.

With rising influence of ESG investment in the secondary market, it is starting to also influence the primary market. In developed markets, ESG investment has been incorporated in the whole process of equity investment — "fund-raising, investing, portfolio-managing and exiting", and has become a part of equity investment due diligence. There have been dozens of private equity institutions in China that signed the PRI. In the future, equity investment institutions should consciously incorporate ESG concept into their investment process, so as to avoid environmental and social risks and better prepare for the secondary market.

第3章

中國內地的綠色及可持續投資

余晨曦
平安科技、壹賬通智慧科技
戰略副總監

崔詩情
平安科技、壹賬通智慧科技
高級投資研究員

摘要

在嚴格的 ESG 披露監管要求以及構建「綠色金融體系」的更廣泛指導下，環境、社會及公司治理（environment、social、governance，簡稱 ESG）在中國內地的採用日益廣泛，呈快速上升之勢。隨着企業 ESG 信息披露的數量和質量不斷上升，投資者在過去幾年裏愈發傾向於選擇與 ESG 相關的投資產品。本章主要介紹了中國內地綠色可持續投資產品的主要類別及其最新發展趨勢，並且深入分析了 ESG 指數和基金，以及可持續投資數據的現狀，預測了未來的發展趨勢並提出具體建議。

中國內地的綠色及可持續投資產品

當前金融產品概述

過去幾年裏，綠色及可持續投資在中國迅速發展。2016 年，七部委和監管部門發佈了《關於構建綠色金融體系的指導意見》，文中明確定義了綠色金融和綠色金融體系。綠色金融是指「為支持改善環境、應對氣候變化和資源節約高效利用的經濟活動提供的金融服務」。綠色金融體系是指「通過綠色信貸、綠色債券、綠色股票指數和相關產品、綠色發展基金、綠色保險、碳金融等金融工具和相關政策支持經濟向綠色化轉型的制度安排」[1]。

在 2030 年前達到碳排放峰值、2060 年前實現碳中和的宏偉目標下，中國內地綠色金融發展速度勢必進一步加快。實現這樣大規模和這樣高速的過渡意味着需要大量投資。綠色金融能夠支持和鼓勵更多對環境和社會負責任的投資，助力對邁向碳中和的轉型有正向貢獻的行業成長。根據清華大學估算，要在 2050 年之前實現這一目標，僅能源系統就需要新增投資約 138 萬億元人民幣（20 萬億美元，佔中國年度國內生產總值的 2.5% 以上）[2]。

就目前的金融產品而言，綠色信貸和綠色債券是兩大主要融資工具，而 ESG（environment、social、governance，即環境、社會和公司治理）投資正在推動更多的資本走向更加綠色和更加可持續的發展領域。

綠色信貸

綠色信貸是銀行業金融機構向公司提供的貸款，旨在鼓勵包括改善環境、應對氣候變化、資源節約高效利用和清潔能源等領域。綠色信貸政策是中國最早、最重要的綠色金融政策之一。中國銀行業監督管理委員會（簡稱「中國銀監會」）於 2012 年發佈的《綠色信貸指引》是一份指引中國綠色信貸發展方向的基礎性政策文件，文件中明確了在銀行組織管理、內部政策、貸款程序、內部管理和信息披露、綠色信貸發行監管等方面的要求[3]。其他監管準則進一步明確了數據收集和監控要求。值得注意的是，中國人民銀行 2018 年發佈的《綠色貸款專項統計制度》要求銀行每季度就貸款餘額（按用途、行業、質量匯報），以及環境風險較高的貸款提交數據。

1　資料來源：《關於構建綠色金融體系的指導意見》，中華人民共和國國務院新聞辦公室發佈，2016年8月31日。
2　資料來源：清華大學氣候變化與可持續發展研究院 〈中國長期低碳發展戰略與轉型路徑研究〉，載於 《中外對話》，2020年10月12日。
3　資料來源：《綠色信貸指引》，中國銀監會發佈，2012年2月24日。

據中國人民銀行和中國銀行保險監督管理委員會（簡稱「中國銀保監會」）的數據顯示，截至 2020 年年底，中國內地的綠色貸款餘額接近 12 萬億元人民幣（約 1.84 萬億美元），居世界首位（見圖 1）。儘管綠色貸款餘額逐年持續增長，但其相對貸款餘額總額的比例仍然偏低 —— 2021 年第一季度該比例為 7.22%。這表明，綠色貸款仍有充足的增長空間。在現有貸款中，綠色交通、可再生能源和節能項目的貸款餘額和增長率均名列前茅。綠色信貸的環境效益逐漸顯現。據估計，21 家主要銀行的綠色信貸每年可支持節約標準煤超過 3 億噸，減少二氧化碳排放量超過 6 億噸[4]。

圖 1：主要金融機構綠色貸款餘額（人民幣和外幣）及其佔貸款總餘額之比重（2018 年 12 月至 2021 年 3 月）

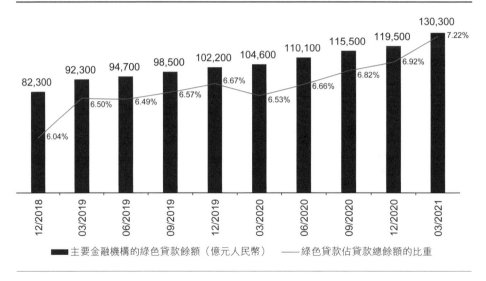

資料來源：Wind。

綠色債券

綠色債券是指「將募集到的資金專門用於支持符合規定條件的綠色產業、綠色項目或綠色經濟活動的有價證券」。它們包括但不限於「綠色金融債券、綠色公司債券、綠色企業債券、綠色債務融資工具和綠色資產支持證券」[5]。此前，中國不同的監管機構對綠色債券的定義不

4　資料來源：〈截至去年末國內21家主要銀行綠色信貸餘額超11萬億元〉，載於《人民日報》，2021年3月26日。
5　資料來源：〈關於發佈綠色債券支持項目目錄(2021年版)的説明〉，載於《氣候債券倡議》（Climate Bonds Initiative，簡稱CBI）網站，2021年4月2日。

同。2021 年，中國人民銀行、國家發展和改革委員會（簡稱「國家發改委」）與中國證券監督管理委員會（簡稱「中國證監會」）聯合發佈了《綠色債券支持項目目錄（2021 年版）》，在 2020 年版的基礎上進行了更新，更重要的是統一了定義和分類標準。新的目錄詳細規定了四個層次的支持項目。其中，第一層次涵蓋了節能環保、清潔生產、清潔能源、生態、基礎設施綠色升級和綠色服務六大領域的項目。

儘管在統一綠色債券指導性文件方面取得了最新進展，但中國的相關指引與國際的相關指引仍存在差異。在項目定義上，國際指引更多地強調氣候變化，而中國指引除應對氣候變化之外，更多地關注減少污染、資源節約和生態保護。中國指引還允許將一部分收益用於企業的一般性經營目的。2019 年，符合《氣候債券倡議》（Climate Bonds Initiative，簡稱 CBI）定義的中國綠色債券在發行金額方面居世界第二位，僅次於美國（見圖 2）。然而，大量中國綠色債券（44%）符合中國指引，卻不符合 CBI 的定義。這表明國際指引與中國指引之間仍然存在較大差異[6]。

圖 2：2019 年全球綠色債券發行額 —— 前 15 個國家

資料來源：《中國綠色債券市場 2019 研究報告》，CBI 與中央國債登記結算公司中債研發中心，2020 年 6 月。

6　資料來源：CBI與中央國債登記結算公司中債研發中心〈中國綠色債券市場2019研究報告〉，2020年6月。

2020 年，內地發行的貼標綠色債券（不包括資產支持證券）從 24.386 億元人民幣跌至 19.615 億元人民幣，跌幅達 19.6%，但發行數量由 163 隻增至 192 隻，有 17.8% 的增幅 （見圖 3）。2016 年至 2020 年年底累計發行貼標綠色債券 618 隻，發行總額達到 1.035 萬億元人民幣[7]。值得注意的是，貼標綠色債券只是整個中國綠色債券市場的一部分。未 貼標綠色債券也有用於資助綠色產業，只是發行實體未給其貼上「綠色」標籤。據估計， 2019 年未貼標綠色債券的發行金額是貼標綠色債券的 2.3 倍[8]。

圖 3：貼標綠色債券（不包括資產支持證券）的發行金額及數量（2016 年至 2020 年）

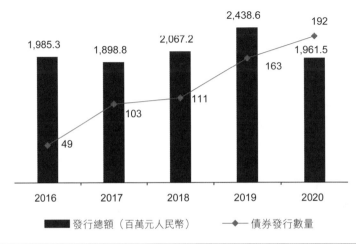

資料來源：綠色金融國際研究院〈中國綠色債券市場 2020 年度分析簡報〉，2021 年 1 月 20 日。

中國內地的綠色債券可分為金融債券、公司債券、資產支持證券、企業債券和其他類別等。 這些類別分別佔 2020 年綠色債券發行總額的 11.45%、33.25%、15.31%、21.68% 和 18.30%，佔比最高的是企業債券（見圖 4）。據平安證券分析，在內地綠色債券發展初期 的 2016 年，金融債券曾佔據主導地位[9]。

7　資料來源：綠色金融國際研究院〈中國綠色債券市場2020年度分析簡報〉，2021年1月20日。

8　資料來源：綠色金融國際研究院〈2019年境內未貼標綠色債券發行情況分析〉，2020年9月1日。

9　資料來源：平安證券研究所〈綠色經濟系列報告(三)：綠色債券方興未艾，助力提高發展質量〉，2021年5月5日。

圖 4：2020 年在中國發行的綠色債券種類及其佔當年發行總額的百分比

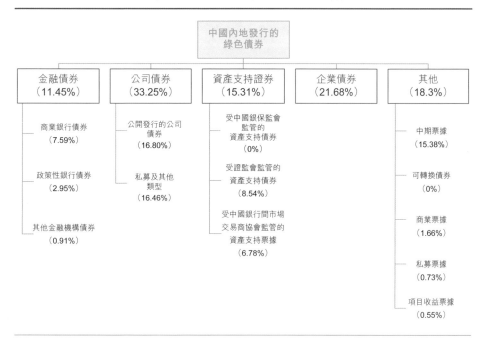

註：(1) 本分類是依據 Wind 的財務數據庫。對於不同類型的債券，可能還有其他分類方式。

　　(2) 由於四捨五入的關係，百分比的總和未必等於總數或 100%。

資料來源：Wind。

在 2060 年前實現碳中和這一宏偉目標的激勵下，綠色債券市場不斷有產品創新。2021 年 2 月 8 日，全國首批 6 隻「碳中和債」在銀行間債券市場成功發行，發行規模共計 64 億元 人民幣。發行人為華能國際、國家電投、南方電網等 6 家國有企業。這是全球首次以「碳 中和」命名的貼標綠色債券產品。碳中和債券是綠色債券的子品種，更關注低碳轉型和減 排領域。這表明了中國在綠色金融產品創新方面所作的積極努力。

ESG 投資

2020 年是 ESG 基金產品發行活躍的時期。於 2020 年年底，中國內地市場共有 19 隻 ESG 指數，其中 9 隻於 2020 年推出。這 19 隻 ESG 指數都在其指數構建策略中明確以 成份股的 ESG 評分作為篩選標準。然而，市場上對綠色基金一直沒有明確的定義。在 對 Wind 數據庫中的 ESG 概念基金進行進一步篩選之後，我們估計市場上有 100 多隻泛 ESG 基金，於 2020 年年底總規模約為 1,310 億元人民幣。

下文對 ESG 基金和指數的發展趨勢進行了更深入的研究。現在，我們用 ESG 主題交易所買賣基金（exchange traded fund，簡稱 ETF）的資金流量來說明 ESG 投資產品的增長，因為它們是拓寬此類產品（尤其是在散戶中）市場准入的重要新興工具。

全球的 ESG 主題 ETF 資金流量在 2019 年創下新高，是 2018 年的三倍。在中國內地，ETF 淨資金流量在 2019 年同比增長 464%，與美國持平，高於日本等其他亞洲國家[10]（見圖 5）。但是，ESG 主題 ETF 基金相對中國內地所有 ETF 的資產管理總規模仍相對較小——低於 1%，而在歐洲，這一比例約為 6%（見表 1）。

圖 5：各投資區域的 ESG 主題 ETF 歷年流進的資金（2012 年至 2019 年）

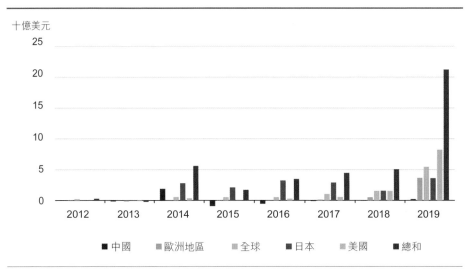

註：投資區域是指資金主要投入的地方。

資料來源：平安數字經濟研究中心按彭博數據的分析。

10 除日本以外的其他亞洲地區因流量太低，無法報告。

表 1：ESG 主題 ETF 淨資金流增長率和 ESG 主題 ETF 的資產管理規模相對所有 ETF 的比重（2019 年）

區域	中國內地	歐洲區域	全球	日本	美國	總計
ESG 主題 ETF 淨資金流同比增長率	464%	639%	254%	132%	433%	305%
ESG 主題 ETF 基金年末資產管理規模佔所有 ETF 的比重	0.42%	5.99%	無數據	5.34%	1.10%	1.25%

註：「區域」是指資金主要投入的地方。在計算 ESG 主題 ETF 淨資金流增長率時，如果基數為負（淨流出），我們將按以下程式：「（新價值 - 舊價值）/（舊價值的絕對值）」計算出百分比增幅。

資料來源：平安數字經濟研究中心按彭博數據的分析。

至於債券型 ESG 投資產品，由於缺乏成熟的評級體系和數據，目前市場上這類產品的數量較少，但它們也在逐漸湧現。2020 年 9 月底，中央國債登記結算有限責任公司（簡稱「中央結算公司」）發佈了「中債 —— 華夏理財 ESG 優選債券策略指數」。該指數根據華夏理財 ESG 和中債 ESG 兩大評估體系篩選成份債券，是國內首個明確使用 ESG 評分篩選成份債券的指數產品。從基金產品的角度來看，目前還沒有明確跡象顯示債券基金均採用 ESG 評分作為篩選標準。市場上的環境主題債券基金僅有 2 隻。

2019 年 4 月至 2020 年 12 月期間，國內銀行的理財子公司共發行了 29 隻 ESG 主題理財產品 [11]。據中國金融網數據顯示，於 2020 年 10 月 13 日，在既有的 27 隻 ESG 概念理財產品中，華夏銀行共發行 16 隻，中國農業銀行共發行 6 隻。ESG 理財產品主要是開放式債券產品。

從第三方研究報告看 ESG 投資的趨勢和重點領域

隨着中國內地資本市場的不斷開放，越來越多具有 ESG 投資理念的國際資本進入了中國，促進了國民對於 ESG 和負責任投資原則的認同和接受。近年來，ESG 投資在內地迅速發展。

證券公司的 ESG 專題研究報告的數量和專題重點是反映市場關注程度和具體關注領域的重要指標。我們收集了 103 份 ESG 專題研究報告 [12]，其中最早的一份於 2017 年發佈。在

11　資料來源：〈銀行財富管理開啟ESG投資探索之路〉，載於《財經新聞》，2020年12月8日。

12　我們從Wind數據庫中共收集到121份包含關鍵詞「ESG」的研究報告，最終採用文本分析技術篩選得出103份ESG專題研究報告。

使用自然語言處理（Natural Language Processing，簡稱 NLP）對報告內容進行分析之後，我們得到了「ESG 概念介紹」、「ESG 在中國」[13]、「ESG 評級體系」、「現有 ESG 產品」和「ESG 投資市場表現」五個主題的結果。通過識別與這些主題相關的關鍵詞，計算各報告中不同主題的相對覆蓋率，我們得出 2017 年以來各主題的年度平均覆蓋率。

自 2017 年以來，ESG 專題報告的數量逐年快速增長，從 2017 年的 1 份增加到 2020 年的 53 份。這表明中國內地資本市場對 ESG 的關注度不斷提高（見圖 6）。在報告內容上，2018 年之前，市場更多關注「ESG 概念介紹」和「ESG 在中國」。2018 年後，「ESG 評級體系」、「現有 ESG 產品」和「ESG 投資市場表現」開始成為市場關注的焦點。這與投資市場逐步接受和歡迎 ESG 概念的發展邏輯是一致的（見圖 7）。

市場的最初焦點是通過引進推廣 ESG 這一新的概念，以及討論 ESG 在中國內地發展的現狀和未來需求來進行市場教育。在初步市場教育階段之後，需要借鑒國際評級供應商的經驗來制定適合當地市場情況的 ESG 評級體系。發展中國特有的 ESG 評級體系和數據，是在國內發展 ESG 投資產品的基礎。隨後，一系列 ESG 指數和投資策略接連在 2019 年和 2020 年推出。隨着 ESG 基金產品數量的增加和規模的擴大，ESG 投資的市場表現和有效性受到越來越多的關注。

圖 6：中國內地歷年 ESG 專題報告的數量（2017 年至 2020 年）

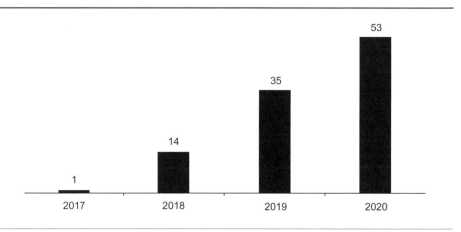

註：截至 2020 年 9 月 10 日的數據。

資料來源：平安數字經濟研究中心按彭博數據的分析。

---

13 「ESG在中國」是指中國ESG發展的現狀和不足，範圍比較寬泛，並不專注於投資產品和投資效果。

圖 7：中國內地 ESG 研究報告主題的年度平均覆蓋率（2017 年至 2020 年）

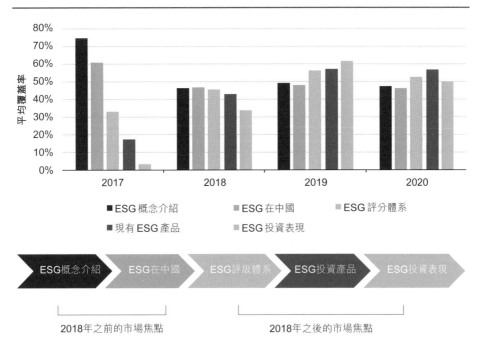

註：(1)　2017 年，只有中國興業證券發佈了 ESG 專題研究報告《興業研究綠色金融報告：上市公司 ESG 披露、評估與應用》。這裏，2017 年的平均覆蓋率僅反映了該報告的主題覆蓋率。

　　(2)　平均覆蓋率不受報告數據採集時間的影響。但是由於關於 ESG 投資市場表現的報告一般在每年年底發佈，2020 年 ESG 投資市場表現的覆蓋率可能會受到影響。

　　(3)　數據乃截至 2020 年 10 月 19 日。

資料來源：平安數字經濟研究中心按彭博數據的分析。

ESG 產品增長的驅動力

近年來，隨着對 ESG 信息披露的監管要求愈發嚴格，以及對構建「綠色金融體系」的指導變得越來越廣泛，中國內地 ESG 信息披露的數量和質量不斷上升，在這方面的投資也越來越多。

在習近平主席宣佈中國在 2060 之前實現碳中和的目標之後，碳中和正式被納入國家的「十四五規劃」，相關政策正在加快出台。中國人民銀行宣佈其將加大力度通過創新金融產品和服務支持綠色產業，從而為實現碳中和目標提供支持。深圳市政府等地方政府也公佈並實施了綠色金融相關政策，以加強信息披露、鼓勵金融產品開發，以及促進碳交易市場的發展。在這樣的政策背景下，預計在未來幾年裏，ESG 和綠色金融在中國內地的發展將進一步加快。

國內資本市場的開放正推動更多以 ESG 為主題和任務的國際資本進入其中，促進 ESG 及其監管的發展。全球有影響力的指數已經將或計劃將內地 A 股納入其中，這會吸引大量外資流入中國內地。由於國際投資者對 ESG 的要求越來越高，信貸評級機構對 ESG 相關的風險愈加重視，因此國際投資者在中國內地進行投資時需要滿足其註冊地對其授權投資的相關要求。這是中國企業實現更好 ESG 相關信息披露和更好表現的又一驅動力。

ESG 指數的最新發展

「純 ESG」指數和債權型 ESG 指數的推出

於 2020 年年底，中國市場共有 19 隻「純 ESG」指數 [14]。於 2019 年之前發佈的只有 4 隻，6 隻發佈於 2019 年，9 隻發佈於 2020 年，其中包含 2020 年 4 月底中證指數有限公司推出的 5 隻 ESG 股票指數（見圖 8）。隨着內地投資市場對於 ESG 關注度的提升、監管部門對於 ESG 數據披露推動力度的增加，以及 ESG 數據的不斷完善，中國市場 ESG 指數自 2019 年以來呈現快速增加的趨勢。

---

14 純ESG指數採用的指數策略，是明確使用公司的ESG評分作為一項篩選準則。本文沒有涵蓋僅考慮與環境保護、扶貧或公司治理相關的主題、且沒有明確將公司的ESG評分納入篩選準則的泛ESG指數。

圖 8：「純 ESG」指數歷年的發行情況（2010 年至 2020 年）

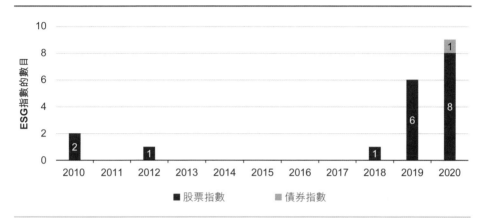

資料來源：平安數字經濟研究中心按 Wind 數據的分析。

從指數類型來看，這 19 隻 ESG 指數中僅有「中債 — 華夏理財 ESG 優選」一隻是債券指數，該指數於 2020 年 9 月推出。由於債券發行人不受上市公司信息披露要求的約束，其相關 ESG 數據的獲得難度較大，因此相應的債券型 ESG 產品評級體系的建立往往較股票型產品滯後。未來，隨着 ESG 債券評級體系的建立和發展，相信債券型 ESG 指數將會有長足發展。

「純 ESG」指數的投資策略

目前市場上主流的 ESG 投資方法主要包括：正面篩選、負面篩選、ESG 因數整合考量、特定主題的可持續發展投資，以及社會影響力投資。由於我們在選取指數時只考慮二級市場中明確將 ESG 評分納入投資策略的指數，而不考慮特定主題（如環保、扶貧等）或者非公開市場的情況，在進一步整合後，我們將集中分析兩種投資策略 —— 正面篩選與負面篩選。

- **正面篩選**：根據各公司的 ESG 評分，從股票池中選擇 ESG 評分高的公司。
- **負面篩選**：根據各公司的 ESG 評分，從股票池中剔除 ESG 評分低的公司。

在正面篩選和負面篩選的基礎上，均可進行因數增強：將 ESG 評分與其他基本因子（如估值和股息率等）相結合。

在可獲得投資策略相關資料的 17 隻 ESG 指數中 [15]，只有 4 隻採用負面篩選策略，14 隻則採用正面篩選策略（「國證 ESG300」採用正面篩選和負面篩選相結合的策略）。其中 9 隻在篩選的基礎上有明確的因子增強策略，主要的增強因子為估值、質量及分紅派息等。可以發現，正面篩選及因子增強是目前市場主流的 ESG 指數投資策略。

2019 年前，所有純 ESG 指數均採用無因子增強的正面篩選。2020 年發佈的 9 隻指數涵蓋了正 / 負面篩選、有或無結合因子增強策略（見表 2），且增強因子類型也更加多樣化。隨着 ESG 數據（包括評級數據）的豐富，ESG 指數採用的投資策略會逐步豐富，投資者在選擇 ESG 投資產品時也會有更大的空間。中國內地市場在結合 ESG 的投資策略發展歷程與國外略有不同。在國外已發展市場的 ESG 投資領域，最早出現的策略大多數以負面篩選為主，剔除武器、煙草、酒精、博彩等「罪惡股票」[16]。隨着 ESG 數據和評分體系的發展，隨後才出現了更全面的 ESG 整合策略。而在中國內地，或許由於 ESG 領域發展可以直接借鑒國際經驗，在早期就直接出現了正面篩選的 ESG 整合策略，而不是只依賴於負面篩選。（表 3 列出 17 隻 ESG 指數及其策略。）

表 2：按投資策略劃分的「純 ESG」指數數量

篩選方式	因子增強	
	有	無
正面篩選	6	5
負面篩選	3[(1)]	3

註：(1) 國證 ESG 300 指數（399378.SZ）採用的是正面篩選和負面篩選相結合的策略，統計分類納入負面篩選一行。
資料來源：平安數字經濟研究中心按 Wind 數據的分析。

---

15 關於「中債 — 華夏理財ESG優選債券策略指數」和「MSCI中國A股國際通ESG通用指數」的資料不詳。

16 資料來源：M. Kelley 與 C. Sardi（2020 年）〈ESG投資 —— 第一部分：ESG投資簡介和歷史〉（"ESG Investments — Part One: An Introduction to and History of ESG Investing"），載於《ESL》網站，2020年10月19日。

表 3：「純 ESG」指數的策略分類

指數代碼	指數名稱	策略類型	有否增強因子	增強因子	樣本範圍（母指數）
399378.SZ	國證 ESG 300 指數	正面篩選 +負面篩選	否	—	國證 1000
000970.CSI	中證 ECPI ESG 可持續發展 40指數	正面篩選	否	—	中證 180
000846.CSI	中證財通中國可持續發展 100（ECPI ESG）指數	正面篩選	否	—	中證 300
931088.CSI	中證 180 ESG 指數	負面篩選	否	—	上交所上市公司
931148.CSI	中證 ECPI ESG 80 指數	負面篩選	有	波動率	中證 300
931168.CSI	中證中財滬深 100 ESG 領先指數	正面篩選	否	—	中證 300
931463.CSI	滬深 300 ESG 基準指數	負面篩選	否	—	中證 300
931476.CSI	中證 ESG 120 策略指數	負面篩選	有	估值、股息收益率、質量和市場因素得分	中證 300
931477.CSI	中證華夏銀行 ESG 指數	負面篩選	有	估值、股息收益率、質量和市場因素得分	中證 300
931465.CSI	滬深 300 ESG 領先指數	正面篩選	否	—	中證 300
931466.CSI	滬深 300 ESG 價值指數	正面篩選	有	估值	中證 300
931525.CSI	中證興業證券 ESG 盈利 100指數	正面篩選	有	股權收益率	中證 300
931565.CSI	中證招銀理財夜光 ESG 指數	正面篩選	有	市值	中證 300
995009.SSI	華證紅利 ESG 指數	正面篩選	有	持續高派息	全市場
980058.CNI	公司治理研究院綠色治理指數	正面篩選	否	—	深交所上市公司
995002.SSI	華證價值傳遞陽光 100 指數	正面篩選	有	流動性、財務實力	A 股
995006.SSI	華證 A 股紅利 ESG 優選指數	正面篩選	有	股息收益率穩定且高、具有一定的市值和流動性	A 股

資料來源：平安數字經濟研究中心按 Wind 數據的分析。

ESG 基金的最新發展

基金類型及投資主題

於 2020 年 12 月 31 日，內地市場共有 14 隻「純 ESG」基金 [17]、50 隻環境主題基金、9 隻公司治理主題基金和 36 隻泛 ESG 概念基金（見圖 9）。從投資資產類別來看，混合型基金有 71 隻（佔主導地位），股票型基金有 34 隻。同期，市場僅環境主題基金有 2 隻債券型基金發行，分別為富國綠色純債（005383.OF）和興業綠色純債一年定開（009237.OF）。

圖 9：按主題和投資類型劃分的 ESG 基金數量分佈情況（2020 年 12 月 31 日）

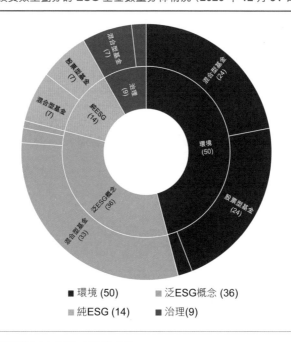

- ■ 環境 (50)
- ■ 泛ESG概念 (36)
- ■ 純ESG (14)
- ■ 治理(9)

資料來源：平安數字經濟研究中心按 Wind 數據的分析。

從規模來看，於 2020 年 12 月 31 日，ESG 基金的總資產管理規模約為 1,303 億元人民幣。其中純 ESG 基金有 14 隻，合計 150 億元人民幣，佔總資產管理規模的 11.5%。泛

---

17 「純ESG」基金是指考慮環境、社會和公司治理其中兩個或以上因素的基金。除專門整合ESG評分的基金產品外，這類別還包括考慮「可持續發展」或「社會責任」等投資主題的基金。

ESG 概念基金的合計規模最大，達 521 億元人民幣，約佔 ESG 基金總資產管理規模的
40%。從投資資產類別來看，混合型基金規模最大，達 985 億元人民幣，佔 ESG 基金總
資產管理規模的 70% 以上。（見圖 10）

圖 10：按主題和投資類型劃分的 ESG 基金資產管理規模分佈情況（2020 年 12 月 31 日）

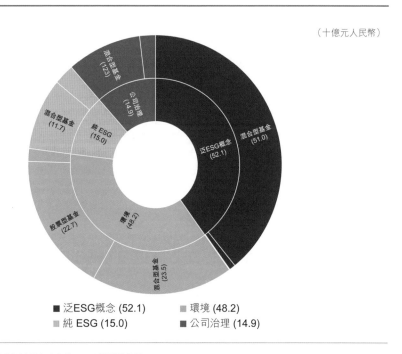

（十億元人民幣）

- 泛ESG概念 (52.1)
- 環境 (48.2)
- 純 ESG (15.0)
- 公司治理 (14.9)

資料來源：平安數字經濟研究中心按 Wind 數據的分析。

ESG 基金的發行趨勢

2014 年至 2016 年是 ESG 主題基金在中國內地的第一個蓬勃發展期。除了市場狀況外，
這也與內地監管政策的發展息息相關。2014 年出台的《環境保護法》對環境污染信息披
露提出了明確規定。2015 年國務院首次明確提出要「建立中國綠色金融體系」。2016 年
七部委發佈了《關於構建綠色金融體系的指導意見》，這些構成了中國首輪 ESG 基金發行
的政策背景。因此，這段時間成立的 ESG 主題概念基金側重於環境主題。2019 年，隨着
ESG 主題基金越來越吸引市場目光，ESG 概念在內地的發展開始加速。ESG 基金數量增
加，類型多種多樣。新的純 ESG 基金發行量明顯增加，市場進入 ESG 基金的第二個集中
發行期。（見圖 11）

專欄 1：ESG 主題基金分類

在我們的列表中，中國內地共有 109 隻 ESG 主題基金。根據它們對投資對象的選擇，我們將其分為四大類：純 ESG 基金、環境主題基金、公司治理主題基金和泛 ESG 概念基金。

- **純 ESG 基金**：在制定投資策略篩選投資標的時，至少考慮了環境、社會和公司治理中兩個或以上維度的基金，除了一些明確將 ESG 評分納入投資策略的產品外，還包括根據投資標的在「可持續發展」特徵或者「社會責任」評分方面表現進行投資的基金。

  註：考慮到目前市場上純ESG基金的數量仍較少，與純ESG指數相比，這裏對純ESG基金的篩選標準相對寬鬆。

- **環境主題基金**：在制定投資策略和選擇投資對象時，主要考慮環境因素的基金。我們選擇的關鍵詞包括：「環保」、「低碳」、「美麗中國」、「新能源」和「綠色節能」等。

  註：環境主題基金不包括「新能源汽車」等更廣泛的行業主題基金。

- **公司治理主題基金**：在制定投資策略及篩選投資標的時，突出強調公司治理能力和水平的基金。

- **泛 ESG 概念基金**：屬於 109 隻 ESG 主題概念基金，但是由於資訊不足，無法納入上述分類的其他 ESG 概念基金。

ESG 主題基金的範圍是基於 Wind 的 ESG 概念基金資料庫。根據 Wind 給出的定義，ESG 概念基金是在其產品名稱 / 投資範圍 / 投資目標 / 業績基準 / 投資理念中包含以下關鍵詞的基金：「ESG」、「社會責任」、「倫理責任」、「綠色」、「環保」、「低碳」、「美麗中國」、「公司治理」或「可持續發展」。

為避免重複計算，我們剔除了類別或等級不同的同一隻基金，以及目前處於募集期的未上市基金產品。最後，於 2020 年 12 月 31 日共有 109 隻基金產品獲納入了我們的分析。

圖 11：按類型劃分的 ESG 基金發行數量分佈情況（2003 年至 2020 年）

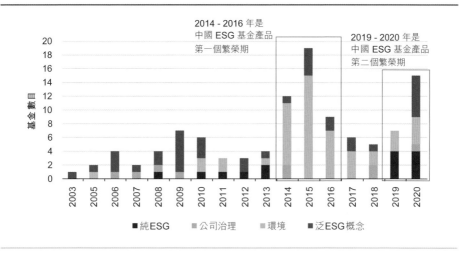

資料來源：平安數字經濟研究中心按 Wind 數據的分析。

從發行規模來看，ESG 主題概念基金自 2018 年以來總體增長較快。2020 年 ESG 主題概念基金總發行規模較 2019 年增長 37%，較 2018 年增長近一倍。增長的主要動力仍然是環境主題基金和泛 ESG 概念基金。2019 年純 ESG 基金的發行規模明顯增加，而 2020 年公司治理主題基金的發行規模增速較快。（見圖 12）

圖 12：按主題劃分的 ESG 基金年度發行規模分佈情況（2015 年至 2020 年）

資料來源：平安數字經濟研究中心按 Wind 數據的分析。

ESG 基金的行業分佈

ESG 基金的第一重倉行業主要集中在電氣設備領域。環境主題基金特別關注電氣設備，這主要是由於很多環境主題基金將選股範圍限定於環保相關產業，而這一產業內電氣設備類公司數量較多。在純 ESG 基金中，食品飲料行業佔權重較高（見圖 13）。2020 年報告顯示，在 28 個行業中，電氣設備行業以及食品飲料行業也是整個基金市場中佔權重最高的兩個行業。電子行業排名第三，生物醫藥行業排名第四。ESG 基金的行業分佈與整體基金市場基本一致。ESG 因素對產業配置影響不明顯。正如我們所見，在中國很少有 ESG 主題基金嚴格使用 ESG 評分作為其核心評估標準，基金經理的主觀意見仍是主導決定因素。

圖 13：按主題劃分的各行業權重排名前三的 ESG 基金數量（2020 年 12 月 31 日）

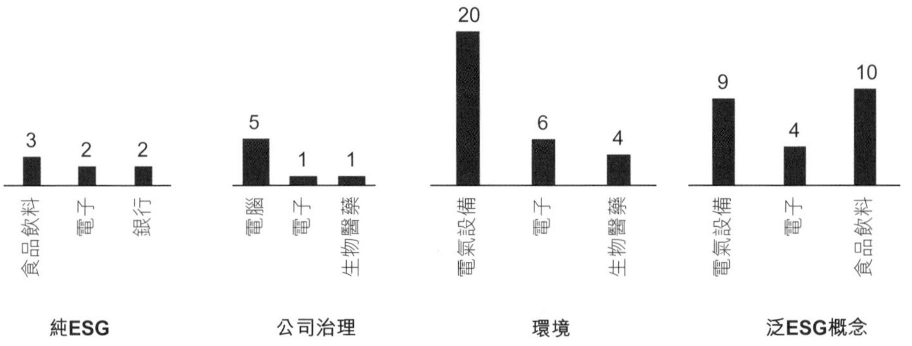

資料來源：平安數字經濟研究中心按 Wind 數據的分析。

ESG 投資產品在中國內地的不足和機會

目前，中國內地的 ESG 金融產品大部分是以綠色債券和貸款產品為主的固定收益類產品。中國綠色債券和貸款產品的總發行規模相對較大，但產品種類的多樣化仍落後於發達市場。其他一些以可持續性為主題的產品也越來越受歡迎，展現出其未來產品發展的機遇。中國的 ESG 債券一直以綠色債券為主，然而社會責任債券在全球也越來越受歡迎。社會責任債券允許將收益用於支持具有積極社會影響的項目，如改善社會福利或為弱勢羣體服務。

在貸款市場，中國的 ESG 產品也以綠色領域為重點，為特定的綠色目的融資。其他 ESG 貸款，例如可持續發展掛鈎貸款，在全球範圍內也很受歡迎。可持續發展掛鈎貸款旨在鼓勵企業實現其可持續目標。如果企業成功地實現某些可持續目標，如減少碳排放或提高能效，貸款利率就可以下調。這種貸款資金的使用範圍不受限制。可持續發展掛鈎貸款已在美國、歐洲和新加坡發行。

雖然部分 ESG 主題 ETF 基金已在中國內地發行，但其總資產管理規模遠小於國際市場。於 2020 年 10 月底，被動型 ESG 主題基金（包括被動型環境主題基金）在內地市場的總資產管理規模僅為 59 億元人民幣 [18]。2021 年 4 月 8 日，貝萊德推出了全球歷來最大的 ESG 主題 ETF 基金——「美國碳轉型準備基金」。僅這隻基金就向機構投資者募集了 12.5 億美元 [19]。一隻投資非美國公司的姊妹基金也在同一天推出，吸引了 4.75 億美元的投資者資金 [20]。

私募市場方面，中國內地與其他主要市場的差距很大。一些內地私募股權公司正積極接納 ESG，例如遠景科技集團和紅杉中國宣佈將共同設立一隻總規模為 100 億元人民幣的碳中和科技基金 [21]。然而，在中國內地，很少有私募股權公司在內部或投資組合中明確採用 ESG 原則。歐洲私募股權公司在採用 ESG 標準方面處於世界領先位置。《全球金融家》（*Financier Worldwide*）雜誌指出，英國的私募股權公司中有近三分之二（63%）在進行投資時將 ESG 原則納入其考慮範圍；有 48% 詳細報告了其投資對 ESG 的影響；而有 25% 有專門的個人或團隊負責將 ESG 融入其投資過程 [22]。

穩健數據：ESG 投資進一步發展的前提條件

全球和國內數據供應商概述

ESG 指數和相關金融產品建基於穩健的 ESG 評級體系和數據。從上述 NLP 分析結果中可以看出，ESG 評級體系和數據是指數與基金產品在中國內地市場進一步發展的基礎。由於在這方面沒有明確的市場領導者，ESG 數據和評級服務供應商的集中程度較信用評級供應商低很多。全球市場中，雖然有像 MSCI 和 Sustainalytics 這樣的老牌公司，但也有許多小眾公司越來越受歡迎。例如，Trucost 擁有全面的環境和氣候相關指標，TruValue Labs

---

18　資料來源：平安數字經濟研究中心〈中國ESG投資〉，2020年11月。

19　資料來源：〈隨着綠色投資浪潮的興起，貝萊德推出了歷來最大規模的ETF基金〉（"BlackRock secures largest-ever ETF launch as green investing wave builds"），載於《金融時報》（*Financial Times*），2021年4月8日。

20　同上。

21　資料來源：〈風險投資和私募股權公司加大在追求綠色效應方面的努力〉（"VC, PE companies expanding green efforts"），載於《中國日報》（*China Daily*），2021年5月6日。

22　資料來源：〈從小眾到主流：私募股權中的ESG〉（"From nice to have to mainstream: ESG in private equity"），載於《全球金融家》（*Financier Worldwide*），2021年2月。

和 Owl Analytics 以其 ESG 另類數據（即非公開披露數據）而聞名。值得注意的是，ESG 數據公司之間出現了一波收購浪潮（見圖 14）：為了將 ESG 數據添加到其產品中，傳統的金融數據供應商開始對小眾公司發起收購。

中國內地與全球 ESG 數據供應商的情況非常不同。首先，ESG 數據供應商在國際市場上的歷史要長得多，它們在上世紀 90 年代已開始嶄露頭角。在內地，ESG 數據和評級服務供應商自 2015 年起才開始出現，是一種新興現象。然而，其發展速度令人驚歎。短短五年時間，內地市場已有 8 家供應商。其次，內地供應商的類型更為多樣化。全球的 15 個供應商中有 9 個是老牌數據供應商，當中一些是傳統的金融數據供應商，如富時羅素、路透社、路孚特和彭博，它們將提供 ESG 數據作為其服務內容的一部分。例如，彭博擁有大量的 ESG 指標，並從 2020 年開始在石油和天然氣行業提供自家的 ESG 評級服務。另外一些是長期專注可持續發展的 ESG 數據供應商，例如 RobecoSAM、RepRisk、MSCI 和 Sustainalytics。自 2014 年以來，一些金融科技公司進入市場，專注於利用新聞和社交媒體等另類數據生成 ESG 信號。然而，在中國內地，供應商的類型包括傳統的指數 / 數據供應商、金融科技公司、資產管理者、資產所有者、學術 / 非營利機構和諮詢公司。我們看到，在更嚴格的監管要求和投資者對可持續金融產品日益增長的需求的推動下，2020 年有一批新的供應商進入市場。

圖 14：全球和中國內地市場的 ESG 數據和評級服務供應商

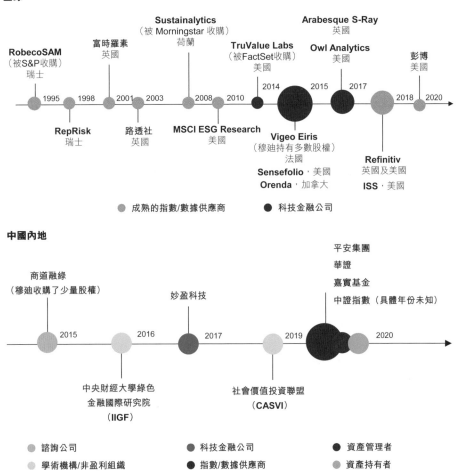

資料來源：平安數字經濟研究中心按公開資料整理。

所需支持因素

中國內地市場的 ESG 評級與數據需進一步提升覆蓋度、增強與內地市場的契合度、為進一步豐富 ESG 主題投資產品提供有效數據支持。中國內地的 ESG 評級與數據發展剛剛起步，但發展速度不容小覷。僅在 2015 年至 2020 年，就出現了 8 家不同類型的數據與評級供應商。然而，因為中國 A 股的 ESG 數據可得性較低，固市場上現有供應商所提供的歷史數據不夠，覆蓋範圍亦不廣。這些因素在很大程度上限制了金融產品的多樣性和 ESG 效果的可驗證性。由於歷史數據不夠，在策略研發時回測也會受到限制。目前，市場上已經有數據供應商逐漸覆蓋全部 A 股的多年數據，如嘉實基金和平安集團研發的 ESG 數據和評級體系。

為債券和債券發行人建立 ESG 評級體系和數據對於加速將 ESG 納入債券型產品投資至關重要。除了覆蓋股票市場以外，債券市場的覆蓋度是另一大挑戰。債券發行人不須遵從適用於上市公司的信息披露要求，其相關 ESG 數據的獲得難度較大，因此相應的債券型 ESG 評級體系的建立往往較股票型滯後。債券投資的複雜性也給 ESG 評級帶來新的挑戰。這在很大程度上限制了現在市場上債券型 ESG 產品的發展。

除了覆蓋度以外，內地市場的數據與評級供應商應注重 ESG 理念在中國的本土化。由於中國的國情和公司發展階段與國外的不同，中國的 ESG 評級體系除應與國際體系接軌之外，也應對指標和評價標準作出相應調整，讓體系充分為中國金融市場提供所需的數據支持。在這方面，我們應發揮現有數據與評級供應商多樣性的優勢：對比海外市場，在中國內地參與 ESG 數據與評級服務的機構更多樣化，包括學術機構、非盈利機構、金融機構和諮詢公司等。每一類型機構都有自己不同的視角。這種多樣性能更好地激發市場研發更適應內地市場情況的 ESG 評價標準。

建議

內地監管機構應該制定統一的準則指引，並匯總一套企業必須披露的核心指標。雖然不同的發行人在其目標和範圍上會有所不同，但應該有一組強制披露的具體指標。內地監管機構和證券交易所應參考《全球報告倡議》（Global Reporting Initiative，簡稱 GRI）和聯合國支持的《責任投資原則》（Principles for Responsible Investment，簡稱 PRI）等國際組織給出的指導方針和建議，並結合針對中國公司的本地市場考慮。他們還應鼓勵公司審計其 ESG 信息披露。ESG 是中國公司治理的一個重要補充環節。更好的 ESG 信息披露和表現有助提高中國公司在全球投資者心目中的可信度和價值。

公司應利用技術解決方案收集和監控 ESG 數據，並從中學習。這個過程應該是一個跨部門自動化的過程，而不是一個手動過程。與其是一項年度實踐，不如進行持續監控。與其對該披露的指標模糊不清，應該根據首選準則制定一份清單，從而減少為應對不同要求所需的資源。公司可以利用技術來簡化 ESG 報告流程。例如，平安集團的 AI-ESG 平台連接了來自不同監管機構的 500 多項指標，並通過行業同行比較，幫助實現數據收集自動化、監測變化，並給出可行的解決方案。

評級服務供應商應提高其方法論的透明度，擴大其 ESG 數據來源，包括取得不依賴公司披露的另類數據，以提高客觀性和及時性。由於涉及知識產權，供應商可能無法披露其方法論的所有細節，但它們仍可以在指標範圍和評分框架方面增加透明度。例如，MSCI 擁有關於其方法論的最詳細的文件，可以提供行業標準。供應商應利用 NLP 和光符識別等先進分析功能，以非披露性質的數據（如政府公告和新聞媒體報告）來對現有的披露性質的數據作出補充，從而擴大數據覆蓋範圍並提高及時性。供應商還應重點關注對投資者具有重要意義的指標，在實踐方面，他們可以測試 ESG 指標對中長期公司估值的影響，並在其評分模型中反映這種影響。

投資者應將 ESG 信息納入其投資決策，開發 ESG 投資工具，發揮股東影響力，並鼓勵中國公司更好地披露 ESG 信息。儘管 ESG 在中國內地的投資尚處於起步階段，但包括華夏基金管理、嘉實基金、平安、南方基金管理和易方達等在內的多家投資管理機構均已開始拓展其以 ESG 為主題的研究和金融產品。我們建議投資者分以下三個階段實踐 ESG 投資：

- 第一，投資經理可以通過市場上幾家主流的 ESG 評級服務供應商，從更簡單的流程開始，如負面篩選和正面篩選。
- 第二，深化 ESG 指標和評級框架的分析和應用，分析 ESG 指標對投資決策的影響，建立符合投資者自身投資風格的自訂評價框架。
- 第三，充分將 ESG 因子納入自己的估值模型當中，並對重要的 ESG 主題（如氣候變化和人口趨勢）開展有針對性的研究。

資產所有者還可以將外部管理人的 ESG 實踐作為其資產管理人選擇標準的一部分。投資者在與公司議合期間，應鼓勵公司提供更為具體且時間更長的 ESG 數據。只有投資者和監管機構都有明確的預期，企業才會更有動力改善其信息披露。

另類數據和技術可以幫助投資者發掘真正實踐 ESG 準則且市場表現優異的公司。隨着 ESG 投資的發展，投資者已越來越關注那些有潛在「漂綠」風險的公司，也就是那些所披露的信息並不反映其真實 ESG 表現的公司。同時，ESG 投資產品本身的界定也比較寬鬆。例如，如本文所示，明確使用 ESG 評分進行篩選的基金和指數，以及重點僅在於「綠色」主題的基金和指數均被納入了 ESG 基金範圍。這讓那些做表面工夫的人有機可乘，所以相關資產的綠色程度還需作仔細審查。因此我們需要開發工具，幫助投資者更好地識別潛在「漂綠」的公司。基於 NLP 的透明度指標有助區分「棕色」和「綠色」企業，並發現「棕色」企業漏報的領域。ESG 評級還可以用於檢測披露信息的公司與不披露信息的公司之間的異常情況。這些工具能作為市場上已有 ESG 評級的補充，來幫助我們更好的識別真正在 ESG 方面有良好表現的公司。

指數與基金公司應開發更加多種類的 ESG 產品，例如被動型指數基金、量化基金的推出，將為投資者提供更多投資選擇空間。 2019 年以來，ESG 指數和基金產品發行都進入了一個爆發期，產品的投資策略也較 2019 年之前更加豐富多樣。從指數市場來看，僅 2020 年 4 月底中證發佈的 5 隻 ESG 指數就運用了 4 種不同的篩選和因子增強策略，這無疑為投資者的未來投資選擇提供了更加豐富的 ESG 產品空間。此外，目前僅有華證發佈的 ESG 指數樣本池覆蓋全 A 股，其他大部分的指數產品仍然是從滬深 300 指數的股票池選股。未來隨着更多評級機構的評級數據實現全 A 股覆蓋，產品的選股範圍將會更加靈活，收益率回報也有望因此而提升。

從基金市場來看，目前市場上的被動型 ESG 指數基金產品仍然較少，而且總規模遠遠低於同類型的主動型 ESG 基金產品。未來隨着 ESG 指數的豐富和 ESG 投資概念的普及，被動型 ESG 基金產品將會有更為廣闊的發展空間。我們還注意到，在 2017 年發行的長信低碳環保行業量化基金之後，2020 年基金市場上出現了一隻純 ESG 量化基金 —— 摩根士丹利華鑫 ESG 量化先行。ESG 數據的完善和規範化未來也將會給量化 ESG 基金提供新的發揮平台。

隨着 ESG 投資在二級市場的影響力不斷加深，其投資理念也開始向一級市場傳導。在已發展的資本市場中，ESG 投資已經被納入了股權投資「募資、投資、組合管理、退資」的全流程，成為股權投資盡職調查考量的常規維度。中國目前已經有數十家私募股權機構簽署了 PRI，未來股權投資機構應當有意識地將 ESG 理念納入其投資管理過程中，在幫助投資機構規避環境與社會風險的同時，更好地完成與二級市場的接軌。

註：本文原稿是英文，另以中文譯本出版。如本文的中文本的字義或詞義與英文本有所出入，概以英文本為準。

Chapter 4

Hong Kong's role as East/West sustainability hub

Dr. E Zhihuan
Chief Economist
Bank of China (Hong Kong) Limited

LOO Jack Lee
Senior Strategic Planner
Economics & Strategic Planning Department
Bank of China (Hong Kong) Limited

JIANG Yinglin, Zoe
Strategic Planner
Economics & Strategic Planning Department
Bank of China (Hong Kong) Limited

Summary

Rapid growth of green and sustainable finance (GSF) has been observed in recent years across the globe. As an important gateway connecting Mainland China and the global market, Hong Kong has been playing the role of a green and sustainability hub in the region. To create a positive market environment and lay solid foundation for the development of GSF, local regulators and policy makers in Hong Kong have proactively introduced a series of supportive measures to regulate the market and unleash market potentials. However, even with the advantages of a mature financial system, a high degree of internationalisation and comprehensive business infrastructures to support the development of GSF, Hong Kong still faces challenges such as an absence of harmonised green standards, the need for more incentives and supporting policies, and the need for further advance in capability building. Collective and coordinated actions across all sectors are essential for Hong Kong to improve market discipline, enhance capabilities, and actively contribute to China's and the world's ambitious blueprint of GSF development, as well as to solidify its position as Asia's green finance centre and to contribute to the achievement of green and sustainable development goals across the world.

Current status of GSF in Hong Kong

While green and sustainable finance (GSF) in Asia commenced relatively late as compared to its western peers, the growth rate has been rapid in recent years. According to the statistics of the People's Bank of China (PBOC) as at the end of 2020, China's outstanding green loan balance in domestic and foreign currencies amounted to RMB 12 trillion, an increase of 17.4% year-on-year, ranking first in the world; and the outstanding green bond balance amounted to RMB 800 billion, ranking the second largest in the world[1]. According to the *2018 Global Sustainable Investment Review* released by the Global Sustainable Investment Alliance (GSIA), sustainable investment in Japan was US$2.18 trillion, second only to Europe and the United States (US). Other Asian regions also show huge potential for GSF development, and as Asian governments and enterprises deepen their understanding of sustainability and pledge to "carbon neutrality" commitments, GSF in the region will continue to flourish.

Hong Kong as an important gateway connecting Mainland China with the global market has assumed the position of a regional GSF hub in the wave of global GSF development. With proactive advocacy efforts from regulators and policy makers, Hong Kong's ability to attract the participation of international stakeholders in green finance with its extensive investor base, comprehensive financial infrastructure and its status as an international financial centre act as a fuel for further development of GSF in Hong Kong. This is likely to be manifested in multiple forms of financial instruments, including green bonds, green loans and green investments.

Hong Kong's green bond and green loan markets are developing rapidly

Grounded in Mainland China, green bonds and green loans are put into practice in Hong Kong and have experienced rapid growth in recent years as two extremely important engines to finance green and sustainable projects. According to *Hong Kong Green Bond Market Briefing 2020* by Climate Bonds Initiative (CBI)[2], the amount of green debt arranged and issued in Hong Kong was US$12 billion in 2020, with a cumulative amount

---

1   Source: The PBOC, "Make full use of China's monetary policy space and promote green finance — Remarks by Governor Yi Gang at the Roundtable of China Development Forum", 21 March 2021.

2   CBI, *Hong Kong Green Bond Market Briefing 2020*, May 2021.

of over US$38 billion by the end of 2020 and a five-year compound annual growth rate (CAGR) of over 100% (see Figure 1).

Figure 1. Cumulative amount of green debt arranged and issued in Hong Kong (2016 – 2020)

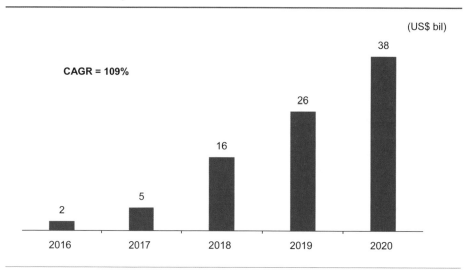

As a mainstream financing tool in Hong Kong, green bonds issued by Hong Kong issuers showed an upward trend in past years. As at the end of 2020, the total amount of green bonds issued by Hong Kong issuers accumulated to US$9.2 billion, exhibiting a five-year CAGR of 66% (see Figure 2).

Figure 2. Cumulative amount of green bonds issued by Hong Kong issuers in Hong Kong (2016 – 2020)

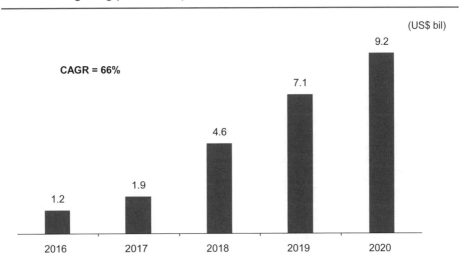

Source: CBI, BOCHK Financial Research Institute.

In respect of issuer origin, Hong Kong has been the prime offshore financing centre for Mainland enterprises. Attributable to its world-class financial services and institutional advantages, and most Mainland issuers consider Hong Kong as an optimal platform for soliciting offshore funding from international investors. As a major driver of the Hong Kong green debt market, green bonds arranged and issued by Mainland entities in total amounted to US$7 billion in 2020, accounting for 60.3% of the total pool[3]. This demonstrates the unique edge of Hong Kong in "backing by the Mainland while engaging the world" within GSF business.

In respect of issuer type, corporations led green bond issuance by issuance amount, accounting for 65.6% of the total green bond issuance in 2020. Of which, real estate was the most prominent sector, accounting for 34%, energy sector accounted for 11.2%, while other sectors in aggregate accounted for 20.4%. The share of financial institutions' issuance fell from 49.4% in 2019 to 29.9% in 2020 and that of issuance by governments, development banks, policy banks and multilateral development banks (MDBs) in aggregate dropped significantly from 14.4% in 2019 to 4.5% in 2020 (see Figure 3).

---

3   Source: CBI, *Hong Kong Green Bond Marketing Briefing 2020*, May 2021.

Figure 3. Distribution of green bond issuance amount in Hong Kong by issuer type (amount issued) (2019 and 2020)

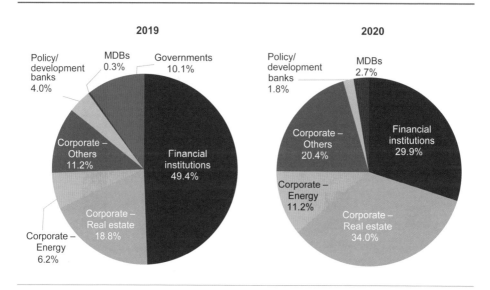

Source: CBI, BOCHK Financial Research Institute.

Overall, the development of the Hong Kong green bond market has been relatively rapid. Nonetheless, there is still room for optimisation in terms of issuer diversity on the path to becoming an international green financial hub.

In addition, Hong Kong has also made significant progress in the green loan market in recent years. According to Bloomberg, Hong Kong green loans increased by US$1.3 billion in 2020, which is 7.5 times that of 2015. Although the total amount of green loans in Hong Kong fell by 38% compared to 2019 due to the pandemic, the Hong Kong green loan market continued to outperform the global and European markets — global green loans fell by 43.2% in 2020 year-on-year while European green loans fell by more than 50%[4]. The green projects supported by Hong Kong green loans have gradually become more diversified. In 2015, green loans only financed energy projects. Within five years, they have supported seven sectors, including finance services, materials, industrial, consumer discretionary, telecommunications, energy and utilities. According to the Hong Kong Quality Assurance Agency, apart from local corporates, a growing number of Mainland corporates are also actively expanding their green loan financed projects.

---

4   Source: *Green Finance Portal* website, viewed on 7 May 2021.

Hong Kong has great potential for sustainable investment

Sustainable investment in Hong Kong has similarly experienced rapid development in recent years. According to Morningstar data, Hong Kong's sustainable fund assets exceeded US$350 million as at the end of 2020, an increase of 20% year-on-year, showing a momentum of robust growth[5]. With fund size in Hong Kong accounting for only 0.8%[6] of the total in the Asian market, it reflects huge future development potential. The sustainable investment ecosystem would continue to improve amidst the favourable macro-environment and collective efforts of stakeholders, facilitating further development of sustainable investment in Hong Kong.

At the outset, investors have been putting investing emphasis on green and sustainability concepts; and countries have become more proactive on climate governance in recent years, proposing concrete roadmaps to reduce greenhouse gas emissions, and establishing timelines for achieving "carbon emissions peak" and "carbon neutrality". Industrial upgrading and transformation in coordination with emissions reduction will trigger tremendous investment opportunities. Along with the outbreak of the COVID-19 pandemic which has garnered greater attention to social and governance considerations, investors will further turn to people's livelihood in the post-pandemic era. Increasing concerns about the importance of good corporate governance have surfaced from the substantial operational risk affecting corporates during the pandemic. Several studies showed that the younger generation of investors in Asia are showing greater concerns over the environmental, social and governance (ESG) performance of corporates[7]. This young generation is likely to drive the boom of green and sustainable investment.

Secondly, the relatively favourable return of sustainable investment is attractive to investors. According to a research conducted by the Bank for International Settlements[8], the Sharpe ratios of green bond indices were slightly higher than those of corporate bond indices with similar credit rating, indicating green bonds could provide a better risk-adjusted return; corporates with emphasis on ESG were also more resilient during

---

5   Source: Walker, R., "Asia ESG funds attract record flows", published on the *Fund Selector Asia* website, 1 February 2021.

6   Source: Walker, R., "Asia ESG funds attract record flows", published on the *Fund Selector Asia* website, 1 February 2021; Chow, W., "Global sustainable fund flows: Q4 2020 in review", published on Morningstar's website, 28 January 2021.

7   Source: Newell, R., "How Asia's family wealth transfers could bolster ESG", published on the *Asian Investor* website, 14 October 2020; Cheuk, W. F., "The rise of social responsible strategy and green investment in Asia" (〈社會責任策略 與綠色投資　亞洲急冒起〉), published on the website of *Hong Kong Economic Journal* (《信報財經新聞》), 8 February 2018.

8   Ehlers, T. and F. Packer. (2017) "Green bond finance and certification", *BIS Quarterly Review*, September 2017.

economic downturn. When the global economy was hit the hardest by the pandemic in 2020, the Bloomberg Barclays MSCI USD Green Bond Index and the Bloomberg Barclays USD Aggregate Corporate Index plummeted followed by a rebound, where the former had a return of 12.6%, higher than the latter's 7.4% (see Figure 4).

Figure 4. The trend of the Bloomberg Barclays MSCI USD Green Bond Index and the Bloomberg Barclays USD Aggregate Corporate Index (2020)

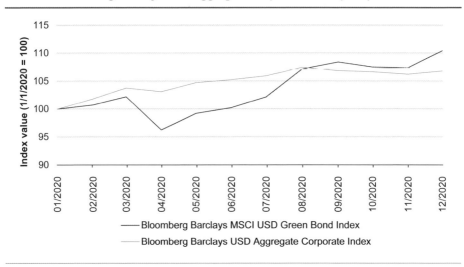

Source: Bloomberg, BOCHK Financial Research Institute.

Thirdly, various efforts have been made by the Hong Kong authorities to create a positive environment for ESG investment. As the investment manager of the Exchange Fund, the Hong Kong Monetary Authority (HKMA) practices responsible investment and incorporates ESG factors into investment considerations. The Hong Kong Exchanges and Clearing Company Limited (HKEX) launched the Sustainable and Green Exchange (STAGE) to allow all stakeholders to share relevant ESG information. These initiatives would facilitate market transparency and further optimise the ESG investment ecosystem.

While the development of GSF in Hong Kong began with only green bonds and green loans, the breadth of GSF has gradually extended from the banking sector to the asset management sector as GSF continues to develop. It is expected that the scope of GSF in Hong Kong will continue to expand comprehensively in breadth and depth to cover green insurance, green securities, and carbon finance in the next development phase.

Hong Kong's regulatory policies and market dynamics

To act in concert with the development of the green financial market and to further reinforce Hong Kong's role as an East/West sustainability hub, Hong Kong regulators are proactively introducing a series of support policies and measures.

Hong Kong regulatory regime for green and sustainable development

The key regulators involved in the green and sustainable development in Hong Kong include HKEX, the HKMA and the Securities and Futures Commission (SFC). Extending the supervision of the overall financial industry from their respective regulatory capacity, the HKMA takes the lead in the development of green banking industry and construction of the Hong Kong green financial hub; HKEX focuses on uplifting the standard of ESG information disclosure of listed companies; and the SFC pushes for the incorporation of sustainability elements into the full management process of securities and futures. In addition, the HKMA and the SFC jointly promoted the establishment of the Green and Sustainable Finance Cross-Agency Steering Group (hereinafter referred to as the Cross-Agency Steering Group), to execute cross-institutional sustainable development actions.

Leading the banking industry in green and sustainable development, the HKMA is committed to promoting Hong Kong as a regional green financial hub. In May 2019, the HKMA announced three major initiatives to promote the development of green and sustainable banking and the alleviation of climate risks — to build green and sustainable banks, to embrace responsible investment and to promote the establishment of a regional centre for green finance in Hong Kong.

HKEX places emphasis on uplifting the standard of information disclosure of listed companies. Since 2011, HKEX has started scrutinising ESG information disclosure of listed companies, and issued a consultation paper on the *Environment, Social and Governance Reporting Guide* in December 2011 for public consultation. Subsequently, HKEX released three editions of the *Environment, Social and Governance Reporting Guide* in 2012, 2015 and 2019 respectively to gradually regulate ESG disclosure requirements of listed companies. To further attract market attention to green and sustainable products and advance product information transparency and distribution, HKEX established the STAGE platform in December 2020 to connect local and foreign investors, serving as a major step to support the inter-connectivity of the green and sustainable financial market between the East and the West.

The SFC promotes the incorporation of sustainability elements into the full management process of securities and futures. In September 2018, the SFC issued the Strategic Framework for Green Finance, which reiterates the importance of disclosure and consideration of ESG elements (especially environmental and climate risks) by listed companies, fund managers and investment products. In April 2019, the SFC issued a circular to the management companies of authorised unit trusts and mutual funds, providing guidance on strengthening the disclosure of green or ESG funds. In October 2020, the SFC issued a consultation paper to the industry to recommend revision of the Fund Manager Code of Conduct to better meet investors' demand for climate risk information disclosure and combat greenwashing behaviour.

The pace of sustainable development within the Hong Kong financial industry is further coordinated by the Cross-Agency Steering Group. Leveraging on the driving forces of the above three major regulators in their respective fields of sustainable development, the Cross-Agency Steering Group was established in May 2020 and released its first strategic plan in December the same year. Five near-term action points were proposed in the plan, including implementing mandatory climate-related disclosures in alignment with the recommendations of the Task Force on Climate-related Financial Disclosure (TCFD) no later than 2025, and aiming to adopt the Common Ground Taxonomy[9], and promoting climate-focused scenario analysis.

Policy support for GSF under the "Carbon Neutrality" commitment

Under China's 14th Five-Year Plan[10], the importance of environmental issues is elevated to national policy level. The Hong Kong Special Administrative Region (HKSAR) ensued

---

9   Taxonomy in this context generally refers to a system that classifies economic activities that are considered environmentally sustainable.
10 *Outline of the Fourteenth Five-Year Plan for the National Economic and Social Development and the Long-Range Objectives Through the Year 2035* (《中華人民共和國國民經濟和社會發展第十四個五年規劃和 2035 年遠景目標綱要》), issued by the National Reform and Development Commission of the People's Republic of China, 23 March 2021.

with announcements of related regulatory policies to promote green and sustainable development in the Chief Executive's 2020 Policy Address and 2021-22 Budget.

To facilitate transition to low-carbon economy, *Hong Kong Climate Action Plan 2030+* was published in 2017, in which the goals of reducing carbon intensity by 65%-70% and reducing absolute carbon emissions by 26%-36% by 2030 were established with reference to the 2005 carbon baseline. Following China's declaration to peak carbon emissions before 2030 and achieve carbon neutrality before 2060, the HKSAR Chief Executive's 2020 Policy Address echoed with the announcement of a long-term commitment to achieve "carbon neutrality" by 2050, and the expected update of the *Hong Kong Climate Action* in 2021 to reflect more aggressive carbon emissions reduction strategies and measures to propel green finance and investments for carbon reduction, thereby supporting the construction of a low-carbon and climate-resilient economy.

In respect of financial budget, the HKSAR Government has allocated over US$47 billion to fund sustainable development projects in renewable energy, energy efficiency measures and waste management over the past decade[11] . The allocation is further increased under the 2020-21 Budget to support carbon-neutrality-related financial projects, such as the development of GSF, sustainable institutional investment, financing and certification activities, and to attract top-notch institutions and talents to provide relevant services in the Hong Kong market.

The HKSAR Government also demonstrates high involvement in the green bond market in two aspects. The first is acting as a model in execution — in April 2021, the HKSAR Government issued the second batch of government green bonds under the Government Green Bond Programme, totalling US$2.5 billion with a 30-year tenor, the longest tenor among US dollar bonds issued by the HKSAR Government to date[12]. The HKSAR Government issues green bonds on a regular basis and expand the scale of the Green Bond Programme by doubling the borrowing ceiling to US$200 billion[13]. The second is to provide incentives to support green bond development — the "Green and Sustainable Finance Grant Scheme" was launched to provide subsidies to eligible bond issuers and loan borrowers on bond issuance and external review expenditure to encourage green borrowing and lending activities[14].

---

11 "The Chief Executive's 2020 Policy Address", webpage on the HKSAR's website, viewed on 23 June 2021.
12 "Provisional financial results for the year ended March 31, 2021", webpage on the HKSAR's website, viewed on 23 June 2021.
13 "Budget Speech", webpage on the HKSAR *The 2020-21 Budget* website, viewed on 23 June 2021.
14 Ditto.

China issued the *Outline Development Plan for the Guangdong-Hong Kong-Macao Greater Bay Area* in February 2019, which clearly affirmed that green finance development in the Guangdong-Hong Kong-Macao Greater Bay Area (GBA) will be actively promoted, and that Hong Kong will be supported to establish itself as a green financial hub in the GBA. In May 2020, the PBOC, the China Banking and Insurance Regulatory Commission, the China Securities Regulatory Commission (CSRC) and the State Administration of Foreign Exchange jointly issued the *Opinions on Financial Support for the Construction of the Guangdong-Hong Kong-Macao Greater Bay Area*, with a focus to promote green finance collaboration within the GBA.

To stimulate continual collaboration, the Hong Kong Green Financial Association, the Guangzhou Green Finance Committee, the Shenzhen Green Finance Committee and the Macau Association of Banks jointly announced the inaugural launch of Guangdong-Hong Kong-Macao Greater Bay Area Green Finance Alliance (GBA-GFA) initiative in September 2020. The initiative will prioritise support for the incubation of green projects in the GBA and tackle the increasingly growing green financial needs in the Guangdong region. Hong Kong will lead the projects of Green Building Platform, Blockchain Solar Project and Carbon Connect out of the five major projects under the initiative. As such, Hong Kong will act as an exertive force, actively participating and supporting the promotion of GBA green finance development.

Hong Kong's advantages and challenges in becoming an East/West sustainability hub

Hong Kong's sound regulatory system and established policy measures have laid a solid foundation for Hong Kong's development as a regional green financial centre. As its next step, Hong Kong should leverage its established competitive advantages and overcome current challenges to add momentum to the GSF development in Hong Kong.

The four advantages of Hong Kong in developing GSF

Hong Kong has the advantages of a solid financial system, a high degree of internationalisation, and well-established supporting facilities. With these advantages, Hong Kong's role as a "super-connector" will be further strengthened under the state's policies of "dual circulation"[15] and "carbon neutrality".

Advantage 1: Hong Kong has a solid foundation as Asia's traditional financial centre

For many years, Hong Kong is consistently among the top places in major international rankings of business centres and financial centres. For instance, according to the 29th Global Financial Centre Index report published by Z/Yen Group Limited and China Development Institute in 2021, Hong Kong's overall ranking moved up one place and ranked fourth globally[16]. In World Bank's 2020 list of *The World's Most Business-Friendly Countries*, Hong Kong ranked third overall[17]. In Forbes' 2019 ranking of *Best Countries for Business*, Hong Kong ranked third, and was the only Asian economy to be ranked among top five internationally[18].

A prominent advantage of Hong Kong is that the city is a highly internalised hub. Under the principle of "One Country, Two Systems", with the name of "Hong Kong, China", Hong Kong can conclude and implement agreements with foreign states, regions and international organisations in the fields of economic, trade, financial and monetary. Hong Kong is not only the founding member of the World Trade Organisation, but also a member of the Asia-Pacific Economic Cooperation, Asian Development Bank, and Asian Infrastructure Investment Bank, and has participated in many international trade agreements between various developed economies, and to date, more than 260 bilateral treaties have been applied to Hong Kong[19].

Moreover, Hong Kong has already established an effective and well-developed financial system. Hong Kong itself is a highly developed free-market economy with a sound

---

15 "Dual circulation": A new economic policy proposed by China which "takes the domestic economic circulation as the mainstay while enabling domestic and foreign markets to interact positively with each other".

16 Source: "GFCI 29 rank", webpage on Z/Yen Group's website, viewed on 23 June 2021.

17 Source: "Doing Business 2020 — Sustaining the pace of reforms", published on the World Bank's website, 25 October 2019.

18 Source: "Best Countries for Business", webpage on Forbes' website, viewed on 23 June 2021.

19 Source: "External Affairs", webpage on the website of Hong Kong SAR's Department of Justice, viewed on 23 June 2021.

business environment. At the same time, the city holds the advantage of free capital flows, linked exchange rate system, investment freedom, and a robust regulatory compliance system. Hong Kong has accumulated abundant liquid capital which is beneficial for reducing funding cost. In recent years, HKEX has implemented a new listing regime targeting new-economy enterprises, increasing the appeal of the Hong Kong market for their financing.

Furthermore, Hong Kong has the advantage of providing strong legal protection with a well-established legal foundation. In Hong Kong, one has the autonomy to draft contracts with a choice of the applicable law and the type of dispute resolution. The city aims to develop into the Asia-Pacific region's main international law and dispute resolution service centre. Moreover, the Hong Kong courts have already established a business case law archive and an international reputation for commercial legal services.

Not to mention Hong Kong has the advantages of low tax rates, a diversified and professional talent pool, Chinese and English bi-literacy and tri-linguicism. These are all strengths for Hong Kong in being Asia's financial centre. These advantages would also translate into the potential for Hong Kong in becoming the region's green financial hub.

Advantage 2: The fortification of Hong Kong's role as connector under China's "dual circulation" policy

Hong Kong has the unique geographical advantage of Mainland-backing and Asia-engagement, playing the role of "super-connector" between Mainland China and the global market. Standing on the crossroads of unprecedented change, China is pivoting to the economic model of "dual circulation", with emphasis on adopting "domestic economic circulation" as a mainstay and positive interaction between the domestic and foreign markets. China market will further open up its market and promote "international economic circulation" with a higher level of interaction, bringing in new development opportunities for Hong Kong.

Firstly, Hong Kong should take this opportunity to strengthen its role as a connector between China and the world, mapping the resources and needs of each party, proactively engage in the construction of the GBA, and support the "Belt and Road" Initiative; it should actively match business opportunities with domestic and international resources, and strengthen its position as a "super-connector" by satisfying the needs of different markets and customers.

Secondly, green and sustainable economy being one of the prerequisites for high-level development, Hong Kong should leverage its advantages of internationalisation, professionalism and highly developed rule of law to assist the region in achieving this ambition. The development of GSF is not merely a new round of business growth opportunity for finance-related industries, it is also a favourable factor for Hong Kong, as a regional financial centre, to grasp for further consolidating its position in this round of historical changes.

Advantage 3: High degree of internationalisation of Hong Kong's GSF for connecting the East and the West

Hong Kong has been actually aligning its GSF standards and regulatory regime with international standards, and has also accumulated experience in international exchanges and cooperation regarding green finance.

Hong Kong is not only the first economy in Asia to require climate-related disclosure in accordance with the TCFD recommendations by 2025, but also the first economy in Asia to sign the Green Bond Declaration[20]. As Hong Kong's central bank for banking and monetary policy, and one of Hong Kong's largest asset owners, the HKMA is also a signatory to the United Nations-supported Principles for Responsible Investment (PRI), and is a member or co-signatory of international green financial organisations such as The Network of Central Banks and Supervisors for Greening the Financial System (NGFS), TCFD, and Global Framework for Climate Services (GFCS).

As a gateway to Mainland China, and a part of the GBA, Hong Kong is also an active participant and facilitator of green finance in Mainland China. Hong Kong is utilising its unique advantages of being the city where the East meets the West to match the needs of the two regions and bridge the gap between the East and the West in GSF.

Advantage 4: Hong Kong is an important window for global investors to participate in China's green economy

Hong Kong has become an important window for global investors to participate in China's capital market and economic development, owing to the gradual advancement of the connectivity mechanism between the two markets. Since the launch of the Shanghai-Hong Kong Stock Connect scheme in 2015 and that of the Shenzhen-Hong Kong Stock

---

20 Source: "HKSAR Government signs the green bond pledge: First signatory from Asia", press release on CBI's website, viewed on 23 June 2021.

Connect scheme in 2016 (the two schemes are collectively called the "Stock Connect" scheme), for the period up to 31 January 2021, the CAGR of the average daily turnover of Northbound trading has exceeded 70%[21]. Bond Connect has also played an important role for the development and opening-up of the Mainland bond market. After the launch of Northbound trading of Bond Connect in 2017, international investors have successfully entered the Mainland bond market through the conventional regulatory and trading platforms in Hong Kong. Since its opening in July 2017 and up to August 2020, Mainland bonds held by foreign institutions increased by RMB 2 trillion — 30% of which were held through Bond Connect[22]. The average daily trading volume surged from RMB 1.48 billion in its first month of operation to RMB 28.1 billion in May 2021[23]. This once again demonstrates Hong Kong's unique strength and role in connecting financial markets and investors in China and abroad.

In addition to attracting foreign investment to participate in the Chinese market, Hong Kong also provides an important channel for Chinese enterprises and capital to "go global". In respect of stocks, for the period from the commencement of Stock Connect in November 2014 to 31 January 2021, the CAGR of the average daily turnover of Southbound trading exceeded 50%[24]. In respect of bonds, along with the active Northbound trading of Bond Connect, the market is increasingly calling for the launch of Southbound trading as well. This was launched in September 2021 to meet the strong demand of onshore investors for investment diversification, improving the connectivity mechanism.

Entering the 21st century, imminent threats from environmental risks such as extreme weather, water resource scarcity, food scarcity loom large on the horizon. The commitment of "carbon neutrality" made by the international community, including China, has accelerated the green, low-carbon transition of the economy. Green and sustainable economic investments across the world have grown rapidly. China is one of the most extensive markets to offer green and sustainable economic investment, providing massive investment and related business opportunities to domestic and foreign investors. Hong Kong has the ability to continue to further advance the breadth and depth of the connectivity mechanism and seize the emerging green and sustainable investment opportunities. It can actively assist global investors in investing in the Mainland market and at the same time provide opportunities for Mainland domestic investors to "go global",

---

21 Source: "HKEX investor presentation", February 2021 version, published on HKEX's website.
22 Source: "Bond Connect — a brief review and the journey ahead", *InSight* article published on the HKMA's website, 28 September 2020.
23 Source: "Flash Report", May 2021 issue, published on Bond Connect Company Limited's website.
24 Source: "HKEX investor presentation", February 2021 version, published on HKEX's website.

thereby opening up the virtuous circulation channel for capital inflow and outflow. This would help fully connecting the domestic and overseas markets and promote the green and low-carbon transition of the regional economy.

The four challenges of Hong Kong in developing GSF

Hong Kong has the foundation and advantages to develop itself into a regional green financial hub. However, Hong Kong also faces challenges such as the lack of common green standards, the need for more incentives and support policies, and the need for continuous improvement of the capacity in developing GSF.

Challenge 1: Absence of common green standards in the market

Green standards are the basis of the GSF ecosystem and these includes standards in policy formulation, certification evaluation, product design, risk assessment and information disclosure. According to a survey conducted by the Hong Kong Institute for Monetary and Financial Research in 2020[25], investors consider difficulties with green certification, low return on investment, and ununified green standards to be currently the significant challenges of green finance. At present, the green finance standards that are internationally recognised are concentrated within the categories of bonds and loans, and there are more than ten green bond standards that are widely used. In China alone, there have been many green bond standards, including *Green Bonds Endorsed Project Catalogue (2015 Edition)* issued by the Green Finance Committee of China Society for Finance and Banking and *Guidelines on the Issuance of Green Bonds* issued by the National Development and Reform Commission (NDRC). In 2021, the PBOC, the NDRC and the CSRC have jointly issued the *Green Bonds Endorsed Project Catalogue (2021 Edition)*, which has strengthened the alignment with international standards with harmonised domestic standards in China. However, there is still much to be done in respect of unifying and aligning GSF standards and rules across different markets and regions. Green definition and disclosure rules also need to be continuously enhanced. For market participants, even subtle differences between different markets and standards would cause confusion in investment and financing activities, limit the scope of investment and financing, affect the cost of capital, and hinder the selection and subsequent review of projects.

---

25 Source: *The Green Bond Market in Hong Kong: Developing a Robust Ecosystem for Sustainable Growth*, published on the website of the Hong Kong Academy of Finance, 24 November 2020.

Challenge 2: Risk associated with emerging green industries

Even though the market for GSF is vast and has great potential, as an emerging market it is still associated with certain risks. For instance, the investment required for emerging green technology research and development is high, the payback period is long, and the industry itself is relatively fragile. In the post-pandemic era, the external environment is highly uncertain. Major economies have generally entered an era of low interest rates. The financial industry, as an important support for industrial development, is facing relatively large business operational pressure. The external environment for the development of green industry is also relatively complex.

Secondly, green financial products are not awarded with special treatment because of their green nature, and the sustainability of financial support remains to be examined. Green bonds, for instance, offer relatively low interest rates compared with global portfolios of a bigger investment scope. Despite the strong global development of green bonds in recent years, ESG corporate bonds are still conservative investment targets in the eyes of investors and the sustainability of the sector's development remains to be further observed.

Thirdly, it may be difficult to identify "greenwashing" behaviour. Governments, regulators and financial institutions all support the development of green finance, with measures to reduce the cost of green financial products. Given that there are diverse green standards across the world, there leaves much space for variation in the definition of "green". Such circumstances could induce by organisations with debatable green businesses to enter the green market, possibly damaging overall market confidence in green products.

Challenge 3: Further deepening of cross-border green finance cooperation is needed

The GBA, which encompasses nine cities in Guangdong and the Hong Kong and Macao Special Administrative Regions, is one of the important engines of China's economic development and sets higher requirements for cross-border cooperation. Cooperation in the field of green finance includes, but not limited to, product exchange, rules integration and resource allocation. Innovative cross-border cooperation should give full play to Hong Kong's connector and transformer roles for connecting the Mainland with the international market and for creating a common market with mutual trust, while respecting the different systems and trading habits of the two places.

Taking the current situation as an example, Guangdong is the main force in green credit, and Hong Kong leads in terms of the scale and growth of green bond issuance. For Hong Kong, it faces the large demand of Mainland enterprises for cross-border green bonds issuance; the existing operations are relatively mature; and the foundation of the connectivity mechanism is good. However, there is room for improvement on issues such as the approval process and ratings, and these areas may become new points of breakthrough in cross-border green cooperation with the Mainland. In the Mainland, the registration and filing process with domestic regulators for overseas bond issuance is relatively long, typically requiring a period of about 2-4 months. There is a quota management system for such issuance by certain types of enterprise, under which quota must be applied for at the beginning of each year and has little flexibility for change afterwards. Besides, these bonds need to be rated overseas, where issuers face problems such as differing standards, long waiting time, the possibility of unexpected results, affecting the time window for their fund-raising, and even the cost of issuance. Moreover, under the current requirements of national foreign exchange management, Mainland enterprises still face many constraints in issuing green bonds or undertaking green investments overseas. Therefore, one can consider creating new cross-border green cooperation approaches, such as opening a green channel to promote the development of green finance in the region.

Challenge 4: Capacity for green finance should be continuously enhanced

The development of GSF is a systematic, long-term and professional ecological system construction project. Talent training and data infrastructure construction are the basic capabilities to support the construction of a green and sustainable financial ecology, but the reality is not ideal. According to KPMG's survey released in 2018 on the development of the Hong Kong ESG market[26], when asked the major obstacles faced by companies in developing ESG, most of the respondents (close to 40%) cited "lack of ESG-related knowledge and experience" as their answer.

As an emerging field, green finance is interdisciplinary in nature, which requires the combination of theory and practice. At present, the problem of talent shortage is not only due to the short-term imbalance of market supply and demand, but also stems from long-term problems such as the difficulty in cultivating cross-discipline talents, an imperfect training system, and the gap between academia and market application. These problems need to be jointly solved by financial institutions and the academia.

26　Source: "ESG: A view from the top (The KPMG, CLP and HKICS Survey on ESG) ", published on KPMG's website, 13 September 2018.

The lack of data is another imminent fundamental problem. Both risk management, which is the core of the financial industry, and front-end product development need to be based on data. A large amount of data must be collected from various markets, industries and customers across different periods to form an analysis model and provide a basis for subsequent judgment. The current inadequacy in relevant data collection in the market is still large, and analysis methods are still being explored, which brings challenges for the financial industry to manage relevant risks.

GSF outlook in Hong Kong

Green and sustainability development is increasingly becoming a common language of the world. As a super-connector between the East and the West, Hong Kong is well equipped with unique and competitive advantages for it to shine in GSF and to further solidify its position as the "Pearl of the Orient" in support of a sustainable future.

Comprehensive common-ground green standards will equip Hong Kong to become the GSF hub

As GSF is at a relatively nascent stage of development, there are no uniform harmonised standards across different financial markets and the difference in standards between the East and the West is big. A set of comprehensive common-ground market standards will facilitate market regulation and the establishment of market consensus, enable efficient allocation of market resources towards green and sustainable projects, and at the same time improve market transparency thereby reducing "greenwashing" risks.

The fundamental question in the market to be addressed is "what activities are green?". Market participants eagerly awaits the roll-out of an international set of harmonised, comprehensive and practically feasible green taxonomy to better define green activities. There are two main types of institutions driving the definition of green activities in the market. The first type is international organisations, such as the International Capital Market Association who issued market principles for reference like the *Green Bond Principles* and the *Sustainability-Linked Bond Principles*, which are voluntary in nature for compliance. The second type is national and regional regulators, who have issued taxonomies that are typically mandatory in nature. The standards issued by China and the European Union (EU) are the two most mainstream taxonomies in the world, but there remain a number of variations between the two in terms of scope. As part of the International Platform on Sustainable Finance, China and the EU worked together towards converging their standards to form the Common Ground Taxonomy, which was released in November 2021.

The formulation of internationally recognised green standards is one of the important cornerstones for Hong Kong to becoming a green financial hub. As announced earlier by the Cross-Agency Steering Group, Hong Kong will adopt the Common Ground Taxonomy to build consensus among market participants, to further promote cross-border issuance and trading of green assets and to realise cross-border green "connectivity" so as to bridge the financing needs of green projects with environmentally-conscious investors across the border.

The Common Ground Taxonomy marks the beginning of a journey, for further harmonisation and enhancement of green standards in the future. Hong Kong has always been one of the most internationalised cities in China where the East meets the West. It has unique competitive advantages to take up in more active role in promoting the harmonisation of green taxonomies of the East and the West, and in further solidifying its position as a green financial centre.

Quality and transparent information disclosure is key to attract international investors in Hong Kong

Enhancing ESG disclosure has become a regulatory consensus among global regulators, while investors are also becoming increasingly concerned about the ESG performances of their investee companies. Quality and transparent ESG disclosure will foster constructive interactions among companies, investors and regulators, and promote efficient allocation of market resources, thereby directing market resources to quality and sustainable corporates.

Hong Kong has always been a market leader in ESG disclosure and HKEX is a leading force driving the ESG disclosure of listed companies. After HKEX released its first *ESG Reporting Guide* in August 2012 and revised it twice thereafter[27], the requirements on the scope and information granularity have been progressively improved. The importance of

---

27 The two amendments were conducted in December 2015 and December 2019 respectively.

quantitative information has come to par with qualitative information, and key indicators within the scope of "Recommended to Disclose" have been upgraded to "Comply or Explain" and are progressing towards "Mandatory Disclosure" in the coming future. An announcement from the Cross-Agency Steering Group mentioned that climate-related disclosures in alignment with the TCFD recommendations would become mandatory across relevant sectors no later than 2025, which makes Hong Kong the first region in Asia to adopt such mandatory requirement. The advanced ESG disclosure requirements will not only enhance the transparency and discipline of Hong Kong's capital market, but also strengthen global investors' confidence in Hong Kong.

In order to have continuous enhancement of ESG information disclosure in Hong Kong, apart from regulatory guidelines imposed by authorities, companies should also get well prepared in advance. Firstly, companies should leverage on big data, blockchain, and financial innovations to enhance data tracking, collection and analysis across front and back offices. Secondly, multinational corporations should consider the different local regulatory requirements when formulating the group's overall information disclosure plan. Thirdly, companies should begin preparation in advance of the relevant technologies and capabilities required in anticipation of further regulatory requirements on climate-related and carbon footprint disclosure, as regulators focus on delivering the "carbon neutrality" commitments.

Local government support will accelerate the development of GSF in Hong Kong

Most green and low-carbon transition industries generally are emerging industries with relatively high risk and long payback period. Government's supportive measures could, to a certain extent, balance the associated risks. This is vital for the development of GSF, especially at the initial stage of development.

First, governmental policy support. Leverage on the recent series of policy support such as "Bond Connect" and "Wealth Management Connect", etc., which aim to improve cross-border financial connectivity between Hong Kong and Mainland China, it is recommended to consider giving priority support to green and sustainable projects by way of administering quota and eligible product types. Furthermore, the "carbon neutrality" commitment has increased the demand for green financing in the Mainland market. Hong Kong, as a main offshore financing centre for Mainland companies, the Hong Kong government could establish "Green Channels" for cross-border green financing activities, simplifying the approval procedures and improve the efficiency of green asset allocations.

Second, incentive schemes. Apart from market regulations and policy support, the industry also expect the government to introduce more incentive schemes to encourage the development of GSF. In the near term, the government may consider increasing subsidies for green activities of small and medium-sized enterprises, and introduce tax concessions for green projects. In the long term, the regulator may consider lowering the risk weightings of green assets of banks to direct market capital towards green and low-carbon transition projects, and away from high-polluting, energy-intensive brown projects.

Building a green financial ecosystem will enhance the GSF capacity of Hong Kong

In becoming a regional GSF hub, talent cultivation and data are two critical cornerstones for Hong Kong GSF capacity building. Capacity building and data establishment are difficult to be accomplished by isolated individual institutions within a short span of time. Instead, it requires a medium- to long-term collective plan, involving collaborative actions between the public and private sectors, as well as cross-border cooperation of Mainland China and Hong Kong. This is fundamental to building a GSF ecosystem and a unified platform that facilitates the sharing of talents, knowledge, experience, as well as resources.

In respect of talent cultivation, market participants can strengthen GSF connectivity in four areas. Firstly, encourage collaboration among the practitioners, academics and research centres to better leverage on Hong Kong's world-class universities and leading global financial institutions for joint industry research and establishment of talent cultivation mechanism. Secondly, the HKSAR Government should seize national policy opportunities in GSF development, and introduce favourable policies and incentive schemes to attract Mainland and global talents to participate in the development of GSF in Hong Kong. Thirdly, fully utilise both public and private GSF collaborative platforms to strengthen cross-industry and cross-institution knowledge and experience exchange, and introduce professional advancement schemes and training courses. Finally, strengthen green finance talents partnerships and introduce market-focused measures to promote flexible talent mobility and efficient placement within the GBA.

In respect of data, credible and high-quality data are the basis of the green financial market. Market participants require a large amount of environmental and market data to assess climate and environmental risks in order to incorporate such cost information into the pricing mechanism. Existing green data in the market is relatively scattered and of questionable accuracy. Institutions across the world are establishing multiple green information databases. Regulators and financial institutions in Hong Kong could consider consolidating efforts to establish a common database on local green data. It will significantly benefit all financial institutions and regulators in identifying, assessing, and managing environmental and climate-related risks, should the database be shared among all in the industry with proper and adequate safeguarding measures.

Integration into the GBA and "Belt and Road" Initiative is an important opportunity for GSF development in Hong Kong

Green economic recovery is a preferred post-pandemic economic recovery strategy of governments around the world. According to data from the National Climate Strategy Centre[28], China will need to invest over RMB 139 trillion into new climate sectors by 2060, with an average annual financing demand of approximately RMB 3.5 trillion, and a long-term financing gap of RMB 1.6 trillion per year. Countries along China's "Belt and Road" Initiative also require large financing needs to support their new and emerging green developments. According to a research conducted by Tsinghua University in collaboration with Vivid Economics[29], the annual demand for green investment along the "Belt and Road" is US$1.7 trillion from 2016 to 2030. Therefore, capitalising on the historical opportunity presented by China's ambitious initiatives is critical for Hong Kong to accelerate its GSF development.

Within the GBA development plan, Hong Kong is strategically positioned as a green financial centre for the region, as it is the world's largest international offshore RMB centre, and has a well-established capital market and financial system and a number of world-class universities and research institutes; Shenzhen is the advanced innovation hub, experienced in commercialisation of innovative technologies with economy of scale;

---

28 Source: "The biggest business opportunity: Carbon neutrality needs 100 trillion yuan investment, where will green assets come from?" (〈最大商機來襲：碳中和需百萬億投資，綠色資產哪裏來？〉), *Caijing* (《財經》), April 2021.

29 Source: Joint Research Group of Tsinghua University, Vivid Economics and ClimateWorks. *Decarbonizing the "Belt and Road" Initiative: A Green Finance Roadmap,* 2019.

Guangzhou has multiple breakthrough innovations in green finance, and the establishment of Guangzhou Futures Exchange is expected to actively promote the development of carbon finance; Macao has its unique advantages in green finance, in respect of its cooperation with Portuguese-speaking countries; and the other cities in the Guangdong Province possess the solid industrial base and market potential for the development of green finance. Hong Kong should therefore give full play to its financial advantages and leverage on the industrial advantages in the GBA to foster differentiation, cooperation and connectivity with other cities in the GBA, in support of the GBA to become the nation's and the world's role model in regional green financial development.

As part of the "Belt and Road" Initiative, many countries along the "Belt and Road" relies on traditional fossil fuels and face tremendous challenges in transitioning to low-carbon economies. On the other hand, a number of developing countries have abundant untapped resources, such as wind and solar power, which could potentially sustain the development of clean energy. At the same time, some other developing countries do not have well-established basic infrastructures like energy and/or transportation, which presents new business opportunities to build brand new infrastructure for them in green and sustainable manner. It is now an international consensus that the developed economies have the responsibility and obligation to support the developing countries in terms of building climate change resilience, amongst which extending investment and financing support is one important means. As an international financial centre, Hong Kong should actively support the inter-connectivity between domestic and foreign investors within the green and sustainable financial market to direct international green capital flow along the "Belt and Road", so as to create mutually beneficial business opportunities.

In conclusion, Hong Kong should integrate into the regional green development of the GBA and "Belt and Road" Initiative under China's "dual circulation" blueprint, to establish itself as an international GSF hub that can support China in boosting high-level opening-up and connectivity in the green and sustainably dimension, and make positive contributions to global green and sustainable developments.

Remark: This paper has been produced in the Chinese language, published with a separate English language translation. If there is any conflict in this paper between the meaning of English words or terms in the English language version and Chinese words in the Chinese language version, the meaning of the Chinese words shall prevail.

第4章

香港 —— 連接東西方的綠色及可持續金融樞紐

鄂志寰博士
中國銀行（香港）有限公司　首席經濟學家

呂潔荔
中國銀行（香港）有限公司　發展規劃部高級策略規劃師

江映林
中國銀行（香港）有限公司　發展規劃部策略規劃師

摘要

近年來全球綠色可持續金融得到快速發展，香港作為連接中國內地與全球市場的重要橋樑，在綠色可持續金融的發展中一直扮演着樞紐角色。為了營造香港綠色可持續金融發展的良好市場環境，以及打好根基，本地監管機構和政策制定者積極推出支持措施，提升市場規範性並激發市場潛力。雖然香港具備金融系統基礎好、國際化程度高、相關配套設施完善等發展綠色金融的優勢，但是也面臨綠色標準未統一、需要更多激勵和支持政策、綠色金融能力需持續提升等方面的挑戰。我們認為，預期未來香港各界將通過聯合力量，持續完善綠色可持續金融規則、提升綠色金融能力，並積極融入中國乃至全球綠色金融發展的宏偉藍圖中，進一步奠定香港作為亞洲綠色金融中心地位，助力全球綠色可持續發展目標實現。

香港綠色可持續金融發展現狀

亞洲地區的綠色可持續金融相比西方國家起步較晚，但近年來得到高速發展。根據中國人民銀行數據顯示，2020 年末，中國本外幣綠色貸款餘額為 12 萬億元人民幣，較去年同期增長 17.4%，存量居世界第一；綠色債券存量約 8,000 億元人民幣，居世界第二[1]。根據全球永續投資聯盟發佈的《2018 年全球可持續投資回顧》[2]，日本的可持續相關投資規模達到 2.18 萬億美元，僅次於歐洲整體和美國。亞洲其他地區亦具備龐大的綠色可持續金融市場潛力，隨着亞洲各地區政府和企業對於可持續發展理念的認知深化及「碳中和」等承諾的提出，綠色可持續金融發展日益蓬勃。

香港一直以來是連接中國內地與全球市場的重要橋樑。在全球綠色可持續金融發展浪潮中，香港定位為區域綠色可持續金融樞紐，在監管機構和政策制定者的積極推動下，以其廣泛的投資者基礎、完善的基礎設施和國際金融中心的市場地位，持續吸引全球綠色金融各方持份者的參與，推動香港綠色可持續金融進一步發展，具體體現在綠色債券、綠色信貸及綠色投資等多方面。

香港綠色債券與綠色信貸市場高速發展

立足中國內地和於香港地區實踐，綠色債券與綠色貸款是為綠色可持續發展金融項目提供資金支持的重要工具，近年來在香港地區得到高速發展。根據氣候債券倡議組織（Climate Bonds Initiative，簡稱 CBI）發佈的 2020 年香港綠色債券市場簡報[3]顯示，2020 年在香港安排和發行的綠色債務（green debt）達到 120 億美元，截至 2020 年年底累計總額超過 380 億美元，從 2016 年到 2020 年的複合年均增長率超過 100%（見圖 1）。

1　資料來源：中國人民銀行〈用好正常貨幣政策空間 推動綠色金融發展 ── 中國人民銀行行長易綱在中國發展高層論壇圓桌會的講話〉，2021年3月21日。
2　The Global Sustainable Investment Alliance《Global Sustainable Investment Review》，2018年版。
3　CBI《Hong Kong Green Bond Market Briefing 2020》，2021年5月。

圖 1：香港累計安排和發行的綠色債務總額（2016 年至 2020 年）

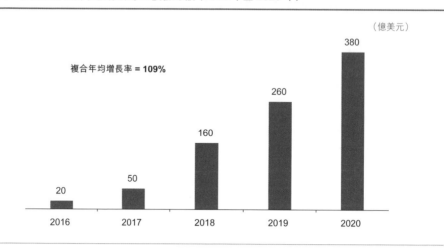

（億美元）

複合年均增長率 = 109%

380

260

160

50

20

2016　2017　2018　2019　2020

資料來源：CBI、中國銀行香港金融研究院。

其中，綠色債券為主要的融資工具，而香港發行人所發行的綠色債券（green bond）過去數年亦呈上升趨勢，截至 2020 年年底香港發行人累計發行總額達到 92 億美元，自 2016 年到 2020 年的複合年均增長率達 66%（見圖 2）。

圖 2：香港發行人在香港發行的綠色債券累計總額（2016 年至 2020 年）

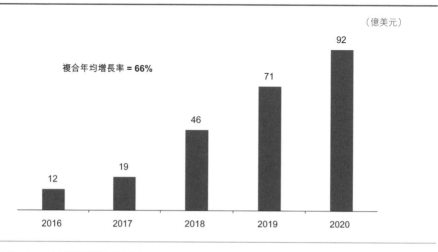

（億美元）

複合年均增長率 = 66%

92

71

46

19

12

2016　2017　2018　2019　2020

資料來源：CBI、中國銀行香港金融研究院。

在發行人來源方面，香港一直是內地企業首選的境外融資中心，具備國際化金融服務和制度優勢，大多數內地發行人將香港作為籌集離岸資金的最佳平台，面向國際投資者，2020 年內地實體在香港安排和發行的綠色債務達到 70 億美元，佔總量的 60.3%[4]，是香港綠色債務市場的主力軍，背靠大陸、連接全球的獨特優勢是香港綠色金融市場繁榮的重要基礎。

在發行人種類方面，以發行金額計，企業成為發行綠色債券的主力，於 2020 年佔比達到 65.6%，其中房地產公司較為突出，佔比位居第一，達到 34%，能源類公司佔比達到 11.2%，而其他類別公司發行佔比合計達到 20.4%；金融機構作為發行人的佔比從 2019 年的 49.4% 下滑至 2020 年的 29.9%；政府、開發銀行、政策性銀行以及多邊開發銀行合計市場佔比出現較大幅度下降，由 2019 年的 14.4% 下降至 2020 年的 4.5%（見圖 3）。

圖 3：香港綠色債券發行人的種類分佈（以發行金額計）（2019 年及 2020 年）

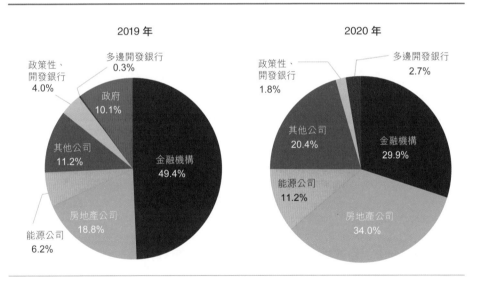

資料來源：CBI、中國銀行香港金融研究院。

香港綠色債券市場整體發展速度較快，但以成為連接東西方的綠色金融樞紐的目標而言，在發行人多元性方面上仍有優化空間。

4　資料來源：CBI《Hong Kong Green Bond Marketing Briefing 2020》，2021年5月。

近年來香港在綠色信貸市場也取得了長足發展。根據彭博數據顯示，2020 年香港綠色貸款新增 13 億美元，是 2015 年的 7.5 倍。香港綠色貸款總額雖然受疫情影響而較 2019 年下降 38%，但香港綠色貸款市場表現明顯好於全球和歐洲地區 —— 2020 年全球綠色貸款同比下降 43.2%，而歐洲地區下降超過 50%[5]。香港的綠色貸款涉及的項目漸趨多元化，2015 年綠色貸款僅涉及能源項目，之後五年的時間裏，綠色貸款涉及了金融、材料、工業、非必需消費品、通訊、能源以及公共事業這七個方面。根據香港品質保證局資料，除香港本地企業外，越來越多的內地企業也在拓展綠色貸款融資項目。

香港可持續投資方面有較大發展潛力

香港的可持續投資領域近年來發展迅速。根據晨星的數據，截至 2020 年年底，香港的可持續基金資產規模逾 3.5 億美元，按年增加 20%，呈現快速增長的勢頭[6]。不過，香港的基金資產規模僅佔亞洲地區的 0.8%[7]，可見未來仍有巨大的發展空間和潛力。在利好的宏觀環境及各持份者的共同努力下，香港的可持續投資生態系統有望不斷完善，推動相關投資進一步發展：

首先，投資者對綠色可持續理念日益重視，近年多國對氣候治理更趨積極，提出了清晰的溫室氣體減排路線圖，制定「碳達峰」和「碳中和」的時間表，在配合減排背景下的產業升級轉型將會催生大量的投資機會。新冠肺炎疫情的爆發，令社會和治理因素得到更大的關注，民生福祉將會在後疫情時代得到投資者更多的重視。疫情也為企業帶來重大的營運風險，令投資者更注重良好企業治理的重要性。此外，多項研究表明亞洲年輕一代投資者更加關注企業的環境、社會和管治（environment、social、governance，簡稱 ESG）等方面的表現[8]，在年輕一代推動下，預計綠色可持續投資將得到蓬勃發展。

其次，可持續投資回報較理想，對投資者有吸引力。國際清算銀行的研究[9]顯示，綠色債券指數的夏普比率，略高於類近信貸評級的企業債券指數，反映在經過風險調整後，綠色債券的回報更佳；而且着重 ESG 的企業在經濟下行時有更強的抗逆能力。在疫情對全球經濟衝擊最嚴重的 2020 年，彭博巴克萊 MSCI 美元綠色債券指數，以及彭博巴克萊美元綜合公司債券指數均先跌後升，前者回報為 12.6%，高於後者的 7.4%（見圖 4）。

5　資料來源：《Green Finance Portal》的網頁，於2021年5月7日閱覽。

6　資料來源：R. Walker〈Asia ESG funds attract record flows〉，載於《Fund Selector Asia》網站，2021年2月1日。

7　資料來源：R. Walker〈Asia ESG funds attract record flows〉，載於《Fund Selector Asia》網站，2021年2月1日；W. Chow〈Global sustainable fund flows: Q4 2020 in review〉，載於Morningstar 的網站，2021年1月28日。

8　資料來源：R. Newell〈How Asia's family wealth transfers could bolster ESG〉，載於《Asia Investor》網站，2020年10月14日；范卓雲〈社會責任策略與綠色投資　亞洲急冒起〉，載於《信報財經新聞》網站，2018年2月8日。

9　資料來源：T. Ehlers 與 F. Packer（2017年）〈Green Bond Finance and Certification〉，載於《國際清算銀行季度回顧》（BIS Quarterly Review），2017年9月。

圖 4：彭博巴克萊 MSCI 美元綠色債券指數及彭博巴克萊美元綜合公司債券指數走勢圖（2020 年）

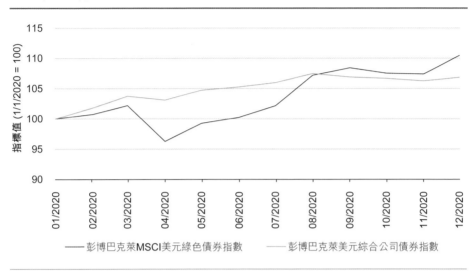

資料來源：彭博、中國銀行香港金融研究院。

再次，香港當局多方面推動以營造更良好的 ESG 投資環境。香港金融管理局（簡稱「香港金管局」）作為外匯基金的管理人，身體力行的實踐負責任投資，將 ESG 因素納入投資考慮當中；香港交易及結算所有限公司（簡稱「香港交易所」）推出的可持續及綠色交易所（STAGE），讓各方持份者能夠分享相關資訊。這些舉措將有利打造透明度更高的市場，進一步優化 ESG 的投資生態系統。

香港的綠色可持續金融發展以綠色債券、綠色信貸等為開端，而隨着綠色可持續金融不斷發展，逐漸從銀行端向資產管理端蔓延，預計下一階段綠色保險、綠色證券、碳金融等將全面發展，推動香港綠色可持續金融市場不斷提升深度和廣度。

香港的監管政策與市場動力

為配合綠色金融市場發展，進一步鞏固香港作為東西方的綠色可持續金融樞紐的地位，香港的監管機構正積極推出新的支持政策及措施。

香港綠色可持續金融發展的監管體系

香港地區推動綠色及可持續發展的主要監管機構包括香港交易所、香港金管局、證券及期貨事務監察委員會（簡稱「證監會」）等。延續其三者在整體金融業的監管分工，香港金管局主導綠色銀行業發展及香港綠色金融中心建設，香港交易所以提升上市公司的 ESG 信息披露為重點，而證監會則主要推動將可持續發展元素納入證券和期貨管理全流程。此外，香港金管局和證監會共同發起成立「綠色和可持續金融跨機構督導小組」（簡稱「跨機構督導小組」），以開展跨機構聯合可持續發展行動。

香港金管局引領銀行業的綠色及可持續發展，並致力推動香港成為區域綠色金融中心。香港金管局於 2019 年 5 月宣佈推出三大舉措，以推動綠色及可持續的銀行業發展和減緩氣候變化帶來的風險，包括建設綠色及可持續銀行、履行負責任投資及推動香港成為區域綠色金融中心。

香港交易所重點着手優化上市公司信息披露質量。早在 2011 年，香港交易所對上市公司的 ESG 信息披露開始進行了探索，並於 2011 年 12 月就《環境、社會及管治報告指引》發表諮詢文件，公開徵詢意見。其後，香港交易所分別於 2012、2015 及 2019 年發佈了三版的《環境、社會及管治報告指引》，逐步規範上市公司的 ESG 披露要求。此外，為提升市場對於綠色可持續產品的關注及促進產品信息透明及流通，香港交易所於 2020 年 12 月成立 STAGE，藉此連接本地與海外發行人及投資者，為支持香港連接東西方綠色可持續金融市場的重要舉措。

證監會推動將可持續發展元素納入證券和期貨管理全流程。2018 年 9 月，證監會發表了《綠色金融策略框架》，強調上市公司、基金經理及投資產品對 ESG 元素（特別是環境及氣候風險）的披露與考量。2019 年 4 月，證監會向其認可的單位信託及互惠基金管理公司發出通函，就如何加強綠色基金或 ESG 基金披露提供指引。2020 年 10 月，證監會向業界發出諮詢文件，建議修訂《基金經理操守準則》，以更好滿足投資者掌握氣候風險信息的需求及打擊「漂綠」行為。

跨機構督導小組進一步協調香港金融業在可持續發展方面的一致步伐。在上述三大主要監管機構各自推動所轄領域的可持續發展基礎上，跨機構督導小組成立於 2020 年 5 月，並於同年 12 月發佈了首個策略計劃，提出了五個短期行動綱領，包括必須在 2025 年或之前按照「氣候相關財務信息披露工作組」（Task Force on Climate-Related Financial Disclosures，簡稱 TCFD）的建議，就氣候相關信息作出披露；以採納《共通綠色分類目錄》[10] 為目標；鼓勵進行以氣候為重點的情境分析等。

---

10 綠色分類目錄是指將被視為在環境方面可持續的經濟活動加以分類的系統。

「碳中和」承諾下對綠色可持續金融的政策支持

隨着中國「十四五規劃」[11] 將環境問題的重要性提至國家政策層面，香港特別行政區（香港特區）亦緊隨其後於 2020 年的行政長官《施政報告》和 2021-22 年度《財政預算案》中宣佈推動綠色及可持續發展的相關監管政策內容。

為邁向低碳經濟方向轉型，香港特區早於 2017 年發佈的《香港氣候行動藍圖 2030+》中，以 2005 年作為基準年訂立了要在 2030 年前實現 65%-70% 的碳強度下降目標，並將絕對碳排放降低 26%-36%。隨着中國宣佈 2030 年「碳達峰」和 2060 年「碳中和」的「雙碳」承諾，香港特區 2020 年度的行政長官《施政報告》亦表明將爭取於 2050 年實現「碳中和」的長遠目標，並預計將於 2021 年更新《香港氣候行動藍圖》，定下更進取的減碳排放策略和措施，大力發展綠色金融以增加有助減碳的投資，建構低碳和更具氣候變化抵禦力的經濟體系。

在財政預算方面，特區政府在過去十年內已投入 470 億美元資助可再生能源、能效措施和廢物管理等可持續發展建設 [12]。2021 年的財政預算將進一步提高分配至實現「碳中和」的相關金融支持，包括通過繼續促進綠色和可持續金融的發展，鼓勵機構開展相關的投資、融資和認證活動，並吸引頂尖的機構和人才來香港提供相關服務等。

香港特區政府在綠債市場參與度較高，主要體現在兩個方面：一是身體力行推出政府綠色債券計劃，特區政府於 2021 年 4 月發行了第二批總額為 25 億美元、為期 30 年的政府綠色債券，是迄今為止政府所發行的最長期限美元債券 [13]。特區政府定期發行綠色債券，並將其借款上限提高一倍至 2,000 億美元，以擴大綠債計劃規模 [14]。二是通過激勵手段支持綠色債券發展，推出「綠色和可持續金融資助計劃」，資助合資格的債券發行人和借款人的發債支出及外部評審服務費用，以鼓勵綠色債券發行和綠色貸款活動 [15]。

---

11 《中華人民共和國國民經濟和社會發展第十四個五年規劃和2035年遠景目標綱要》，中華人民共和國國家發展和改革委員會發佈，2021年3月23日。
12 資料來源：中華人民共和國香港特別行政區網站上的〈行政長官2020年司政報告〉網頁，於2021年6月23日閱覽。
13 資料來源：中華人民共和國香港特別行政區網站上的〈二○二○至二一年度財務狀況的臨時數字〉網頁，於2021年6月23日閱覽。
14 資料來源：中華人民共和國香港特別行政區2020至21財政預算案網站上的〈預算案演詞〉網頁，於2021年6月23日閱覽。
15 同上。

在粵港澳大灣區規劃下，香港可發揮作為大灣區綠色金融中心的角色

中國於 2019 年 2 月印發《粵港澳大灣區發展規劃綱要》，當中明確提出將在大灣區大力發展綠色金融，以及肯定和支持香港打造大灣區綠色金融中心。2020 年 5 月，中國人民銀行、中國銀行保險監督管理委員會、中國證券監督管理委員會和中國國家外匯管理局共同發佈《關於金融支持粵港澳大灣區建設的意見》，重點推動粵港澳大灣區綠色金融合作。

為促進持續的合作模式，2020 年 9 月，香港綠色金融協會、廣東金融學會綠色金融專業委員會、深圳經濟特區金融學會綠色金融專業委員會及澳門銀行公會宣佈成立粵港澳大灣區綠色金融聯盟（GBA-GFA）的聯合倡議，重點促進大灣區的綠色項目孵化及應對廣東日益增長的綠色金融需求，而香港將主導五個重點項目當中的「綠色建築」、「區塊鏈光伏」和「碳市通」。由此可見，香港是推動大灣區綠色金融發展的堅實力量之一，可扮演積極參與者及助力者的重要角色。

香港成為東西方的綠色可持續金融樞紐的優勢及面對的挑戰

完善的監管體系及政策措施已為香港發展成為區域綠色金融中心奠定穩固基礎。下一步，香港需發揮固有的競爭優勢，以及克服當前的挑戰障礙，為綠色可持續金融發展增添動力。

香港發展綠色可持續金融的四項優勢

香港具備金融系統基礎好、國際化程度高、相關配套設施完善等優勢，而在「雙循環」[16]、「碳中和」等國家政策帶動下，香港連接東西的「超級聯繫人」角色將進一步得到強化。

優勢 1：香港作為傳統亞洲金融中心基礎良好

多年以來，香港一直在國際各大營商和金融中心的排名中名列前茅。例如，2021 年由英國 Z/Yen 集團與中國（深圳）綜合開發研究院聯合發佈的第 29 期《全球金融中心指數》報

---

16 「雙循環」是指「以國內大循環為主體、國內國際雙循環相互促進的新發展格局」，是中國在2020年提出的一項新經濟政策。

告中，香港的總排名上升一位，為全球第四位 [17]；在世界銀行 2020 年《營商環境報告》中排名第三 [18]；在福布斯（Forbes）2019 年《最佳營商地》的排名中同樣列第三，是前五名中唯一的亞洲經濟體 [19]。

首要原因，香港是一個高度國際化的樞紐城市，在「一國兩制」的制度下，香港可以「中國香港」為名，自行與其他國家、地區以及國際組織簽訂經濟、貿易、金融、貨幣等方面的協定。香港不僅是世界貿易組織的創始成員，也是亞太經合組織、亞洲開發銀行和亞洲基礎設施投資銀行的成員之一，而且還參與國際多個發達經濟體之間的貿易協定，迄今國際上有超過 260 條的雙邊條約適用於香港 [20]。

其次，香港已經建立起一套行之有效且優勢穩固的金融體系。香港本身就是高度自由的經濟體，具有良好的營商環境，同時，還擁有貨幣流通自由、聯繫匯率制度、投資自由以及完善合規監管體系等金融體系優勢，積累了充裕的流動資金，降低資金成本。近年，香港交易所又針對新經濟企業進行上市制度改革，讓香港融資市場變得更具吸引力。

此外，香港具有強大的法治保障和優勢，法律基礎設施完善，擁有制定合約和選擇適用法律以及爭端解決機制的自由，致力發展成為亞太區主要國際法律及爭議解決服務中心，並且香港法院已建立一套完善的商業案例法檔案庫，在商事法律服務上享有國際聲譽。

除此之外，低稅率、多樣化且專業的人才儲備、中英兩文三語工作環境等，都是香港成為亞洲金融中心的優勢，也是未來繼續發展成為區域綠色金融樞紐的潛力所在。

優勢 2：中國「雙循環」政策下香港橋樑角色強化

香港擁有得天獨厚的地理優勢，背靠大陸、輻射亞太，一直以來扮演着聯通內地與全球市場「超級聯繫人」的角色。站在百年未有之大變局的十字路口，中國正積極發展以國內大循環為主體、國內國際雙循環相互促進的「雙循環」新發展格局。其中，強調要以高水平開放推進經濟的「外循環」及相互促進，為香港帶來新的發展機遇。

其一，香港要藉此機會強化自身連接內外的橋樑作用，串聯各方的資源與需求，積極參與大灣區建設，支持「一帶一路」倡議，應積極撮合境內外資源和機會，在滿足不同市場和客戶需求中強化香港「超級聯繫人」的地位；

其二，發展綠色可持續經濟必是「高水平」的要求之一，香港應積極發揮自身國際化、專

---

17 資料來源：Z/Yen集團網站上的〈GFCI 29 Rank〉網頁，於2021年6月23日閱覽。
18 資料來源：〈2020年營商環境報告 —— 保持改革步伐〉，載於世界銀行網站上的專題報導，2019年10月25日。
19 資料來源：Forbes 網站上的〈Best Countries for Business〉網頁，於2021年6月23日閱覽。
20 資料來源：香港特別行政區律政司〈對外事務〉網頁，於2021年6月23日閱覽。

業化、法治化程度高等優勢，助力區域實現高水平發展。發展綠色可持續金融，不僅是金融相關產業新一輪業務增長的機遇，也是香港作為區域金融中心在本輪歷史變局中可以把握、進一步鞏固自身地位的有利因素。

優勢 3：香港綠色可持續金融連接東西方國際化程度較高

香港在綠色及可持續金融標準和監管制度方面正在積極與國際主流接軌，在國際綠色交流合作方面已經積累起較為成熟的經驗。

香港不僅是亞洲第一個要求必須在 2025 年或之前按照 TCFD 建議就氣候相關資料作出披露的經濟體，還是亞洲第一個簽署《綠色債券宣言》的經濟體 [21]。作為香港制定銀行和貨幣政策的中央銀行、以及香港最大的資產擁有者之一的香港金管局也簽署了聯合國支持的《責任投資原則》（Principles for Responsible Investment），並且是央行與監管機構《綠色金融體系網絡》（Network for Greening the Financial System）、TCFD、《全球氣候服務框架》（Global Framework for Climate Services）等國際綠色金融機構的成員或聯署人。

香港作為通向中國內地的門戶、粵港澳大灣區的一部分，同時也是中國內地綠色金融的積極參與者和助力者，正在利用自身橫貫東西的獨特優勢，對接兩地需求，拉近東西方綠色可持續金融的距離。

優勢 4：香港是全球投資者參與中國綠色經濟發展的重要窗口

有賴於兩地市場互聯互通機制的逐步推進，香港已經是全球投資者參與中國資本市場和經濟發展的重要窗口。股票市場的「滬港通」機制自 2015 年開通及「深港通」機制自 2016 年開通以來（「滬港通」與「深港通」合稱「滬深港通」）直至 2021 年 1 月 31 日止，北向交易日均成交金額的複合年均增長率超過 70%[22]。「債券通」也為內地債券市場的發展和開放起了重要作用，自 2017 年「債券通」的北向交易推出後，國際投資者利用熟悉的香港監管和交易平台，順利便捷地進入內地債券市場，自 2017 年 7 月開通至 2020 年 8 月，境外機構持有境內債券淨增加約兩萬億元人民幣，其中三成是通過債券通持有 [23]，日均交易量從首月的 14.8 億元人民幣，上升至 2021 年 5 月的 281 億元人民幣 [24]，再一次印證香港在溝通中外金融市場和投資者上的獨特優勢和作用。

除了吸引外資參與中國市場，香港還為中國企業和資本「走出去」參與國際資本市場提供了重要通道。股票方面，「滬深港通」自 2014 年 11 月開通至 2021 年 1 月 31 日止，股票南

---

21 資料來源：〈香港特別行政區政府簽署了綠色債券宣言 成為亞洲區首個簽署單位〉，載於 CBI 網站上的新聞稿，2019 年 5 月 6 日。
22 資料來源：〈香港交易所投資者簡報〉，2021 年 2 月版，載於香港交易所的網站。
23 資料來源：〈債券通的回顧與展望〉，載於香港金管局網站的《匯思》文章，2020 年 9 月 28 日。
24 資料來源：〈運行報告〉，2021 年 5 月版，載於債券通公司的網站。

向通日均成交額的複合年均增長率超過 50%[25]；債券方面，隨着蓬勃的「債券通」北向交易，南向交易已於 2021 年 9 月推出，以滿足在岸投資者對投資多元化的強勁需求，完善互聯互通機制。

進入 21 世紀，來自極端天氣、水資源危機、糧食危機等氣候環境相關風險的威脅迫在眉睫，包括中國在內的國際社會作出「碳中和」承諾，加速經濟的綠色低碳轉型進程，各地綠色和可持續經濟相關的投資增長突飛猛進，中國又是其中最為遼闊的市場之一，給包括香港在內的國內外投資者提供海量投資和相關業務機遇。香港有能力繼續推進「互聯互通」機制朝着更深更廣領域發展，抓住新湧現的綠色可持續投資機會，主動協助全球投資者投資中國內地市場，同時也給內地投資者提供出海良機，打通資本進出和良性循環的通道，充分聯通海內外市場，推動區域經濟的綠色低碳轉型。

香港綠色可持續金融發展面臨的四項挑戰

香港有基礎也有優勢發展成為區域綠色金融樞紐，但與此同時，也面臨綠色標準未統一、需要更多激勵和支持政策、綠色金融能力需持續提升等方面的挑戰。

挑戰 1：市場綠色標準尚未統一

綠色分類標準是包括政策制定、認證評估、產品設計、風險評估和信息披露在內的整個綠色及可持續金融生態鏈的基礎。根據香港貨幣及金融研究中心 2020 年的調查[26]，綠色認證問題、投資回報低和綠色標準不一，是投資者認為目前面臨的重大挑戰。當前國際公認度較高的綠色金融標準主要集中在債券和信貸領域，影響力較大的綠色債券標準就超過 10 個。僅在內地過往就有多個綠色債券標準，包括中國金融學會綠色金融專業委員會的《綠色債券支持項目目錄 (2015 年版)》和國家發展和改革委員會 (簡稱「發改委」) 的《綠色債券發行指引》等。雖然中國人民銀行、發改委和中國證券監督管理委員會已經在 2021 年聯合發佈了《綠色債券支持項目目錄 (2021 年版)》，在統一內地市場基礎上加強與國際標準對接，但不同市場和地區之間綠色及可持續發展金融中標準和規則的統一和銜接工作仍有很長的路要走，綠色定義、披露規則等也需要持續優化。對市場參與者來說，不同市場和標準之間的細微差別足以對投融資活動造成困擾，限制投融資範圍，影響資金成本，阻礙對項目的選擇和後續評審。

挑戰 2：新興綠色產業有一定風險性

雖然綠色及可持續金融市場廣闊，潛力巨大，但作為新興產業，依然有一定的風險性，例

25　資料來源：〈香港交易所投資者簡報〉，2021年2月版，載於香港交易所的網站。

26　資料來源：《香港綠色債券市場：為可持續增長建設健全的市場生態》，載於香港金融學院的網站，2020年11月24日。

如新興綠色科技研發投入大風險高、項目回報週期長，產業本身就較為脆弱等。當前適逢後疫情時代，外圍環境不確定性強，各大經濟體普遍進入低利率時期，作為產業發展重要支持力量的金融業面臨較大經營壓力，綠色產業發展的外部環境較為複雜。

第二，市場也並未因為金融產品的綠色屬性就對其另眼相看，金融支持的可持續性仍需考察。以綠色債券為例，相較於投資範圍更廣的全球投資組合，綠色債券的利率屬於較低水平。雖然近年全球綠色債券發展強勁，但在投資者眼中依然是保守型的投資標的，發展的可持續性仍待進一步觀察。

第三，「漂綠」行為較難辨別。目前各國政府、監管機構和金融機構紛紛支持綠色金融發展，降低綠色金融產品成本，加上各地綠色標準不統一，給綠色概念的演繹留下較大空間，可能會有一些無關綠色的業務趁機混入，有可能損害市場對綠色金融產品的信心。

挑戰 3：跨境綠色金融合作需不斷深化

粵港澳大灣區囊括廣東九市、香港和澳門特別行政區，是中國經濟發展的重要引擎之一，給跨境合作提出更高要求。綠色金融領域的合作包括但不限於產品交流、規則融和、資源配置，而創新跨境合作即是在尊重兩地不同制度和交易習慣的前提下，充分發揮香港連接內地和國際市場的橋樑和轉換器作用，打造雙方市場皆可信任的共同市場。

以現狀為例，廣東是綠色信貸主力，香港在綠色發債的規模和增速方面領先。對香港來說，內地企業跨境發行綠色債券的需求大、現有操作較為成熟、互聯互通基礎好，但在審批流程、評級等問題上都存在改進空間，有可能成為與內地綠色跨境合作的新突破點。目前，境內監管機構對境外發債的登記備案流程較長，一般週期需 2-4 個月左右；針對某一類型企業有額度管理制度，需要年初申請，後期改動的靈活性較小；債券需進行境外評級，面臨標準不一、時間長、結果可能不如預期等問題，影響企業募資窗口期，甚至發行成本。並且在現行中國外匯管理要求下，內地企業境外發行綠色債券或作綠色投資依然面臨較多制約因素，可以考慮通過創新綠色跨境合作方式，如開通綠色通道來促進區內綠色金融發展。

挑戰 4：綠色金融能力需持續提升

發展綠色可持續金融，是一項系統化、長期化、專業化的生態體系建設工程，人才培養、數據基礎設施建設等是支持綠色可持續金融生態建設的基礎能力，但現實並不理想。據畢馬威 2018 年發佈關於香港 ESG 市場發展的調查顯示[27]，在問及公司發展 ESG 面臨的主要挑戰的選項當中，最多受訪者（佔比近四成）選擇了「缺乏 ESG 相關的知識和經驗」。

27　資料來源：〈ESG: A view from the top（The KPMG, CLP and HKICS Survey on ESG）〉，載於 KPMG的網站，2018年9月13日。

作為新興領域，綠色金融本質上屬於交叉學科，需要理論和實踐雙結合。目前人才短缺的問題既來源於短期市場供求不平衡，又有跨界人才難培養、培養體系不健全，以及學界與市場應用之間存在缺口等長期問題，有待金融機構和學界共同解決。

數據缺失是擺在眼前的另一個基礎性難題。無論是作為金融行業核心的風險管理，還是前端的產品開發，都需要以數據為基礎，大量收集不同時期來自各個市場、行業、客戶的數據，才能形成分析模型，為後續判斷提供基礎。目前市場上相關數據的收集缺口依然較大，分析方法也在摸索階段，為金融業管理相關風險帶來挑戰。

香港綠色可持續金融的展望

綠色可持續發展已成為全球的共同語言。香港作為東西方的交接點，具備獨特的優勢條件，將可在綠色可持續金融上大放異彩，成為可持續發展的「東方明珠」。

完善、共通的綠色標準有助於香港成為綠色可持續金融樞紐

綠色可持續金融作為新興領域，目前其多項市場標準尚未統一，東西方綠色標準差異較大。共通的、完善的市場標準有助於規範市場及統一共識，引導資本向綠色可持續項目準確配置，提升市場透明度並減少「漂綠」風險。

在綠色市場標準中，最基本的就是需要回答「哪些屬於綠色活動」的問題。因此，業界期盼監管機構儘快出台國際間共通的、清晰可執行的綠色分類標準（Green Taxonomy），劃定綠色活動邊界。主導市場綠色分類的機構主要有兩類：一是國際組織，如國際資本市場協會（International Capital Market Association）制定了綠色債券原則、可持續掛鈎債券原則等，為市場提供綠色定義參考，以自願遵守為主；二是各國家和地區的監管機構，其出台的綠色分類標準具有一定強制性，較為主流的是中國和歐盟的綠色分類標準，但兩者的具體範圍存在不少差異。中國與歐盟在可持續金融國際平台（International Platform on Sustainable Finance）下合作，於 2021 年 11 月發佈「共通綠色分類目錄」（Common Ground Taxonomy），統一中國和歐盟兩大市場的綠色項目邊界。

構建國際認可的綠色標準對於香港發揮綠色金融樞紐作用意義重大。香港的跨機構督導小組此前宣佈香港將採納此「共通綠色分類目錄」，其出台後將有利於凝聚境內外共識，推動綠色資產的跨境發行和交易，真正實現跨境綠色「互聯互通」，在境內外有綠色投資需求的投資者與有資金需求的綠色項目之間搭建起橋樑。

以此「共通綠色分類目錄」為起點，預期未來全球的綠色標準將得到不斷統一和完善。香港一直以來是中國國際化程度最高的城市之一，在東西方綠色標準的碰撞和交融過程中，香港有基礎也有優勢扮演更加活躍的角色，推動東西方綠色金融標準的接軌，並進一步奠定香港作為綠色金融中心的地位。

高質透明的信息披露是香港吸引國際投資者的關鍵

當前強化 ESG 信息披露已成為各地監管共識，市場投資者也更加關注標的企業的 ESG 表現。高質透明的 ESG 信息披露有利於促進企業、投資者、監管部門之間的良性互動，促進市場資金的高效配置，讓市場資源流向真正高質量、有可持續發展能力的企業。

香港地區對於企業 ESG 信息披露要求一直走在市場前列，香港交易所是推動上市企業 ESG 信息披露的主導力量。香港交易所自 2012 年 8 月首次發佈《環境、社會及管治報告指引》後對該指引作了兩次修訂[28]，其對於信息披露的範圍和細緻度要求不斷提升，從定性信息為主到定性與定量信息並重，關鍵指標從最初的「建議披露」逐步過渡為「不遵守就解釋」，並將繼續朝「強制披露」的方向邁進。此前跨機構督導小組也提出在 2025 年前相關行業應按 TCFD 的要求就氣候相關資料作出披露，是亞洲第一個提出該強制要求的地區。ESG 信息披露方面的先進性有利於提升香港資本市場的透明度和規範性，增強國際投資者對香港市場的信心。

為持續提升香港資本市場的 ESG 信息披露，除了監管機構的規則引導，香港的企業也應作好充分準備：一是善用大數據、區塊鏈等金融科技力量，加強前中後台 ESG 信息的追蹤、搜集和分析；二是對於跨區域的企業，統籌兼顧好各地監管對於 ESG 信息披露的不同要求；三是在「碳中和」趨勢帶動下，預期企業的氣候和碳足跡信息披露將會是監管關注重點，企業應提前作好相關技術和能力部署。

政府支持措施將提速香港綠色可持續金融發展

大部分的綠色及低碳轉型產業屬於新興領域，風險較高且回報週期長，政府的支持措施可一定程度平衡綠色可持續金融的風險，對促進起步階段的綠色可持續金融發展至關重要。

一是政策支持。一方面，近年來中國內地與香港推動的一系列如「債券通」、「理財通」等金融市場互聯互通機制中，建議可在額度管理、產品種類管理等方面優先支持綠色可持續發

---

28 兩次修訂分別於2015年12月及2019年12月進行。

展項目，提升綠色市場要素的雙向開放和聯通。另一方面，「碳中和」等政策推動下內地市場對於綠色資金需求較大，香港亦是內地企業首選的離岸融資平台，建議可針對跨境綠色融資項目設置「綠色通道」，簡化審批程序，提升綠色資本配置效率。

二是激勵措施。除了市場規範和政策引導，業界也期許香港特區政府未來可出台更多激勵措施，短期來看可加大對中小企業綠色金融活動的補貼、對於綠色投資項目實施稅收減免等，長期來看可考慮降低銀行綠色金融資產風險權重，以經濟手段引導市場資金流向綠色及低碳轉型項目，遠離高污染、高能耗棕色項目。

打造綠色金融生態圈將提升香港綠色可持續金融能力

香港要成為區域綠色可持續金融樞紐，離不開綠色可持續金融能力的建設，兩大關鍵在於人才與數據。人才培育與數據建設均無法靠單一機構力量、在短時間內完成，而需要中長期的建設，需要公營私營、境內境外的聯合行動，建立起香港綠色可持續金融的生態系統，實現統一平台下人才、知識、經驗與資源的共享和流通。

在人才培育方面，業界參與者可通過以下四方面加強聯動：一是產學研結合，發揮香港擁有世界一流的大學和匯集全球領先金融機構的優勢，加強企業與大學在綠色金融方面的科研合作與人才聯合培養機制；二是充分借力國家大力推動綠色金融發展的政策紅利，香港特區政府可考慮推出更多人才優惠和激勵政策，吸引境內外優秀人才參與香港綠色可持續金融建設；三是充分利用各類官方和民間的綠色金融合作平台，加強跨行業、跨機構的知識和經驗交流，推出有針對性的專業能力提升計劃及培訓課程；四是加強粵港澳大灣區綠色金融人才合作，以市場為導向推動大灣區內的人才便捷流動和高效配置。

在數據建設方面，可信和高質量的數據是建設綠色金融市場的基礎，市場參與者需要大量的環境數據和市場數據，以量化評估氣候及環境風險，並將風險成本納入金融市場的定價體系中。目前市場上存在的綠色數據較為分散，數據準確性亦難以統一驗證，全球許多機構正在建設多個綠色信息數據庫，香港的監管機構、金融機構等可考慮整合力量，建設香港地區統一的、本土化的綠色數據庫，在保障安全的基礎上將該數據庫開放給業界共享，這將大大裨益金融機構和監管機構識別、評估及管理與環境和氣候相關的風險。

融入大灣區及「一帶一路」發展大局是香港綠色可持續金融的重要機遇

綠色經濟復甦是各地政府在後疫情時代共同的選擇。根據國家氣候戰略中心數據顯示[29]，到2060年中國新增氣候領域投資需求規模將達到139萬億元人民幣，年均資金需求約為3.5萬億元人民幣，長期資金缺口年均1.6萬億元人民幣。「一帶一路」沿線國家也有龐大及新興的綠色發展需求，根據清華大學與生動經濟學（Vivid Economics）合作的研究表明[30]，2016年至2030年「一帶一路」沿線每年綠色投資需求為1.7萬億美元。因此，融入中國國家發展大局是香港綠色可持續金融發展的重要機遇。

在粵港澳大灣區發展方面，香港擁有發達的資本市場和金融體系，是世界上最大的人民幣國際離岸中心，具備世界一流的大學和科研機構，定位為大灣區綠色金融中心；深圳具有先進的科創能力，擅長快速實現技術的商業化和規模化應用；廣州在綠色金融創新方面開展諸多嘗試，廣州期貨交易所的成立預計將大力推動碳金融發展；澳門在與葡語國家綠色金融合作方面具有獨特優勢，可發展特色綠色金融；而廣東省內多個城市則具有扎實的產業基礎和市場優勢。因此，香港在大灣區綠色發展中應發揮自身的金融優勢，結合大灣區的產業優勢，與區內其他城市錯位發展、合作互促，在互聯互通中不斷提升香港綠色金融中心地位，並支撐大灣區建成全國乃至世界性的區域化綠色金融發展典範。

在「一帶一路」發展方面，「一帶一路」沿線多是對於燃煤依賴嚴重的傳統地區，整體經濟向綠色低碳轉型的挑戰較大。但另一方面，部分發展中國家具備豐富的、待開發的自然資源，有先天優勢大力發展風能、光伏等清潔能源；部分發展中國家尚未建立完善的能源、交通等基礎設施體系，反而提供了建成全新的綠色產業商機。當前的國際共識是全球主要經濟體有責任也有義務幫助發展中國家提高應對氣候變化的韌性，其中擴大國際投融資支持是重要的實現手段。香港可以憑藉其國際金融中心的優勢，積極發揮橋樑作用，對接國內與國際綠色資本對「一帶一路」沿線經濟體的投資需求，創造多贏的商業機會。

綜上所述，在中國構建國家「雙循環」的宏偉藍圖中，香港應主動融入綠色大灣區及「一帶一路」等區域發展大局，成為境內外綠色可持續金融聯動的樞紐，助力國家在綠色可持續方面實現更高水平的對外開放和互聯互通，為全球綠色可持續發展作出積極貢獻。

29　資料來源：〈最大商機來襲：碳中和需百萬億投資，綠色資產哪裏來？〉，載於《財經》雜誌，2021年4月。
30　資料來源：清華大學國家金融研究院、Vivid Economics 與 ClimateWorks聯合課題組《支持「一帶一路」低碳發展的綠色金融路線圖》，2019年。

2

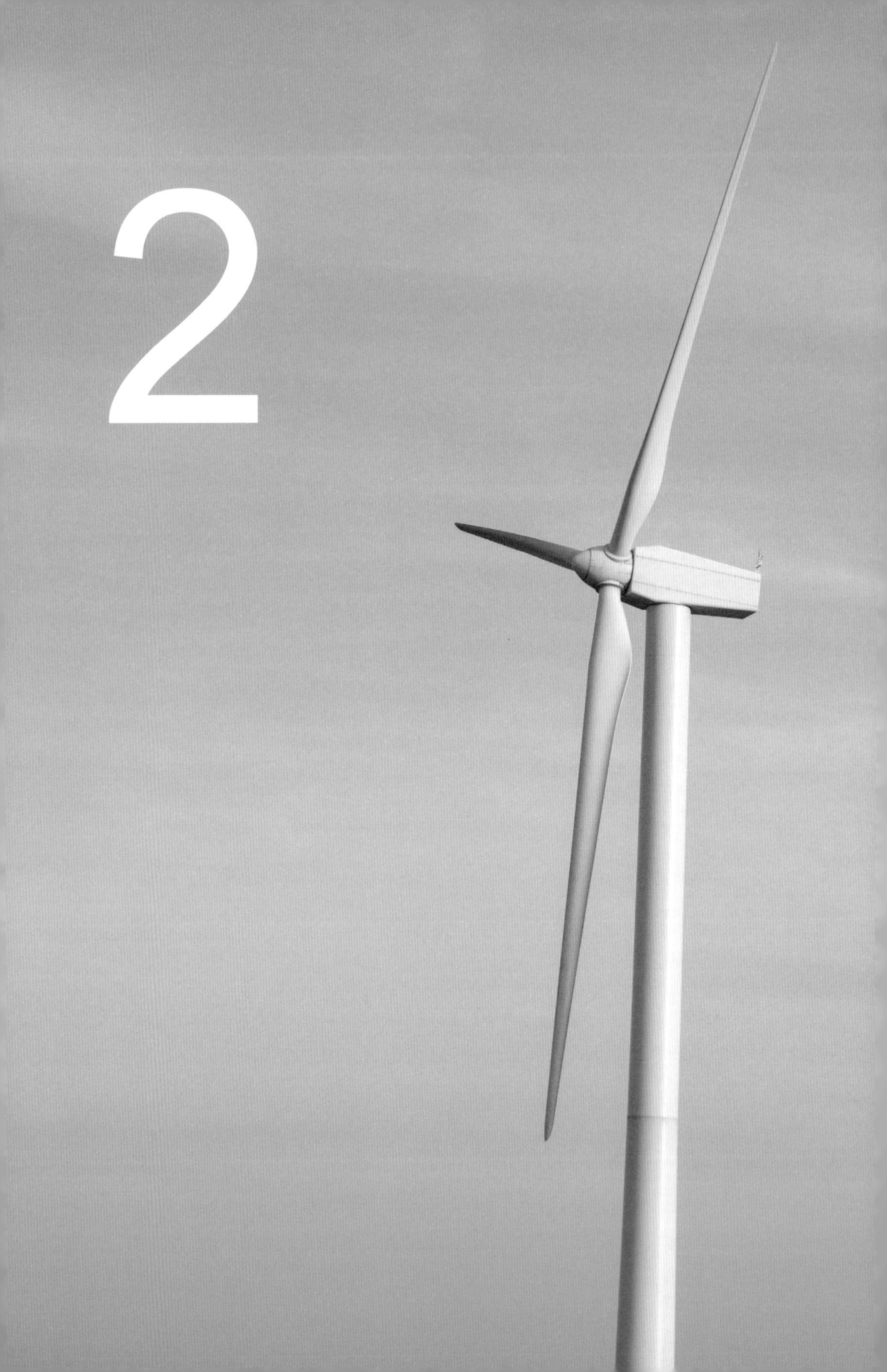

Market practice and infrastructure

市場實踐與基礎設施

Chapter 5

Shifting mindsets and embracing common metrics for GSF and ESG investment: From global to China

Rebecca IVEY
Chief Representative Officer, World Economic Forum, Greater China

Emily BAYLEY
Project Lead, ESG, Future of Investing
World Economic Forum

Kai KELLER
Platform Curator, The Future of Financial Services in China
World Economic Forum

Sha SONG
Specialist, China Partnerships, Circular Economy & Value Chains
World Economic Forum

Summary

This chapter addresses several factors that influence the readiness of companies (including those founded and/or publicly listed in Mainland China and Hong Kong) to measure, report and improve upon environmental, social and governance (ESG) performance, as a prerequisite to developing or obtaining green and sustainable financing (GSF) to further fund their long-term value creation and sustainability agendas. It shares lessons from a multi-stakeholder consultation effort led by the World Economic Forum to identify a foundational set of universal, material ESG metrics and disclosures from among the existing frameworks and put forward a cross-industry recommendation for consistent ESG reporting.

Introduction

Developing and obtaining green and sustainable financing (GSF) presents a critical opportunity for companies to further fund the long-term value creation and sustainability agendas demanded by shareholders among other stakeholders. The readiness of companies in Mainland China and Hong Kong, among other regions, to measure, report and improve upon their environmental, social and governance (ESG) performance will provide a credible foundation for the evolution of GSF globally.

Corporate leaders have strengthened their public commitments to corporate citizenship, stakeholder engagement and private-sector contributions towards achieving the United Nations (UN) Sustainable Development Goals (SDGs). Such commitments over the past two years include the World Economic Forum's Davos Manifesto[1] and the US Business Roundtable[2], among others.

Yet there are continued obstacles for companies globally, including those based in Greater China, to make the necessary strategic and operational shifts to transition from articulating values and principles to reporting on ESG metrics to the full extent requested by investors as well as other stakeholders, including employees, regulators and the civil society. Not least, the multiplicity of ESG frameworks put forward by a wide range of institutions involved in setting ESG standards has inadvertently led to caution and uncertainty among businesses examining the way forward for their sustainability reporting and practices.

Since 2019, in response to interest and concern voiced by leading global businesses, including Chinese firms, about the measurement and reporting burden associated with the multitude of ESG metrics, the World Economic Forum has worked in collaboration with the International Business Council (IBC), a group of 120 leading businesses drawn from across the World Economic Forum's most engaged partner companies, and the "big four" accounting firms[3]. The aim is to identify a foundational set of universal, material ESG metrics and disclosures from among the existing frameworks and put forward a

---

1   Schwab, K., "Davos Manifesto 2020: The universal purpose of a company in the Fourth Industrial Revolution", published on "Agenda" webpage on World Economic Forum's website, 2 December 2019.
2   "Business Roundtable redefines the purpose of a corporation to promote 'an economy that serves all Americans' ", published on the website of US Business Roundtable, 19 August 2019.
3   These are Deloitte, EY, KPMG and PwC.

cross-industry recommendation for consistent ESG reporting. Following the consultation exercise, a white paper was published in September 2020[4].

In an effort to further facilitate and shape the development of ESG in China, the World Economic Forum has been expanding on this initial global work and convening leading industry voices and system experts to explore how China's embrace of ESG concepts aligns with practices elsewhere and how the country's approach will remain distinct. Over a nine-month period from July 2020 to March 2021, this multi-stakeholder community examined the World Economic Forum's global ESG metrics work and discussed its applicability in the Chinese context. Discussions focused in particular on enablers and roadblocks to further advancing ESG frameworks in China[5].

This community of Chinese ESG champions may eventually leverage the global work stream of World Economic Forum member companies to coalesce common, industry-agnostic ESG metrics and will complement the Green Investment Principles for the "Belt and Road" Initiative that were jointly developed with the World Economic Forum by a group of Chinese and global stakeholders.

Defining common and comparable ESG metrics: Addressing a global challenge

A solid foundation of ESG reporting will be needed to lay the groundwork of trust, credibility and interoperability that can enable new opportunities in green financing or value-generating products and services that further support ESG transitions across markets. While the financial sector has developed an advanced understanding of ESG and green financial instruments, corporate leaders in other industry sectors are relatively less aware or less engaged in ESG and GSF issues and opportunities.

Working closely with company chief executive officers and chairpersons, the World Economic Forum identified a strategic understanding of the business case for reporting on material ESG factors and the continued consolidation of the primary ESG metrics and disclosure requirements as essential steps to make it possible for more companies to go beyond a compliance or philanthropy mindset.

---

4   See World Economic Forum et al., *Measuring Stakeholder Capitalism: Towards Common Metrics and Consistent Reporting of Sustainable Value Creation*, White Paper, September 2020.
5   See World Economic Forum, *A Leapfrog Moment for China in ESG Reporting*, White Paper, March 2021.

Establishing the business case for ESG reporting

ESG reporting is a global trend: assets under management by signatories to the United Nations-supported Principles for Responsible Investments (PRI) surpassed US$100 trillion in 2020, an increase of 75% over 2015[6].

Even under the economic and financial pressure of the COVID-19 pandemic, investor interest in sustainable assets has continued to rise. Globally, sustainable assets recorded a 96% increase in investments coming from mutual funds and exchange traded funds compared to 2019, totalling US$288 billion in the first 11 months of 2020[7].

The rising emphasis placed on ESG reporting by the investor community has shifted from niche impact investing to the mainstream, particularly driven by institutional investors with a focus on climate-related risks and disclosures. For example, since early 2020, prominent asset managers such as BlackRock, representing clients that include foundations and pension funds, have requested all companies they invest in to issue reports aligned with the recommendations of the Task Force on Climate-related Financial Disclosures (TCFD) and the Sustainability Accounting Standards Board (SASB)[8].

Thus, quality and credible ESG reporting is a critical issue for companies seeking investment and financing, as well as maintaining a continued "licence to operate" in a societal and regulatory context that is increasingly cognizant of climate change and other environmental and social risk factors.

However, earlier research published by the World Economic Forum in January 2019 in collaboration with Allianz SE and Boston Consulting Group[9] highlighted three barriers to meaningful ESG disclosure: the complexity and burden of ESG reporting, the incomparability of company ESG data, and a poor understanding of, and interaction with, ESG ratings agencies.

---

6   Source: "PRI growth 2006–2020" dataset on the *PRI* website, downloaded on 9 February 2021.

7   As cited in BlackRock, "Larry Fink's 2021 letter to CEOs", 2021 (published on BlackRock's website, viewed on 1 April 2021), citing the original source: Simfund, Broadridge, GBI, data as of November 2020 (closed-end funds, funds of funds excluded, money market funds included).

8   See BlackRock, "Larry Fink's 2020 letter to CEOs — A fundamental reshaping of finance", published on BlackRock's website, viewed on 1 April 2021.

9   World Economic Forum in collaboration with Allianz SE and Boston Consulting Group, *Seeking Return on ESG: Advancing the Reporting Ecosystem to Unlock Impact for Business and Society*, White Paper, January 2019, published on World Economic Forum's website.

Consolidating ESG reporting metrics and disclosures

In 2020, on behalf of its largest global private sector partners as organised in the IBC, the World Economic Forum focused on building consensus around a set of common metrics for ESG disclosure. The intent was to transform the reporting ecosystem and encourage convergence and standardisation for material ESG and longer-term value considerations.

The expertise of the institutions involved in setting ESG standards and the complexity of managing a paradigm shift in investor and corporate responsibility should not be underestimated. The World Economic Forum, as the International Organisation for Public-Private Cooperation, offers a complementary platform for these stakeholders to meet, exchange insights and concerns, and develop joint action plans to address global challenges.

The value of engaging this particular group of business stakeholders was recognised throughout the ecosystem of ESG standard-setters as a highly influential collective who could, through their own leadership of ESG performance, induce momentum across other companies to engage in ESG best practices and reporting.

More than 75% of over 200 companies, investors and other stakeholders who were consulted over six months agreed that "reporting on a set of universal, industry-agnostic ESG metrics would be useful for their company, financial markets and the economy more generally"[10].

Definition of materiality and the relevance of ESG to achieving strategic goals

A major challenge faced by businesses to transition to meaningful ESG reporting is to identify the most material metrics on which to report. Materiality is defined as "information that is important, relevant and/or critical to long-term value creation" (while noting that "the issue of materiality and what should be disclosed in annual reports varies according to regional regulations and expectations")[11].

---

10 See World Economic Forum et al., *Measuring Stakeholder Capitalism: Towards Common Metrics and Consistent Reporting of Sustainable Value Creation*, White Paper, September 2020, op. cit., p.6.
11 Ibid., pp.13 and 14.

Establishing which issues among the major elements of ESG disclosure are most relevant to a given company or industry's long-term financial performance is an essential strategic step for companies on the ESG journey.

And yet, "some 'pre-financial' information […] may not be strictly material in the short term, but are material to society and planet and therefore may become material to financial performance over the medium or longer term. Materiality is a dynamic concept, in which issues once considered relevant only to social value can rapidly become financially material"[12].

This is explored in greater depth in the white paper, *Embracing the New Age of Materiality: Harnessing the Pace of Change in ESG*, released by the World Economic Forum in collaboration with Boston Consulting Group in March 2020.

Criteria for selecting consolidated ESG metrics

The following criteria were used to filter and prioritise ESG metrics as published in the corresponding World Economic Forum white paper in September 2020 and endorsed by the IBC members[13]:

- Consistency with existing frameworks and standards;

- Materiality to long-term value creation;

- Extent of actionability;

- Universality across industries and business models; and

- Monitoring feasibility of reporting.

Ultimately, 21 core indicators and 34 expanded disclosures were selected through a rigorous consultation process, condensed into four thematic pillars, listed below.

Four thematic pillars for ESG reporting

Granular ESG metrics serve a useful function for businesses, investors and regulators to assess, compare and reward non-financial corporate performance and risk factors.

---

12 Ibid., p.14.
13 See World Economic Forum et al., *Measuring Stakeholder Capitalism: Towards Common Metrics and Consistent Reporting of Sustainable Value Creation*, White Paper, September 2020, op. cit., p.13.

However, breaking down social purpose into minute detail is not the only purpose that participating businesses are seeking to fulfil in establishing the narrative on their long-term value proposition to investors and society at large.

Thus, four pillars were identified, which are interdependent but communicate the fundamental purpose underlying the reporting and performance improvements for which companies and investors strive, as follows[14]:

1. **Principles of Governance:** Principles of agency, accountability and stewardship recognised as vital for truly "good governance", despite the evolving definition of governance as organisations are increasingly expected to define and embed their purpose at the centre of their business.

2. **Planet:** An ambition to protect the planet from degradation, including through sustainable consumption and production, sustainably managing its natural resources and taking urgent action on climate change, so that it can support the needs of the present and future generations.

3. **People:** An ambition to end poverty and hunger, in all their forms and dimensions, and to ensure that all human beings can fulfil their potential in dignity and equality and in a healthy environment.

4. **Prosperity:** An ambition to ensure that all human beings can enjoy prosperous and fulfilling lives and that economic, social and technological progress occurs in harmony with nature.

Each of the four pillars around which more granular ESG metrics are adhered reflects the principle that all actors in the economic system should also consider how their operations contribute towards the achievement of the SDGs, a roadmap for a more inclusive and sustainable world, to which businesses that create long-term and sustainable value can contribute.

---

14 Ibid., Figure 2.

Table 1. Four thematic pillars and 21 core metrics for ESG reporting (linked with relevant SDGs)

Principles of governance	Planet	People	Prosperity
1. Setting purpose 2. Governance body composition 3. Material issues impacting stakeholders 4. Anti-corruption 5. Protected ethics advice and reporting mechanisms 6. Integrating risk and opportunity into business process	7. Greenhouse gas (GHG) emissions 8. TCFD implementation 9. Land use and ecological sensitivity 10. Water consumption and withdrawal in water-stressed areas	11. Diversity and inclusion (%) 12. Pay equality (%) 13. Wage level (%) 14. Risk for incidents of child, forced or compulsory labour 15. Health and safety (%) 16. Training provided (#, $)	17. Absolute number and rate of employment 18. Economic contribution 19. Financial investment contribution 20. Total research and development expenses ($) 21. Total tax paid
Related SDGs: #12 Responsible consumption and production #16 Peace, justice and strong institutions #17 Partnerships for the goals	**Related SDGs:** #6 Clean water and sanitation #7 Affordable and clean energy #12 Responsible consumption and production #13 Climate action #14 Life below water #15 Life on land	**Related SDGs:** #1 No poverty #3 Good health and well-being #4 Quality education #5 Gender equality #8 Decent work and economic growth #10 Reduced inequalities	**Related SDGs:** #1 No poverty #8 Decent work and economic growth #9 Industry, innovation and infrastructure #10 Reduced inequalities

Source: World Economic Forum et al., *Measuring Stakeholder Capitalism: Towards Common Metrics and Consistent Reporting of Sustainable Value Creation*, White Paper, September 2020.

Examining specific metrics related to green and sustainable finance

In a world that is increasingly aware of the urgency of action needed to redress the issues of climate change, biodiversity loss and other planetary effects of human activity, the mandate for business has moved beyond "do no harm" towards making meaningful contributions to national and global emissions reduction targets and other resource management plans.

In line with the intention to consolidate rather than proliferate the set of ESG metrics for corporate reporting, the below metrics related to environmental sustainability were largely sourced or expanded upon existing recommendations for ESG reporting from across a wide range of respected sources, including but not limited to: the Global Reporting Initiative (GRI), the International Organisation for Standardisation (ISO), the Sustainability Accounting Standards Board (SASB), the TCFD, the Climate Disclosure Standards Board (CDSB), the Greenhouse Gas Protocol (GHG Protocol), the Science Based Targets Initiative (SBTi), the Natural Capital Protocol, the US Environmental Protection Agency (EPA), the World Business Council for Sustainable Development (WBCSD) Circular Transition Indicators, the World Resources Institute (WRI) Aqueduct water risk atlas tool, the Value Balancing Alliance, and the Ellen MacArthur Foundation.

Core metrics for "Planet"

From among the shortlist of 21 core metrics, four under the pillar of "Planet" directly relate to corporate performance on environmental factors, thus providing a necessary foundation for companies that seek to eventually develop or attract green and sustainable finance:

Table 2. Core metrics for "Planet"

Theme	Description
Climate change	**Greenhouse gas (GHG) emissions** • For all relevant greenhouse gases (e.g. carbon dioxide, methane, nitrous oxide, F-gases, etc.), report in metric tonnes of carbon dioxide equivalent (tCO2e) GHG Protocol Scope 1 and Scope 2 emissions. • Estimate and report material upstream and downstream (GHG Protocol Scope 3) emissions where appropriate. **TCFD implementation** • Fully implement the recommendations of the TCFD. If necessary, disclose a timeline of at most three years for full implementation. • Disclose whether you have set, or have committed to set, GHG emissions targets that are in line with the goals of the Paris Agreement — to limit global warming to well below 2°C above preindustrial levels and pursue efforts to limit warming to 1.5°C — and to achieve netzero emissions before 2050.
Nature loss	**Land use and ecological sensitivity** • Report the number and area (in hectares) of sites owned, leased or managed in or adjacent to protected areas and/or key biodiversity areas (KBA).
Freshwater availability	**Water consumption and withdrawal in waterstressed areas** • Report operations where material: megalitres of water withdrawn, megalitres of water consumed and the percentage of each in regions with high or extremely high baseline water stress, according to WRI Aqueduct water risk atlas tool. • Estimate and report the same information for the full value chain (upstream and downstream) where appropriate.

Source: World Economic Forum et al., *Measuring Stakeholder Capitalism: Towards Common Metrics and Consistent Reporting of Sustainable Value Creation*, White Paper, September 2020.

Expanded metrics for "Planet"

In addition, 12 expanded metrics related to "Planet" indicate a "direction of travel" for companies or industry sectors that are more advanced in ESG reporting, as these indicators may soon (in the coming 3-5 years) meet the criteria of materiality, universality and feasibility that were set for the core metrics.

The expanded metrics reflect a mature approach to impact assessment that goes beyond basic figures of inputs and outputs, involving innovative methods for calculating socialised or monetised estimates of the effects of a company's operations in interaction with other contextual information (e.g. the impact of air pollution is magnified by local population density). Companies that master some or all of the expanded metrics may advance their relative position and opportunities in the market for GSF.

Table 3. Expanded metrics for "Planet"

Theme	Description
Climate change	**Paris-aligned GHG emissions targets** Define and report progress against time-bound science-based GHG emissions targets that are in line with the goals of the Paris Agreement — to limit global warming to well below 2°C above pre-industrial levels and pursue efforts to limit warming to 1.5°C. This should include defining a date before 2050 by which you will achieve net-zero GHG emissions, and interim reduction targets based on the methodologies provided by the SBTi, if applicable. **Impact of GHG emissions** Report wherever material along the value chain: the valued impact of GHG emissions. Disclose the estimate of the societal cost of carbon used and the source or basis for this estimate.
Nature loss	**Land use and ecological sensitivity** Report for operations (if applicable) and full supply chain (if material): • Area of land used for the production of basic plant, animal or mineral commodities (e.g. the area of land used for forestry, agriculture or mining activities). • Year-on-year change in the area of land used for the production of basic plant, animal or mineral commodities. • Percentage of land area in the first point above or of total plant, animal and mineral commodity inputs by mass or cost, covered by a sustainability certification standard or formalised sustainable management programme. **Impact of land use and conversion** Report wherever material along the value chain: the valued impact of use of land and conversion of ecosystems.
Freshwater availability	**Impact of freshwater consumption and withdrawal** Report wherever material along the value chain: the valued impact of freshwater consumption and withdrawal.
Air pollution	**Air pollution** Report wherever material along the value chain: nitrogen oxides (NOx), sulphur oxides (SOx), particulate matter and other significant air emissions. **Impact of air pollution** Report wherever material along the value chain: the valued impact of air pollution, including nitrogen oxides (NOx), sulphur oxides (SOx), particulate matter and other significant air emissions.

(continued)

Theme	Description
Water pollution	**Nutrients** Estimate and report wherever material along the value chain: metric tonnes of nitrogen, phosphorous and potassium in fertilizer consumed.
	Impact of water pollution Report wherever material along the value chain: the valued impact of water pollution, including excess nutrients, heavy metals and other toxins.
Solid waste	**Single-use plastics** Report wherever material along the value chain: estimated metric tonnes of single-use plastic consumed. Disclose the most significant applications of single-use plastic identified, the quantification approach used and the definition of single-use plastic adopted.
	Impact of solid waste disposal Report wherever material along the value chain: the valued societal impact of solid waste disposal, including plastics and other waste streams.
Resource availability	**Resource circularity** Report the most appropriate resource circularity metric(s) for the whole company and/or at a product, material or site level as applicable.

Source: World Economic Forum et al., *Measuring stakeholder capitalism: Towards common metrics and consistent reporting of sustainable value creation*, White Paper, September 2020.

Assessing the outlook for common ESG metrics

Several trends appear in the search to identify common ESG metrics, including those most closely related to environment and GSF opportunities:

1. **The dynamic materiality of intersectional issues:** Linkages between pillars, particularly the effects of planetary management on the health and well-being of people, have a significant impact on companies' risk factors. Additionally, the future financial materiality of factors, which are currently still mainly classified as social materiality, may present an opportunity to seize for companies ready to report on and improve their performance on the next generation of ESG metrics.

2. **Expanded metrics:** As mentioned, the expanded metrics indicate a likely "direction of travel" from core metrics, not only for the specific outputs that could be measured but also regarding the methodologies of impact assessment, which will represent the next frontier for corporate ESG reporting.

3. **Further institutional collaboration and consolidation:** This collaboration has brought together many of the key institutions that set ESG standards globally, including those that are referenced in the core and expanded metrics listed above, that have committed to working towards a joint ESG vision. Collaboration on data sharing may also take place in the near future between major providers of ESG-related data to allow more seamless input of corporate ESG information into databases and simplified access for investors and other consumers of sustainability-related information.

The World Economic Forum will continue to provide a platform for all relevant stakeholders, including from Greater China, to further explore these trends and seek common solutions where needed.

Insights from corporates and boards on the ESG journey in China

Recognising the importance of global metrics, a group of chief executive officers and chairpersons from leading Chinese corporates asked the World Economic Forum to lead an exploration of the state of ESG understanding, thinking and preparedness in China. Over the course of 2020, the World Economic Forum convened business leaders and subject matter experts in workshops and leadership discussions and complemented these dialogue opportunities with extensive desk research and expert interviews[15].

These explorations generated a number of key insights, discussed below.

Board-level commitment

All contributors to the World Economic Forum-facilitated roundtables and discussions identified the active engagement and support of the board as a prerequisite to a company's successful ESG journey. Initial motivations to embrace ESG frameworks and develop capacity to report on ESG performance may vary — including shareholder

---

15 Findings from this work were summarised in the White Paper, *A leapfrog moment for China in ESG reporting*, March 2021.

expectations, regulatory pressure, or personal convictions — yet at some point they have to manifest themselves in the explicit and active support of the company's board.

Once board commitment has been achieved, leadership must then communicate its ESG strategy to all levels of the organisation and develop the internal capacity to pursue and report on the strategy. Although an ESG or sustainability committee may support a firm's ESG efforts and take on responsibility for certain aspects of the strategy, it is the board that owns outcomes and provides organisational guidance.

Beyond traditional corporate social responsibility (CSR)

Chinese companies are at very different stages of their respective ESG journeys. While some are very sophisticated and global leaders in the area possessing sophisticated reporting capabilities, others, while ambitious and motivated, are just starting to develop frameworks and resources. What oftentimes complicates, even hinders, their efforts is the proliferation of concepts and acronyms, many of which are interchangeably used in China. Three in particular are repeatedly discussed and require clarification: ESG as compared to SDG investment, and CSR. While many regard ESG and SDG investing as synonymous, SDG-aligned investment strategies focus on companies producing products and services that seek to achieve the SDGs, whereas ESG focuses on the environmental, social and governance aspects of business operations with an eye towards enhancing risk management[16]. CSR activities, often in the form of volunteer programmes or the provision of funding to charitable foundations, are not necessarily integrated into a company's core business and managed as standalone efforts.

ESG and CSR efforts are thus inherently different sets of activities serving different goals through the employment of differing means.

Capacity-building and coordination

A shortage of ESG professionals has been identified as a major obstacle to broad-based adoption of ESG metrics and reporting in China. This shortage hinders the establishment

---

16 See the UN Secretary-General's Task Force on Digital Financing of the Sustainable Development Goals and World Economic Forum, "Unlocking capital markets to finance the SDGs", September 2019.

of processes, capacity buildout across business units, subsidiaries and partners and ultimately impacts a company's ability to gather and process relevant data. Extensive training is needed to equip employees with the tools to manage risks associated with environmental, inclusion or dignity issues and further develop understanding of ESG to include evolving issues such as climate or data privacy.

As the language to describe and address these issues differs somewhat in China compared to other jurisdictions, capacity and skill-building efforts have to be localised and expertise generally cannot be imported. This need for local skill building presents an additional bottleneck.

Sustainability in supply chains

While Chinese manufacturers are increasingly focused on developing their own, company-specific, ESG capacities, they are also focused on aligning practices and reporting throughout their supply chains. In some instances, these efforts originate downstream, for example by global — oftentimes European — brands requiring an upgrade of sustainability practices through the employment of frameworks such as the GRI Sustainability Reporting Standards, in others, Chinese firms proactively probe their suppliers and demand accountability. Manufacturers in the technology industry, for instance, have set up supplier social responsibility codes of conduct that also speak to ESG management requirements. Frameworks cover not only risk identification mechanisms but also processes for rectification, progress monitoring and the provision of coaching resources.

Insights from investors and shareholders

Investors are a major driver of the adoption of ESG frameworks and the deployment of resources to enhance reporting capacity. The removal of the investment quotas under China's Qualified Foreign Institutional Investor (QFII) and Renminbi (RMB) Qualified Foreign Institutional Investor (RQFII) programmes paired with ongoing pension reform efforts and the long-term shift of wealth tied up in traditional savings or real estate investments into capital-market-driven investments will continue to transform Chinese capital markets. Equity markets in particular will rapidly mature and institutionalise[17]. This institutionalisation of markets that are currently driven by retail investors will have consequences for listed companies that will increasingly be examined not only for their financial performance but also their non-financial performance as measured by ESG metrics.

Asset owners, asset managers and retail investors

2020 marked a pivotal year for ESG investing globally. ESG funds largely outperformed the broader market during the COVID-19-driven market selloff in February and March of 2020. ESG funds in the US also recorded record inflows[18]. Market commentators observed that ESG investing "can future-proof investments and in some cases boost return, all while helping to shape a better future"[19]. These demand dynamics, accelerated by the pandemic, are a major driver of the adoption of ESG frameworks by listed corporates in Mainland China. Forward-looking companies realise that access to financing and a high-quality investor base requires them to demonstrate their alignment with and strong performance on globally accepted ESG metrics.

In addition, demand is not only coming from global investors. Chinese asset managers and financing providers equally realise the benefits of employing an ESG lens to investment decisions. These benefits include the ability to offer differentiated products and enhance risk management practices. As the influence of professional asset managers on shaping Chinese markets will continue to accelerate and global capital allocations towards China will continue to increase as the Mainland capital market continues to open further, the pressure on Mainland listed corporates to build and enhance ESG reporting capabilities will only continue to grow.

Furthermore, investor demand for ESG disclosures and reporting is not only impacting listed companies. Private enterprises feel similar pressure from private equity investors who employ ESG frameworks in their investment decisions as risk management tools just like their peers managing public equities. In addition, these private equity firms see also similar demand dynamics for ESG products and funds from their Limited Partners.

---

17 See World Economic Forum in collaboration with Oliver Wyman, "China Asset Management at an Inflection Point", *Insight Report*, July 2020.

18 Source: Whieldon, E. and R. Clark, "ESG funds beat out S&P500 in 1st year of COVID-19; how 1 fund shot to the top", published on *S&P Global Market Intelligence* website, 6 April 2021.

19 See Fiona Reynolds, "COVID-19 accelerates ESG trends, global investors confirm", published on the *PRI* website, 3 September 2020.

State-owned enterprises (SOEs) and public-sector investment funds

While retail investors continue to drive market movement and volatility in the Mainland equity markets, the largest ownership group of listed companies in Mainland China are public investors which include central governments, local governments, public pension funds, state-owned enterprises (SOEs) and sovereign wealth funds. China's basic pension programme and National Social Security Fund (NSSF) together account for 80% of Mainland China's pension assets[20] and could thus be a significant trailblazer for ESG-aligned investment processes if policymakers decided to align these investment and pension vehicles accordingly. Government entities acting as SOE shareholders are attuned to national priorities, particularly on environmental and social welfare priorities. Any alignment between investment decisions and public policy should thus most likely occur around the 'E' of ESG, or green investments.

Green Investment Principles (GIP)

From ESG to green investment

Investment allocations in the wake of the COVID-19 pandemic showed that investors seek resilience. They are looking for companies that are able to weather any short-term storm and are positioning the business for long-term success. The Green Investment Principles for the "Belt and Road" Initiative (GIP in short) provide an important tool helping investors consider environmental risks with the goal of accelerating the green transition.

Theory of change and closing the gaps

"Belt and Road" Initiative (BRI) has unrealised potential to support the UN SDGs and Paris Agreement. Bringing together major financiers of BRI projects that will touch up to

---

20 Source: World Economic Forum in collaboration with Oliver Wyman, "China Asset Management at an Inflection Point", *Insight Report*, July 2020.

4.6 billion people, or 61% of the world's population[21], the GIP has a unique opportunity to support transformative environmental and social impacts.

To accelerate progress on implementation and address the lock-in risk of the BRI, the Secretariat of the GIP and the World Economic Forum are introducing a theory of change. Institutions and countries are at different starting points on green BRI investments. A consistent implementation gap exists between GIP signatories and economies along the "Belt and Road" on the resources, policies and measures to assess and manage climate risk, track and report data and ultimately drive a shift in capital allocations to green projects.

Unlocking green investment through regional chapters and "green BRI"

The GIP's diversified membership base from 14 economies in Asia, Europe and Africa, and practitioner-led Working Groups mean the GIP is in a unique position to build capacity. Integration and alignment with other international principles and standard-setting organisations, senior members of whom sit on the GIP Steering Committee, enables the GIP to tap into other networks and expertise to work towards Vision 2023, the strategy articulates a holistic picture of how the GIP will function with five key aims, respectively: access, disclose, commit, invest and grow.

GIP members collectively have great potential to contribute to scaling green project financing along the "Belt and Road". Combined global assets held by the 39 signatory institutions are in excess of US$41 trillion[22]. The majority of signatories who reported are actively engaging in developing or expanding their green financing activities and capabilities, and encouragingly close to 90% refer to national and/or international reference standards and taxonomies for defining what constitutes "green" investing[23].

---

21 Source: Refinitiv. *BRI Connect: An Initiative in Numbers, 3rd Edition: Understanding Risks and Rewards of Infrastructure Projects.*
22 Source: Calculated from annual reports published by GIP members.
23 Source: Calculated from annual reports published by GIP members.

The outstanding balance of green loans among GIP signatories amounted to over US$754 billion in 2019, and total issuance of green bonds in excess of US$138 billion[24]. Increasing quantitative reporting on green transactions is one of the priorities identified.

GIP members committed to the following five strategies:

- **Assess:** all GIP members will integrate climate risk into their governance structures;
- **Disclose:** all GIP members will make their first climate disclosures;
- **Commit:** 60% of GIP members will set quantitative green investment targets;
- **Invest:** green investment flows to the BRI will rise by over 35% from a 2020 baseline; and
- **Grow:** continue to expand the GIP's reach, aiming to bring on board major financing institutions while growing the global network of regional chapters.

Until now, the GIP has concentrated on the supply side, by focusing on the providers of capital to infrastructure projects, a vital lever. However, in order for the GIP to create the impact needed, there is a need for a next stage, a sprint from now to 2023, which will bring a more holistic approach to de-carbonisation, including a significant focus on recipient countries (the demand side).

This strategy is born out of consultations with GIP members, who have identified consistent barriers to green investment at the recipient country level. These barriers include the lack of the need for demand signals from emerging economies supported by robust enabling environments; a pipeline of bankable green projects; forums for discussions with key policy makers; and an understanding of the investment landscape and green investment potential. To overcome these barriers, stakeholders will launch the GIP Global Action Platform.

At the core of the GIP, next phase through 2023 will be a series of regional chapters. Regional chapters bring the current strength of the GIP — a core of major investors — into a local context with the potential to engage and transform regional financial institutions. This regional focus will zero in on structural barriers to green investment and work for the benefit of all major stakeholder groups: investors seeking to grow green investments, project developers seeking capital, and local communities seeking a better living environment.

---

24 Source: Data collated from GIP members.

By bridging supply and demand for green investment, the regional chapter approach will reinforce a virtuous cycle where climate-risk-sensitive capital flows to key countries and regions proactively, acting to deliver a green recovery.

Regional chapters will initially be set up in three countries in Central Asia, South East Asia and Africa, in a staggered timeline until 2023. Host countries will be selected on a set of criteria including carbon intensity of the economy, gross domestic product, implementation capacity, regional influence, and the scale of planned investments.

Through the GIP, it is important to facilitate the implementation of the standards and mobilise the local resources to achieve the SDGs and address climate risks. Local financial institutions need to learn from the international green investment champions on ESG investment to upscale the impact of green investment.

Outlook

As companies, investors and public sector stakeholders are not only accepting but also increasingly embracing the notion that non-financial disclosures and reporting is equally material to financial performance, dynamics advancing global common metrics efforts and adoption of ESG reporting processes will only accelerate. ESG metrics will move into integrated reports, reporting will get audited and assured, and capital allocation processes involve due diligence on sustainability performance.

While China will shape its own, distinct, ESG journey, there are strong incentives for corporates and public sector leaders to align approaches with global efforts and accepted best practices. Sophisticated ESG reporting capabilities also provide an important, widely accepted tool to Chinese businesses to articulate their story to a global audience. This audience is larger than merely investors and includes customers, potential employees and supervisors and regulators.

Policymakers — both globally and in China — are accelerating efforts particularly on climate. Given the important role they play in advancing ESG practices, their involvement will build momentum and drive adoption. This momentum is already visible, for example in the context of climate-related disclosures in filing materials, and the GIP offers a promising tool to streamline efforts within the boundaries of the BRI.

Given ESG investment's momentum, business leaders are well advised to drive the adoption of common metrics and the buildout of ESG reporting capacities, globally and China. The World Economic Forum's global metrics work and the GIP both are important tools at the disposal of corporate executives, policymakers and subject matter experts as they shape the green and sustainable finance area going forward.

第5章

轉變觀念，實行通用指標，促進GSF和ESG投資：全球實踐，中國落地

艾瑞碧
世界經濟論壇　大中華區首席代表

Emily BAYLEY
世界經濟論壇　「投資的未來」ESG 項目主管

姚凱力
世界經濟論壇　「中國和世界金融服務的未來」倡議負責人

宋莎
世界經濟論壇　循環經濟和價值鏈中國合作專家

摘要

針對公司（包括在中國內地和香港註冊成立及 / 或上市的公司）為衡量、報告和改善環境、社會及管治（environment、social、governance，簡稱 ESG）方面的績效而開展的工作，本章介紹了影響公司這方面工作就緒度的幾大因素，指出這些因素是企業發展或獲得綠色及可持續金融、為其長期價值創造和可持續發展願景提供更多資金支持的前提條件。報告分享了世界經濟論壇牽頭發起的多方利益相關者合作項目的經驗洞察，旨在現有框架基礎上制定一套根本性的、通用的和重要的 ESG 指標和披露標準，並針對如何開展一致的 ESG 報告提出了跨行業建議。

引言

發展並獲得綠色及可持續金融（green and sustainable finance，簡稱 GSF）能為企業提供重要機遇，幫助它們按照股東等利益相關者的要求，為長期的價值創造和可持續發展願景提供進一步的資金支持。中國內地、香港以及其他地區的企業在衡量、報告和改善環境、社會及管治（environment、social、governance，簡稱 ESG）績效方面若能一切就緒，將為全球 GSF 的發展奠定堅實基礎。

企業領導者已經加強公開承諾，切實履行企業公民責任，促進利益相關者合作，擴大私營部門貢獻，助力實現聯合國可持續發展目標。過去兩年間，企業作出的此類承諾包括世界經濟論壇《達沃斯宣言》[1] 和美國商業圓桌會議 [2] 等。

然而，包括大中華區企業在內的世界各地企業仍然面臨許多障礙，難以作出必要的戰略和營運變革，從單純闡述價值理念和指導原則，轉向全面開展 ESG 指標報告工作，從而達到投資者和員工、監管者和社會組織等其他利益相關者的要求。尤其是，各行各業的機構參與了 ESG 標準的制定，提出了各式各樣的 ESG 框架，這為廣大企業帶來了不確定性，使得它們在可持續發展報告和實踐的過程中變得小心謹慎。

2019 年以來，為了回應包括中國企業在內的全球一流企業的關切，助力解決 ESG 指標不一致給衡量和報告工作帶來的負擔，世界經濟論壇和國際工商理事會（成員包括積極參與世界經濟論壇交流合作的 120 家世界一流企業）以及「四大」會計師事務所 [3] 展開合作，旨在現有框架的基礎上，制定一套根本性的、通用的和重要的 ESG 指標與披露標準，並針對如何開展一致的 ESG 報告提出跨行業建議。合作各方經過協商研究，於 2020 年 9 月發佈了一份白皮書 [4]。

為了進一步促進和推動中國 ESG 的發展，世界經濟論壇一直致力於拓展這項初步的全球性工作，不斷召集頂級行業領袖和系統專家，探討中國如何將 ESG 理念與世界其他地區的實踐結合起來，同時還能保持鮮明的中國特色。從 2020 年 7 月到 2021 年 3 月，世界經濟

1　克勞斯·施瓦布，〈達沃斯宣言2020：第四次工業革命時代企業的普遍性目標〉（"Davos Manifesto 2020: The universal purpose of a company in the Fourth Industrial Revolution"），載於世界經濟論壇的網站上的〈Agenda〉網頁，2019年12月2日。

2　〈商業圓桌會議重新界定企業的目標，即推動發展「造福所有美國人」的經濟〉（"Business Roundtable redefines the purpose of a corporation to promote 'an economy that serves all Americans'"），載於美國商業圓桌會議的網站，2019年8月19日。

3　「四大」會計師事務所包括德勤、安永、畢馬威和普華永道。

4　參閱世界經濟論壇等《衡量利益相關者理念：制定通用指標和一致性報告，促進可持續價值創造》（*Measuring Stakeholder Capitalism: Towards Common Metrics and Consistent Reporting of Sustainable Value Creation*）白皮書，2020年9月。

論壇的多方利益相關者羣體花了九個月，審視了全球 ESG 指標工作，探討了將其推廣至中國的可行性。討論聚焦於在中國推廣 ESG 框架的主要動力和限制因素[5]。

中國 ESG 領軍者羣體最終可能會在世界經濟論壇會員企業在全球開展的工作基礎上，整合跨行業的各項通用 ESG 指標，與《「一帶一路」綠色投資原則》形成補充，後者由中國和全球利益相關者與世界經濟論壇攜手共同制定。

制定通用、可比的 ESG 指標：應對全球挑戰

要建立高可信度和可操作性，釋放綠色金融領域的新機會，或者催生價值創造型產品和服務，進一步推動各大市場的 ESG 轉型，就必須為 ESG 報告工作奠定堅實基礎。雖然金融行業對於 ESG 和綠色金融工具已有深入理解，但其他行業的企業領袖對 ESG 和 GSF 的領域和機遇缺乏認識或參與不足。

為此，世界經濟論壇與企業的首席執行官和董事長緊密合作，幫助他們從戰略層面了解報告重大 ESG 因素的商業理由，並繼續整合主要的 ESG 指標和披露要求，使更多企業不僅將 ESG 工作視為合規要求或慈善行為，而是必要之舉。

確定 ESG 報告的商業理由

ESG 報告是一個全球趨勢：2020 年，聯合國支持的責任投資原則組織（Principles for Responsible Investment，簡稱 PRI）各簽約機構管理的資產規模超過了 100 萬億美元，比 2015 年增加了 75%[6]。

即使面對新冠疫情帶來的經濟和金融壓力，投資者對可持續資產的興趣依然有增無減。全球範圍內，公募基金和交易所開放式指數基金對可持續資產的投資比 2019 年增長了 96%，在 2020 年的前 11 個月達到了 2,880 億美元[7]。

5　參閱世界經濟論壇《ESG報告，助力中國騰飛聚勢共贏》白皮書，2021年3月。

6　資料來源：《PRI》網站上的〈2006-2020年期間負責任投資原則組織的發展〉（"PRI growth 2006—2020"）數據集，於2021年2月9日下載。

7　間接引自貝萊德〈勞倫斯·芬克致企業首席執行官函〉（載於貝萊德的網站，於2021年4月1日閱覽），源自：Simfund、Broadridge、GBI，截至2020年11月的數據（未包括封閉式基金和母基金，但包括貨幣基金）。

投資者將對 ESG 報告的日益重視，逐漸從投放於其對 ESG 有影響力的投資轉向其主流投資，尤其是機構投資者更是重視氣候風險的報告和披露。例如從 2020 年初開始，為基金會和養老金提供服務的貝萊德集團等知名資產管理公司對其投資的所有公司提出了新的要求，要求它們按照氣候相關財務信息披露工作組（Task Force on Climate-related Financial Disclosures，簡稱 TCFD）和永續會計準則委員會（Sustainability Accounting Standards Board，簡稱 SASB）的建議來發佈報告[8]。

因此，對於尋求投融資的企業來說，可靠、優質的 ESG 報告至關重要。在日益關注氣候變化和其他環境與社會風險因素的社會和監管形勢下，企業要想維持「營運執照」也必須進行這樣的 ESG 報告。

但是，世界經濟論壇和安聯集團以及波士頓諮詢公司在 2019 年 1 月發佈的研究[9]顯示，有效的 ESG 披露面臨三大障礙：ESG 報告事項非常複雜，給企業帶來了負擔；企業 ESG 數據之間缺乏可比性；以及企業對 ESG 評級機構了解不夠，雙方之間缺少互動交流。

統一 ESG 報告的指標和披露標準

2020 年，世界經濟論壇通過國際工商理事會召集了全球最大規模的私營部門合作夥伴，致力於凝聚各方共識，圍繞 ESG 披露工作制定通用指標，旨在改變報告生態系統，促進重大 ESG 因素和長期價值考量的統一和標準化。

對於參與制定 ESG 標準的機構所需具備的專業性，以及對投資者和企業責任的管理模式轉變涉及的複雜性，我們不能低估。作為推動公營與私營部門合作的國際組織，世界經濟論壇提供平台，讓這些利益相關者會面、交流觀點和關注事項，以及採取共同行動，以應對全球挑戰。

讓這些商業利益相關者參與制定 ESG 標準具有重要價值，這一點已經得到了整個生態系統的認可。作為極具影響力的羣體，他們能夠在 ESG 績效方面發揮自身領導力，引領並推動其他企業開展 ESG 的最佳實踐和報告工作。

8　參閱貝萊德〈勞倫斯‧芬克致企業首席執行官函 —— 迎接金融新變局〉，載於貝萊德的網站，於2021年4月1日閱覽。

9　世界經濟論壇、安聯集團和波士頓諮詢公司《尋求ESG的回報：推動報告生態系統的發展，釋放商業和社會效益》（*Seeking Return on ESG: Advancing the Reporting Ecosystem to Unlock Impact for Business and Society*）白皮書，2019年1月，載於世界經濟論壇的網站。

在六個多月內對 200 多家企業、投資者和其他利益相關者所進行的諮詢調研結果顯示,他們當中超過 75% 認同「按照一套通用的、跨越行業的指標來報告 ESG 事項,對公司、金融市場以至整個經濟都非常有利」[10]。

界定 ESG 對實現戰略目標的重要性和相關性

企業進行有效的 ESG 報告面臨一項重大挑戰,即如何確定最重要的指標作匯報。重要性是指「對於長期價值創造具有重要性、相關性及 / 或關鍵性的信息」(同時也指出「隨着各地區監管政策和期望的不同,具重要性的事項以及應當在年報中披露的內容也會有所差異」)[11]。

在推進 ESG 工作的過程中,企業必須採取的一個戰略步驟是確定在需要披露的各項 ESG 要素中,哪些事項是與該企業或行業的長期財務績效最為相關。

然而,「一些『財務前』信息 […] 或許嚴格來説在短期內不具重要性,但對社會和地球具有重要性,因此對於中長期財務績效可能具有重要性。重要性是一個動態概念,原本只與社會價值相關的一些事項可能會迅速具有財務重要性」[12]。

世界經濟論壇和波士頓諮詢公司在 2020 年 3 月聯合發佈的《迎接新的「重要性原則」時代,加快 ESG 的發展步伐》(*Embracing the New Age of Materiality: Harnessing the Pace of Change in ESG*)白皮書對此進行了深入分析。

選擇通用 ESG 指標的準則

在篩選 ESG 指標、並對指標進行優先排序時,我們採用了下列準則。這些準則載列於世界經濟論壇 2020 年 9 月發佈的相關白皮書,並獲得了國際工商理事會成員的認可[13]:

- 與現有框架和標準的一致性;
- 對於長期價值創造的重要性;
- 可實施的範圍;
- 在各行各業和各種商業模式中的通用性;以及
- 監測相關報告的可行性。

---

10 參閱世界經濟論壇等《衡量利益相關者理念:制定通用指標和一致性報告,促進可持續價值創造》白皮書,2020年9月,第6頁。
11 同上,第13與14頁。
12 同上,第14頁。
13 世界經濟論壇等《衡量利益相關者理念:制定通用指標和一致性報告,促進可持續價值創造》白皮書,第6頁。

通過嚴格的磋商程序後，最終甄選出了 21 項核心指標和 34 項擴展的披露標準，並將這些指標和標準歸納入下列四大主題性支柱要素。

ESG 報告的四大主題性支柱

精細化 ESG 指標能為企業、投資者和監管者提供有用工具，幫助他們評估、對比和獎勵非財務性的公司績效和風險因素。但是，將社會目標細化成若干細節並非參與企業的唯一目標，因為他們致力於為投資者和整個社會建立長期價值主張。

有鑒於此，世界經濟論壇和利益相關者確定了下列四大支柱要素。這些主題相互關聯，表達了企業和投資者開展 ESG 報告和改善績效、實現繁榮發展背後的根本目標 [14]：

1. **管治原則**：隨着人們日益希望各機構能夠確定其發展目標，並將其置於業務經營的核心，關於管治的定義也在不斷變化，但代理、問責和管理等原則還是真正意義上「善治」的關鍵。

2. **地球**：致力於保護地球，使其免遭生態惡化，包括採取可持續的消費和生產方式、可持續地管理地球上的自然資源，以及採取應對氣候變化的緊急行動，以確保地球能夠滿足當前和未來世代的需求。

3. **人類**：致力於消除一切形式和層面的貧困和飢餓，建設平等、健康和有尊嚴的環境，讓所有人充分釋放發展潛力。

4. **繁榮發展**：致力於確保全體人類享有繁榮社會和有意義的生活，確保在人類與自然和諧共生的同時，實現經濟、社會和技術的進步。

---

14 同上，圖2。

表 1：ESG 報告的四大支柱要素和 21 項核心指標（與聯合國可持續發展目標相關）

管治原則	地球	人類	繁榮發展
1. 設定目標	7. 溫室氣體排放	11. 多元化和包容（%）	17. 絕對就業人數和就業率
2. 管治機構構成	8. 落實 TCFD 的建議	12. 薪酬平等（%）	18. 經濟貢獻
3. 影響利益相關者的重要問題	9. 土地利用和生態敏感性	13. 工資水平（%）	19. 投資
4. 反腐敗	10. 用水緊張地區的淡水消耗和抽取	14. 童工或強制性勞動力遭遇事故的風險	20. 研發總開支（$）
5. 保密道德建議與舉報機制		15. 健康和安全（%）	21. 納稅總額
6. 將風險和機遇納入業務流程		16. 所提供的培訓（#, $）	
相關的可持續發展目標：	**相關的可持續發展目標：**	**相關的可持續發展目標：**	**相關的可持續發展目標：**
#12 負責任消費和生產	#6 清潔飲水和衛生設施	#1 無貧窮	#1 無貧窮
#16 和平、正義和強大機構	#7 經濟適用的清潔能源	#3 良好健康與福祉	#8 體面工作和經濟增長
#17 促進目標實現的夥伴關係	#12 負責任消費和生產	#4 優質教育	#9 產業、創新和基礎設施
	#13 氣候行動	#5 性別平等	#10 減少不平等
	#14 水下生物	#8 體面工作和經濟增長	
	#15 陸地生物	#10 減少不平等	

資料來源：世界經濟論壇等《衡量利益相關者理念：制定通用指標和一致性報告，促進可持續價值創造》白皮書，2020 年 9 月。

上述每一支柱都包含了更加精細化的 ESG 指標，反映了經濟系統中的所有相關者在思考如何通過其營運來實現可持續發展目標的過程中需要遵守的原則，也為企業提供了創造長期、可持續價值的路線圖，幫助它們為建設包容、可持續的世界作出貢獻。

審視與綠色及可持續金融相關的特定指標

當今世界，人們愈發認識到亟需採取行動，來解決人類活動造成的氣候變化、生物多樣性喪失和其他地球生態問題，因此企業的使命已經不再局限於「無害」，而是進而為國家和全球減排目標以及其他資源管理計劃作出積極貢獻。

為了整合（而不是制定大量的）企業 ESG 報告指標，下文關於環境可持續性的各項指標基本是在現有建議的基礎上制定或拓展而來。這些現有建議來自廣泛的可信資源，包括但不限於：全球報告倡議組織（Global Reporting Initiative，簡稱 GRI）、國際標準化組織（International Organisation for Standardisation，簡稱 ISO）、SASB、TCFD、氣候信息披露標準委員會（Climate Disclosure Standards Board）、溫室氣體核算體系（Greenhouse Gas Protocol）、科學基礎減碳目標倡議組織（Science Based Targets Initiative，簡稱 SBTi）、《自然資本議定書》、美國國家環境保護局、世界可持續發展工商理事會（World Business Council for Sustainable Development）循環轉型指標、世界資源研究所「水道水風險地圖集」工具、價值平衡聯盟（Value Balancing Alliance）和艾倫 · 麥克阿瑟基金會（Ellen MacArthur Foundation）。

有關「地球」的核心指標

在 21 項核心指標中，「地球」支柱下有四項和企業環境績效直接相關，因此能為企業提供必要基礎，幫助它們最終開發或吸引綠色及可持續金融。

表 2：有關「地球」的核心指標

主題	描述
氣候變化	**溫室氣體排放** • 對於所有相關的溫室氣體（如二氧化碳、甲烷、一氧化二氮、含氟氣體等），報告溫室氣體核算體系範圍 1 和 2 的排放情況，以二氧化碳當量噸（tCO2e）為單位。 • 如具重要性，還需估計和報告上下游（溫室氣體核算體系範圍 3）的排放情況。 **TCFD 的建議落實情況** • 充分落實 TCFD 的相關建議。如有必要，披露長達三年的建議落實時間表。 • 披露公司是否已經設定或承諾設定溫室氣體排放目標，以實現《巴黎協定》的目標 —— 在工業前水平基礎上將全球氣溫升幅控制在攝氏 2 度以內，努力控制在攝氏 1.5 度以內，力爭在 2050 年前實現淨零排放。
自然損失	**土地利用和生態敏感性** • 報告在保護區及 / 或生物多樣性關鍵區域附近擁有、租賃或管理的場地數量和面積（公頃）。
淡水可用性	**用水緊張地區的淡水消耗和抽取** • 報告具有重要性的營運情況：使用世界資源研究所「水道水風險地圖集」工具，報告抽水量（百萬公升）和耗水量（百萬公升），及其在水資源高度或極度緊張地區的比例情況。 • 如恰當，估計和報告整個價值鏈的同類信息（上下游）。

資料來源：世界經濟論壇等《衡量利益相關者理念：制定通用指標和一致性報告，促進可持續價值創造》白皮書，2020 年 9 月。

有關「地球」的擴展指標

對於處在 ESG 報告較高級階段的企業或行業部門來說，有關「地球」的 12 項擴展指標為其指出了「前進的方向」，因為這些指標或許在未來 3-5 年內就能符合重要性、通用性和可行性等核心指標的準則。

這些擴展指標體現了成熟的影響力評估方法，不僅包含基礎的投入和產出數據，而且結合其他情境化信息（如當地人口密度能夠放大空氣污染的影響），採取創新的方式來估計公司營運所產生的社會或貨幣成本。滿足部分或全部擴展指標的企業或許能在 GSF 市場上獲得更多的優勢和機遇。

表 3：有關「地球」的擴展指標

主題	描述
氣候變化	**與《巴黎協定》一致的溫室氣體減排目標** 對照有時間限制的科學減排目標，確定和報告減碳進展，助力實現《巴黎協定》的目標——在工業前水平基礎上將全球氣溫升幅控制在攝氏 2 度以內，努力控制在攝氏 1.5 度以內。為此，需要在 2050 年前設定一個日期，實現公司的淨零排放，並在適用的情況下，按照 SBTi 提供的方法，制定中期減排目標。
	溫室氣體排放的影響 報告溫室氣體排放對整個價值鏈的量值影響。披露對所使用碳的社會成本的估值，及其來源或依據。
自然損失	**土地利用和生態敏感性** 報告營運情況（如適用）和整個供應鏈情況（如具重要性）： • 用於生產基本植物、動物或礦物的土地面積（如林業、農業或礦業用地面積）。 • 用於生產基本植物、動物或礦物的土地面積的年度同比變化。 • 使用可持續認證標準或遵循正規的可持續管理計劃，報告上述第一點各類土地的佔比或植物、動物和礦物生產要素（按投入量或成本）的佔比。
	土地利用和轉換的影響 報告對整個價值鏈的重要性影響：土地利用和生態系統轉換所產生的量值影響。
淡水可用性	**淡水消耗和抽取的影響** 報告對整個價值鏈的重要性影響：淡水消耗和抽取產生的量值影響。
空氣污染	**空氣污染** 報告對整個價值鏈的重要性影響：氮氧化物、硫氧化合物、顆粒物和其他重要的空氣排放物。
	空氣污染的影響 報告對整個價值鏈的重要性影響：空氣污染產生的量值影響，包括氮氧化物、硫氧化合物、顆粒物和其他重要的空氣排放物。
水污染	**營養物** 估計和報告對整個價值鏈的重要性影響：消耗的化肥中的含氮量、含磷量和含鉀量（公噸）。
	水污染的影響 報告對整個價值鏈的重要性影響：水污染所產生的量值影響，包括多餘營養物、重金屬和其他毒素。

（續）

主題	描述
固體 廢棄物	**一次性塑料** 報告對整個價值鏈的重要性影響：估計消耗的一次性塑料的數量（公噸）。披露一次性塑料的最重要用途、所採用的量化方法和對一次性塑料的定義。
	固體廢棄物處理的影響 報告對整個價值鏈的重要性影響：處理固體廢棄物（包括塑料和其他廢棄物）對社會產生的量值影響。
資源 可用性	**資源的可循環性** 在整個公司及 / 或相關產品、材料或工廠層面，報告最適合的資源可循環性指標。

資料來源：世界經濟論壇等《衡量利益相關者理念：制定通用指標和一致性報告，促進可持續價值創造》白皮書，2020 年 9 月。

評估通用 ESG 指標的前景

在尋求制定通用 ESG 指標的過程中，出現了幾個趨勢，其中有些和環境以及 GSF 機遇密切相關：

1. **跨部門事項的動態重要性**：幾大支柱之間的關聯性，特別是通過管理地球而對人類健康和福祉的影響，能夠極大影響企業的風險因素。此外，一些因素目前雖仍然主要屬於社會重要性，但未來可能會具有財務重要性，企業可以把握這個機會，按下一代 ESG 指標來報告和改善其績效。

2. **擴展指標**：如前所述，擴展指標可能代表着核心指標的「前進方向」，不僅關乎被衡量的具體產出，而且也涉及影響力評估的方法體系，這將代表着企業 ESG 報告的下一個前沿領域。

3. **機構之間的進一步協作和整合**：這種協作已經匯集了全球範圍內參與制定 ESG 標準的多個關鍵機構，包括上文所述核心和擴展指標中提及的那些機構，這些機構都致力於實現共同的 ESG 願景。不久的將來，ESG 數據的主要供應商之間可能會進行數據共享協作，從而將企業 ESG 信息無縫融入數據庫，並為投資者和其他可持續信息消費者提供更加簡化的訪問流程。

世界經濟論壇將繼續為包括大中華區利益相關者在內的各方提供平台，進一步探討這些趨勢並酌情制定共同的解決方案。

企業和企業董事會關於 ESG 在中國發展的洞察

正是認識到全球性指標的重要性，中國一流企業的多位首席執行官和董事長希望世界經濟論壇牽頭開展研究，探討目前中國對 ESG 的認識、看法和準備程度。因此，世界經濟論壇在 2020 年召集商業領袖和相關專家舉行多次研討和領導人會談，並開展了廣泛的案頭研究和專家訪談，以此補充會談的成果[15]。

這些研究產生了大量重要洞察，於以下各節作討論。

董事會層面的支持

所有參加世界經濟論壇圓桌會議和討論會的人士都認為，董事會的積極參與和支持是企業成功開展 ESG 工作的前提條件。企業接納 ESG 框架並建立對 ESG 績效進行報告的能力的初始動機可能各有不同 —— 包括股東期望、監管壓力或個人信念，但不管如何，企業董事會明確而積極的支持都至關重要。

一旦董事會承諾給予支持，領導層就必須向機構內各層面傳達其 ESG 戰略，並建設相應的內部能力，來實施和報告這一戰略。雖說 ESG 委員會或可持續發展委員會能夠支持企業的 ESG 工作，並能承擔起 ESG 戰略的某些責任，但歸根結底，是由董事會對結果負責並向整個機構提供指導。

超越傳統的企業社會責任

中國企業處於 ESG 事業的不同階段。有些企業已經成為這一領域的全球領導者，具備了非常專業的報告能力，而有些企業雖然雄心勃勃、動力十足，卻才剛開始制定框架和籌集資源。通常讓這項工作變得非常複雜，甚至阻礙這項工作開展的，是各式各樣的概念和縮略語，其中有許多在中國往往被混用。尤其被反覆討論的是三大概念，需要加以澄清：環境、社會及管治（ESG）、可持續發展目標（sustainable development goals，簡稱 SDG）和企業社會責任（corporate social responsibility，簡稱 CSR）。雖然許多人認為 ESG 和 SDG 投資意思相同，但與 SDG 保持一致的投資戰略通常關注那些以 SDG 為導向來生產產品和提供服務的企業，而 ESG 則更關注企業經營過程中的環境、社會及管治環節，着眼於提高

15　這項工作的研究成果已在《ESG報告，助力中國騰飛聚勢共贏》白皮書作出總結，2021年3月。

風險管理能力 [16]。CSR 活動通常表現為志願者項目或者為慈善基金會提供資助，但並不一定會納入企業的核心業務，而是作為一種單獨的活動加以管理。

因此，ESG 和 CSR 是通過採取不同方式來追求不同目標的兩種不同性質的活動。

能力建設和協調

缺乏 ESG 專業人才一直是 ESG 指標和報告在中國廣泛應用的主要障礙。這不僅會影響業務部門、分支機構和合作夥伴的流程部署和能力建設，更會最終影響企業採集和處理相關數據的能力。因此，需要開展廣泛的培訓，為員工提供工具，幫助他們管理與環境、包容或尊嚴問題有關的風險，加深對 ESG 工作的理解，包括氣候或數據隱私等不斷演變的問題。

在中國，描述和解決這些問題所用的語言與其他司法權區略有不同，且相關專長無法從國外引入，因此必須建立本地化的能力和技巧。這種對本地技能的需求構成了 ESG 工作的另一個瓶頸。

供應鏈的可持續發展

雖然中國製造業企業日益注重建立自身的 ESG 能力，但它們也着重在整條供應鏈上採取一致做法和報告方式。有些情況下，這樣的工作由下游發起，例如全球（尤其是歐洲）的品牌會要求採用 GRI 可持續報告標準等框架，來升級可持續實踐。中國企業也會積極調查其供應商的情況，要求其承擔起 ESG 責任。舉例説，技術行業的製造商已經按照 ESG 管理要求，制定了供應商社會責任行為規範。這些框架不僅包括風險識別機制，也包括問題整改、進展監測和提供輔導資源的流程。

投資者和股東的洞察

投資者是企業採用 ESG 框架和部署資源來提高報告能力的主要推動力量。下列幾項因素將共同發揮作用，繼續推動中國資本市場的轉型：中國取消了合格境外機構投資者和人民

16　參閱聯合國秘書長數字金融工作組和世界經濟論壇〈釋放資本市場的力量，為可持續發展目標提供資金支持〉（"Unlocking capital markets to finance the SDGs"），2019年9月。

幣合格境外機構投資者計劃下的投資額度;中國持續推進養老金改革;以及傳統儲蓄和房地產投資蓄積的財富持續轉向資本市場投資。尤其是證券市場將快速發展成熟並實現制度化[17]。當前,零售投資者推動下的市場制度化將會給上市公司帶來影響:不僅要評估其財務績效,也要通過 ESG 指標來衡量其非財務績效。

資產所有者、資產管理者和零售投資者

2020 年是全球 ESG 投資的關鍵之年。2020 年 2 月和 3 月,在新冠疫情引發市場拋售的情況下,ESG 主題基金的表現大多跑贏了大市。美國 ESG 基金也吸引了創紀錄的資金流入[18]。市場評論人士指出,ESG 投資「是能夠防範未來風險的投資,有時候能夠提高投資回報,同時還能助力塑造更加美好的未來」[19]。在新冠疫情的推動下,這些需求的動態變化成為中國內地上市企業採用 ESG 框架的主要動力。具前瞻性的企業意識到,要獲得融資和優質的投資者,它們就必須展現它們實行了全球通用的 ESG 指標,並在此方面取得了卓越表現。

此外,需求不僅來自於全球投資者。中國的資產管理公司和資金提供者同樣已認識到從 ESG 角度考慮投資決策的價值所在。這些價值包括能夠提供差異化的產品和完善風險管理實踐。隨著專業資產管理公司對中國市場產生的影響持續增速,以及全球資本在中國內地資本市場加大開放力度下不斷增加在中國市場的配置份額,中國內地上市企業面臨着越來越大的壓力,去建立和加強其 ESG 報告的能力。

而且,投資者對 ESG 披露和報告的需求不僅影響着上市企業,私營企業同樣也感受到了來自私募股權投資者的壓力,這些投資者將 ESG 框架作為風險管理工具,用於投資決策,這和其他投資者管理公共股權的做法一樣。此外,私募股權公司的有限合夥人也會圍繞 ESG 產品和資金,向私募股權公司提出類似的需求。

---

17 參閱世界經濟論壇與奧緯諮詢〈中國資產管理行業進入發展拐點〉,《洞察力報告》,2020年7月。

18 資料來源:E. Whieldon, 與 R. Clark〈新冠疫情第一年,ESG基金跑贏標普500指數:一基金如何登頂〉("ESG funds beat out S&P500 in 1st year of COVID-19; how 1 fund shot to the top"),載於《標普全球市場資訊》(*S&P Global Market Intelligence*)網站,2021年4月6日。

19 參閱Fiona Reynolds〈全球投資者證實,新冠疫情加速ESG 發展趨勢〉("COVID-19 accelerates ESG trends, global investors confirm"),載於 *PRI* 網站,2020年9月3日。

國有企業和公共投資基金

雖然個人投資者持續推動中國內地證券市場的行情和波幅，但內地上市企業的最大股東卻是公共投資者，包括中央政府、地方政府、公共養老金、國有企業和主權財富基金。中國基本養老計劃和全國社會保障基金合共持有中國內地養老金資產的 80%[20]，因此如果政策制定者決定將 ESG 投資和養老資金掛鈎，它們即可以成為這一投資流程的開拓性力量。作為國有企業股東的政府實體非常了解國家重點事項，尤其是環境和社會福利領域的重點事項。投資決策和公共政策的協同最有可能在 ESG 的 E 領域（即環境）或者是綠色投資領域發生。

綠色投資原則

從 ESG 到綠色投資

新冠疫情之後的投資配置趨勢表明，投資者尋求的是韌性。他們希望投資的公司要能抵禦短期風暴，而業務經營要着眼長遠。《「一帶一路」綠色投資原則》（Green Investment Principles for the "Belt and Road" Initiative，簡稱 GIP）為投資者提供了重要工具，幫助他們考慮環境風險，加快推動綠色轉型。

變革理論和消除差距

在助力實現聯合國可持續發展目標和《巴黎協定》方面，「一帶一路」倡議有很大潛力。GIP 匯集了「一帶一路」項目的主要供資者，項目覆蓋 46 億人（世界人口的 61%）[21]，故能提供獨特機會，支持實現環境和社會的轉型。

為了加快實踐和應對「一帶一路」倡議所蘊藏的風險，GIP 秘書處和世界經濟論壇正在引入一種變革理論。在「一帶一路」綠色投資方面，各個機構和各個國家的起點不同。GIP 簽約方和「一帶一路」沿線經濟體在實踐上一直存在差距，雙方需要共同部署資源、政策和措施，旨在評估和管理氣候風險，追蹤和報告數據，最終引導資本流向綠色項目。

20　資料來源：世界經濟論壇與奧緯諮詢〈中國資產管理行業進入發展拐點〉，《洞察力報告》，2020年7月。

21　資料來源：路孚特《「一帶一路」倡議背後的數字 —— 第三期報告：了解基礎設施項目的風險和回報》（*BRI Connect: An Initiative in Numbers, 3rd Edition: Understanding Risks and Rewards of Infrastructure Projects*）。

通過區域分支和「綠色一帶一路」，釋放綠色投資的力量

GIP 的成員非常多元化，涵蓋亞洲、歐洲和非洲的 14 個經濟體，並組建了由從業者領導的工作小組，這表明 GIP 具有能力建設的獨特優勢。GIP 和其他國際原則和標準制定組織進行了協調和對接，邀請其高級成員加入 GIP 指導委員會，這使得 GIP 能夠利用其他網絡和專長，共同致力於實現 2023 年願景。GIP 的戰略清晰闡述了全面的發展願景，顯示了 GIP 的五大目標：評估、披露、承諾、投資和發展。

從整體來看，GIP 成員能夠釋放巨大潛力，有望加大綠色項目融資力度，支持「一帶一路」建設。39 個 GIP 簽約機構持有的全球總資產超過 41 萬億美元 [22]，其中絕大多數簽約機構正在積極開展或擴大綠色金融活動和能力。尤其令人鼓舞的是，近 90% 的簽約機構在定義「綠色」投資時，參照了國家及 / 或國際參考標準和分類標準 [23]。

2019 年，GIP 簽約機構的綠色貸款餘額超過 7,540 億美元，綠色債券的發行總額超過 1,380 億美元 [24]。加大對綠色交易的量化報告力度是已確定的重點工作之一。

GIP 成員承諾實行下列五大戰略：

- **評估**：所有 GIP 成員將會把氣候風險納入其治理架構；
- **披露**：所有 GIP 成員將首次進行氣候信息披露；
- **承諾**：60% 的 GIP 成員將制定可量化的綠色投資目標；
- **投資**：流向「一帶一路」項目的綠色投資金額將在 2020 年基礎上增加 35% 以上；以及
- **發展**：繼續擴大 GIP 的覆蓋範圍，旨在吸納更多大型金融機構，同時壯大由區域分支組成的全球性網絡。

截至目前，GIP 主要關注供給側，即基礎設施項目的資本提供者（是為重要槓桿）。但是，為了建立必要的影響力，GIP 必須進入下一個發展階段，向 2023 年衝刺，這將實現更加全面的脫碳策略，包括關注投資接受國（需求側）。

這項戰略是與 GIP 各成員共同協商的結果。各成員已經認清了接受國發展綠色投資面臨的長期障礙，包括新興經濟體缺少有利的穩定政策環境，因而無法傳遞有效的需求信號；缺少絡繹不絕的可融資綠色項目；缺少與關鍵政策制定者對話的討論平台；以及缺乏對投資格局和綠色投資潛力的認識。為了消除這些障礙，利益相關者將發起「GIP 全球行動平台」。

---

22 資料來源：根據GIP成員年度報告進行的計算。
23 資料來源：根據GIP成員年度報告進行的計算。
24 資料來源：經GIP成員核對的數據。

在向 2023 年衝刺的新階段，一系列區域分支將發揮核心作用。區域分支能匯聚 GIP 當前的優勢（主要投資者的核心平台），將其融入本地環境，有望將區域性金融機構起動與轉型。這種區域化的運作方式將能凸顯和消除綠色投資的結構性障礙，努力造福所有主要的利益相關者羣體：投資者希望加大綠色投資；項目開發者尋求資本；而當地社區希望獲得更加優質的生活環境。

通過對接綠色投資的供需關係，區域分支的運作策略有助於建立良性循環，促進氣候風險敏感性資本主動流向關鍵國家和地區，推動經濟的綠色復甦。

在 2023 年之前，將首先在中亞、東南亞和非洲的三個國家相繼設立區域分支。這三個國家將依據一套準則甄選產生，包括經濟的碳強度、國內生產總值、實踐能力、區域影響力和已計劃投資的規模。

各相關方必須通過 GIP，促進各項標準的實施，動員當地資源，實現可持續發展目標和應對氣候風險。當地金融機構需要向 ESG 投資領域的國際綠色投資領軍者學習，共同擴大綠色投資的影響力。

前景展望

非財務信息的披露和報告相對於財務績效同樣重要，這種理念正在日益受到企業、投資者和公共部門利益相關者的接受和歡迎。在此背景下，制定全球通用指標和推廣 ESG 報告的動力會不斷增強。ESG 指標會被納入合併報告，ESG 報告會接受審計和獲得鑒證，資本配置流程亦會增加對可持續績效的盡職調查。

雖然中國會在 ESG 方面建立自身特色，但企業和公共部門領導者也有強大的動力，按照國際經驗和公認的最佳實踐來積極建立 ESG 發展策略。專業的 ESG 報告能力也能為中國企業提供一項獲得各方認可的重要工具，向全球受眾講述它們的故事。全球受眾不僅包括投資者，也包括客戶、潛在員工、監督者和監管者。

中國與全球的政策制定者正在不斷努力，加快應對氣候變化。鑒於他們在推進 ESG 工作方面的重要性，他們的參與有助於普及 ESG 並形成勢頭。這種趨勢已經清晰可見，尤其是氣候相關的信息正在通過各類匯報文件進行披露，而 GIP 在這方面正提供了一個很有前景的工具，能夠在「一帶一路」框架下簡化各項工作。

鑒於 ESG 投資已經獲得良好的發展勢頭，我們建議中國和世界各國的商業領袖推廣使用通用指標，建設和完善 ESG 報告能力。在企業高管、政策制定者和專家學者努力塑造綠色及可持續金融的過程中，世界經濟論壇開展的全球指標工作和 GIP 可以為他們提供重要的工具。

Chapter 6

Classification of ESG investment products in the global market

Mary LEUNG, CFA
Head, Advocacy, Asia Pacific
CFA Institute

Sivananth RAMACHANDRAN, CFA
Director, Capital Markets Policy
CFA Institute

Summary

In this chapter, we examine the classification of environmental, social, and governance (ESG) investment products in the global market to shed light on both the progress and challenges. This includes an overview and outlook of the global regulatory landscape, voluntary industry standards, ESG investment approaches, application of labels and classification to investment products, as well as opportunities and challenges in the area.

Having a clear ESG classification system for investment products, be it through regulations, voluntary labels or standards, can offer significant benefits to both investors and investment managers. Investors looking for ESG or sustainability products would thereby save time and effort when navigating a large universe of investment products, and would have greater confidence in the features that such products claim to offer. For investment managers, a well-defined system can help them communicate their investment philosophy, approach and commitment to ESG and sustainability to their clients.

This is a fast-evolving area. Although the opportunities are immense, the rising demand for ESG-themed products and the growing number of such products on the market have given rise to the need for greater scrutiny, and for more informed labels, classification and standards. A higher level of transparency that allows investors to better understand the ESG and sustainability features of such products will go a long way toward fostering trust and sustaining growth in the system.

Introduction

Since the launch of the first sustainable mutual fund in 1970, an increasing number of investors are focused on widening the scope of their analyses to criteria beyond the traditional financial metrics by incorporating environmental, social, and governance (ESG) factors into their investment analyses. In recent years, this focus has been elevated to a new level for the following reasons:

- Increased awareness by investors of the potential impact that ESG factors may have on the value of an investment;

- Greater availability of ESG disclosures by issuers, as well as ESG data and information from third-party providers that aid in investment decision making; and

- Intensifying regulatory scrutiny of "greenwashing"—"greenwashing" refers to the situation where investment products that make claims around being green, meeting ESG criteria, or being sustainable, more so than they really are.

As a result, a myriad of terms used to label investment approaches and investment products have evolved, including, for example, socially responsible investing, sustainable investing, ethical investing, green finance, ESG integration, best-in-class, ESG overlay, ESG tilt, and values-based investing. The benign view may be that this proliferation of terminology is a sign of product innovation that caters to a growing and diversifying market. These terms, however, do not have a standardised meaning. They refer to a range of methodologies, characteristics, and benefits that are not always clear or distinctive and that sometimes overlap. These terms can be confusing not just to end investors but also those operating within the finance industry.

Given the explosion of interest in the market for ESG investment products worldwide, concern is rising that inconsistencies and differences in terms related to ESG investment approaches may lead to misunderstandings, allegations of mis-selling, and rising mistrust between investors and asset managers, which in turn will prevent efficient capital allocation and impede the market from reaching its full potential. They also create opportunities for issuers to engage in greenwashing. In a global survey[1] of CFA Institute members carried out in March 2020, in which CFA Institute surveyed 325 C-suite executives and 373 ESG specialists, 78% of respondents thought that standards are needed to mitigate greenwashing.

---

1   Source: CFA Institute, "Future of sustainability in investment management: From ideas to reality", December 2020.

In response to such concerns, regulators, standard setters, and professional bodies are increasing their efforts to impose some order and structure on product classification by establishing regulations, standards, labels, and other initiatives.

Global regulatory and standards development for ESG investment products

The growing shifts of assets into ESG and sustainability investing has prompted regulators and industry bodies to strengthen rules and practices in a number of ways. These include the following:

- establishing taxonomies and catalogues to determine which activities are green and sustainable;

- mandating ESG disclosures by issuers;

- setting standards and guidelines on the naming, labelling, and disclosures of investment funds;

- setting standards for green instruments; and

- setting relevant benchmarks.

On a relative basis, the development of standards and guidelines relating to investment products, including collective investment schemes and investment funds, has lagged behind those for corporate issuers and green financial assets. To enable proper disclosures at the product level, asset managers need to have timely access to consistent, relevant data from issuers; hence, in many markets, the initial priorities have been on agreeing a taxonomy that defines green and sustainability activities, and improving and standardising issuer disclosures.

That said, regulations and industry standards relating to investment product naming and disclosures are catching up quickly. The most far-reaching piece of legislation is the Sustainable Finance Disclosure Regulation (SFDR) in the European Union (EU), which came into effect in March 2021. SFDR requires asset managers to disclose how they integrate ESG factors into their investment and risk management processes and such disclosures apply at both the entity and the product level.

An overview of the regulatory environment for the classification and labelling of ESG products in selected jurisdictions is provided below. The focus is on regulations and guidance that pertain to collective investment schemes (such as equity and fixed-income funds), rather than financial assets (such as green or sustainability bonds) or corporate disclosures. We also review voluntary disclosures and industry efforts in standardising labels and disclosures for ESG products.

EU

The EU's commitment to transition to a low-carbon, more sustainable economy is a key driver in its efforts to build a financial system that supports sustainable growth. This approach is encapsulated in the Sustainable Finance Action Plan, published in 2018, which features three key objectives:

- reorient capital flows towards sustainable investment;

- mainstream sustainability into risk management; and

- foster transparency and long-termism in financial and economic activity.

To achieve these objectives, the EU introduced, and is now in the process of implementing, a wide range of new legislative measures. Table 1 provides an overview of ESG regulations in the EU.

These measures complement pre-existing legislation that has indirect ESG implications, such as the second Shareholder Rights Directive, which imposes obligations on asset managers on ESG investment strategies, corporate engagement, and related disclosures.

The EU Taxonomy Regulation (the EU Taxonomy), SFDR, and the Non-Financial Reporting Directive (NFRD) are the three key components of the EU ESG Regulatory Regime and are interlinked. The EU Taxonomy provides the official ESG classification and associated technical criteria, while the NFRD mandates ESG data disclosures from EU corporations. These data are collected and analysed by asset managers to determine whether an investment is classified correctly as being sustainable in accordance with the EU Taxonomy. According to these analyses, asset managers then make their own disclosures as stipulated in the SFDR.

Table 1. Overview of selected ESG regulation in the EU

Regulation	Brief description	Effective date
Taxonomy Regulation	Establishes a unified classification system on environmentally sustainable economic activities. In time, disclosures required under the Non-Financial Reporting Directive and SFDR must be aligned with this taxonomy.	July 2020. Delegated Act published in April 2021
SFDR	Introduces disclosure obligations for asset managers on how they integrate sustainability factors in their investment and risk management processes.	Level 1 disclosures became effective in March 2021, and level 2 in 2022
Non-Financial Reporting Directive	Requires large public interest companies (i.e. those with more than 500 employees) in the EU to report on four sustainability issues, namely, (1) environmental, (2) social and employee issues, (3) human rights, and (4) bribery and corruption.	First introduced in 2018; a proposal to strengthen existing rules and established a new Corporate Sustainability Reporting Directive was published in April 2021 by the European Commission
Climate Benchmarks Regulation	Establishes standardised sustainability benchmarks that take into account climate transition and Paris Agreement-aligned targets. Aims to raise transparency by requiring benchmark administrators to disclose benchmark methodology and explain how ESG factors are reflected in the benchmark in a standardised and comparable way.	Delegated Acts published and became effective in December 2020
EU Ecolabel for Retail Financial Products	Establishes common product labels for retail sustainable financial products across the EU.	Under development

Source: CFA Institute; European Commission, see, for example, "Sustainable finance" webpage on its website.

Regulators and market practitioners outside the EU are closely monitoring these developments. While some believe that these EU ESG regulations could provide a blueprint to other markets, others are looking for an intermediate way to establish an ESG-related disclosures regime that is less costly and time-consuming.

SFDR

The SFDR consists of rules that apply to asset managers and financial advisors with two key objectives: first to increase transparency and comparability for end investors, and second to combat greenwashing. Level 1 disclosure requirements of the SFDR came into effect in the EU on 10 March 2021. Asset managers have to make such disclosures at both the investment firm level (e.g. governance and investment decision-making processes) and at the product level (e.g. the sustainability of the underlying securities in an investment fund). These disclosures are made on a comply-or-explain basis and are broadly based on the following three categories:

- how sustainability risks are managed and integrated;
- substantiation of their ESG credentials of their products; and
- disclosure of principal adverse impacts their investments have on sustainability objectives.

The most visible impact of SFDR is the three-way split of all European investment products based on the degree of commitment to ESG goals. All financial institutions manufacturing and selling investment products in the EU must classify the products they manage, market, or advise into one of the following three categories:

- Article 9 (referred to as "dark green"): These financial products actively pursue a sustainable investment strategy. All of their holdings must meet the definition of sustainable investments[2].
- Article 8 (referred to as "light green"): These products promote environmental or social characteristics. These funds have the discretion to invest a portion of their portfolio in sustainable investments.
- Article 6 (referred to as "pale green" or "grey"): This category encompasses all other products not classified as Article 8 or 9, including those that do not integrate any kind of sustainability into the investment process.

Article 8 and 9 products are subject to higher standards of disclosures, including the obligation to describe how such levels of sustainability have been attained, as well as whether and how a designated index is aligned with the investment objective.

For Article 6 products, pre-contractual disclosures are required on which sustainability risks are integrated and the likely impacts of the sustainability risks on the returns of the product. Otherwise, firms can explain why they do not consider such sustainability risks as relevant.

---

2   The SFDR defines a sustainable investment as an investment in an economic activity that contributes to an environmental or social objective or an investment in human capital or disadvantaged communities, provided that such investments do not significantly harm those objectives; and where the investee follows good governance practices.

As part of the Level 1 requirements, these disclosures must be made available on an asset manager's website as well as provided on a pre-contractual basis. When Level 2 requirements become effective in 2022, periodic disclosures also will be required.

Many asset managers are adapting their existing strategies to comply with the new requirements. Some of these managers are already making claims about the extent to which their fund offerings are Article 8 or Article 9 compliant. Some are working with consultants to improve the sustainability characteristics in their funds so that they can move up from Article 6 to Article 8.

Other asset managers are more circumspect. Although ESG funds are gaining popularity, it is unclear how categorising a fund as Article 6, 8, or 9 will affect investor demand. Furthermore, when Level 2 requirements become mandatory, it will be important for asset managers to support any sustainability claims they make with hard data. This is challenging as many of the key performance metrics under the EU Taxonomy and the NFRD are still works-in-progress, and there are persistent data gaps. Hence, some asset managers have categorised their funds under Article 6 or 8 for the time being, as these categories have a lower burden of proof[3].

The SFDR will have an extra-territorial impact on financial institutions not based in the EU. Asset managers who market their funds into the EU, or who provide portfolio management or investment advisory services to EU firms, will come under scope and will need to provide SFDR-compliant disclosures, even if their products are not specifically ESG related.

Notwithstanding these considerations, the SFDR is expected to transform the financial services industry in the EU. It is an important step in raising transparency, combating greenwashing, and enhancing trust and authenticity in how investors approach ESG and sustainability. More important, this will help direct capital flows to more sustainable activities, a key policy objective for the EU, and contribute to achieving its target of mobilising €1 trillion (US$1.2 trillion) in sustainable investments in the next decade[4].

---

3 Source: Adrian Whelan, "Sustainable finance disclosure regulation: So much to do, so little time", *BBH Insights*, 8 February 2021.

4 See, for example, "Targeted consultation on the establishment of an EU Green Bond Standard", webpage on the EU's website.

United States

Listed companies in the US are required to disclose ESG risks if such risks are deemed material to their businesses. To date, however, the Securities and Exchange Commission (SEC) has not mandated or standardised ESG disclosures. As a result, ESG regulations in the US are relatively underdeveloped, both in the area of corporate disclosure or investment product disclosure. That said, regulatory activity around ESG issues has been gaining momentum.

In March 2020, the SEC sought public comments on the issue of Fund Names (the "Names Rule"), specifically on whether this rule is still relevant or needs to be updated given that it has never been updated since its first adoption in January 2001. The Names Rule requires a fund to invest at least 80% of its assets in the manner suggested by its name, whereas previously, funds typically would select fund names based on a 65% threshold.

Much of the impetus behind revisiting the rule is the rising popularity of ESG or sustainable investment products, including exchange traded funds (ETFs). A lack of standardisation of terms, such as ESG or sustainable investing, and improper monitoring of this rule has allowed product manufacturers to find loopholes in existing regulations and engage in mislabelling of investment products. The SEC was concerned that the names of these products may be misleading and investors are overly reliant on labels such as "ESG" or "sustainability" without properly understanding the types of assets the fund invests in, the strategy used, or the non-financial objectives of the fund.

Since the beginning of 2021, the SEC has signalled a notable shift in its approach to ESG and has positioned itself for a holistic assessment of this issue. The most relevant actions include:

- creating a task force on climate and ESG issues;
- reviewing funds that claim to be ESG funds and assessing whether they live up to such claims;
- placing an emphasis on climate and ESG in examinations for registered investment advisors; and
- consulting the public on the future of climate change disclosures by issuers.

Asia Pacific

Hong Kong Special Administrative Region (SAR)

The topic of sustainable finance and ESG has become increasingly important in Hong Kong SAR and the level of government and regulatory attention has accelerated in the past few years. To position Hong Kong SAR as a hub for green finance, the government has launched several initiatives at the policy level, including, for example, announcing a climate action plan with the goal of achieving carbon neutrality by 2050, approving a green bond issuance programme, and launching the Green Bond Grant Scheme that would allow issuers to recoup additional costs relating to a green bond issuance, such as external reviews.

One crucial milestone in this effort is the establishment of the Green and Sustainable Finance Cross-Agency Steering Group led by the Hong Kong Monetary Authority and the Securities and Futures Commission (SFC) to provide strategic direction on regulatory policy and market development in the financial sector[5]. In December 2020, the Steering Group published a strategic plan outlining six key focus areas, one of which is to promote the flow of climate-related information to facilitate risk management, capital allocation, and investor protection[6].

As the regulator responsible for asset managers and investment products, the SFC has focused on setting expectations and new policies, as well as providing practical guidance in this area. In November 2020, SFC issued a consultation on the management and disclosure of climate-related risks by fund managers. The proposal outlines baseline requirements and enhanced standards on governance, investment management, risk management, and disclosures. There are two levels of disclosure requirements: (1) the entity level, which focuses on approach, process, and structure for governance, investment management, and risk management; and (2) the fund level, on weighted average carbon intensity, which is applicable if the assets under management (AUM) of the manager exceeded a certain size.

In 2019 the SFC published a circular on disclosure requirements for green and ESG funds,

---

5   Other members of the Steering Group include the Environment Bureau, the Financial Services and the Treasury Bureau, Hong Kong Exchanges and Clearing Limited, the Insurance Authority, and the Mandatory Provident Fund Schemes Authority.

6   Source: Green and Sustainable Finance Cross-Agency Steering Group, "Strategic plan to strengthen Hong Kong's financial ecosystem to support a greener and more sustainable future", 17 December 2020.

and updated it in 2021[7] by adding new requirements. The objectives of the disclosures are to improve transparency, comparability and visibility. For ESG funds, in addition to the original requirement of providing a description of their investment focus, strategy, expected proportion of ESG investment, and risks, the updated rules require the following:

- How the ESG focus is measured and monitored throughout the lifecycle of the fund;

- The methodologies adopted to measure such ESG focus;

- Due diligence carried out in relation to the ESG-related attributes of the fund's assets;

- Engagement and proxy voting policies; and

- Sources of ESG data.

Further, there is a new requirement for ESG funds to review and report periodically on how they have attained their ESG focus.

The SFC has considered the EU SFDR and has determined that UCITS[8] funds that incorporate ESG factors as their key investment focus are acceptable as ESG funds in Hong Kong. Moreover, the UCITS funds that meet the disclosure and reporting requirements for SFDR Article 8 or Article 9 are deemed to have satisfied the new SFC disclosure requirements.

The SFC maintains a central list of green and ESG funds on its website. As of August 2021, 65 listed and unlisted products meet these criteria[9].

Singapore

In 2019, the Monetary Authority of Singapore announced the development of a new and comprehensive long-term strategy to make sustainable finance a defining feature of Singapore's role as an international financial centre.

One key area of focus includes the development of a set of Environmental Risk Management Guidelines across the banking, insurance, and asset management sectors. The final guidelines, published in December 2020, require asset managers to implement

---

7   See SFC, "Circular to management companies of SFC-authorized unit trusts and mutual funds — ESG funds", 29 June 2021.

8   UCITS stands for Undertakings for the Collective Investment in Transferable Securities, which is a EU regulatory framework that allows for the sale of cross-Europe mutual funds.

9   Source: "List of green and ESG funds", webpage on SFC's website, viewed on 19 August 2021.

robust environmental risk management policies and procedures and embed such risks into their research and portfolio construction processes if they are material.

Shortly after the publication of the guidelines, Singapore followed up with a consultation in January 2021 on a proposed green taxonomy that will be aligned with the EU Taxonomy.

Although many regulatory initiatives are in progress, one notable gap is in the area of investment fund naming and labelling. As concerns over greenwashing increase, investors have called for the development of an ESG fund label to improve comparability and transparency and to grow the market.

Malaysia

In Malaysia, sustainable and responsible investing (SRI) has a relatively long track record and high level of acceptance in the market as a result of the similarities between SRI and Islamic finance principles. In positioning Malaysia as an Islamic finance hub, the development of SRI has been a key focus for the Securities Commission Malaysia (SC), the industry regulator. To support this market, the SC established facilitative regulatory frameworks, such as the SRI Sukuk Framework and published an SRI Roadmap in 2019. The roadmap set out a clear action plan to strengthen the ecosystem that encompasses investors, issuers, instruments, internal culture and governance, and information architecture.

With respect to investment funds, the SC issued a set of guidelines[10] on SRI funds in 2017 to encourage further growth and set expectations on what would constitute an SRI fund. By introducing additional disclosure and reporting requirements, the SC aims to encourage greater transparency in investment policies and strategies of SRI funds, thereby widening the range of products available and attracting more investors into the segment.

Other voluntary standards

In addition to mandatory regulatory frameworks, a number of other voluntary guidelines, labels, and standards are in use and being developed around the world, such as those below.

---

10 Securities Commission Malaysia, *Guidelines on Sustainable and Responsible Investment Funds*, SC-GL/4-2017, 19 December 2017.

CFA Institute ESG Disclosure Standards for Investment Products

CFA Institute is in the process of developing a set of global, voluntary ESG disclosure standards for investment products (the Standard). The purpose of the Standard is to provide greater transparency and comparability for investors by enabling asset managers to clearly communicate the ESG-related features of their investment products. The Standard will establish fundamental requirements for investment products with ESG-related features, procedures for independent examination of disclosures, and a classification of ESG-related features according to ESG-related needs. A consultation[11] was launched in August 2020 as part of this process, and there was significant support for such a standard, as well as support for this standard to adopt a descriptive approach.

The Standard aims to elicit information about the use of ESG factors in an investment product and will explicitly avoid attempting to define what is or what is not an ESG product. As mentioned in previous sections, regulations are increasingly focused on the naming of products, and on the setting of minimum thresholds for a product to qualify as ESG or sustainable. The Standard will neither require nor prohibit the use of particular terms in investment product names, descriptions, or presentations. Further, it will not require investment products to have specific ESG-related features or meet minimum thresholds for portfolio-level ESG characteristics or performance. As a result, the Standard will not conflict with local rules and regulations and can be globally applicable. The Standard is expected to be available in the fourth quarter of 2021.

EU fund labels

In the EU, the two main categories of labels for ESG investment products, are as follows:

- National labels, including, for example, the ISR Label and Greenfin Label in France, Towards Sustainability in Belgium, LuxFLAG in Luxembourg, and Umweltzeichen in Austria; and

- Cross-border labels, including, for example, the Nordic Swan Ecolabel and FNG-Siegel for German-speaking financial markets.

Most of the national labels follow similar guidelines based on a particular theme, such as environmental, social issues, microfinance, or energy transition[12]. The Belgian Towards

---

11 CFA Institute, *Consultation Paper on the Development of the CFA Institute ESG Disclosure Standards for Investment Products*, August 2020.

12 Source: Candriam, "SRI Labels in Europe: What to Choose?", 5 September 2016.

Sustainability Label and the French ISR Label are two prominent national labels in the EU. A common feature that runs across most of the national sustainable finance labels in the EU is the exclusion of fossil fuels, except for the ISR Label and the LuxFLAG ESG and Environment Label.

EU Ecolabel for retail financial products

Currently, various national Ecolabels within the EU have diverging requirements. The European Commission is in the process of developing a harmonised EU Ecolabel under the Sustainable Finance Action Plan for retail financial products to facilitate cross-border trading in sustainable financial products.

In late 2020, the European Commission consulted the market on the product scope and criteria for the EU Ecolabel. Responses to the consultation suggested that the industry would like to see greater alignment with the EU Taxonomy[13], while others noted the importance of maintaining "the right balance between the strictness of the criteria that gives the label its credibility" and ensuring "a sufficiently large pool of eligible investment opportunities"[14].

Eurosif SRI Transparency Code

This is a voluntary code aimed at increasing the accountability and socially responsible investing practices of asset managers of such funds in Europe. This code allows retail investors to make better investment decisions by ensuring accurate, timely, and honest information disclosure on policies and practices by funds claiming to be socially responsible. The two core principles guiding this code are transparency and accountability.

Responsible Investment Certification Program

The Responsible Investment Association Australasia (RIAA) is a network of individuals and organisations actively engaged in responsible investing in Australia and New Zealand. RIAA developed a voluntary Responsible Investment Certification Program under which financial products may apply for a certification symbol that signifies that a product or provider is delivering on its responsible investment promise and meeting the required

---

13 See, for example, AMIC, "AMIC response: EC consultation on the EU Ecolabel for retail financial products", 11 December 2020.

14 See, for example, European Fund and Asset Management Association, "EFAMA's answer to the JRC consultation on the 3rd technical report on development of EU Ecolabel criteria for retail financial products", 11 December 2020.

standards for responsible investing. The programme applies to investment products, investment management services, and superannuation (pension) funds. As part of the process, RIAA assesses all applicants against a set of criteria, and in addition, asset managers must also seek independent verification.

The objective of the certification is to provide a degree of comfort and assurance to investors that an investment product or service has implemented an investment style and process that systematically takes into account ESG or ethical considerations, and this investment process reliability has been verified by an external party. Strict operational and disclosure requirements also ensure that standards are upheld.

For a product to be certified as a responsible investment, some of the following requirements[15] must be met:

- having formal, consistent, documented, and auditable responsible investment strategies and processes;

- making honest claims and be appropriately labelled;

- avoiding significant harm;

- accounting for ESG factors in the investment process; and

- having relevant and accessible responsible investment disclosures.

RIAA also set up a platform called Responsible Returns, which allows investors to find, compare, and choose responsible and ethical superannuation, banking, and investment products that best match their needs. All products and funds that feature on the platform have been certified in accordance with RIAA's certification programme.

Global framework for ESG investment approaches

ESG investing encompasses a range of approaches addressing different investment objectives, from "value-based" objectives to "values-based" objectives. A value-based

---

15 Source: RIAA, "Responsible Investment Certification Program: RI Certification Standard", 15 August 2020.

approach, in which material ESG factors are integrated in the evaluation of an investment opportunity, either to mitigate risk or to generate alpha, is perhaps the closest to traditional financial investing. In contrast, a values-based approach takes into account an investor's beliefs, or values, and these non-financial objectives may supersede the financial return objective. Between these two ends of the spectrum, there is a continuum of approaches with different characteristics, some of which overlap. Portfolio managers may apply more than one approach to a given investment strategy. The approaches used to label or classify an investment product are sometimes incorporated in its name, and some fund labels requires the adoption of certain approaches, such as exclusion or engagement.

Even though such approaches have been around for some time, the terminology can vary considerably without consensus or standardisation. Several organisations, including the Global Sustainable Investment Alliance, Principles for Responsible Investment, and RIAA, have attempted to create a framework to describe such approaches. Table 2 shows six generic ESG investment approaches and their financial and impact objectives, each is examined in detail below.

Table 2. ESG investment approaches

		Focus	Impact Goals	Financial Goals
Traditional Investing		No regard for environment, social or governance factors	No consideration	Focus on superior risk-adjusted returns
ESG Investing Approaches	**ESG Integration**	Explicit consideration of ESG factors in investment decision making	Avoids harm and/or mitigate ESG risks / Benefit stake-holders / Make positive impact	Baseline expectations of market-rate returns
	Exclusion/ Negative Screening	Exclusion of certain companies to avoid risk or align with stated values, ethics or beliefs		
	Best-in-Class/ Positive Screening	Target companies with better ESG performance in a segment		
	Voting and Engagement	Exercise voting rights and engage actively to influence company's activities and behaviour regarding ESG matters		
	Thematic Investing	Target ESG-specific themes and trends		
	Impact Investing	Generate positive environmental or social impact alongside financial returns		Below-market to market-rate returns
Philanthropy		Generate positive environmental or social impact with no consideration of financial returns		Accept partial or full loss of capital

Source: RIAA Responsible Investment Framework; *Handbook on Sustainable Investments*, CFA Institute.

ESG integration

ESG integration is the most popular approach with around US$25.2 trillion in total managed assets, according to the 2020 Global Sustainable Investment Review (GSIR)[16]. It refers to an explicit consideration of material ESG factors into traditional financial analysis and investment decisions to improve the risk-return characteristics of a portfolio. Portfolio managers usually start with a predefined investment strategy, while also incorporating material ESG factors through a variety of approaches, such as impact investing and positive screening.

ESG concerns generally are integrated by targeting material ESG issues that are considered highly likely to have a negative or positive impact on the company's finances. One approach for such an analysis comes from the Sustainability Accounting Standards Board Materiality Map, which helps investors and portfolio managers assess financially material issues across sectors and industries.

The consideration of ESG concerns, however, is not limited to security selection and portfolio construction. In terms of valuation and credit analysis, ESG integration involves an understanding of the impact that ESG factors have on matters such as revenue forecasting, valuation multiples, spread analysis, and management quality. In risk management, ESG factors are used to perform scenario analysis and stress testing.

Exclusion or negative screening

The exclusion approach is considered to be the earliest form of ESG investing. It involves excluding certain companies, industries, or governments whose behaviours or activities are inconsistent with the beliefs, ethics, or values of investors. Exclusions may also be applied in an investment strategy to comply with laws and regulations in a given region. Normally, the screening process starts with a broad market benchmark, and investments that do not meet a particular set of criteria are excluded from the investment portfolio. Such exclusions can be categorised into the following two main types:

- **Product-based exclusions:** This category excludes businesses that are involved in products and activities, including such things as controversial weapons, gambling,

---

16　Global Sustainable Investment Alliance, "2020 Global Sustainable Investment Review".

tobacco, or fossil fuels. According to GSIR, it is the second largest sustainable investment strategy globally with about US$15 trillion in AUM, or 42% of total ESG-related managed assets.

- **Behaviour and norms-based exclusions:** This category refers to exclusions based on either ongoing controversies, such as human rights violations and corruption, or a principles-based framework, such as the United Nations (UN) Global Compact. This screening is generally applied to manage reputation and potential financial risks associated with businesses.

Best-in-class or positive screening

Typically, the best-in-class approach can take the following forms:

- **Best-in-sector:** This approach focuses on the best performing companies in their sectors in terms of ESG.

- **Best-in-universe:** In this approach, the portfolio manager identifies the highest-ranked companies in a given universe, regardless of sector. This may lead to the exclusion of certain sectors if their ESG performance is worse than others.

- **Best-effort:** This includes those companies that have demonstrated substantial improvements in their ESG performance over time.

The best-in-class approach differs from ESG exclusions in that it does not exclude an entire segment of companies based on their activity (e.g. exclusion of tobacco stocks), but rather it selects or weights companies on relative ESG performance. In contrast to ESG integration, in the best-in-class approach, the ESG performance metrics have an explicit focus on asset allocation, security selection, and portfolio construction decisions. In contrast to thematic investing, this approach does not select or weight companies based on a structural long-term trend. Last, compared with impact investing, best-in-class strategies are not designed to achieve a measurable change in outcomes.

Voting and engagement

Voting and engagement refers to the process in which investors use their shareholder rights to influence company's activities and behaviour regarding ESG matters through voting of shares, corporate engagement, and filing shareholder resolutions. Shareholders generally use annual general meetings as the platform in which to engage with the company's board of directors and to assess whether the business complies with their voting policy. A shareholder like to actively engage with the company for two main reasons:

- to exert influence on the company's policies and decisions to improve their ability to tackle long-term challenges; and

- to assess management quality and commitment to ESG issues through better disclosures, which will inform investment and voting decisions.

The impact pertinent to such engagement can be measured either qualitatively (e.g. quality of disclosures, extent of commitment, or change in strategy) or quantitatively (e.g. carbon emissions reduction or ESG ratings improvement).

Thematic investing

Thematic investing refers to an approach in which investments are made based on long-term macroeconomic or structural themes or trends linked to ESG matters. This approach usually contributes to addressing sustainability challenges, such as climate change, biodiversity loss, or water scarcity, with a purpose of generating strong financial returns. As a result, these portfolios often display size, regional, and sector biases with respect to a market benchmark. There are two main approaches:

- **Single theme:** This approach usually consists of identifying a particular trend, such as health or biodiversity loss, and investing in businesses that are active in that area.

- **Multiple themes:** A fund manager may wish to pursue multiple themes, typically linked to one or more goals outlined by the United Nations Sustainable Development Goals (SDGs). Unlike the single-themed approach, the goal is to create a diversified portfolio while also contributing toward a more sustainable world.

Impact investing

Impact investment is one of the fastest-growing industries to address environmental and social issues. According to the Global Impact Investing Network (GIIN), a global alliance of more than 250 impact investing organisations, impact investing refers to investments that are made with the intention of generating positive and measurable environmental and social impacts alongside a financial return. The overriding objective is to make a positive impact that will benefit the community and the environment. Hence, it is often considered to be an extension of philanthropic efforts, in which the investor looks for below-market to market-rate returns, depending on the strategic outcomes and circumstances. It covers a range of asset classes — from real estate to private equity and debt — related to such areas as microfinance, clean energy, and social housing.

Benefits and challenges of ESG investment approaches

Table 3 below presents the benefits and challenges of each of the ESG investment approaches.

Table 3. Benefits and challenges of ESG investment approaches

Investment approach	Benefits	Challenges
ESG integration	• Broad and flexible and allows the consideration of any strategies or criteria an investor may want to use • The focus on increasing returns and / or reducing risks allows investors to avoid investing in overvalued companies, even if their ESG performance is outstanding	• The quality of investment decisions can vary considerably — asset managers need to communicate clearly their objectives and processes
Exclusion / negative screening	• Simple approach that allows investors to assess easily if a portfolio is tailored to their needs • Performance highly correlated with market benchmarks when compared with other approaches	• Narrows the investment universe • Limits diversification opportunities by restricting the range of available sectors
Best-in-class / positive screening	• Allows investors to take a more precise view of a company's ESG impact • Allows investors to identify long-term leaders and avoid poor ESG performers	• Requires a high level of resources to support this analysis, such as sourcing and calculation of ESG performance metrics, construction of portfolio based on ESG metrics and ongoing monitoring

(continued)

Investment approach	Benefits	Challenges
Voting and engagement	• Positive impact on returns • Raises awareness of ESG factors within the portfolio companies • Allows better investment decision making	• Perceived as not as relevant for fixed income investors • Growth of low-cost passive investing is seen to discourage voting and engagement
Thematic investing	• Provides opportunities to take advantage of secular, macro trends • Creates a risk-and-return profile that differs from broad market benchmarks and provides superior returns over multiple business cycles	• Tends to have lower correlation with market benchmarks, hence higher variances • Allows investment into companies with a weak ESG profile
Impact investing	• Allows investors to deliver on their commitments • Relatively more straightforward • Latest data suggest that investors may not need to compromise their returns[17]	• Relatively more concentrated and constrained • Potential liquidity issues with limited exit options as investments tend to be small and unlisted • Lack of standardised impact measurement so investors may find it difficult to assess the impact of their investments

Source: RIAA Responsible Investment Framework; CFA Institute, *Handbook on Sustainable Investments*.

Application of labels and classification

Sustainable funds are marked with a long and increasingly sophisticated list of names, from ESG, green and environmental to ethical and socially responsible, to thematic water, biodiversity or carbon funds. The wide array of choices has also led to much confusion on the part of investors and an average investor is likely to be bewildered and confused by these terms and the inconsistencies between them. The application of standardised labels and classification go some way in alleviating some of these concerns, as we will see below.

---

17 See, for example, Global Impact Investing Network, "Impact investing decision making: Insights on financial performance", 14 January 2021.

Investment funds

Use of labels by asset managers and investors

The national and cross-regional investment product labels in the EU offer an interesting case study on how labels are used by asset managers and investors. The objective of these labels is to provide investors with a minimum level of quality guarantee on the validity of a product's sustainability claims. Each label has its own assessment criteria, reporting requirements and governance structures. Labels are gaining in popularity: at the end of 2020, 1,418 investment funds in the EU had an ESG or green label, representing an AUM of €690 billion, an increase of 128% over the previous year[18]. The two leading labels in Europe are the ISR from France and Towards Sustainability from Belgium. The ISR Label had 645 labelled funds with €359 billion AUM and Towards Sustainability had 494 labelled funds with €284 billion AUM[19]. The growth in number of funds and AUM indicates increased recognition by investors of the utility of labels in selecting sustainable investment products. Despite this growth, so far sustainability labels represent a small portion of the overall fund universe in the EU.

Since labels are voluntary, there is intense competition between them for the attention of asset managers who are the ultimate decision makers as to which label (if any) their products should obtain. According to Novethic (a green finance research institute), an emerging trend is that more funds are opting to be certified with multiple labels. This is because investors are more familiar with national labels and asset managers selling into a market would often gain better access and recognition for their products if they were certified with national labels.

Sustainable labels typically apply to UCITS-type equity and bond funds, including UCITS ETFs. The Greenfin label can be applied to unlisted funds such as private equity and infrastructure and the ISR label can be applied to real estate funds. Although labels are useful to all investors, more sophisticated investors such as institutional investors, fund selectors and high-net-worth individuals, are relatively more experienced in evaluating and investing in fund products and may not rely on them as much. For these users, the focus is on getting a detailed understanding on whether an investment manager has a clear commitment to ESG and sustainability, how their policy around sustainable investments is implemented, and how ESG criteria are assessed.

---

18 Source: Novethic, "Market data: Sustainable fund labels, Europe", published on the website of Novethic, 31 December 2020.
19 Ibid.

Differences between labels in the EU

At present, there are nine labels in the EU: with seven national and two cross-border. There are two categories of labels, one focusing on ESG and the other focusing on environmental investing.

Table 4. Overview of sustainable finance labels in the EU

Label	Country	Governance	Type
FNG-Siegel	Germany, Austria and Switzerland	Expert committee under the stewardship of FNG, a sustainable investment forum	Sustainable / ESG investment process with climate exclusions
Greenfin Label	France	Standalone stakeholder committee, chaired by the Ministry for the Ecological and Fair Transition	Thematic investments and ESG criteria; climate exclusions
ISR Label	France	Standalone stakeholder committee, supported by the Ministry of France	Sustainable / ESG investment process
LuxFLAG ESG	Luxembourg	LuxFLAG, a cross-border labelling agency	Sustainable / ESG investment process
LuxFLAG Environment	Luxembourg	LuxFLAG	Thematic investments and ESG criteria
LuxFLAG Climate Finance	Luxembourg	LuxFLAG	Thematic investments and ESG criteria; climate exclusions
Nordic Swan Ecolabel	Nordic countries	Nordic Ecolabelling Board (mandated by Nordic governments)	Sustainable / ESG investment process with climate exclusions and green reporting
Towards Sustainability	Belgium	Central Labelling Agency	Quality standard combining requirements on the investment process and exclusions
Umweltzeichen	Austria	Austrian Federal Ministry for the Environment	Sustainable / ESG investment process with climate exclusions

Source: Novethic, "Overview of European Sustainable Finance Labels", published on the website of Novethic, June 2020.

As Table 4 shows, these labels are typically managed by professional responsible investment associations or specialised environmental labelling organisations. The only exception is France, where the government has created and supports two public labels: ISR and Greenfin. The ISR label is dedicated to responsible investment and the Greenfin label is committed to environmental funds.

What is perhaps most instructive is the different approaches and methodologies each label adopts in setting requirements for security selection, portfolio allocation and portfolio disclosure. Set out below are some examples:

- **ESG analysis coverage:** Although analysis of ESG factors is mandatory for all labels, their threshold requirements vary from one label to another, with some requiring ESG screening for 100% of the portfolio (e.g. FNG-Siegel, Towards Sustainability) and others requiring a coverage of 90% or more (e.g. ISR label).

- **Exclusion:** As discussed in the preceding section, exclusion of non-qualifying or undesirable investments is one of the most common ESG investment approaches and is also widely adopted by EU labels. Some labels combine the exclusion approach with ESG analysis, either excluding companies known for breaches of human rights, or excluding sectors that are engaged in controversial activities such as anti-personnel mines.

- **Fossil fuels:** All environmental labels exclude fossil fuels, in particular coal, to various degrees. Aside from coal, each label sets technical criteria for different types of fossil fuel production and extraction as well as for electricity generation. Such criteria may include the revenue share (say 5% or 10%) a company derives from an excluded activity.

- **Green activities:** Some labels have the explicit objectives relating to climate or environment (e.g. LuxFLAG Climate Finance, LuxFLAG Environment, Greenfin and Nordic Swan). These labels set thresholds both at the holding level and at the portfolio level to ensure that investments are directed towards environmentally sustainable activities. For example, the LuxFLAG Climate Finance label defines a "green" company as one with a turnover of at least 50% from sustainable activities, and sets a threshold of 75% of green companies that a portfolio has to invest in. For the definition of sustainable activities, the labels rely on taxonomies of sustainable activities, such as one from the Climate Bonds Initiative (CBI).

- **Portfolio disclosure:** Reporting intervals vary across different labels. Several are required to make full portfolio disclosures on an annual basis (LuxFLAG Environment,

LuxFLAG Climate Finance, Greenfin). Others are on shorter reporting cycle (half-yearly for Towards Sustainability and quarterly for Nordic Swan), and one, Umweltzeichen, reports on a monthly basis.

While labels were designed to solve one problem, the proliferation of labels gives rise to another — that of confusion and lack of comparability. There are costs involved in maintaining a label, and they add up quickly if a fund is multi-labelled. Unsurprisingly, there is call for more harmonisation of different labels. One potential solution, the EU Ecolabel, is under development as part of the EU's sustainable finance agenda and has been through several rounds of consultation. While the EU Ecolabel is not expected to replace the national labels, an EU-wide fund label may provide further impetus for the development of sustainable investments in the region.

Fund ratings

In addition to regulators and voluntary standard-setters, for-profit data providers such as Morningstar and Sustainalytics provide fund-level sustainability ratings. These ratings provide an indication of the ESG performance of the investments in the fund. Many investors rely on them to support their investment decisions and to make comparisons between funds.

There is a crucial difference between ratings and labels: labels are attained on the investment manager's initiative, whereas fund ratings are assigned by data providers, and can be attributed to any funds, regardless of whether that fund has a dedicated strategy. The ratings process may not involve any effort from the investment manager, but may still act as an incentive. Another difference is that fund ratings typically assess the outcomes of various sustainability metrics of a fund (depending on the methodology of individual providers), while labels typically focus more on an investment manager's approach and process.

Green, social, sustainability, transition and sustainability-linked bonds

Overview

In simple terms, green, social, and sustainability (GSS) bonds are essentially a type of bond instrument the proceeds of which are used solely for eligible environmental and social projects, or a combination of the two.

- **Green bonds:** Within the GSS category, green bonds represent the largest segment and have the longest track record. The proceeds of green bonds are exclusively applied to financing or re-financing, in part or in full, of new and / or existing eligible green projects, including, for example, renewable energy, pollution prevention and control, climate change adaptation, water and biodiversity, or green buildings.

- **Social bonds:** They are the second category, after green bonds, that have seen a substantial growth in recent years. The proceeds of these bonds are intended to fund projects that address specific social issues or seek to achieve positive social outcomes for a segment of population. Such projects may include affordable housing, affordable basic infrastructure, and access to basic services. Examples of target populations include those living below the poverty line, people with disabilities or other vulnerable groups.

- **Sustainability bonds:** These are issues proceeds of which are used to finance or re-finance a combination of green and social projects or activities. These bonds can be issued by companies, governments and municipalities for operations as well as for specific assets and projects. They can be unsecured, backed by the creditworthiness of the corporate or government issuer, or secured with collateral on a specific asset.

- **Transition bonds:** This is a relatively new category that is targeted at industries with high greenhouse gas emissions. Transition bonds do not require an issuer to be green. Rather, the objective is to enable companies in "brown" industries, such as mining and coal, to raise capital to finance transition projects that would allow them to become less brown and switch to more sustainable business activities.

The above four categories are typically termed "use-of-proceeds" bonds. Their proceeds go towards specific, dedicated uses, which are vetted against lists of eligible projects or other taxonomies of green and sustainable activities. The focus of these bonds is on the projects rather than the issuers themselves. In addition to these use-of-proceeds bonds, there is another relatively new category of instruments, called the sustainability-linked bonds (not to be confused with sustainability bonds).

- **Sustainability-linked bonds, or SLBs:** Unlike GSS bonds, the funds raised from SLBs do not need to be allocated to specific environmental or social projects but rather are for general corporate purposes. This type of bonds is intended to support the key role that debt markets can play in funding companies that contribute to sustainability, scaling up de-carbonisation while serving a broader range of issuers. They incorporate predefined sustainability-linked key performance targets which issuers commit to achieve. If they fail, the bond coupon would step up, typically by between 10 and 75 basis points.

Classification of GSS, transition and sustainability-linked bonds

What makes a bond "green", "social" or "sustainable"? Often they are not defined by regulation but by a series of voluntary, market-based principles and standards, such as those from the International Capital Market Association (ICMA), which aims to build a common language within sustainable capital markets (see Table 5). The ICMA principles that have the longest track record include the Green Bond Principles (GBP) and the Social Bond Principles (SBP).

Table 5. Selected ICMA principles

Name	Applies to	Core components	Year first published
Green Bond Principles	Green bonds	• Use of proceeds • Process for project evaluation and selection • Management of proceeds • Reporting	2014
Social Bond Principles	Social bonds	• Aligned with the GBP	2017
Sustainability Bond Guidelines	Sustainability bonds	• Aligned with the GBP and SBP	2018
Climate Transition Finance Handbook	Transition bonds	• Issuer's climate transition strategy and governance • Business model environmental materiality • Climate transition strategy to be "science-based," including targets and pathways • Implementation transparency	2020
Sustainability-Linked Bond Principles	SLBs	• Credible key performance indicators • Calibration of sustainability performance targets • Bond characteristics that include financial and structural impact involving trigger events • Reporting of key performance indicators and information pertaining to sustainability performance targets • Verification by qualified external reviewers	2020

Source: ICMA.

The GBP does not provide definitions of what constitutes "green" and leaves the decision to the discretion of the issuers. Examples of project categories that are considered green include energy, buildings, transport, water management and waste management, and pollution control. The latest version of the GBP, published in 2021, recommends that issuers explain the alignment of their green bonds with the four core GBP components in a green bond framework. In their green bond frameworks, issuers are encouraged to make reference to their own sustainability strategy as well as the high-level environmental objectives of the GBP.

In addition to ICMA, the CBI has also established a set of green bond standards, the Climate Bonds Standard, which provides sector-specific eligibility criteria for assets and projects that can be used for green bonds. There are other national and regional green bond standards, such as China's Green Bonds Endorsed Project Catalogue, and the ASEAN Green Bond Standards. The EU is also developing a set of uniform green bond standards which are expected to be published in 2021.

While alignment with international principles such as ICMA and CBI is voluntary and subject to the discretion of issuers, there are significant pricing and reputational advantages which render the classification of GSS bonds important from an issuer's perspective. Because demand for GSS bonds has exceeded supply, we have seen the phenomenon of a green premium, or "greenium", in which a green bond trades at a lower yield than a traditional bond of the same issuer with the same horizon. An example is a twin bond structure introduced by the German government. It involves issuing a conventional bond and a green bond, sharing similar characteristics, within a short period. According to CBI[20], the green twin yielded one basis point lower than the conventional twin, suggesting that issuers were able to achieve better terms with green issues.

Furthermore, GSS bonds address themes that are not traditionally covered by companies and investors, allowing issuers to build relationships with investors who want more insight into business processes and operations. By issuing a GSS bond, issuers can diversify their bondholder base and reach different investors.

The classification of bonds into green or other categories is also important from an investor's perspective. Asset managers rely on such classifications to identify these instruments, and some investment mandates may explicitly require that funds can only be invested in GSS bonds. As investors are increasingly looking to deploy funds into sustainable projects, GSS bonds provide a fast and ready means for them to do so.

---

20 Caroline Harrison, "Green bond pricing in the pricing market: July-December 2020", published on the website of CBI, March 2021.

Although the availability of voluntary principles has strengthened the integrity of GSS bond market, issuers still face challenges while setting their targets because of a lack of unified international green bond taxonomy and standards. Cross-border coordination is underway to ensure better alignment of international, regional and domestic guidelines and standards, to ensure the development of a robust GSS bond market.

External review and certification

The proliferation of GSS bonds has given rise to the concerns of not only greenwashing, but also social washing — the misrepresentation of a bond's social benefits. Investors desire a high level of assurance that the securities they invest in are genuine and authentic, that the proceeds are being deployed in accordance with the ICMA principles mentioned above. In the case of SLBs, investors also want to know that the selection of key performance indicators and the setting of targets are credible.

As a solution, the market has looked to external reviews to provide additional comfort to investors. The GBP (2021 version) recommends that, prior to issuance, issuers appoint an external reviewer to confirm, among other things, the alignment of their issues with the four core components. Post issuance, the GBP also recommends that the management of proceeds to be tracked and verified by an external auditor.

Examples of external reviews include second-party opinions, verification, certification and bond rating and scoring. ICMA has published a set of voluntary guidelines for external reviewers, which include professional and ethical standards for external reviewers as well as guidance on the organisation, content and disclosure for their reports.

Although external reviews are voluntary and recommended under the ICMA principles, they are required under the Climate Bonds Standard. CBI requires third-party verification from an approved verifier, so that investors can receive assurance that the bond in question does indeed meet with the Climate Bonds Standard.

Retaining the services of external reviewers generates additional costs that issuers have to bear. To encourage issuers, some governments provide incentives to offset such costs (e.g. Singapore, Hong Kong SAR). Third-party reviews and verifications are key to boosting transparency and are indispensable to a successful and credible issue. In many instances, the positive profile, reputation benefits and pricing advantages more than make up for the extra costs incurred.

Opportunities and challenges

Benefits and limitations of labels

For investors attempting to navigate the complex landscape of sustainable investments, labelling and classifications of ESG investment products provide an appealing, simple, and straightforward solution. In particular, labels offer a level of assurance on the quality of the investment product, the ESG criteria used and the alignment of the product with pre-determined criteria, principles and guidelines. They have gone a long way in allaying concerns about greenwashing and enabling investors to identify and select investment products that best suit their needs.

However, the wide range of labels on offer, particularly in a region like Europe, can also cause confusion. It is not always easy for investors to comprehend fully the methodologies and approaches between competing labels and differentiate between them. There are no standardised requirements for labels and products certified by different labels can have vastly different features and characteristics, making like-for-like comparisons across funds difficult.

In Asia Pacific, the issue is different: with the exception of the RIAA certification programme in Australia and New Zealand, there are no voluntary product labelling frameworks for ESG and sustainable investment products. However, in some markets such as Hong Kong SAR and Malaysia, regulators have provided guidance on fund names to raise transparency and reduce confusion.

Labels typically stipulate a certain minimum standard and are usually process-oriented, focusing on verifying what and how ESG or green securities are selected into the portfolio and on ensuring that funds provide periodic, comprehensive reporting to fund investors. For investors, it is important to understand that being certified with a label is no guarantee of financial or ESG performance, and even for funds with the same label, there will be significant differences in approaches and strategies.

Making the best use of labels and classifications

Despite the ability of labels and classifications to condense and convey a great deal of information into one single number, icon or phrase, the reality is much more nuanced and may not reflect accurately a product's ESG processes or outcomes. This, again, has its roots in the lack of standardised terminology for ESG and sustainability investment. So what should an investor do? Investors should be cognisant if and how they match with their own objectives — some investors may be looking for a fund that has strict criteria in selecting their investments, while others are only looking for a fund that integrates ESG factors in a very broad sense. Either way, investors need to look beyond the label and do proper due diligence to better understand the meaning of a label or a classification. As an example, investors can review the investment criteria of a fund, top fund holdings, what screens (if any) a fund applies and whether this is consistent with their own objectives. Labels are an important first step, but will not completely eliminate the need for thoughtful due diligence on the part of the investors.

The role of exchanges in labelling and classification

The fundamental business of an exchange is to provide an efficient platform for buyers and sellers to execute transactions at a price that best reflects the market value, a platform that provides liquidity and access to a broad range of products, promotes price discovery and has a robust investor protection framework that ensures a high level of trust. Exchanges' roles as gatekeeper and standard setter and enforcer are crucial to the development of capital markets.

As we have mentioned throughout this chapter, a key concern that is hindering development of sustainable finance is a lack of standardised terms and common terminology. Labels and classifications are useful in this regard: they are relatively easy to use, help build trust in the system, and are particularly valuable to the investing public. Notwithstanding this, no single label or classification will cater to the full spectrum of investor needs or the entire universe of investment products, hence exchanges need to be open but selective in the labels and classifications they implement on their platform.

To fulfil its role, an exchange can reduce the friction of information and maximise the utility of its platform to users, by improving the visibility of sustainable securities and by standardising disclosures. For example, sustainable funds that are not listed can opt to be "displayed" on an exchange if certain criteria are met. This is also pertinent for GSS bonds, which can be displayed in a separate, dedicated segment to improve transparency, access and visibility to investors. Exchanges can also encourage further issuance of green bonds by creating effective procedures for the issuance process while also ensuring the highest standards for the listing of GSS bonds. Given the lack of investment product labels in Asia, there is scope for regional exchanges to take on the initiative to develop appropriate labelling frameworks and standards for investment products.

Closing thoughts

The increased focus on sustainability and issues such as climate change by governments, regulators, the corporate sector, the financial services industry, and investors means that the emphasis on allocating capital to ESG and sustainability investments will only intensify. To ensure efficient capital allocation, the issue of greenwashing needs to be addressed urgently. Existing labelling and classifications systems provide some order in a vast market of ESG products, diminishing the opportunities for greenwashing, but as yet, there are no universally accepted standards. However, as new regulations and industry standards are implemented, we are on the cusp of substantive progress that will see significant improvements in transparency and delivery of desired outcomes. It will not be all plain sailing — the challenge of achieving regional and international convergence on terminology and definitions will remain for some time. Successfully navigating this landscape is tricky but has the potential to be a huge source of opportunities for growth and innovation and a means to reduce the reputational and regulatory risk for both investors and the financial services industry.

第6章

環球ESG投資產品的分類

梁家恩，CFA
CFA 協會　亞太區行業倡導總經理

Sivananth RAMACHANDRAN, CFA
CFA 協會　資本市場政策總監

摘要

這一章檢視環境、社會及管治（即 environment、social、governance，簡稱 ESG）投資產品在環球市場的分類，從中說明有關進展及挑戰。我們會探討 ESG 投資產品的監管環境、自願遵守的行業標準、ESG 投資方法、標籤的應用及分類等不同方面的概覽和前景，以及這範疇的機遇和挑戰。

為投資產品建立清晰的 ESG 分類系統（不管是通過監管規例、自願性標籤或標準），對投資者和基金經理來說都有極大好處。對希望涉足 ESG 或可持續產品的投資者來說，面對五花八門的投資產品時可省去不少時間和心力，對產品聲稱的特徵會符合預期也有較大信心。對基金經理來說，要向客戶解說公司在 ESG 和可持續發展方面的投資理念、方法及承擔，定義明確的系統也大有幫助。

這個範疇的發展非常迅速，雖有海量機會，但市場對 ESG 主題產品的需求越來越大，加上這類產品的數目不斷遞增，市場顯然需要更嚴謹的監管，以及更清晰的標籤、分類和標準。提高透明度有助於投資者加深了解相關產品的 ESG 及可持續特徵，對鞏固金融系統的信譽及促進其持續增長發展將有極大幫助。

引言

自 1970 年推出首隻可持續發展互惠基金以來，越來越多投資者將投資分析範圍擴大至傳統財務指標外，將環境、社會及管治（即 environment、social、governance，簡稱 ESG）因素加進分析框架裏。而近年，投資者對 ESG 的熱衷有增無減，並因以下原因提升至更高層次：

- 投資者日益了解 ESG 因素對投資價值造成的潛在影響；

- ESG 信息及數據倍增：發行人披露的 ESG 資料，以至來自第三方供應商的 ESG 數據及資料都比過去多，有助於作出投資決策；及

- 監管機構從嚴打擊「漂綠」行為 ——「漂綠」是指投資產品宣傳注重環保、符合 ESG 準則或可持續發展，但卻言過其實。

因此，市場出現各種各樣標籤投資方法及投資產品的詞彙，例如「社會責任投資」、「可持續投資」、「道德投資」、「綠色金融」、「ESG 整合」、「同類最佳」、「ESG 覆蓋」、「ESG 傾斜」和「價值為本的投資」等。從好的方面來看，新詞彙的湧現，意味產品不斷創新以迎合市場的多樣化及持續發展。然而，這些詞彙並沒有統一標準，它們代表一系列不同的方法、特徵及好處，未必完全清晰也不易分辨，有時更互相重疊，投資者固然容易混淆，即使業內人士亦難以理解清楚。

在市場對 ESG 投資產品熱烈追捧下，令人關注與 ESG 投資相關詞彙的缺乏一致性所帶來的一系列問題，例如：令投資者對產品的期許與現實產生落差、增加投資者對不當行銷的指控，使投資者與基金經理之間互不信任，繼而令資金無法有效分配、市場無法完全發揮潛力。有部分發行人亦可能會趁機進行「漂綠」，混水摸魚。CFA 協會於 2020 年 3 月向全球會員進行意見調查[1]，訪問了 325 名公司高層行政人員及 373 名 ESG 專家，在所有受訪者當中，**78%** 認為應制定相關標準以遏止「漂綠」行為。

對此，監管機構、標準制定者及專業團體紛紛加把勁，透過制定規例、標準、標籤及其他措施，希望為有關的產品分類，增添一些結構和秩序。

1　資料來源：CFA協會〈投資管理可持續性的前景：由理想到現實〉（"Future of sustainability in investment management: From ideas to reality"），2020年12月。

ESG 投資產品的全球監管與標準制定

ESG 及可持續投資的普及，促使監管者與行業機構從各方面加強各種規則及做法，包括：

- 制定分類標準及目錄，以釐定哪些活動符合綠色及可持續定義；

- 規定上市公司須披露 ESG 資料；

- 就投資基金的命名、標籤及披露制定標準及指引；

- 就綠色金融工具設立標準；及

- 設立相關基準。

有關投資產品（包括集體投資計劃及投資基金）的標準及指引方面的發展，比起適用於公司發行人及綠色金融資產的標準及指引相對落後。基金經理若要在產品層面作出適當的披露，必須從發行人取得及時和一致的相關資料；因此從市場發展角度來說，首要工作亦是協議一套分類標準，清晰界定何謂綠色及可持續活動，以及提升發行人的披露，並將之規範化。

不過，有關投資產品的命名及披露的規例和行業標準亦正迅速跟上。影響力最大的法例是 2021 年 3 月起生效的歐盟《永續金融披露規範》（Sustainable Finance Disclosure Regulation，簡稱 SFDR）。該項規範規定基金經理須披露如何在投資及風險管理程序中加入 ESG 因素，而有關披露同時適用於投資公司及投資產品層面。

下文載列某些司法權區有關 ESG 產品分類及標籤的監管環境概覽，當中側重於股本證券及定息基金等集體投資計劃（而非綠色或可持續發展債券等財務資產）或公司披露的相關規例及指引。我們亦會檢視 ESG 產品的自願性披露，以及業界在標準化 ESG 產品的標籤及披露方面所作的努力。

歐盟

致力轉型至低碳及較可持續發展的經濟，是歐盟積極建立可持續發展金融體系之一大動力。2018 年發佈的《永續金融行動計劃》（Sustainable Finance Action Plan）亦有涵蓋，而計劃的三大目標如下：

- 將資金流重新調配至可持續投資；

- 將可持續發展納入風險管理範疇；及

- 提升金融和經濟活動的透明度並促進長遠發展。

為實現上述目標，歐盟推出了一系列新的立法措施，現正一一實施。表 1 是歐盟的 ESG 規例概覽。

表 1：歐盟部分 ESG 規例概覽

規例	簡介	生效日期
《可持續金融分類標準條例》(Taxonomy Regulation)	就支持可持續環境的經濟活動設立統一分類系統。未來，《非財務報告指令》(Non-Financial Reporting Directive) 及 SFDR 項下規定的披露須跟從此分類準則。	2020 年 7 月。授權法案於 2021 年 4 月頒佈
《永續金融行動計劃》(SFDR)	引入適用於基金經理的披露責任，規定其須於投資及風險管理程序中加入可持續因素。	「1 級披露」於 2021 年 3 月生效，「2 級披露」將於 2022 年生效
《非財務報告指令》(Non-Financial Reporting Directive)	規定歐盟的大型公共利益公司（員工超過 500 人的公司）就四個可持續項目進行報告，即 (1) 環境；(2) 社會和員工事宜；(3) 人權；及 (4) 賄賂和貪污。	2018 年首次引入；有關加強現有規則及設立新的《企業可持續發展報告指令》(Corporate Sustainability Reporting Directive) 的建議於 2021 年 4 月由歐洲委員會 (European Commission) 發佈
《氣候基準規範》(Climate Benchmarks Regulation)	設立標準化的可持續發展基準，當中計及氣候轉型及符合《巴黎協定》(Paris Agreement) 的目標，旨在規定基準管理人員披露基準的方法論，並說明有關基準如何在標準化及可比較的情況下反映 ESG 因素，以提升透明度。	授權法案於 2020 年 12 月發佈及生效
《適用於零售金融產品的歐盟生態標籤》(EU Ecolabel for Retail Financial Products)	為歐盟各地的可持續零售金融產品設立通用的產品標籤。	制定中

資料來源：CFA 協會；歐洲委員會，請參閱（例如）其網站上的〈Sustainable finance〉網頁。

上述措施補充了對 ESG 事宜有間接影響的現有法例，例如對基金經理施加有關 ESG 投資策略、企業議合及相關披露等責任的《第二項股東權益指令》(Shareholder Rights Directive II)。

歐盟的《可持續金融分類標準條例》（以下稱為「歐盟分類標準」）、SFDR 及《非財務報告指令》（Non-Financial Reporting Directive，簡稱 NFRD）是歐盟 ESG 監管制度的三大元素，彼此環環相扣。歐盟分類標準提供正式的 ESG 分類及相關技術準則，而 NFRD 規定歐盟的公司須披露 ESG 資料。基金經理會收集及分析這些資料，釐定相關投資是否按歐盟分類標準正確歸類為可持續投資。根據此等分析，基金經理再按 SFDR 的規定作出披露。

有關的歐盟 ESG 規例能為其他市場提供藍圖，所以區外的監管機構及市場從業員正密切觀察有關進展，考慮是否全面或局部仿效，以節省在制定 ESG 披露制度中所涉及的成本與時間。

SFDR

SFDR 包括適用於基金經理及財務顧問的規則，當中有兩大目標：第一是為投資者提升透明度及可比性，第二是打擊「漂綠」行為。SFDR 的「1 級披露」規定於 2021 年 3 月 10 日在歐盟生效。基金經理作出的披露須同時涵蓋基金投資公司層面（例如管治及投資決策程序）及產品層面（例如投資基金所持相關證券的可持續性）。有關披露是按「不遵守就解釋」的基礎作出，意思是指不作披露就須給予解釋，並大致基於以下三個範疇：

- 如何管理及整合可持續風險；

- 產品的 ESG 績效的證明；及

- 披露其投資對可持續發展目標造成的主要不利影響。

SFDR 最明顯的影響，就是所有歐洲投資產品須按其實現 ESG 目標的承諾分為三大類。所有在歐盟生產及銷售投資產品的金融機構均須將其管理、推廣或推薦的產品納入下述三個類別之一：

- 第 9 條（「深綠」）：此類金融產品積極追求可持續投資策略，持有的所有投資均須符合可持續投資的定義 [2]。

- 第 8 條（「淺綠」）：此類產品推廣環保或社會特徵。有關基金可酌情決定將其中一部分資金投資於可持續投資。

- 第 6 條（「淡綠」或「灰色」）：非第 8 或第 9 條的其他產品均屬此類，包括在投資程序中並無考慮任何類型可持續因素的產品。

2　SFDR將可持續投資定義為在經濟活動中，對環境或社會目標帶來貢獻或對人力資本／弱勢社羣作出的投資，前提是這些投資者不會對其他目標造成重大損害，及所投項目須遵守良好的管治操守。

第 8 及第 9 條產品須遵守較高的披露標準，包括如何實現有關的可持續水平，以及個別的指定指數如何符合投資目標。

就第 6 條產品而言，有關金融機構須於訂立合約前披露產品含有哪些可持續風險，以及該等風險可能會對產品回報造成的影響，又或解釋為何認為該等可持續風險並不相關。

按照「1 級披露」規定，有關資料必須於訂立合約前在基金經理的網站上披露。及至 2022 年「2 級披露」規定生效後，有關機構亦須進行定期披露。

不少基金經理均在調整策略以符合新規定。部分已開始宣稱其基金符合第 8 條或第 9 條的若干規定。也有一些與顧問合作，改良基金的可持續特徵，以便從第 6 條升級至第 8 條。

另一些基金經理則比較審慎。儘管 ESG 基金備受歡迎，但將基金歸入第 6、第 8 或第 9 條會如何影響客戶需求，仍是未知之數。此外，待「2 級披露」規定強制執行後，基金經理作出的任何有關可持續發展的聲明便須有實質數據支持。這倒不容易，因為歐盟分類標準與 NFRD 裏不少細節和指標仍在制定中，數據缺口的問題尚未解決。因此，部分基金經理暫時先將基金分類為第 6 條或第 8 條，因為這兩類的舉證責任相對較輕[3]。

SFDR 會對歐盟以外的金融機構有治外法權影響。向歐盟推廣基金或向歐盟公司提供投資組合管理或投資顧問服務的基金經理亦在此範圍內，故須作出符合 SFDR 的披露（即使其產品並不特別與 ESG 有關）。

儘管有上述考慮因素，但預期 SFDR 仍會改變歐盟的金融服務業。這是舉足輕重的措施，可以提升透明度、打擊「漂綠」行為，以及加強投資者所接觸並須了解的 ESG 及可持續發展事宜的可信性。更重要的是，這將有助於將資金導向更可持續的活動（這亦是歐盟的一項主要政策目標），並可促使歐盟達到未來十年調動 1 萬億歐元（1.2 萬億美元）投入可持續投資的目標[4]。

美國

在美國，上市公司若認為 ESG 風險對其業務會有重大影響，便須披露有關風險。然而，到目前為止，美國證券交易委員會（Securities and Exchange Commission，簡稱 SEC）仍未

3　資料來源：Adrian Whelan〈可持續金融披露規例：工作量繁多，時間卻很少〉（Sustainable finance disclosure regulation: So much to do, so little time），《BBH Insights》，2021年2月8日。

4　可參閱的資料例子有歐盟網站上的〈擬就設立歐盟綠色債券標準進行的市場諮詢〉（"Targeted consultation on the establishment of an EU Green Bond Standard"）網頁。

強制規定 ESG 披露要求或將之標準化。因此,相對而言,美國的 ESG 規例,不論在公司披露或投資產品披露兩方面均未成熟。不過,圍繞 ESG 事宜的監管活動已日漸增加。

2020 年 3 月,SEC 就有關基金命名的規例(Names Rule,以下稱為《命名規則》)徵詢公眾意見,當中特別提到有關規則是否仍然相關或需要更新(因為該規則自 2001 年 1 月首次採納至今從未更新)。根據《命名規則》,每隻基金的資產至少要有 80% 是按基金名稱所述方式投資,相比之下,此前基金一般只按 65% 的界線選擇基金名稱。

SEC 重新檢視此規則的其中一個原因,是由於 ESG 或可持續投資產品(包括交易所買賣基金 —— exchange traded fund,簡稱 ETF)越來越受歡迎。但 ESG 或可持續投資等詞彙並未標準化,加上《命名規則》缺乏適當監管,導致產品發行商能在現行規例中尋找漏洞,以投資產品的命名誤導投資者。SEC 憂慮有關產品的名稱可能會造成誤導,而投資者又過份依賴「ESG」或「可持續」等詞彙作為產品標籤,未有確切了解基金所投資的資產類型、投資策略或非財務目標。

自 2021 年初起,SEC 已示意將顯著改變其在 ESG 方面的做法,並表明會就此事進行全面評估。SEC 與投資行業最息息相關的行動包括:

- 就氣候及 ESG 事宜成立工作小組;

- 檢視名稱中標榜「ESG」的基金,並評估當中是否言過其實;

- 在對註冊投資顧問的審查中強調有關氣候及 ESG 的事宜;及

- 就發行人對氣候變化所需作出的相關信息披露向公眾諮詢。

亞太區

香港特別行政區

在香港,有關可持續金融及 ESG 的議題越來越重要,而政府及監管機構近年對這方面的關注程度亦與日俱增。為使香港成為綠色金融中心,政府在政策層面推出了多項措施,包括:公佈氣候行動計劃,期望 2050 年前實現碳中和;通過綠色債券發行計劃;及推出《綠色債券資助計劃》,就有關發行綠色債券的額外成本(例如外部評審)向發行人提供補助。

當中的一項重大里程碑,就是成立由香港金融管理局與證券及期貨事務監察委員會(簡稱「香港證監會」)帶領的《綠色和可持續金融跨機構督導小組》,為金融業的監管政策及市場發展提供策略性方向[5]。2020 年 12 月，該督導小組發佈策略規劃，列出六大重點範疇，當中包括推動氣候相關信息在各層面的流通，以便利風險管理、資金分配及投資者保障[6]。

作為基金經理及投資產品的監管機構，證監會專注於設立預期目標及新政策，以及就有關範疇提供實務指引。2020 年 11 月，香港證監會刊發有關基金管理人管理及披露氣候相關風險的諮詢文件，概述管治、投資管理、風險管理及披露等各方面的最低規定，以及提升後的標準。披露規定分為兩個層面：(1) 機構層面：披露重點在管治、投資管理及風險管理的方法、過程及架構；及 (2) 基金層面：披露加權平均碳強度（若管理人的資產管理規模超過某水平便適用）。

香港證監會於 2019 年發佈一份對綠色和 ESG 基金作出披露要求的通函，並於 2021 年對此作更新及增加新的要求[7]。披露目的旨在提高透明度、可比性和可見度。對於 ESG 基金，除了需要提供投資重點、策略、ESG 投資預期比例和風險等描述外，還需要作以下的額外披露：

- 如何在整個基金週期中衡量和監控 ESG 重點投資；

- 衡量此類 ESG 重點投資的方法；

- 對基金資產的 ESG 屬性進行的盡職調查；

- 公司議合和授權投票政策；及

- ESG 數據來源。

此外，通函新加一項規定，就是要求 ESG 基金定期審視及報告如何實踐其 ESG 重點投資。

香港證監會已考慮過歐盟 SFDR，容許以 ESG 因素作其投資重點的「可轉讓證券集體投資計劃」(UCITS[8]) 基金在香港可作為合規的 ESG 基金。此外，已經符合 SFDR 第 8 及第 9 條披露和報告要求的 UCITS 基金也被視為已經滿足香港證監會新的披露要求。

香港證監會整理了一份綠色和 ESG 基金的中央名單，於其網站上列出。截至 2021 年 8 月，共有 65 個已上市或未上市的產品符合這要求[9]。

5　其他成員包括環境局、財經事務及庫務局、香港交易及結算所有限公司、保險業監管局和強制性公積金計劃管理局。

6　資料來源：綠色和可持續金融跨機構督導小組〈有關「鞏固香港金融生態系統，共建更綠和更可持續未來」的策略計劃〉，2020年12月17日。

7　參閱香港證監會〈致證監會認可單位信託及互惠基金的管理公司的通函——環境、社會及管治基金〉，2021年6月29日。

8　UCITS (Undertakings for the Collective Investment in Transferable Securities) 是歐盟一個監管框架，容許互惠基金於歐盟各國之間銷售。

9　資料來源：〈綠色基金和環境、社會及管治基金列表〉，香港證監會網站上的網頁，於2021年8月19日閱覽。

新加坡

2019 年，新加坡金融管理局（Monetary Authority of Singapore）宣佈制定嶄新而全面的長遠策略，旨在令可持續金融成為新加坡作為國際金融中心的關鍵特色。

重點之一是就銀行、保險及資產管理範疇制定一套《環境風險管理指引》。最終指引於 2020 年 12 月發佈，規定基金經理須實施健全的環境風險管理政策及程序，若有關風險對業務構成重大影響，則必須於研究及投資組合建構程序中顧及有關風險。

新加坡於公佈該套指引後不久的 2021 年 1 月再進行市場諮詢，建議推出符合歐盟分類標準的綠色分類標準。

儘管不少監管措施的制訂正在進展中，但投資基金的命名與標籤方面仍有明顯落差。隨着「漂綠」問題日益受到關注，投資者紛紛要求建立 ESG 基金標籤，以提升可比性及透明度，並促進市場發展。

馬來西亞

可持續及責任投資（sustainable and responsible investing，簡稱 SRI）與伊斯蘭金融原則相似，因此在馬來西亞有相對較長的往績紀錄，市場的認受度亦相當高。為了將馬來西亞打造成為伊斯蘭金融中心，發展 SRI 一直是業內監管機構馬來西亞證券監督委員會（Securities Commission Malaysia，以下稱為「馬來西亞證監會」）的重點工作。馬來西亞證監會制定了配套式的監管框架，以促進這個市場的發展，例如 SRI 伊斯蘭債券框架（SRI Sukuk Framework），並於 2019 年發佈 SRI 藍圖，當中載列清晰的行動規劃，旨在加強由投資者、發行人、投資工具、內部文化和管治，以及資訊架構組成的整個生態圈。

投資基金方面，馬來西亞證監會於 2017 年就 SRI 基金發佈了一套指引 [10]，鼓勵 SRI 基金進一步發展，並令市場對此類基金的組成或結構有一定概念。馬來西亞證監會希望透過引入額外披露及匯報規定，鼓勵提升 SRI 基金投資政策及策略的透明度，從而增加市場上的產品種類，吸引更多投資者。

其他自願性標準

除強制性的監管框架外，全球各地亦已採用和正在研究制訂多種其他的自願性指引、標籤及標準，以下是其中一些例子。

---

10 馬來西亞證監會《有關可持續及責任投資基金的指引》（*Guidelines on Sustainable and Responsible Investment Funds*），SC-GL/4-2017，2017年12月19日。

CFA 協會有關投資產品的 ESG 披露標準

CFA 協會正就投資產品制定一系列全球自願性 ESG 披露標準（簡稱「CFA 披露標準」，下同）。CFA 披露標準旨在透過讓基金經理清晰表達其投資產品的 ESG 相關特點，為投資者提供較高的透明度及可比性。CFA 披露標準會訂立適用於具有 ESG 相關特點的投資產品的基本規定、有關披露資料的獨立審查程序，以及根據 ESG 相關需要而作出的 ESG 相關特點分類。CFA 協會並為此而於 2020 年 8 月諮詢市場[11]，結果發現市場非常支持這套標準，亦支持這套標準採用描述性質的做法。

CFA 披露標準旨在令投資產品闡釋其運用 ESG 因素的有關資料，並明確表示不會試圖定義某隻產品是否 ESG 產品。正如前文所述，監管規例已日益着重產品的命名，如產品要定名為 ESG 或可持續產品，須通過監管機構所設的最低門檻。CFA 披露標準既不會要求，亦不會禁止投資產品的名稱、描述或介紹使用特定詞彙。此外，CFA 披露標準亦不會要求投資產品須有特定的 ESG 相關特點，又或是須符合投資組合層面 ESG 特徵或表現的最低門檻。因此，CFA 披露標準不會與本地的監管規例產生矛盾，而可以全球通用。CFA 披露標準預期於 2021 年第四季實施。

歐盟基金標籤

在歐盟區內，ESG 投資產品的標籤有以下兩大類：

- 歐洲國家標籤，例子包括法國的 ISR 及 Greenfin 標籤、比利時的 Towards Sustainability、盧森堡的 LuxFLAG 及奧地利的 Umweltzeichen；及

- 跨境標籤，例子包括德語系金融市場的 Nordic Swan Ecolabel 及 FNG-Siegel。

大部分國家標籤均跟從以特定主題（例如環境、社會議題、微型金融或能源轉型）為基礎的類似指引[12]。比利時的 Towards Sustainability 及法國的 ISR 標籤是歐盟兩個重要的可持續金融標籤。歐盟大部分國家的可持續金融標籤的共通點是排除化石燃料（ISR 及 LuxFLAG ESG 與環境標籤除外）。

零售金融產品的歐盟生態標籤

目前，歐盟不同國家綠色或可持續標籤的規定各有差異。歐洲委員會正就《永續金融行動計劃》制定一個適用於零售金融產品的統一生態標籤（Ecolabel），以促進可持續金融產品的跨境交易。

11　CFA協會《有關就投資產品制定CFA協會ESG披露標準的諮詢文件》（*Consultation Paper on the Development of the CFA Institute ESG Disclosure Standards for Investment Products*），2020年8月。

12　資料來源：Candriam〈歐洲的SRI標籤：應作何選擇？〉（"SRI Labels in Europe: What to Choose?"），2016年9月5日。

2020 年末，歐洲委員會就歐盟生態標籤的產品範圍及準則徵詢市場意見。回應顯示，業界都希望歐盟生態標籤能進一步與歐盟分類標準對齊[13]，當中亦有一些回應提到必須確保準則嚴謹、標籤可信，而又確保市場上有充足的符合要求的投資機會，兩者兼顧[14]。

《Eurosif SRI 透明度守則》(Eurosif SRI Transparency Code)

這是一套自願性守則，旨在令歐洲有關基金的基金經理採用具問責性並符合社會責任的投資做法。有關守則確保自稱有社會責任的基金在披露其政策及做法時，提供準確、適時及無誤導成分的資料，讓散戶投資者可作出更佳的投資決策。有關守則的兩大核心原則是具透明度和問責性。

責任投資認證計劃 (Responsible Investment Certification Program)

澳大拉西亞責任投資協會 (Responsible Investment Association Australasia，簡稱 RIAA) 是由澳洲及紐西蘭積極參與責任投資的個人和機構所組成的網絡。RIAA 制定了自願性的「責任投資認證計劃」，可讓金融產品申請認證標記，以代表有關產品或供應商履行了責任投資的承諾，並按規定符合責任投資的標準。該項計劃適用於投資產品、投資管理服務及退休基金。當中流程包括根據一套準則來評估所有申請人，另外基金經理亦須尋求獨立驗證。

要求認證的目的是給予投資者一定程度的信心和保證，令他們相信投資產品或服務採用的投資風格和程序，均有系統地考慮到 ESG 或道德因素，而這個投資程序亦經由外部專家驗證為可靠可信。嚴謹的營運及披露規定亦可確保產品或服務遵守相關標準。

任何產品如要獲認證為責任投資產品，均須符合以下部分規定[15]：

- 設有正式、一致、有記錄並可審核的責任投資策略及程序；

- 陳述符合事實，標籤恰如其名；

- 避免重大損害；

- 在投資程序中考慮到 ESG 因素；及

- 就責任投資作出相關及可查閱的披露。

---

13 相關例子請參閱AMIC〈AMIC回應：歐洲委員會就適用於零售金融產品的歐盟生態標籤之市場諮詢〉("AMIC response: EC consultation on the EU Ecolabel for retail financial products")，2020年12月11日。

14 相關例子參閱歐洲基金暨資產管理協會 (European Fund and Asset Management Association)〈歐洲基金暨資產管理協會對JRC就適用於零售金融產品的歐盟生態標籤發展之第三份技術報告的市場諮詢所作回應〉("EFAMA's answer to the JRC consultation on the 3rd technical report on development of EU Ecolabel criteria for retail financial products")，2020年12月11日。

15 資料來源：RIAA〈責任投資認證計劃：RI認證標準〉("Responsible Investment Certification Program: RI Certification Standard")，2020年8月15日。

RIAA 亦設立了一個名為「責任回報」(Responsible Returns) 的平台，讓投資者搜尋、比較及選擇最能滿足自身需要、負責任並合乎道德的退休基金、理財及投資產品。平台上的所有產品和基金均已根據 RIAA 的認證計劃獲得認證。

環球 ESG 投資框架

ESG 投資方式有許多，涉及的投資目標或方針不一而足，從以「價值為本」到以「價值觀為本」的方針都有。以價值為本的投資方針，會在評估投資機遇時顧及重要的 ESG 因素，以減低風險或賺取高於基準的回報，這或許是最接近傳統的金融投資方式。相對而言，以價值觀為本的投資方式，則會在投資時考慮投資者的信念或價值觀，這些非財務目標甚至可能較財務回報更重要。而在這兩者的中間，則是許多各具特色的投資方式，部分更有重疊。基金經理可針對某個投資策略而採取多於一種投資方式。有時候，投資產品會以其標籤或分類方式命名，而有部分基金的標籤已限定了其必須採用某些方式，例如排除篩選式或議合式投資。

即使這些方式已沿用多時，但因為一直沒有統一標準，所以存在各式各樣的稱呼。市場上有多個組織亦嘗試建立可描述此等方式的框架，包括全球永續投資聯盟 (Global Sustainable Investment Alliance)、責任投資原則組織 (Principles for Responsible Investment) 及 RIAA。表 2 顯示六類典型的 ESG 投資方式及其財務性和影響性目標，下文將逐一檢視。

表 2：ESG 投資方式

		焦點	影響性目標	財務性目標
傳統投資		不理會ESG因素	不考慮	着重調整風險後有高額回報
ESG投資方式	ESG整合	作投資決定時明確考慮ESG因素	避免損害及/或緩減ESG風險	
	剔除 / 負面篩選	剔除若干公司，以避險或切合所定的價值觀、道德觀或信念		期望市場回報達一定基準
	拔尖 / 正面篩選	挑選行業內ESG表現較佳的公司	惠及持份者	
	表決和議合	行使表決權，積極監察公司對公司ESG方面的活動及行為發揮影響力		
	主題投資	以ESG主題和趨勢為投資焦點		
	影響力投資	爭取財務回報之餘，也對環境或社會有正面影響	帶來正面影響	低於市場水平至市場水平的回報
慈善事業		致力為環境或社會帶來正面影響，不計財務回報		接受會損失部分或全數資本

資料來源：《RIAA負責任投資框架》（*RIAA Responsible Investment Framework*）；CFA 協會《可持續投資手冊》（*Handbook on Sustainable Investments*）。

ESG 整合

根據《2020 年全球可持續投資回顧》（2020 Global Sustainable Investment Review，簡稱 GSIR）[16]，ESG 整合是最受人歡迎的投資方式，相關管理資產總額約 25.2 萬億美元。ESG 整合是指在傳統財務分析及投資決策中明確考慮重要的 ESG 因素，以改善組合的風險回報。投資組合管理人通常先有既定投資策略，再通過各類不同方式（例如影響力投資及正面篩選）加入重要的 ESG 因素。

在 ESG 整合過程中，一般是找出可能對公司財政帶來正面或負面影響的重要 ESG 議題。相關的分析方法之一是利用永續會計準則委員會（Sustainability Accounting Standards Board）的重要性圖譜（Materiality Map），這圖譜可協助投資者和基金經理針對不同行業而評估一些會大幅左右財務狀況的議題。

---

16 全球永續投資聯盟〈2020年全球可持續投資回顧〉。

不過，考慮 ESG 議題並不僅限於挑選證券和構建投資組合。就估值及信貸分析而言，整合 ESG 需了解 ESG 因素對若干事宜（例如收入預測、估值倍數、差價分析及管理質素）的影響。在風險管理上，則意味用上 ESG 因素作情景分析和壓力測試。

剔除或負面篩選

剔除法可說是最早出現的 ESG 投資方式，即剔除一些其所作所為與投資者信念、道德觀或價值觀不符的公司、行業或政權。另外，投資策略亦可為了符合指定地區的法律和法規而採用排除法。篩選時通常以一個廣泛的市場基準作起點，不符合特定準則的投資便剔出投資組合。排除法可分為兩大類：

● **以公司的產品作剔除基礎**：剔除產品和活動具爭議性的公司，包括武器、賭博、煙草或化石燃料。根據 GSIR，這種方式是全球第二最大的可持續投資策略，管理資產總值約 15 萬億美元，佔 ESG 相關管理資產總額的 42%。

● **以公司的行為及既定標準作剔除基礎**：剔除一些涉及持續有爭議事項（例如違反人權、貪污）或不合乎某個原則框架（例如聯合國全球契約）的公司，投資者通常是在管理其聲譽和潛在財務風險時作出如此篩選。

拔尖或正面篩選

拔尖通常採取以下形式：

● **業界龍頭**：鎖定業內 ESG 表現最佳的公司。

● **界域龍頭**：基金經理找的是特定界域（而非特定板塊）裏所有公司的最高評級者。倘若某些板塊的 ESG 表現遜於其他板塊，可能整個板塊會被剔除在外。

● **最努力求進**：包括 ESG 表現進步良多的公司。

拔尖法與剔除法相異之處，在於前者並非按公司業務活動而剔除整個板塊的公司（例如剔除煙草股），而是按相對的 ESG 表現作篩選或附以權重。有別於 ESG 整合法，在拔尖方式下的 ESG 表現指標，明確着重資產配置、證券選擇及組合構建決策等。拔尖方式亦不像主題投資，並非因應結構性長期趨勢來篩選公司或改變其權重。若與影響力投資作比較，拔尖策略的目標並非要達到有實質的改變。

表決和議合

表決和議合是指投資者利用股東投票權利，爭取對公司在 ESG 的活動和行為上發揮影響力，具體方法包括投票表決、與公司議合及提交股東議案等。股東通常以股東週年大會作平台，與公司董事會溝通，並評估公司業務是否符合他們的表決政策。股東積極與公司議合不外乎兩大原因：

- 對公司政策及決策發揮影響力，提高應對長遠挑戰的能力；及
- 藉着掌握更佳的披露資料以評估管理層的質素及對 ESG 議題的承擔，有助於作出投資和投票決定。

此類議合所帶來的影響可以質化（例如披露質素、公司對 ESG 的熱衷和承擔程度或公司策略的變動）或量化（例如碳排放減量或 ESG 評分上升）的方式來衡量。

主題投資

主題投資是指根據與 ESG 事宜相關的長遠宏觀經濟或結構性主題或趨勢作投資。這種投資方式通常着眼於可持續發展的挑戰（例如氣候變化、喪失生物多樣性或水源短缺），追求的是龐大財務回報。因此，這類組合的規模、涉及地區和行業往往有別於市場基準。主題投資有兩大方式：

- **單一主題投資**：通常是認定某個行業趨勢（例如健康護理或喪失生物多樣性），然後投資於在該領域有積極發展的公司。
- **多主題投資**：基金經理或有意尋求多個主題，通常是與聯合國可持續發展目標所列的一個或多個目標有關。有別於單一主題投資，多主題投資的目的是構建多元化的組合，同時促進全球可持續發展。

影響力投資

影響力投資是應對環境及社會問題而衍生、增長最迅速的領域之一。根據全球超過 250 個影響力投資機構組成的「全球影響力投資網絡」（Global Impact Investing Network），影響力投資泛指在爭取財務回報的同時，亦期望對環境和社會產生正面而可衡量的影響的投資方式。最重要的目的是帶來能夠造福社會和環境的正面影響。正因如此，影響力投資常被視作慈善工作的延伸 —— 投資者只是追求市場水平甚或較低的回報，視乎策略成果與情況而定。這種投資涵蓋多類資產，包括房地產以至私募投資和債務，涉及微型金融、清潔能源及社會住房等領域。

各 ESG 投資方式的好處與挑戰

各類 ESG 投資方式的好處與挑戰載於表 3。

表 3：ESG 投資方式的好處與挑戰

投資方式	好處	挑戰
ESG 整合	• 範圍廣、靈活性高，投資者可以考慮任何有意採用的策略或準則 • 專注提高回報及／或減低風險，讓投資者避免投資於估值過高的公司，即使其 ESG 表現出眾	• 投資決策的質素可以相當參差，基金經理需要清楚表明投資目標及流程
剔除／負面篩選	• 簡單易明，方便投資者評估組合是否切合自己所需 • 與其他投資方式相比，其表現與市場基準有密切關係	• 收窄投資選擇 • 限制了可選行業的範圍，令分散投資的空間減少
拔尖／正面篩選	• 投資者可更精準評核公司的 ESG 表現 • 可助投資者找到 ESG 方面長期領先的表表者，避開 ESG 表現遜色者	• 分析過程須用上許多資源，例如尋找和計算 ESG 表現、按 ESG 指標建立投資組合並持續監察
表決和議合	• 對投資回報有正面影響 • 提高投資組合所持公司對 ESG 因素的意識 • 有助作出更佳投資決策	• 由於定息投資者沒有投票權，對定息投資者意義不大 • 低成本的被動式投資日益盛行，可能會削弱參與表決和議合的意慾
主題投資	• 有機會把握長期的宏觀趨勢 • 締造有別於廣義市場基準的風險回報，可以經歷多個業務週期起跌而持續提供卓越回報	• 與市場基準關聯較少，令變數更大 • 或會投資 ESG 欠佳的公司
影響力投資	• 投資者可表現其承擔 • 相對較直接 • 最新數據顯示投資者所得回報未必比傳統回報遜色 [17]	• 相對較集中、約束較多 • 投資規模通常較小且不公開買賣，故離場選擇不多，或有流動性問題 • 沒有劃一的影響力衡量基準，投資者或難以評估其投資的影響

資料來源：《RIAA 負責任投資框架》（*RIAA Responsible Investment Framework*）；CFA 協會《可持續投資手冊》（*Handbook on Sustainable Investments*）。

17　參閱例子：Global Impact Investing Network〈Impact investing decision making: Insights on financial performance〉，2021年1月14日。

標籤與分類的應用

可持續基金的數目不斷上升，其名稱也日趨複雜：由 ESG、綠色與環境，到道德與社會責任，以至用水、生物多樣性或減碳為主題的基金。選擇花多眼亂亦令投資者混淆。名稱各異，亦欠一致，眼花繚亂下令一般投資者不知所措。如下文所述，在某程度上，採用標籤與分類有助減輕這些問題。

投資基金

基金經理與投資者如何使用標籤

歐盟區內國家及跨區投資產品標籤，是極具參考價值的案例，能讓我們加深了解當地基金經理及投資者如何有效利用這些標籤。首先，這些標籤能給予投資者最低限度的質量保證：產品確實包含所聲稱的可持續元素。每個標籤的評審準則、匯報要求及管治架構各不相同。採用標籤的基金數目持續上升：至 2020 年年底，歐盟共有 1,418 隻投資基金帶有 ESG 或綠色標籤，涉及的管理資產規模為 6,900 億歐元，較前一年增加 128%[18]。歐洲兩大主要標籤為法國的 ISR 與比利時的 Towards Sustainability，其中使用 ISR 標籤的基金有 645 隻，涉及管理資產規模為 3,590 億歐元；而帶有 Towards Sustainability 標籤的基金則有 494 隻，涉及管理資產規模為 2,840 億歐元[19]。基金數目和管理資產規模均有增長，顯示在挑選可持續投資產品時投資者對標籤的參考價值益發重視。不過，即使標籤越來越普及，但只佔基金整體市場很小部分。

不同標籤之間存在激勵競爭：一個投資基金要否加上標籤、要加哪個標籤，純是基金經理的決定，所以他們每每是被遊說的對象。根據綠色金融研究機構 Novethic，選擇附帶多個標籤的基金數目開始湧現，原因是投資者對本地認證的標籤更為熟悉，若產品帶有此類標籤，其銷售和取得認可都能事半功倍。

可持續標籤一般適用於 UCITS 類股權及債券基金，包括 UCITS ETF。Greenfin 標籤可用於非上市基金（例如私募股權或基建），ISR 標籤則可用於房地產基金。儘管標籤能惠及所有投資者，但如機構投資者、挑選基金者及高資產淨值人士等資深投資者對評估和投資基金產品的經驗相對較豐富，毋須依賴標籤。對這些用戶來說，重點反而是深入了解基金經理是否對 ESG 及可持續發展有清晰的承擔、如何實行其可持續投資政策，以及如何審視投資對象的 ESG 準則。

---

18 資料來源：Novethic〈市場數據：可持續基金標籤（歐洲）〉（"Market data: Sustainable fund labels, Europe"），載於 Novethic的網站，2020年12月31日。

19 同上。

歐盟區內各標籤的差別

現時歐盟區內共有九個標籤，其中七個是國家標籤，兩個是跨境標籤。這些標籤可分為專注於 ESG 和專注於環境投資兩類。

表 4：歐盟可持續金融標籤概覽

標籤	國家	規管	類型
FNG-Siegel	德國、奧地利及瑞士	FNG（一個可持續投資論壇）之下管理的專家委員會	可持續 / ESG 投資流程（以氣候議題作負面篩選）
Greenfin	法國	獨立持份者委員會，由生態與公平轉型部（Ministry for the Ecological and Fair Transition）主理	主題投資與 ESG 準則（以氣候議題作負面篩選）
ISR	法國	獨立持份者委員會，由財政部支持	可持續 / ESG 投資流程
LuxFLAG ESG	盧森堡	跨境標籤機構 LuxFLAG	可持續 / ESG 投資流程
LuxFLAG 環境	盧森堡	LuxFLAG	主題投資與 ESG 準則
LuxFLAG 氣候金融	盧森堡	LuxFLAG	主題投資與 ESG 準則（以氣候議題作負面篩選）
Nordic Swan Ecolabel	北歐國家	北歐環保標籤委員會（Nordic Ecolabelling Board）（由北歐政府授權）	可持續 / ESG 投資流程（以氣候議題作負面篩選）；有綠色匯報
Towards Sustainability	比利時	中央標籤機構（Central Labelling Agency）	質量標準結合投資流程和剔除法的要求
Umweltzeichen	奧地利	奧地利環境部（Austrian Federal Ministry for the Environment）	可持續 / ESG 投資流程（以氣候議題作負面篩選）

資料來源：Novethic〈歐洲可持續金融標籤概覽〉("Overview of European Sustainable Finance Labels")，載於 Novethic 的網站，2020 年 6 月。

從表 4 可見，這些標籤一般由專責投資團體或專業環保標籤組織管理。唯獨法國的是由政府創立並支持的兩個公共標籤：ISR 和 Greenfin。ISR 用於負責任投資，Greenfin 則用作識別環保基金。

每個標籤為挑選證券、組合配置及組合披露定下要求時，所採納的方式和方法也不盡相同。例如：

- **ESG 分析的涵蓋範圍**：雖然所有標籤都必須分析 ESG 因素，但門檻各異，有些要求對投資組合進行全面的 ESG 篩選（例如 FNG-Siegel、Towards Sustainability），有些只要求 90% 或以上的覆蓋率（例如 ISR）。

- **剔除法**：正如前文所述，剔除不合資格或不符期望的投資是最常見的 ESG 投資方式，許多歐盟標籤亦有採用。部分標籤結合剔除法與 ESG 分析，要求基金剔除違反人權的公司，或從事放置反步兵地雷等具爭議活動的行業。

- **化石燃料**：所有環保標籤均在不同程度上排除化石燃料（尤其是煤）。除了煤，各標籤亦對生產及提取不同類型的化石燃料以及發電制定相關的技術準則，若某公司從此類活動獲得的收入佔比過高，如超過公司收入的 5% 或 10%，基金則不能投資該公司。

- **綠色事務**：一些列明與氣候或環境日標有關的標籤（例如 LuxFLAG 氣候金融、LuxFLAG 環境、Greenfin 及 Nordic Swan），在持有比例和投資組合兩個層面均設有門檻，確保所作投資都是推動環境可持續發展的活動。舉例，LuxFLAG 氣候金融標籤將「綠色」公司定義為至少一半營業額來自可持續事務，並規定綠色公司須佔投資組合的 75%。至於何謂可持續，標籤以可持續活動的分類標準為準，例如「氣候債券倡議組織」（CBI）的分類標準。

- **組合披露**：不同標籤的匯報頻次不一。有些須每年對投資組合作全面披露（LuxFLAG 環境、LuxFLAG 氣候金融、Greenfin），其餘的匯報週期則較短（Towards Sustainability：每半年；Nordic Swan：每季），Umweltzeichen 更須每月匯報。

標籤的本意是解決投資產品得到認證的問題。但形形色色的標籤卻衍生其他問題：令投資者眩惑，難以將產品互相比較。而且，要維持一個標籤涉及成本，若基金有多個標籤，成本更越滾越大，因此市場上開始出現要求協調不同標籤的聲音。其中一個潛在方案是使用歐盟生態環保標籤（EU Ecolabel）。這個標籤尚在制定中，是歐盟的可持續金融議程之一，亦已通過多輪諮詢。EU Ecolabel 並非用來取代國家標籤，只是若使用全歐盟適用的基金標籤，或可進一步推動區內可持續投資的發展。

基金評級

除監管當局及自發訂立標準者外，Morningstar 和 Sustainalytics 等商業數據供應商亦有提供基金層面的可持續發展評級，評定基金的 ESG 表現。許多投資者亦依據這些評級來作投資決定和比較。

評級和標籤最明顯的分別在於，附加標籤與否是由基金經理決定，而基金評級則是數據供應商賦予，無論基金是否有特別制定與 ESG 相關的策略，亦可獲得評級。評級過程或不需要基金經理作出任何行動，但對一些基金經理來說，取得高評級可能會成為誘因。另一分別是，基金評級評估的往往是基金在各種可持續指標的表現（視乎個別供應商的方法），而標籤通常更着重投資經理的投資方針及過程。

綠色、社會責任、可持續發展、轉型及可持續發展掛鈎債券

概覽

綠色、社會責任及可持續發展（green、social、sustainability，簡稱 GSS）債券屬於一種債券工具，其所得款項須完全用於合資格的環境或社會項目，又或兩者俱備的組合。

- **綠色債券**：GSS 類別中，綠色債券佔份額最大，歷史亦最長。綠色債券的所得款項只能用於對合資格的既有或新立的綠色項目進行部分或全面融資或再融資，有關項目包括再生能源、污染防控、適應氣候變化、用水及生物多樣性或綠色建築等。

- **社會責任債券**：社會責任債券是近年綠色債券以外第二種有強勁增長的類別。這類債券的所得款項用於資助一些可以處理特定社會議題，或對某部分羣眾產生正面社會影響的項目，可能包括建設可負擔的房屋、基本設施，以及基礎公共服務。目標羣眾的例子有生活在貧窮線下、肢體傷殘或其他弱勢社羣。

- **可持續發展債券**：可持續發展債券的所得款項用於對綠色與社會項目或活動進行融資或再融資。債券可由公司、政府和市政當局發行，用於營運特定資產及項目，可以是無抵押、以企業或政府發行人的信用作支持，又或是以特定資產作抵押品擔保。

- **轉型債券**：這類債券相對較新，適用於溫室氣體排放高的行業。轉型債券的發行人不一定是綠色發行人。其目標是讓「棕色」行業（例如煤礦）的公司集資轉型，轉投更可持續的業務活動，逐漸褪去棕色。

上述四類債券常被稱為「募集資金用途債券」。它們的所得款項有特定用途，並參照合資格項目或綠色及可持續活動的其他分類列表審批。這些債券的焦點在於相關項目，而不是其發行人。除了這些「募集資金用途債券」，還有一種相對較新的工具類別，稱為「可持續發展掛鈎債券」（切勿與可持續發展債券混淆）。

- **可持續發展掛鈎債券**（Sustainability-linked bonds，**簡稱 SLB**）：有別於 GSS 債券，SLB 籌集的資金不一定要用於特定的環境或社會項目，而是可作一般企業用途。這類債券旨在支持債券市場向公司提供資金，讓它們朝着可持續方向發展、擴大減碳規模，同時可幫助不同類別的發行人。這類債券須預定一些與可持續發展掛鈎的重要表現目標，若發行人未能達標，債券票息會提升，一般是提高 10 至 75 個基點。

GSS、轉型債券及 SLB 的分類

怎樣才算是「綠色」、「社會責任」或「可持續發展」債券？一般而言並非由監管條例界定，而是由一系列以市場為基準的自發原則及標準所界定。如國際資本市場協會（International Capital Market Association，簡稱 ICMA）便是例子之一，該會的目標是為可持續資本市場建

立一套共通語言（見表 5）。ICMA 可追溯最久遠的原則包括《綠色債券原則》（Green Bond Principles，簡稱 GBP）及《社會責任債券原則》（Social Bond Principles，簡稱 SBP）。

表 5：ICMA 部分原則

名稱	適用於	核心部分	首次刊發年份
綠色債券原則（GBP）	綠色債券	• 所得款項用途 • 項目評估及篩選過程 • 所得款項的管理 • 匯報	2014
社會責任債券原則（SBP）	社會責任債券	• 與 GBP 一致	2017
可持續發展債券指引（Sustainability Bond Guidelines）	可持續發展債券	• 與 GBP 和 SBP 一致	2018
氣候轉型融資手冊（Climate Transition Finance Handbook）	轉型債券	• 發行人的氣候轉型策略及規管 • 業務模式對環境影響的輕重 • 氣候轉型策略以「科學為本」，包括目標及路徑 • 實施透明度	2020
可持續發展掛鈎債券原則（Sustainability-Linked Bond Principles）	SLB	• 具公信力的主要表現指標 • 為可持續發展表現目標定標 • 包括涉及觸發事件的金融及結構性影響的債券特徵 • 匯報主要績效指標及與可持續表現目標有關的資料 • 合資格外部審核者的核證	2020

資料來源：ICMA。

GBP 並沒有提出「綠色」的定義，讓發行人自行酌情界定。被視為綠色的項目類型包括能源、樓宇、運輸、用水管理和廢物管理，以及污染控制。於 2021 年發佈 GBP 最新版中，建議要求發行人解釋其綠色債券如何透過其綠色債券框架，與 GBP 的四個核心部分保持一致性。GBP 並鼓勵發行人在其綠色債券框架中，為其可持續發展策略及對 GBP 的五個高層次環境目標貢獻作出描述。

除了 ICMA，CBI 亦設立了一系列綠色債券標準，稱為「氣候債券標準」（Climate Bonds Standard），為不同行業用以發行綠色債券的資產和項目提供相關的資格準則。除此之外，其他國家和地區亦設有綠色債券標準，例如中國的「綠色債券支持項目目錄」和東南亞國家聯盟的「綠色債券標準」（Green Bond Standards）。歐盟亦正訂立一系列劃一的綠色債券標準，預期於 2021 年發佈。

依循 ICMA 及 CBI 等國際原則與否全屬自發性及視乎發行人的決定，而對發行人來説，當中最大誘因在於發債時在定價及聲譽上所享的優勢。由於 GSS 債券供不應求，市場出現了綠色溢價現象：由同一發行人發行的傳統債券與其綠色債券相比，即使年期一樣，後者的價格每每較高而收益率較低。例子之一是德國政府推出的雙債券架構，即在短時間內發行特徵相似的傳統債券和綠色債券。根據 CBI[20]，綠色債券的收益率較相對應的那隻傳統債券低一個基點，顯示發行人發行綠色債券的條款更佳。

此外，GSS 債券所關注的主題並非企業與投資者慣常接觸到，發行人有機會與一些渴望多了解業務流程和運作的投資者建立關係。通過發行 GSS 債券，發行人可分散債券持有人的基礎，接觸不同投資者。

對投資者而言，將債券分類為綠色或其他類別亦很重要。基金經理憑着這些分類來辨別相關工具，有些投資授權條文或會明文規定基金只可投資 GSS 債券。當越來越多投資者有意將資金投入可持續發展項目之際，GSS 債券可説為他們大開快捷方便之門。

儘管自願性原則的出現加強了 GSS 債券市場的持正操作，但國際綠色債券的各種標準（包括分類標準）不一，發行人在制定目標時始終面對不少挑戰。跨地區合作的工作現正進行中，希望國際、地區和本地的各種指引和標準可以有更好的接軌，確保 GSS 債券市場得以蓬勃發展。

外部評審與認證

GSS 債券的盛行不止令人關注「漂綠」問題，還有「漂社」（即扭曲債券可對社會帶來的裨益）的風氣。投資者渴望獲保證所投資的證券皆真實可信，而所得款均按上述的 ICMA 原則使用。就 SLB 來説，投資者亦想確保制定主要績效指標和目標的程序同樣可靠可信。

為解決這個問題，市場選擇通過外部評審來令投資者安心。2021 年版本的 GBP 建議發行人於發行前需委任外部評審者以確認所發行的產品與四個核心部分保持一致性，及符合其他相關要求；還建議在發行後，由外部審計者為收益管理進行追蹤及驗證。

外部評審的例子包括第二方意見、核證、認證以及債券評級和評分。ICMA 為外部評審者發佈了一系列的自願性指引，包括專業和道德標準，以及報告編排、內容和披露等方面的指引。

20　Caroline Harrison〈定價市場的綠色債券定價：2020年7月至12月〉（"Green bond pricing in the pricing market: July-December 2020"），載於CBI的網站，2021年3月。

雖然在 ICMA 原則下，發行人進行外部評審只是自願和建議性質，但在「氣候債券標準」之下，外部評審是強制規定的。CBI 要求認可評審者進行第三方核證，向投資者保證有關債券符合「氣候債券標準」。

聘用外部評審服務的額外費用須由發行人自行承擔。為鼓勵發行人進行外部評審，新加坡、香港等地的政府均有提供獎勵以抵銷相關費用。第三方評審與核證是提高透明度的關鍵，亦是成功發行可信度高的債券不可或缺的因素。許多時候，正面形象、聲譽上裨益和定價優勢已蓋過所涉及的額外費用。

機遇及挑戰

標籤的好處與限制

投資者面對市場上五花八門的可持續投資產品，難免眼花繚亂。適當的標籤和分類，當然是簡單直接，亦很吸引的解決方案。尤其是有了標籤後，投資產品的質素、採用的 ESG 準則，以至產品是否符合預設準則、原則和指引等，亦有一定保證。設立標籤後，市場毋須太擔心「漂綠」的行徑，投資者亦可選出最切合本身需要的投資產品。

然而，市場上各式各樣的標籤（尤其是在歐洲等地），亦可能會造成混淆。面對類似的產品標籤，投資者不易充分理解不同標籤的方法及取向，未必能分辨出當中差異。標籤並無劃一規定，具不同標籤認證的產品在產品特點及特徵上可以截然不同，難以將產品直接比較。

在亞太區，問題又不一樣：除澳州與紐西蘭的 RIAA 認證計劃外，便沒有其他適用於 ESG 及可持續投資產品的自願性標籤框架。然而，部分市場（例如香港和馬來西亞）的監管機構亦就基金名稱提供指引，以提升透明度及避免造成混淆。

標籤一般設有特定最低標準，且通常以程序為本，着重驗證投資組合裏面所持的 ESG 或綠色證券，以及這些證券是如何獲挑選的，並確保基金向投資者定期作出全面匯報。投資者必須明白即使基金有標籤認證，並不代表對其財務或 ESG 表現作出保證；而且，有着同一標籤的不同基金，其做法及策略亦可能大相逕庭。

善用標籤及分類

標籤和分類的好處是可將大量資料壓縮成一個數字、標誌或詞彙來傳遞信息，但不足的地方是有關資料的細微差別遠超想像，不一定準確反映產品的 ESG 流程或結果。這個問題的根源又在於 ESG 及可持續投資缺乏劃一詞彙。那麼投資者應如何自處？投資者應充分掌握產品如何達到自己的投資目標 —— 有些投資者可能想尋找嚴選投資項目的基金，而另一些投資者可能只要求其投資的基金廣義上已加入了 ESG 因素。不論是哪一類，投資者還須考慮標籤以外的其他因素，並進行適當的盡職審查，以進一步了解標籤或分類的涵義。舉例而言，投資者可檢視基金的投資準則、持倉最多的投資、採用哪種篩選方法（如有），以及是否符合投資者本身的目標。標籤是重要的第一步，但不能完全取代周詳的盡職審查。

交易所在進行標籤及分類上的角色

交易所的基本角色是為買賣雙方提供一個有效率的平台，讓雙方以最能反映市場價值的價格進行交易。有關平台須為市場提供各式不同產品和相關流動性，並能促進市場定價，且設有健全的投資者保障框架，確保市場得到投資者的信任。交易所作為把關人、設定標準及執行規則者，對資本市場的發展起着關鍵作用。

正如前文多次提到，妨礙可持續金融發展的一大疑慮是缺乏標準化、劃一的通用詞彙。就此而言，標籤及分類極具實用價值：不僅相對易用，亦有助市場建立對有關系統的信心，這對公眾投資者更大有裨益。儘管如此，世上並無任何單一標籤或分類系統可完全滿足投資者的各種需要，又或是適用於所有投資產品。因此，交易所需要對自身平台上使用的標籤和分類保持開放但謹慎的態度。

交易所要履行職能，可以透過提升可持續證券的可見度，並將披露資料規範化，以減少信息矛盾，發揮平台對使用者的最大效用。舉例而言，非上市的可持續基金若符合若干條件，亦可選擇在交易所「展示」。這亦適用於 GSS 債券，為此可另設特定板塊作為展示渠道，將此類產品的透明度及可見度提高，方便買賣。交易所亦可透過建立有效的發行程序，同時確保 GSS 債券上市達到最高標準，以鼓勵發行人發行更多綠色債券。由於亞洲缺少投資產品標籤，區內交易所可在一定範圍內實行相關措施，就投資產品建立適當的標籤框架及標準。

結語

隨着各國政府、監管者、企業、金融服務業及投資者對可持續發展及氣候變化等議題日益重視，對 ESG 及可持續方面提供資金會是愈益重要的議題。為確保資金有效配置，「漂綠」問題亟待解決。現有標籤及分類制度總算為五花八門的 ESG 產品市場帶來一些秩序，亦減少「漂綠」的機會，但至今仍未有國際劃一的標準。然而，隨着新的規例及業界標準陸續面世，市場已達致轉捩點，重大進展指日可待。只要跨得過去，當可大大提高透明度，實現所期待的結果。這條路不會一帆風順 —— 要將地區及國際的詞彙和定義劃一和規範化，仍需要一段時間。要在這環境下摸索出一條康莊大道殊不容易，但卻可能帶來大量增長與創新的機會，亦有助於投資者和金融服務業降低在聲譽和監管上面對的風險。

註：本文原稿是英文，另以中文譯本出版。如本文的中文本的字義或詞義與英文本有所出入，概以英文本為準。

Chapter 7

GSF for issuers and borrowers: A solution to sustainable development

Radek JÁN
Infrastructure & Green Finance Specialist
Natixis

Summary

This chapter provides a practitioners' perspective on the value chain of green and sustainable finance (GSF) instruments from the standpoint of an investment bank. Assessing what constitutes a "green" or "sustainable" financial instrument is an intricate task, which draws upon knowledge from multiple domains of natural and social sciences alike. Over the past few years, given the absence of universally accepted scientific taxonomies that would readily provide such answers, market practitioners have taken a pragmatic approach and together conceived voluntary principles and guidelines, defining conditions under which bond and loan instruments can be labelled as "green", "social", "sustainability" or "sustainability-linked". Labelled bonds and loans within the GSF space can be divided into two groups based on their underlying mechanism: use of proceeds, and, general purpose.

While this chapter focuses on labelled GSF bond and loan instruments because these financial instruments are well-defined and easily identifiable, it should be emphasised that many other types of financial instruments can contribute to environmental, social and/or sustainability objectives. As such, labelled GSF instruments constitute a subset of financial instruments that can claim varying degrees of GSF credentials.

The issuance of labelled GSF bonds reaches record highs each year, but investors' demand continues to be higher still. The supply-demand imbalance has persistent pricing consequences in primary markets, which also spills into secondary markets. This chapter presents an empirical analysis of oversubscription rates, spreads tightening at reoffer versus initial pricing talk, and new issuance premia in euro-denominated bond markets. This analysis shows that investors have a stronger appetite for labelled GSF bonds than for comparable conventional bonds, which in turn results in the more favourable pricing of the former. Moreover, our analysis shows the existence of "greenium", a premium for GSF bonds in secondary markets. While far from being a homogeneous phenomenon (both positive and negative greenium can be observed), the existence of a greenium was shown to be persistent over time and its magnitude tends to increase with the maturity of the bond and the credit risk of the issuer.

As GSF moves away from the niche into the mainstream, several evolutions are taking place in the market. Several jurisdictions are currently preparing "taxonomies" to officially define what can be considered as "green" or "sustainable". The adoption of such taxonomies will likely be reflected in the evolution of market principles governing labelled GSF instruments. The diversification of available labelled GSF bond and loan formats has been particularly accentuated by the COVID-19 pandemic. With social and socioeconomic issues thrust into the spotlight, attention thus pivoted to social and sustainability GSF instruments. While green bonds remain the largest labelled GSF instrument in terms of issuance volumes and amount outstanding in the market, the share of social and sustainability bonds has been rising since the onset of the COVID-19 pandemic, and the trend is likely to continue in the foreseeable future. Sustainability-linked bonds and loans offer an entirely different mechanism with the promise of vastly expanding the GSF universe by appealing to issuers and borrowers who were not particularly interested in the use-of-proceeds mechanism of green, social and sustainability bonds and loans. The extent to which sustainability-linked bonds and loans manage to extend the appeal of GSF remains an open question for the time being. Given the absence of requirements to earmark proceeds and the focus on improvements over time, these instruments could be particularly suitable for financing the "transition" of carbon-intensive and/or heavily polluting industries towards a low-carbon economy. However, it remains unclear whether "sustainability-linked" shall become interchangeable with "transition" or whether an entirely new type/category of "transition" GSF instruments might be created in the future.

Issuers' motives for sustainable development through GSF

Climate change and sustainable development are becoming increasingly visible topics, and the past few years have been marked by rising activity at all levels: from companies and investors to states and international organisations. Much emphasis has been placed on understanding how to ensure economic development becomes more sustainable and what the implications of transition towards a low-carbon economy are for the financial landscape. There is an ongoing effort to understand how to align the financial system with the Paris Agreement[1] and investors are increasingly looking at the carbon footprint and climate risks and impacts of their portfolios. This momentum is in turn driving the supply of green and sustainable finance (GSF) solutions, most of which did not exist just ten years ago.

Central banks, financial regulators and supervisors are increasingly paying attention to the relationship between financial stability and climate change, which in turns incentivises financial institutions to consider these topics with rising interest. Climate and environmental focused momentum within the financial sector has been gathering pace ever since 2015, when two particularly impactful events occurred: the signing of the Paris Agreement and the *"Breaking the tragedy of the horizon"* speech[2] by Mark Carney, then Governor of the Bank of England. While the Paris Agreement set the stage in general terms, Carney's speech marked the first time that environmental and climate considerations were framed in terms that resonated with the financial community. Research and development of methodologies related to understanding, measuring and managing climate-related risks to financial stability have proliferated ever since, and much of the latest knowledge in this rapidly developing domain can be accessed via the Network for Greening the Financial System[3] (NGFS). The NGFS regroups central bankers, financial regulators and supervisors who together conduct analytical work about green finance and develop and share best practices in order to *"enhance the role of the financial*

---

1 The goal of the Paris Agreement is to limit average global temperature increase in this century to 2 degrees Celsius (°C), while pursuing efforts to limit the increase even further to preferably 1.5°C, compared to pre-industrial levels. (See "the Paris Agreement" webpage on the *United Nations Climate Change* website.)

2 Full speech of Mark Carney (dated 29 September 2015) is available at the "Speeches" webpage of the Bank of England's website.

3 Also known as The Network of Central Banks and Supervisors for Greening the Financial System.

system to manage risks and to mobilise capital for green and low-carbon investments in the broader context of environmentally sustainable development[4].

Within this context, more and more issuers are arriving to the market with GSF instruments. Some are frequent issuers well familiar with the market, but many more are arriving with inaugural issuances, whether they be in green, social, sustainability or sustainability-linked bond formats (the short form "GSS" will be used throughout this chapter to refer to these labelled formats). Consequently, there were nearly 1,300 individual issuers of labelled GSS bond instruments at the end of the second quarter of 2021 (2021Q2) (see Figure 1).

Figure 1.   Number of individual issuers of GSS bond instruments (2011 – 2021Q2) (all currencies)

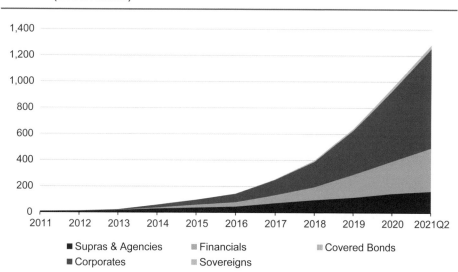

Source: Analysis by Natixis based on data from Bloomberg.

An increasing number of entities are devising their green and sustainable strategies and looking for means to align their funding mechanisms with environmental, social and governance (ESG) topics and sustainable development. As a consequence, GSF

---

4   Source: The "Joint statement by the Founding Members of the Central Banks and Supervisors Network for Greening the Financial System", available at Banque de France's website, 12 December 2017.

instruments thrive as they provide a concrete way of financing environmental, social or other sustainability-themed topics. In practical terms, accessing capital via GSF instruments brings several benefits to the issuer/borrower, these are discussed below.

Image and communication

By entering the GSF market, an issuer/borrower sends a clear message of commitment to ESG/sustainability topics. Use-of-proceeds bonds/loans show that the issuer/borrower has secured funding allocated to projects and activities with recognised environmental and/or social added value. Sustainability-linked bonds and loans send the message that the issuer/borrower commits to long-term improvements in the ESG space. Using either use-of-proceeds or sustainability-linked formats usually tends to have a positive impact on the issuer's/borrower's reputation and credibility, and potentially increases its ESG evaluation in the future. Depending on the nature of the GSF financing, the issuer/borrower is able to claim contribution to climate change adaptation or mitigation, positive environmental impact, support of social progress or economic empowerment/ development, or sustainable development in general.

Internal engagement

Embarking on the sustainability journey by means of GSF instruments can set in motion virtuous cycles of long-term improvement in operational/energy efficiency and/ or management in general. For instance, in fulfilling the conditions required for the issuer/borrower, a labelled GSF instrument can result in the setting up or enhancing of internal environmental management systems (environmental and climate accounting and reporting for example) or the evolution of company practices or procurement policies and requirements.

Regulatory environment

Entering into the GSF markets also presents opportunities to anticipate and align with future regulatory and policy changes/targets/commitments related to climate change, energy transition and sustainable development in general. For instance, green and sustainability-linked instruments present an opportunity for issuers/borrowers to align with national and international agendas related to climate change and environment.

Responding to investors' calls for a greater degree of clarity surrounding the environmental and sustainability credentials of different financial instruments and economic activities, several jurisdictions have begun to create legislation providing official definitions and taxonomies of GSF. The most prominent manifestations of this recent development are the European Union (EU) Taxonomy Regulation and "the Chinese taxonomy", officially known as the Green Bonds Endorsed Project Catalogue. The EU Taxonomy Regulation is the foundation of the EU Sustainable Finance Action Plan, a broader legislative and regulatory GSF push which also includes the creation of a new financial instrument, the "EU Green Bond", based on the EU Green Bond Standard, as well as the creation of EU Ecolabel, which clearly defines which retail investment funds can be marketed as "green". Ongoing efforts are taking place within the International Platform on Sustainable Finance (IPSF), a multilateral forum of public authorities, to ensure consistency and cooperation in ongoing effort in several jurisdictions to create regulatory frameworks and legislation for defining and scaling up GSF.

Appetite of investors and lenders for GSF instruments

Given the aforementioned ongoing developments, GSF bonds and loans are met with an increasing degree of interest in the market. Institutional Investors and asset managers are evermore focused on the climate footprint of their investment portfolios in order to gauge their potential exposure to the financial implications of climate policies and energy transition towards a low-carbon economy. Many players on the buy side have made quantified commitments to increase the share of GSF instruments in their portfolio, which is in turn driving the demand for these instruments in the market. The same can be said about lenders. For instance, sustainability-linked loans are a well-suited response to sustainability considerations and ESG criteria in a lender's credit assessment policies. Thanks to sustainability-linked loans, lenders can claim support of the broader sustainability/ESG agenda by directing capital towards borrowers committed to improving their performance in these areas. Generally speaking, labelled GSF instruments provide increased availability of information and accountability of issuers/borrowers. This in turn, enhances the integrity of financial markets and gives investors better information to evaluate their investments in terms of ESG risks and impacts.

Consequently, the past few years have been marked by an increasing demand for assets and investment opportunities with tangible green/social/ESG credentials. Labelled GSF instruments are particularly suitable to respond to this demand as the core principles of relevant bond/loan principles address investors'/lenders' expectations in terms of eligibility criteria, reporting, transparency and expected environmental and/or social impact. Both use-of-proceeds and sustainability-linked bond formats are intended for a broad range of fixed-income investors. Fixed-income funds with responsible investment strategies (such as ESG integration, best-in-class, thematic investing or ESG tilting) may find sustainability-linked bonds largely appealing due to their forward-looking perspective. There are also numerous dedicated GSS bond funds which are especially interested in use-of-proceeds bonds. Whether such dedicated funds would also consider including sustainability-linked bonds in their portfolio would depend on the relevance of given key performance indicators (KPIs) and sustainability performance targets (SPTs) for the fund.

As a consequence, issuing a GSS bond can result in diversification of the investor base, as issuers can gain access to a wider range of investors or attract different types of investor who were previously not considering issuances from the issuer.

Empirical insights from euro-denominated markets

The imbalance between supply and demand for euro-denominated GSS bonds has pricing consequences observable in both primary and secondary bond markets.

GSS bonds supply-demand imbalance in primary markets

Analysis of empirical data from euro-denominated markets reveals that despite rapidly increasing issuance volumes of GSS bonds, demand for these instruments is higher still. This supply-demand imbalance results in pricing advantages for GSS bonds, which are consistent over time. Our empirical analysis of market data between 2018 and 2021H1 shows that investors have stronger appetite for GSS securities[5] relative to their conventional peers (same type of issuer, similar size, similar issuance time) as shown by differences in oversubscription rates between the two formats. Stronger investor appetite then results in pricing differences in terms of spread tightening at launch and in terms of new issuance premia (NIP).

---

5   This section uses the term "securities" rather than "financial instruments" to make an explicit reference to bonds only (loans are not securities). While the rest of the chapter refers to both bond and loan instruments bearing green, social, sustainability and sustainability-linked labels, the sections about pricing in primary markets and greenium in secondary markets refer exclusively to bonds.

Oversubscription rate

Oversubscription rate indicates the magnitude of investor appetite for bonds at the moment of their issuance. While bond issuances in general tend to be oversubscribed, the oversubscription rates tend to be, on average, higher for GSS bonds, pointing to higher investor appetite for GSS bonds. Stronger investor appetite would have pricing consequences.

Comparison of average quarterly oversubscription rates between GSS and conventional bonds presented in Figure 2 reveals that investors tend to have a stronger appetite for issuances in GSS format. GSS BBB-rated corporate debt has displayed higher oversubscription rates than issuances in conventional format in every quarter since 2021Q1. Similarly, GSS senior preferred financial debt has exhibited higher oversubscription rates in every quarter since 2019Q2 and GSS senior non-preferred financial debt displayed the same tendency since 2020Q3. Only A-rated corporate debt offered a more nuanced picture — much higher average GSS bonds' oversubscription rates between 2019Q4 and 2020Q2, similar levels for both GSS and conventional formats between 2020Q3 and 2021Q1 and lower GSS oversubscription rates in 2021Q2.

Figure 2. Oversubscription rates of euro-dominated GSS bond vs conventional bonds (2018Q1 – 2021Q2)

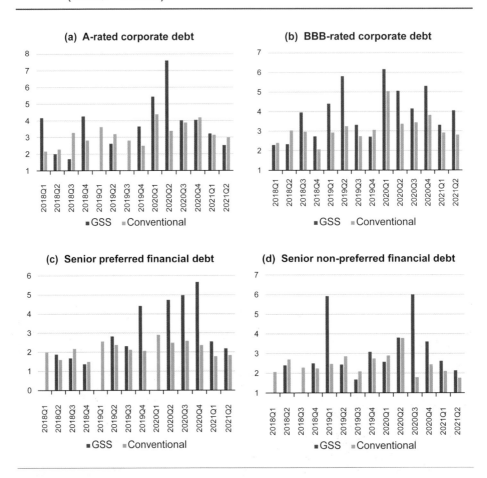

Source: Analysis by Natixis based on data from Bloomberg.

Spread compression at launch

Spread compression between the time of the initial pricing talk (IPT) and the time of the final pricing is closely related to the oversubscription rate. As part of the pricing process, bonds experience spread tightening. Stronger investor demand for a bond (reflected in higher oversubscription rates) results in a higher spread compression between the time of the IPT and the time of the pricing.

Overall, this indicator displays consistent pricing advantages for issuances in GSS formats relative to their conventional peers. As a consequence of stronger investor demand for GSS issuances, euro-denominated BBB-rated GSS corporate debt has, on average, experienced higher spread compression versus the IPT, when compared to conventional peers issued at a similar time. This holds for every quarter observed in our sample, with the exception of 2018Q2. Similar trends in favour of GSS formats can be observed in every quarter since 2019Q2 for senior preferred financial debt and since 2020Q4 for senior non-preferred financial debt. Only A-rated corporate debt offers a more nuanced picture, with the average spread tightening stronger for GSS formats in some quarters and stronger for conventional formats in others. (See Figure 3.)

Figure 3. Spread compression vs IPT of euro-dominated GSS bond vs conventional bonds (2018Q1 – 2021Q2)

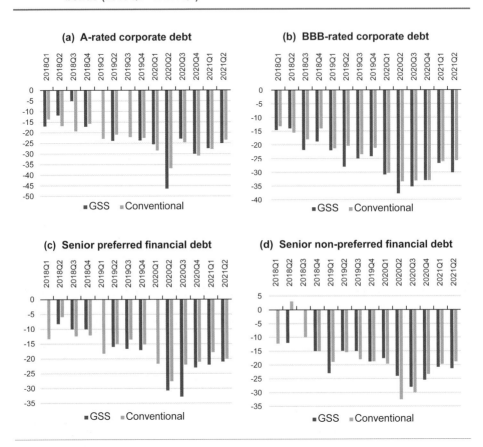

Source: Analysis by Natixis based on data from Bloomberg.

New issuance premium (NIP)

NIP refers to the extra yield received by the buyer (paid for by the seller) for a newly issued bond relative to the yield of other bonds by the same issuer, which are being traded in the secondary market at the time the new bond is priced. To calculate NIP, we built zero-volatility spread (z-spread[6]) curves for each issuer in our sample and interpolated the secondary curve on the maturity of the newly issued bond.

Due to higher investor appetite for GSS bonds in euro-denominated issuances, all observed asset classes in our sample exhibit a pricing advantage for issuers in terms of lower (and sometimes negative) NIP for issuances in GSS rather than conventional format. This trend is consistent over time. Moreover, numerous inaugural or otherwise innovative GSS issuances tend to be "awarded" by NIP that is not only considerably lower than for conventional formats, but also negative. As observed in Figure 4, the average NIP for euro-denominated BBB-rated GSS corporate debt was negative between 2020Q3 and 2021Q2, while the average NIP displayed by conventional issuances remained positive throughout this period. Moreover, the average NIP for GSS issuances, both senior preferred and senior non-preferred financial debt, turned negative for the first time in 2021Q1, while the NIP displayed by their conventional peers remained positive during the same period. Interestingly, even A-rated corporate debt has exhibited a lower average NIP for GSS issuances since 2020Q2, even though GSS and conventional issuances in this category tend to be similarly oversubscribed and exhibit similar levels of spread tightening at launch.

---

6   Z-spreads are used to quantify what the market thinks about the value of bond's cashflows: defined as the basis point spread that would need to be added to the implied spot yield curve such that the discounted cash flows of the a bond are equal to its present value (its current market price). We use z-spreads because they are the best measure of credit risk (no maturity bias) and the best tool to measure the relative value between different issuances and in terms of spread history. This is because z-spreads are not influenced by the evolution of the yield curve.

Figure 4. NIP of euro-dominated GSS bond vs conventional bonds (2018Q1 – 2021Q2)

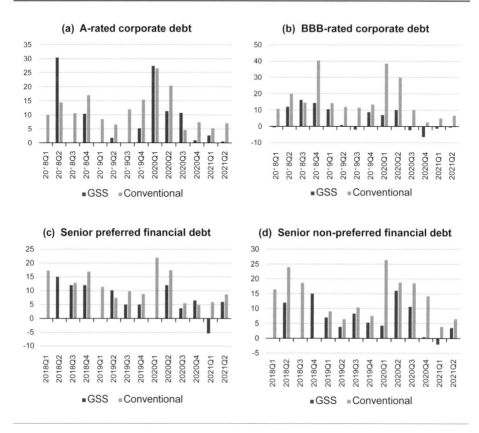

Expanding greenium in the secondary market [7]

The growing imbalance between investor demand for GSS bonds and its supply, although the latter has proven very dynamic over the past years (see Figures 1 and 10), is translating into a significant premium for GSS bonds versus their respective conventional counterparts in the secondary market (the so-called "greenium"), as it is the case in the primary market (see Figure 4).

In order to measure the greenium, one needs to compare the yield (or more precisely the z-spread) of instruments of a given issuer at a given date in the GSS market with the equivalent yield (or rather z-spread) of instruments offered by the same issuer, of the same seniority, comparable maturity as well as liquidity. Measured as the difference in z-spread between a given GSS bond and its conventional counterpart, the greenium tends to be negative when investors accept to pay a premium for GSS assets.

In the euro-denominated non-financial corporate bond market, where GSS bonds have the longest track record for comparison with their conventional counterparts, we noticed that the greenium (calculated over a panel of 78 GSS bonds representing about €60 billion outstanding) has been constantly negative since the second half of 2017, except during a few days in March 2020 in the midst of the COVID-19 crisis in Europe. Since March 2020, the greenium in the euro-denominated corporate bond market has been trending almost continuously more negative (i.e. larger greenium) and is worth around 3.2 basis points (bps) in early August 2021. (See Figure 5.)

---

7   This section on greenium has been prepared by Thibaut Cuillière, Head of Real Asset Research at Natixis.

Figure 5. Trend in the average greenium for euro-denominated corporate bonds (2 Jul 2018 – 12 Aug 2021)

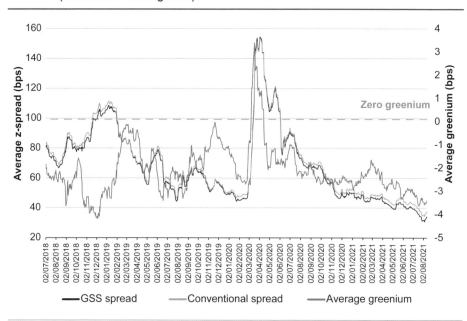

Source: Analysis by Thibaut Cuillière (Natixis) based on data from Bloomberg.

Moreover, one also needs to consider the greenium as a function of the spread paid by the issuer for issuing a bond, either GSS or conventional. Indeed, the higher the credit risk of a given issuer, the greater the GSS premium as more appetite for GSS bonds will make greater difference for a riskier issuer (for which the investor demand is much lower, be it for conventional or GSS format).

As shown in Figure 6(a), the greenium as a percentage of the average corporate z-spread has become larger since March 2020, with another phase of acceleration since February 2021 — the average greenium for a given corporate non-financial issuer by mid-August 2021 amounted to 9% to 10% of its z-spread on average, compared with 4%-5% at the start of the year, further demonstrating how the strong demand for GSS assets is impacting the pricing of these instruments.

As shown in Figure 6(b), the average greenium (in bps) as of 12 August 2021 in the euro-denominated corporate bond market is largely correlated with the level of spread.

Figure 6. Greenium as a % of spread and average greenium by spread level for euro-denominated corporate bonds

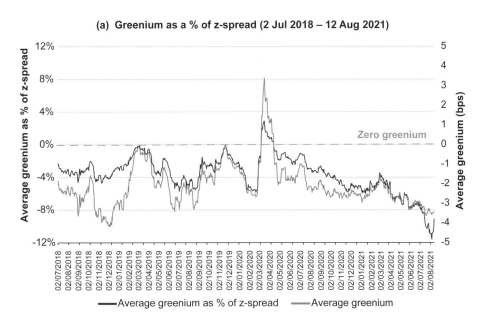

(a) Greenium as a % of z-spread (2 Jul 2018 – 12 Aug 2021)

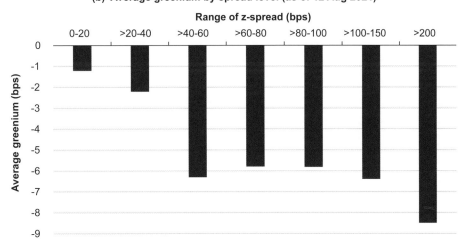

(b) Average greenium by spread level (as of 12 Aug 2021)

Source: Analysis by Thibaut Cuillière (Natixis) based on data from Bloomberg.

Not only has the greenium been growing in the euro-denominated corporate bond market, but it has also extended to markets in other bond types. In the euro-denominated financial debt market, one could hardly find any significant pricing difference between a GSS bond and a conventional one until the COVID-19 crisis in spring 2020 (see Figure 7). Since the summer of 2020, banks have been more actively issuing GSS bonds (especially green and social bonds) funding their needs and the fixed income market has been increasingly differentiating its pricing between these growing GSS bonds and conventional ones. As shown in Figure 7, the average greenium for senior non-preferred financial debt issued in euros amounted to around 4 bps, compared to an average z-spread of 45 to 50 bps for these instruments (as of 12 August 2021). The greenium in these instruments has been rising particularly fast since September 2020.

Figure 7. Trend in the average greenium for euro-denominated non-preferred senior financial debt (1 Aug 2019 – 12 Aug 2021)

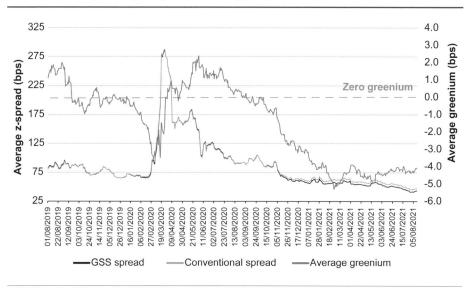

Source: Analysis by Thibaut Cuillière (Natixis) based on data from Bloomberg.

The same could be said for some other market segments such as the euro-denominated senior preferred financial debt or the USD corporate debt market — Figure 8 shows the average pricing difference between GSS and conventional bonds for different segments and currencies as of 12 August 2021:

- All the market segments under study displayed significant greenium — from 2.5 bps to 6 bps in z-spread terms, which demonstrates that the current supply-demand imbalance in the GSS market is now generalised in the fixed income market;

- The greenium calculated for each market segment is a function of the average z-spread observed in each market. It tends to be more negative for United States dollar (USD) corporate debt where spreads are generally wider than in the euro credit universe. The greenium is also more negative in euro-denominated senior non-preferred financial debt than euro-denominated senior preferred financial debt, which corroborates our above analysis (the riskier the debt, the higher the greenium in absolute terms as it tends to be a function of spread).

Figure 8. Average greenium by market segment and by currency (as of 12 Aug 2021)

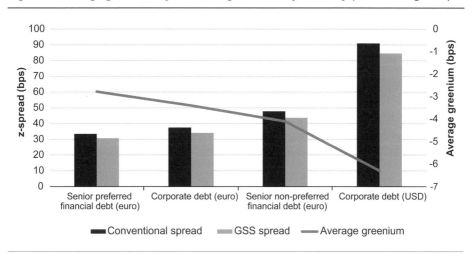

Source: Analysis by Thibaut Cuillière (Natixis) based on data from Bloomberg.

Finally, our observations show that the greenium depends on the maturity of the GSS bond. Figure 9 shows that the greenium tends to be more negative when maturity increases in the corporate bond market, for euro-denominated as well as for USD-denominated bonds. This can be explained by two factors: (1) the average spread of a given issuer itself (since the magnitude of greenium is found to be in proportion to the magnitude of z-spread in general); and (2) buy-and-hold investors are more focused on maturities above 7 years, for which the trend in greening their investment portfolio is deeper.

Figure 9. Average greenium by maturity of euro- and USD-denominated corporate bonds (as of 12 Aug 2021)

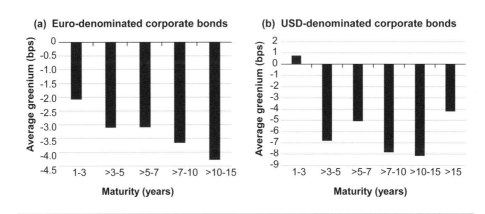

Source: Analysis by Thibaut Cuillière (Natixis) based on data from Bloomberg.

Implications for GSF financial instruments denominated in other currencies

The pricing dynamics observed in euro-denominated primary bond markets can be attributed to the persistent imbalance between the supply of GSS bonds and investor demand for these instruments. As the demand still far exceeds available supply, new GSS bond issuances in euro-denominated markets tend to be more strongly oversubscribed than their conventional peers issued by the same type of issuer within the same period of time. This strong demand, in turn, results in pricing advantages for GSS issuances in terms of spread tightening between the time of the IPT and the time of pricing, and in terms of NIP displayed at issuance. Moreover, this supply-demand imbalance also has consequences in euro-denominated secondary bond markets, as shown by the persistent existence of a "greenium".

The same case would apply to GSS bonds in other currencies. The Renminbi (RMB) market in GSS bonds, for example, could potentially benefit from similar pricing dynamics in primary markets and from the emergence of "greenium" in secondary markets, should similar supply-demand imbalances (as currently observed in European markets) also occur in China. This will, to a large extent, depend on the speed at which supply of RMB-denominated GSS bonds could be scaled up, and how fast RMB fixed-income investors might develop appetite for GSS bonds.

Choices of GSF instruments and potential challenges

Debt markets can play an essential role in funding projects and economic activities that contribute to sustainable development and transition towards a low-carbon economy. But how do market participants know what is *"green"* or *"sustainable"*? As far as debt markets are concerned, the answer is provided by voluntary market principles and guidelines which define conditions under which bond and loan products can be labelled as *"green"*, *"social"*, *"sustainability"* or *"sustainability-linked"*. These labels can be given to any product that is aligned with relevant principles and guidelines, which have been created to ensure the integrity of these products, while contributing to the improvement of overall transparency of debt markets. Interestingly, these labels were created by market participants themselves rather than being *"imposed"* by regulators or legislators. Nevertheless, several jurisdictions are in the process of preparing official definitions of "green" and/or "sustainable" economic activities, so called "taxonomies" (discussed below). Current market principles governing GSF instruments will likely evolve to reflect the content of these taxonomies.

All labelled GSF debt instruments can be divided into two groups: use-of-proceeds instruments and general-purpose instruments. Labelled use-of-proceeds GSF instruments are "green", "social" and "sustainability" bonds and loans. Use-of-proceeds instruments bring clarity and transparency about what is being financed, as they require proceeds or equivalent amounts to be earmarked for specific eligible projects. Labelled general-purpose GSF instruments are "sustainability-linked" bonds and loans. Their proceeds can be used for any purpose, but the issuer/borrower commits to the improvement of its sustainability performance over time. The financial characteristics of these instruments will vary depending on whether these predefined sustainability objectives are achieved or not. As such, sustainability-linked bonds and loans are forward-looking financial instruments, offering a more holistic perspective of issuer's/borrower's commitments. These two financial instruments are relative newcomers to the GSF landscape and the markets for these instruments are in their early stages of development. Markets for use-of-proceeds GSF instruments are, on the other hand, relatively more well established.

It should be stressed that not every bond or loan used to finance environmental/social projects and related expenditures uses an official label. Some issuers/borrowers simply consider that their sustainability credentials speak for themselves and do not wish to go through the process of officially labelling their financing means. Furthermore, several institutions almost exclusively finance activities that fall within the eligible categories of use-of-proceeds for green or social bonds/loans, but these institutions do not align their bond/loan instruments to the relevant market standards. As such, the data presented below accounts for the labelled portion of GSF debt markets, rather than for all debt market activities channelled towards green/social/ESG themes.

The market for GSS bonds is expanding fast. As illustrated by Figure 10, GSS bond issuance amounted to €420 billion in the first half of 2021 (2021H1) alone, an increase of 134% vs 2020H1.

Figure 10. GSS bond issuance by currency (2013 – 2021H1)

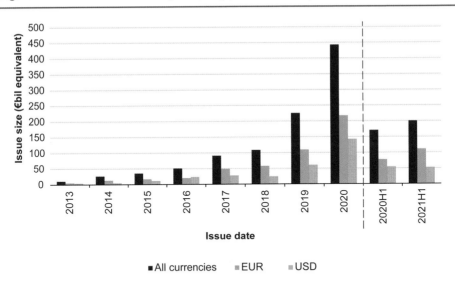

Source: Analysis by Natixis based on data from Bloomberg.

The total outstanding of GSS bonds at the end of 2021H1 was €1.4 trillion, a 40% increase versus outstanding levels at the end of 2020. GSS bonds in USD and euro accounted for 82% of the total outstanding (see Figure 11).

Figure 11. Outstanding amount of GSS bonds by currency (2006 – 2021H1)

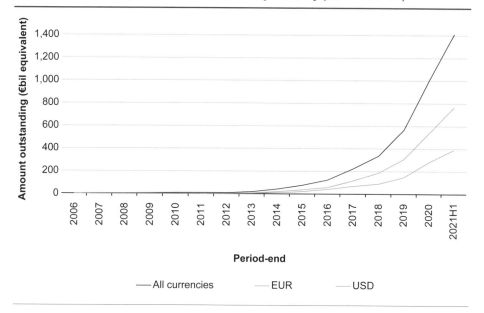

Source: Analysis by Natixis based on data from Bloomberg.

Use-of-proceeds GSF instruments

The essential feature/requirement of any use-of-proceeds financial instrument is that the proceeds from these instruments may only be used for the financing of specific projects or activities. In the case of green bonds and loans, proceeds are used to fund projects with environmental benefits. In the case of social bonds and loans, proceeds must be allocated to projects with socioeconomic benefits. Sustainability bonds can be thought of as a mixture of green bond and social bond in the sense that proceeds are allocated to projects with environmental and socioeconomic benefits. This does not mean that green bonds/ loans would not finance projects with socioeconomic co-benefits or that projects financed with social bonds/loans cannot be environmentally virtuous. Rather, sustainability bonds finance projects that intentionally mix environmental and socioeconomic benefits from the onset.

Green bonds and loans

Green bonds are the most mature labelled debt securities available in GSF markets. They are formally defined and governed by the Green Bond Principles (GBP)[8], a set of widely used voluntary issuance guidelines. The GBP were launched to provide parameters which describe what has to be done in terms of project selection, transparency, disclosure and reporting in order to launch a credible green bond. Issuers benefit from these principles, which describe the key steps that have to be taken to minimise the risk of being accused of "*greenwashing*". Investors, correspondingly, benefit by having an investment opportunity with clearly defined and transparent environmental credentials which also provides some insight into estimated environmental impacts.

The type of projects and economic activities that can be defined as "green" is subject to ongoing debate. Several catalogues and taxonomies of environmentally sustainable activities to provide authoritative and detailed answers to this question are currently being developed. Rather than trying to provide an exhaustive list of criteria under which different projects and economic activities could claim to be "*green*" (which would take years to create), the GBP took a pragmatic approach based on five high-level environmental objectives: *climate change adaptation and mitigation, natural resource conservation, biodiversity conservation, and pollution prevention and control.* Based on these categories, the GBP provides a list of Eligible Projects with several illustrations, which are represented in Table 1. The list is not meant to be exhaustive as related projects or supportive expenditures such as research and development (R&D) are also eligible for financing with green bonds and loans.

---

8   The GBP are administered by the International Capital Market Association (ICMA), which also administers all other voluntary market principles governing all the other labelled bond instruments within the GSF space (that is social bonds, sustainability bonds and sustainability-linked bonds).

Table 1. List of green projects as outlined by the GBP

Indicative category of eligibility	Illustration / precision
Renewable energy	Including production, transmission, appliances and products
Energy efficiency	Such as in new and refurbished buildings, energy storage, district heating, smart grids, appliances and products
Pollution prevention and control	Including reduction of air emissions, greenhouse gas control, soil remediation, waste prevention, waste reduction, waste recycling and energy/emission-efficient waste-to-energy
Environmentally sustainable management of living natural resources and land use	Including environmentally sustainable agriculture, environmentally sustainable animal husbandry; climate smart farm inputs such as biological crop protection or drip-irrigation; environmentally sustainable fishery and aquaculture, environmentally sustainable forestry, including afforestation and reforestation, and preservation or restoration of natural landscapes
Terrestrial and aquatic biodiversity conservation	Including the protection of coastal, marine and watershed environments
Clean transportation	Such as electric, hybrid, public, rail, non-motorised, multi-modal transportation, infrastructure for clean energy vehicles and reduction of harmful emissions
Sustainable water and wastewater management	Including sustainable infrastructure for clean and/or drinking water, wastewater treatment, sustainable urban drainage systems and river training and other forms of flooding mitigation
Climate change adaptation	Including information support systems, such as climate observation and early warning systems
Eco-efficient and/or circular economy adapted products, production technologies and processes	Such as development and introduction of environmentally sustainable products, with an eco-label or environmental certification, resource-efficient packaging and distribution
Green buildings	Which meet regional, national or internationally recognised standards or certifications

Source: GBP (2021), printed with permission from ICMA.

In addition to financing/refinancing Eligible Projects, bonds/loans labelled as "green" must also be aligned with the four core components of the GBP or the Green Loan Principles (GLP)[9], whichever is applicable. These are outlined below.

---

9   The GLP have been developed by the financial industry, which build on and refer to the GBP.

All the labelled used-of-proceeds GSF instruments currently available in the market are governed by dedicated principles (Green Bond/Loan Principles, Social Bond/Loan Principles) or guidelines (Sustainability Bond Guidelines) framed around four core components:

(1) **Use of proceeds** — This is the key concept to ensure credibility and integrity of use-of-proceeds instruments. The very idea of a green bond/loan is that the proceeds are only used to finance "Green Projects". Issuers/borrowers should clearly assess the environmental benefits of these projects, and quantify them where feasible[10]. If proceeds are being used for the refinancing of existing projects, this should be clearly stated. If a green loan takes the form of one or more tranches of a loan facility, the green tranche(s) have to be clearly designated.

(2) **Process for project evaluation and selection** — Issuers/borrowers should communicate to investors/lenders three elements:

   • The issuer's/borrower's environmental sustainability objectives;

   • Processes used by the issuer/borrower to determine that the project(s) fit the description of eligible Green Project(s); and

   • Eligibility criteria used to determine the previous element and, if applicable, identification and management of material environmental or social risks that could be associated with financed project(s).

(3) **Management of proceeds** — This aspect is important for the transparency and integrity of any use-of-proceeds product. As such, proceeds of a green loan have to be either credited to a dedicated account (not necessarily a particularly popular option) or tracked by the borrower (often the preferred option). Similarly, the proceeds raised by a green bond (or an amount equivalent to these proceeds) have to be tracked by the issuer (which may, but does not necessarily have to, take form of crediting proceeds to a sub-account or moving them to a sub-portfolio).

(4) **Reporting** — Information on the use of proceeds should be updated at least annually until the loan is fully drawn or the bond's proceeds are fully allocated. The key difference between loans and bonds is, that in the case of a loan, the information only needs to be provided to institutions participating in the loan, while information

---

10 For instance, quantifying emissions reductions resulting from shift to renewables tend to be considerably easier than quantifying impacts on biodiversity.

about the allocation of proceeds from a bond should be included in the issuer's annual report. For both bonds and loans, in the case that detailed information (list of Green Projects, their description and expected impact) cannot be provided due to confidentiality and/or competitive reasons, and/or the large number of projects, disclosure should be made at least in general terms or on a portfolio basis. When it comes to the assessment of the expected impact of financed projects, both qualitative indicators and quantitative measures (subject to feasibility) are recommended, as is the disclosure of the underlying methodology and key assumptions.

There are four different types of green bonds currently available in the market as summarised in Table 2.

Table 2. Currently available types of green bonds

Type of bond	Description
Standard Green Use-of-Proceeds Bond	Standard recourse-to-the-issuer debt obligation aligned with the GBP.
Green Revenue Bond	Non-recourse-to-the-issuer debt obligation aligned with the GBP in which the credit exposure in the bond is to the pledged cash flows of the revenue streams, fees, taxes etc., and whose use of proceeds go to related or unrelated Green Project(s).
Green Project Bond	Project bond for a single or multiple Green Project(s) for which the investor has direct exposure to the risk of the project(s) with or without potential recourse to the issuer, and that is aligned with the GBP.
Green Securitised Bond	Bond collateralised by one or more specific Green Project(s), including but not limited to covered bonds, asset-backed securities (ABS), mortgage-backed securities (MBS), and other structures; and aligned with the GBP. The first source of repayment is generally the cash flows of the assets.

Source: GBP (2021), printed with permission from ICMA.

As for green loans, it is noteworthy that the GLP were updated in February 2021, to account for the growing importance of social topics: social risks are now among the aspects to be considered during project evaluation when determining what can be labelled as a green facility. There are several interesting points specific to the loan market, as discussed below.

(1) Term loans and revolving credit facilities (RCFs)

The GLP are intended for application to a wide variety of loan instruments, which also includes term loans and RCFs. Since term loans are often used by companies to purchase fixed assets, the use-of-proceeds identification is relatively straightforward. Matters are more complicated for RCFs, as RCFs are often not able to provide a similar level of detail in identifying the use of proceeds from the outset. For an RCF to be labelled as green, the proceeds must still be allocated to some of the eligible categories defined by the GLP (just as for any other green loan). If the borrower is not able to designate a Green Project when entering into the loan, the facility agreement has to contain sufficiently identifiable eligible categories of Green Projects which may be financed by proceeds of the RCF. As such, it is up to the concerned parties to jointly find the best way to show that funds from the RCF are indeed flowing towards achieving an agreed-upon sustainability objective. This needs to be done on a case-by-case basis between lenders and borrowers. Similarly, lenders and borrowers need to agree whether there will be any additional conditions or reporting requirements at the moment of the drawdown under the RCF.

(2) Green clauses to be included in loan documents

While a case-by-case approach is required for green loan documentation, there are at least four considerations to be kept in mind when drafting a new green loan. First, given the importance of the use of proceeds, the "purpose provision" or "use-of-proceeds provision" should clearly state the eligible green project categories to be financed. Second, the facility agreement should clearly identify information undertakings and/or covenants relevant to the financed green projects. Third, the accuracy of any reporting should be an obligation for the borrower. Fourth, the facility agreement of each deal should provide clarity on what would constitute a "*green breach*" — a breach of the use-of-proceeds provision which would result in the loss of the right to use the green label for the given product from the time of the breach onwards. The GLP do not take a stance as to whether such a breach (when proceeds are not used for a green project) should trigger a default (and any resulting cross-default for outstanding loans), this is left for the consideration of the concerned parties for each loan.

Social bonds and loans

The launch of Social Loan Principles (SLP) in April 2021 illustrates how the ESG/GSF category continues to expand beyond its original environmental roots to incorporate a broader range of sustainability themes, including socioeconomic issues. While Social Bond Principles (SBP) were first released in 2017, issuance volumes remained marginal until the COVID-19 pandemic. In terms of possible bond/loan types that can be labelled as "social", everything described previously in the case of green bonds/loans, also holds for the social label. Aligning a bond/loan with the SBP/SLP in order to obtain the "social" label requires adherence to the four core components of SBP/SLP: (1) Use of Proceeds; (2) Process for Project Evaluation and Selection; (3) Management of Proceeds; and (4) Reporting.

The understanding of social issues, their consequences and possible remedies is evolving, and views may differ based on cultural and geographical differences. Bearing this in mind, the SBP/SLP provide a high-level list of broad categories considered to be eligible for financing social bonds or loans (SLP reference SBP for this). This list presented in Table 3 is not meant to be exhaustive, but rather, aims to capture the most usual types of projects that can be financed/refinanced with social bonds and loans.

Table 3. Indicative (non-exhaustive) categories of eligibility for social projects

Category	Illustration
Affordable basic infrastructure	Clean drinking water, sewers, sanitation, transport, energy, basic telecommunications
Access to essential services	Education and vocational training, public health/healthcare, public health emergency response energy (including electricity), financing and financial services, other governmental offices servicing selected populations (and/or in low /low-middle income countries)
Affordable housing	Increase of quantity and/or quality of affordable and social housing. For instance, via renovation of existing housing stock and construction of new affordable and social accommodation
Employment generation, and programmes designed to prevent and/or alleviate unemployment stemming from socioeconomic crises, including through the potential effect of small and medium enterprise financing and microfinance	Professional training and retraining programmes, unemployment insurance schemes and similar socioeconomic buffers

(continued)

Category	Illustration
Food security and sustainable food systems	Physical, social, and economic access to safe, nutritious, and sufficient food that meets dietary needs and requirements; resilient agricultural practices; reduction of food loss and waste; and improved productivity of small-scale producers
Socioeconomic advancement and empowerment	Equitable access to and control over assets, services, resources, and opportunities; equitable participation and integration into the market and society, including reduction of income inequality

Source: Adapted from SBP (2021), printed with permission from ICMA.

An important difference between green and social bonds/loans is that the social label puts more emphasis on the target populations expected to benefit from the use of proceeds. The very purpose of social financing is to help address some social issues and achieve better social outcomes. As such, the SBP/SLP provide indicative categories of the populations which may be particularly in need of social financing. These are summarised in Table 4. The list is non-exhaustive and social financing can also benefit a population as a whole, rather than a specific subset of it.

Table 4. Target populations

Categories	
• Living below the poverty line	• Excluded and/or marginalised populations and/or communities
• People with disabilities	• Migrants and/or displaced persons
• Undereducated	• Underserved, owing to a lack of quality access to essential goods and services
• Unemployed	• Women and/or sexual and gender minorities
• Aging populations and/or vulnerable youths	• Other vulnerable groups, including as a result of natural disasters

Source: SBP (2021), printed with permission from ICMA.

Joint use of SLP and SBP

The SLP were conceived with the possibility of being used together with the SBP. The SLP explicitly state that an issuer of a social bond (aligned with the core components of the SBP) may use the proceeds of such bond as a lender providing social loans (aligned with the core components of the SLP) to other borrowers.

Original borrower also acting as a lender

Borrowers, such as governments, development finance institutions or municipalities, often act as a lender to other borrowers. If the original borrower borrows a social loan and then acts as a lender to other borrowers, SLP can be used to qualify each loan as social, as long as all the loan products are aligned with the core components of the SLP.

Sustainability bonds

Sustainability bonds are a mixture of green and social bonds. As such, they have the same structure, need to align to the same four core components of the GBP and the SBP, and exist under the same aforementioned types of bonds (Standard Use-of-Proceeds Bond, Revenue Bond, Project Bond and Securitised Bond). This label has been created for projects that explicitly combine green and social aspects. Similarly, several organisations in the development finance area issue bonds which could be classified under this label, but they have chosen not to.

General-purpose GSF instruments

Sustainability-linked bonds (SLBs) and sustainability-linked loans (SLLs) are the most recent labelled instruments added to the GSF family. As both labels were formally defined much later than their use-of-proceeds peers, some market participants sometimes refer to these products as *"KPI bonds/loans"*, *"ESG-linked bonds/loans"* or possibly even *"SDG-linked bonds/loans"*[11]. Moreover, there may be several financial instruments using the aforementioned labels which may or may not fulfil the criteria to be considered as SLBs or SLLs. To be considered as an SLB, a bond has to align with the five core components of the Sustainability-linked Bond Principles (SLBP)[12] described below. Similarly, a loan can use the SLL label only if it is aligned with the five core components of the Sustainability-linked Loan Principles (SLLP)[13] described below.

SLBs and SLLs aim to promote sustainable development more generally by supporting environmental and/or social and/or governance improvements over time. In other words,

---

11 SDG refers to United Nations Sustainable Development Goals (see the SDG webpage on the website of the United Nations).

12 SLBP are voluntary market principles developed by the ICMA.

13 SLLP are voluntary market principles developed by a trio of market associations: Loan Market Association (LMA), Loan Syndications and Trading Association (LSTA) and Asia-Pacific Loan Market Association (APLMA).

these instruments are meant to incentivise achieving improvements in the issuer's/ borrower's performance in one or several areas of the broad set of ESG topics.

Unlike all the other GSF instruments discussed above, SLB and SLL are not use-of-proceeds instruments. Rather, they are used for general-purpose financing. Instead of determining eligible categories for financing through the use-of-proceeds format, SLBs and SLLs focus on the improvement of the borrower's/issuer's sustainability profile over time. As such, these instruments are inherently forward-looking and performance-based, while use-of-proceeds bonds and loans are focused on financing eligibility *"as-of-now"*, without taking future evolutions into consideration. In this sense, SLBs and SLLs may be particularly appropriate for issuers and borrowers in sectors which traditionally have not been so interested in GSF (e.g. oil and gas, carbon-intensive industries), either due to lack of eligible projects for use-of-proceeds GSF instruments or because they feared market backlash and accusations of *"greenwashing"*.

Improvements in the sustainability/ESG performance of the issuer/borrower are assessed using SPTs. These SPTs are established at the outset and the issuer's/borrower's progress (or lack of it) towards their achievement is measured by KPIs, external ESG ratings or a combination of both. An overview of commonly used SPT categories is presented in Table 5. These categories and examples are intended to be illustrative only: given the broad scope of topics and issues related to sustainable development, the set of potential SPTs is very large. Moreover, SPTs and KPIs tend to be sector specific. Given the relative novelty of these concepts, it is reasonable to assume increasing market sophistication in the coming years, in terms of methodologies and best practices for KPI selection, SPT setting, reporting and evaluation.

Table 5. Common categories of KPIs and examples

Category	Example
Energy efficiency	Improvements in the energy efficiency rating of buildings and/or machinery owned or leased by the issuer/borrower
Greenhouse gas emissions	Reductions in greenhouse gas emissions in relation to products manufactured or sold by the issuer/borrower or to the production or manufacturing cycle
Renewable energy	Increases in the amount of renewable energy generated or used by the issuer/borrower
Water consumption	Water savings made by the issuer/borrower

(continued)

Category	Example
Affordable housing	Increases in the number of affordable housing units developed by the issuer/borrower
Sustainable sourcing	Increases in the use of verified sustainable raw materials/supplies
Circular economy	Increases in recycling rates or use of recycled raw materials/supplies
Sustainable farming and food	Improvements in sourcing/producing sustainable products and/or quality products (using appropriate labels or certifications)
Biodiversity	Improvements in conservation and protection of biodiversity
Global ESG assessment	Improvements in the borrower's ESG rating and/or achievement of a recognised ESG certification

Source: Adapted from SLLP (2021), printed with permission from LMA.

Sustainability-linked bonds and loans

Bonds/loans bearing the "sustainability-linked" label have to align with the five core components of SLBP/SLLP. Prior to the 2021 revision, SLLP used to have four core components, but this has been aligned with the five core components of SLBP (see below) in order to avoid confusion and to ensure a unified approach to sustainability-linked labels.

(1) **Selection of KPIs.** If SLBs and SLLs are to succeed as a new asset class, great care has to be taken to avoid selecting meaningless KPIs which would compromise the credibility of the whole financial instrument and render the issuer/borrower vulnerable to accusations of *"greenwashing"*. KPIs will be used to assess the sustainability performance of the issuer/borrower and this assessment will in turn be used to modify the financial and/or structural characteristics of the SLB/SLL. As such, the KPIs must be material to the issuer's/borrower's business and address some of the ESG/sustainability challenges in their sector. KPIs can eventually be selected at project level, although selecting KPIs at issuer/borrower level appears more obvious in most cases. The four key characteristics of KPIs suitable for the structuring of sustainability-linked instruments are presented in Table 6.

Table 6. Key considerations for KPIs for SLBs and SLLs

- Relevant, core and material to the issuer's/borrower's overall business, and of high strategic significance to the issuer's/borrower's current and/or future operations
- Measurable or quantifiable on a consistent methodological basis
- Externally verifiable
- Able to be benchmarked, i.e. as much as possible using an external reference or definitions to facilitate the assessment of the SPT's level of ambition

Source: SLBP (2020), printed with permission from ICMA.

It is in the issuer's/borrower's best interests to ensure that selected KPIs are under their own control. In this sense, selecting KPIs dependent on commercially unproven technologies would leave the issuer/borrower dependent on technology and policy elements beyond their control. Similarly, choosing to use an external ESG rating as a KPI could be risky, as such rating might be subject to methodological changes which may or may not be favourable.

(2) **Calibration of SPTs** is an essential aspect of structuring of sustainability-linked instruments. Once KPIs tracking the issuer's/borrower's progress on material ESG/ sustainability topics are selected, SPTs are calibrated to set the target levels these KPIs should eventually reach over time. As such, SPTs represent the issuer's/ borrower's commitment and ambition. SPTs ought to aim for material improvements of KPIs beyond the "business as usual" trajectory, and should be consistent with the issuer's/borrower's sustainability strategy and overall approach to ESG. Subject to feasibility, SPTs should be set based on an issuer's/borrower's own past performance (KPI values for at least past three years), its peers (average and best-in-class performances in the sector, industry or sectorial standards) and science (science-based scenarios, climate targets[14], best available technologies). Several initiatives now provide data and analysis that could inspire SPT selection, for instance the *Transition Pathway Initiative* (TPI)[15] or the *Science Based Targets initiative* (SBTi)[16].

As a rule, SPTs should be meaningful, ambitious, relevant to the issuer's/borrower's core business and applicable over the lifetime of the financial instrument for which

---

14 Either "net zero" carbon emissions or referencing the Paris Agreement.

15 TPI is an initiative seeking to assess the extent to which companies are prepared for a transition to a low-carbon economy. All methodological notes and tools are publicly available at the TPI's website.

16 SBTi provides tools showing how fast and how much companies have to reduce their emissions to align with the goals of the Paris Agreement. This can be accessed at the SBTi's website.

they are set. For instance, SPTs for an oil and gas company would relate to greenhouse gas emissions/intensity, rather than the amount of recycled paper used at the company's headquarters.

Second-Party Opinion (SPO) can be elaborated by external reviewers to provide an independent assessment evaluating how relevant, reliable and robust the selected KPIs are, whether SPTs are ambitious and relevant, and if the issuer's/borrower's strategy to achieve them appears credible. However, SPOs are not mandatory[17] and some issuers/borrowers may prefer to demonstrate/develop their own internal expertise with regards to the aforementioned points. In this case, relevant documentation should be communicated to investors/lenders.

While SPTs fixed at the outset offer transparency and an easy way to assess whether they are achieved or not, some issuers/borrowers may prefer to select SPTs whereby the range or final target value may change at some point during the lifetime of the SLB/SLL. An illustration of such SPTs could, for instance, be *"staying within the top decile/quartile of the industry for selected KPIs"*. Moreover, SPTs and KPIs can be eventually adjusted to account for impacts of mergers and acquisitions (M&A). Such potential adjustments would be tailor-made to each SPT and related KPI(s) and have to be clearly specified.

(3) **Sustainability-linked characteristics.** Unlike the use-of-proceeds GSF instruments (green, social, sustainability bonds and loans), the economic outcome of sustainability-linked instruments can be modified by a *"trigger event"*. Trigger events are situations in which KPIs reach or fail to reach predefined SPT(s) within a predefined timeframe. For SLBs, this results in the modification of the financial and/or structural features. In practice, coupon variation is the most frequently used feature, but several other options could be considered (repayment amount, maturity, interest payment date, …). Similarly, the margin of SLL is reduced/increased if the borrower meets/fails predefined SPT(s). Given the novelty of the whole "sustainability-linked" concept, these practices may evolve in the coming years, thanks to market innovation.

(4) **Reporting.** Issuers of SLBs should publish information regarding the evolution of KPIs at least annually. A summary checklist of both mandatory and recommended disclosures pre-issuance and post-issuance is available online in Appendix II of SLBP[18]. In the case of SLLs, public reporting is not a requirement due to the private

---

17 Both SLBP and SLLP recommend using SPO, but financial instruments can bear SLB or SLL labels without being evaluated by SPO.

18 ICMA, *Sustainability-Linked Bond Principles: Voluntary Process Guidelines*, June 2020.

nature of the loan market, and the borrower may choose to share this information only privately with lender(s).

(5) **Verification.** An independent external verification of the issuer's/borrower's performance for each SPT has to be elaborated at least annually for both SLBs and SLLs until after the last SPT trigger event. While this SPT performance verification should be made public in the case of SLBs, borrowers of SLLs may instead choose to share this information only with lenders.

Challenges related to SLBs and SLLs

Given the relative novelty of SLBs and SLLs, there are several interrogation points related to these products. Some of these are discussed below.

(1) Greenwashing / "ESG washing"

SLBs and SLLs have to be structured properly to avoid risks of greenwashing — a situation when sustainability credentials are inflated, inaccurate or presented in a misleading manner. Given the unique structure of sustainability-linked instruments, there are two specific circumstances under which suspicion of greenwashing/ESG washing could arise:

- In the case that SPTs are not sufficiently ambitious and/or meaningful for issuer's/ borrower's business; and

- In the case that the issuer's/borrower's performance is improperly monitored/ evaluated/disclosed against its SPTs.

This risk can be mitigated by following the SLBP/SLLP guidelines and potentially seeking the assistance of independent external parties in setting the SPTs and choosing an appropriate SPT performance benchmark and timeline.

(2) Information asymmetry

Another point of attention when it comes to SLBs and SLLs, relates to information asymmetry between the issuer/borrower and other parties of the transaction. The issuers/borrowers have the best understanding of their own business and, therefore, ought to act in good faith throughout the whole process of target setting and provide accurate input.

(3) Setting the SPTs for SLBs/SLLs

There are several possible approaches that can be taken for the selection of SPTs and relevant metrics for tracking their progress. None of these approaches is "*superior*" or "*more credible*" on its own. They are simply suitable for different clients depending on the client's familiarity with ESG and sustainability issues. If the issuer/borrower already has well-formulated ESG/sustainability policies and strategies, metrics and targets used, they can simply be used for SLBs/SLLs as well. Conversely, issuers/ borrowers who are just embarking on their ESG/sustainability journey may prefer to rely on external analysis to provide them with ESG criteria and best sustainability practices specific to their sector, or to use pre-existing industry metrics reported against established frameworks.

(4) Materiality assessment for SLBs/SLLs

Ensuring that SPTs and related metrics are actually relevant may be a challenging task in some cases, especially in the early stages of development of the SLB and SLL markets, as there is little market precedent for the time being. Materiality assessments can be a helpful tool in this task, as they identify the most important/ impactful ESG factors for each sector of economic activity and for concerned stakeholders. As such, a materiality assessment of the borrower's/issuer's sector can serve as a confirmation that improvement of ESG issues being sought through the SPTs, is indeed relevant. For instance, the Sustainability Accounting Standards Board (SASB) developed a materiality map[19] which can be used to compare financially material ESG issues across industries. Similar services are also offered by several ESG rating agencies and consultancies.

(5) Ambitiousness assessment for SLBs/SLLs

Similarly, making sure that SPTs are ambitious enough, rather than merely following a "*business as usual*" trajectory, may seem challenging given the relative novelty of the concept and the resulting lack of market experience. Several initiatives can lend a helping hand. **TPI** assesses corporate preparedness for a low-carbon transition by evaluating their carbon trajectories and the extent to which climate-related topics are integrated to the company's strategic goals and decision-making processes. All the

---

19 See the "Materiality Map" webpage on the SASB's website.

assessments (available by sector and by company) are publicly accessible online[20]. Similarly, **SBTi** provides guidance, resources and an assessment of corporate greenhouse gas emissions reduction targets[21]. For SPTs related to renewable energy, another useful source to consult is **RE100** — an initiative bringing together companies which are committed to sourcing all their electricity from renewable sources, as fast as feasible[22].

Moreover, regional and cultural differences should be taken into consideration when assessing the ambitiousness of SPTs. For instance, SPTs related to carbon intensity or environmental protection, which may be considered moderately or even little ambitious in the context of OECD countries, may well be ambitious and impactful in the context of developing countries. The same can be true for social issues related, for example, to gender equality or demographics.

(6) Specific reporting for SLBs/SLLs

Given the novelty of both SLBs and SLLs, there is currently no globally accepted SPT reporting methodology. As such, appropriate reporting methodologies to monitor the progress towards the achievement of SPTs are chosen on a case-by-case basis considering the nature of the issuer/borrower and the chosen SPTs. There are several sustainability reporting methodologies to choose from (see above sections on SLBP and SLLP).

(7) Combining the use-of-proceeds and sustainability-linked bond/loan formats

Issuers may decide to combine a green/social bond with an SLB. In this setting, proceeds of an SLB would be earmarked for the financing or refinancing of projects deemed eligible by either the GBP or SBP, and the bond would align with all the core components of both SLBP and either the GBP or SBP. Similarly, a loan can be structured in a way that it can be considered as both a green/social loan and as an SLB. For instance, Verbund issued the world's first bond combining use-of-proceeds and sustainability-linked mechanisms in March 2021[23]. Verbund's "Green Financing Framework"[24] has been designed to align with both GBP and SLBP. The proceeds

---

20 See the "Sectors" webpage on TPI's website.
21 See SBTi materials and guidelines on its website.
22 See the *RE100* website.
23 Source: Press release on Verbund's website, 22 March 2021.
24 The Verbund Green Financing Framework (March 2021) is available on Verbund's website.

from the issuance of this bond will be allocated exclusively to "green" projects as defined by the Framework and the bond's coupon will increase in case Verbund fails to meet two SPTs defined in terms of newly installed renewable energy production capacities and newly installed transformer[25] capacities. Nevertheless, such transactions remain rare as of 2021.

GSF outlook

While the GSF bond and loan markets have developed under voluntary market principles, regulators and legislators are stepping in to create new binding definitions, "taxonomies" of what can be considered as "green" or "sustainable" activities or financial instruments. While the aim is to improve the credibility and trustworthiness of markets for GSF instruments, the development of taxonomies also creates challenges for issuers/borrowers, notably in terms of data collection and reporting. Furthermore, COVID-19 brought socio-economic issues into the public spotlight and to investors' attention, which led to multiple issuers issuing social and sustainability bonds, thus diversifying the GSS bond market, which was predominantly green until 2020. Sustainability-linked bonds and loans have the potential to extend the reach of GSF market as these instruments do not require earmarking of proceeds to specific eligible projects. Moreover, the topic of "transition" towards a low-carbon and possibly net-zero emissions economy appears ever more important but "transition" GSF instruments are not yet defined.

Ongoing development of GSF taxonomies

While the recent uptake of GSS bond issuance provides some reasons for optimism, we are still far from the trillions of dollars of green investments required to flow into low-carbon sectors and activities each year, in order to enable the global transition towards a low-carbon economy and limit the global temperature increase to 2°C, as set out by the Paris Agreement (which has been signed by over 190 countries). Even though public financing will continue to play an important role, the scale and magnitude of the challenge at hand is such that a substantial part of these "green trillions per year" will have to be provided by the private sector.

---

25 This is to enable feeding this electricity from newly installed renewable sources into high-voltage grid.

The private sector is increasingly willing to take its part as investors are rapidly integrating climate change considerations as well as broader environmental and sustainability concerns into their investment decision-making processes and portfolio allocations. Several jurisdictions, including the EU and the People's Republic of China, have put in place legislation intended to scale-up and further develop GSF. Part of this legislative effort has led to the adoption of "taxonomies", providing official definitions of what economic activities can be considered as "green". If well designed, such taxonomies can increase the transparency and integrity of GSF markets, increasing investors' confidence and willingness to allocate more capital towards "green" or "sustainable" projects and economic activities, while also increasing issuers'/borrowers' willingness to raise capital using GSF instruments.

Interestingly for issuers, the climate change mitigation and adaptation part of the EU Taxonomy also covers some notoriously "brown" or "hard-to-abate" sectors whose decarbonisation is nonetheless essential for the transition towards a low-carbon economy. These sectors are notably steel, aluminium and cement. While the eligibility thresholds are far from where these sectors currently stand in terms of carbon footprint, they could potentially serve for the selection of SPT trajectories, thus unlocking sustainability-linked financing for these sectors, which have a crucial role to play in the ongoing decarbonisation of the global economy.

One of the key challenges of every GSF taxonomy for issuers and investors alike, relates to data availability. For instance, the EU Taxonomy requires numerous data points which are not usually tracked, collected and disclosed by issuers, meaning that much work needs to be done regarding reporting on the issuer's side. On the investor's side, the data challenge resulting from the EU Taxonomy will relate to the aggregation of available data and its consistent and comparable assessment. More market data standardisation will be required in the future.

Taking into consideration the essential importance of coherence across jurisdictions in terms of GSF definitions and taxonomies, the IPSF was launched in 2019 as a multilateral forum for public authorities active in developing environmental finance policies and incentives, notably finance and economy ministries, central banks, financial regulators and supervisors. This forum aims to facilitate exchanges, cooperation and coordination about GSF amongst its members, who combined, represent half the world's population, 55% of global greenhouse gas emissions and 55% of world's gross domestic product[26].

---

26 Source: "International Platform on Sustainable Finance", webpage on the European Commission's website, viewed on 15 July 2021.

Although IPSF is not intended to create binding global GSF standards and taxonomies to be imposed on its members, the sharing of best practices and a coordinated approach to GSF taxonomies could potentially entail more consistent frameworks and approaches. This would, in turn, enable global investors to better allocate their capital to GSF opportunities across various jurisdictions, thus taking us one significant step closer to the "green trillions per year".

Diversification of GSF instrument formats

The year 2020 marked an important milestone in terms of the breakdown of labelled GSS bonds, as shown in Figure 12. While green bonds accounted for the vast majority of GSS bond issuance each year until the end of 2019, the year 2020 saw social and sustainability bond issuance really take off. This was primarily due to the COVID-19 pandemic and the spotlight it placed upon social and socioeconomic issues. Both social and sustainability bonds are well suited to channelling capital towards projects contributing to such causes. As such, the issuance of social bonds surpassed €130 billion in 2020, which is 7.5 times the amount seen in 2019. Sustainability bond issuance reached over €100 billion in 2020 and SLBs also started to take off the same year, albeit with much lower volumes. At the same time, green bond issuance grew by "only" 17% relative to 2019 levels, suggesting that this bond format is becoming more mature and hence growing less rapidly.

These structural trends which reshaped the labelled GSS bond market in 2020 are continuing in 2021. While all formats of labelled GSS bonds have increased in supply and outstanding at a record pace during 2021H1, the sharpest increase has come from social bonds, suggesting that green bonds are no longer the indisputably dominant GSF instrument (see Figure 12).

Figure 12. Labelled GSS bond issuance by type (all currencies) (2014 – 2021H1)

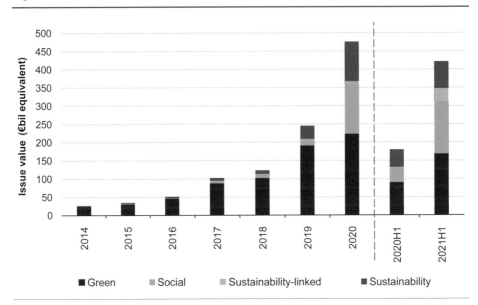

Source: Analysis by Natixis based on data from Bloomberg.

As of 2021, there are no official labels for GSF "transition" instruments. Nevertheless, the thematic label "transition" is sometimes used in the market for instruments used by issuers/borrowers who want to finance their decarbonisation strategy and their transition towards business models compatible with a low-carbon economy. The ICMA's *Climate Transition Finance Handbook* provides guidelines about what type of disclosure is recommended to issuers, to convince investors about the credibility of their transition strategy. The handbook is sector agnostic and does not aim to define a set of use-of-proceeds categories or economic activities that can claim to be eligible for such financing. This leaves the "transition finance" space open for both use-of-proceeds and sustainability-linked GSF instruments, and for carbon intensive industries such as cement, steel, aluminium, and oil and gas.

Several illustrations are given below to exemplify how GSF instruments create links between sustainability ambitions, growth strategy and funding strategy.

Green real estate investment trust (REIT)

Masdar Green REIT ("MGR") was incorporated within the Abu Dhabi Global Markets ("ADGM") on 19 December 2020 as a private REIT under the regulations of the Financial Services Regulatory Authority (FSRA) in Abu Dhabi. Abu Dhabi Future Energy Company PJSC (or Masdar), a company engaged in renewable energy and sustainable urban development and currently the sole shareholder of MGR, seeded the instrument with four income-producing assets totalling AED 949 million (US$258 million). MGR is the first green REIT in the United Arab Emirates (UAE) with a mandate to invest solely into sustainable, income-producing real estate assets within Masdar City, and the UAE[27]. The sustainable portfolio of real estate assets are benchmarked against "Leadership in Energy and Environmental Design" (LEED) and Estidama certifications[28], as well as a range of sustainability performance measures including utility consumption, transportation, waste management, design and construction within Masdar City.

MGR is in the process of securing a Green Finance Facility to support future MGR growth and acquisition objectives. The facility is being negotiated to meets lenders' sustainable finance commitments and LMA Green Loan Principles with MGR management tracking and reporting on energy efficiency and performance of each asset within its portfolio on an ongoing, quarterly basis against relevant sustainability measures.

Green convertible bonds: NEOEN, EDF and Voltalia

NEOEN, an independent producer of renewable energy focused on solar, wind and energy storage, placed the first ever European green convertible bond (€170 million) in May 2020[29]. The proceeds are intended to finance and/or refinance renewable energy production (solar photovoltaic and wind power) and energy storage activities.

In September 2020, EDF (Électricité de France), a frequent issuer of green bonds, launched its inaugural offering of green senior unsecured bonds convertible into new shares and/or exchangeable for existing shares for a nominal amount of approximately €2.4 billion[30]. The proceeds from this issuance, the largest green convertible bond issuance at the time, will be used for the financing and/or refinancing of projects in line

---

27 Source: Press release on Masdar's website, 15 January 2020.
28 Estidama is the Arab word for sustainability. Estidama certification is associated with a green building rating system used to evaluate sustainable building development practices in Abu Dhabi.
29 Source: Media release on NEOEN's website, 27 May 2020.
30 Source: Press release on EDF's website, 8 September 2020.

with the company's Green Bond Framework, which are the construction of renewable power generation projects, investments in existing hydropower facilities and investments in energy efficiency and in biodiversity protection.

Voltalia, an international player in renewable energies, issued its inaugural €200 million green convertible bond in January 2021[31]. The use of proceeds is dedicated to financing and/or refinancing of development, construction, operation and maintenance of renewable energy plants (wind, solar, biomass, hydro or hybrid) and storage units and majority or minority acquisitions of companies significantly active in any of the renewable energy technologies. Voltalia has developed an innovative Green & Sustainability-linked Financing Framework, which combines key features of both use-of-proceeds and general-corporate-purpose GSF, hereby enabling Voltalia to issue both use-of-proceeds and sustainability-linked bonds in the future.

Green margin loan: Ivanhoé Cambridge

Ivanhoé Cambridge ("IC"), the real estate subsidiary of Caisse de dépôt et placement du Québec ("CDPQ"), sought finance linked to the improvement of its sustainability profile via a first ever green margin loan in 2019. As such, the margin of the loan has been tied to a basket of four KPIs over the life of the facility: (1) the score of the Global ESG Benchmark for Real Assets (GRESB); (2) the rating of GRESB; (3) the value of all of IC's LEED Gold-certified assets (or the equivalent or higher); and (4) a reduction in the portfolio's carbon footprint, certified by an independent expert.

"Green" initial public offers (IPOs)?

This chapter focused on labelled GSF instruments as these are clearly defined and easily identifiable. There are, of course, other means for companies to raise capital for environmental and/or social purposes without using these official labels — for instance, through issuing conventional debt securities or new equity. The difficulty with ascertaining what does or does not constitute a "*green stock*" is that there are no universally accepted market principles as there are for bonds or loans. Instead, there are plenty of data providers and ESG rating agencies using a wide range of methodologies to "colour" different stocks. The IPOs of companies considered as "pure players" in the GSF space, i.e. "green IPOs", make for an interesting case. An illustration of a company raising funds while positioning itself as a "pure green player" is, for instance, the US$2.4 billion IPO of

---

31 Source: Press release on Voltalia's website, 6 January 2021.

the Swiss smart metering company, Landis & Gyr Holding, in 2017. Another example is the listing of Acciona's renewable energy unit, Acciona Energía, in summer 2021 as the group sought to raise funds for an almost doubling of its renewable energy capacity by 2025.

Further thoughts

The increasing popularity and diversification of GSF instruments, the ongoing development of taxonomies in several jurisdictions and the ever-increasing attention to climate and environmental aspects of financial stability from central banks, financial regulators and supervisors, suggest that GSF has successfully moved from a "nice-to-have" niche into the mainstream of the financial system.

Much attention has been paid to channelling capital towards climate change mitigation by funding greenhouse gas emissions reduction and prevention. However, as the Intergovernmental Panel on Climate Change (IPCC) reminds us, some adverse impacts of climate change are already inevitable, regardless of the success (or the failure) of global greenhouse gas emissions reduction. This grim realisation could bring climate change adaptation more increasingly into the spotlight due to the increasing need for adjustments to the changing climate and its impacts. Moreover, there are several other important environmental topics for which GSF instruments could play a more prominent role in the future, such as biodiversity protection and enhancement, the circular economy and the stewardship of water resources and oceans. The framework of the Planetary Boundaries defines the key environmental processes whose active stewardship should allow human society to remain within a "safe operating space" on Earth. The extent to which GSF instruments could draw inspiration from the concept of the Planetary Boundaries and from other scientific insights, remains to be seen.

Several jurisdictions are in the process of creating taxonomies of "green" and/or "sustainable" economic activities and/or financial instruments. While the existing voluntary market principles are likely to reflect the content of such taxonomies in their future updates, the process will take some time. In the meantime, could taxonomies result in the emergence of a "deep green" or "dark green" niche within the GSF market? Moreover, conflicting definitions and diverging eligibility criteria across jurisdictions could cause labelling and communication challenges for issuers and investors alike.

Sustainability-linked instruments are showing their potential and while at an early stage, these general-purpose instruments have the potential to significantly increase the perimeter of GSF. The pervasive question regarding these instruments is "how much is enough?" in terms of ambitiousness of the targets (SPTs). For instance, should every greenhouse gas related SPT aim at reaching net-zero emissions at some point? Alternatively, could "transition" finance one day become a subset of sustainability-linked financing explicitly targeting the deep decarbonisation of the issuer/borrower?

Finally, there is the question of financial attractiveness of GSF instruments relative to conventional financial instruments. The supply-demand imbalance for euro-denominated GSS bonds results in pricing advantages for GSS bonds in primary bond markets and the emergence of "greenium" in secondary bond markets. Could similar pricing dynamics actually take place in other markets too?

第7章

服務發行人與借款人的綠色及可持續金融：可持續發展的解決方案

Radek JÁN
Natixis　基建及綠色金融專員

摘要

本章以投資銀行的視角，闡述相關從業者關於綠色及可持續金融（green and sustainable finance，簡稱 GSF）工具價值鏈的觀點。評估金融工具的「綠色」或「可持續」元素是一項錯綜複雜的任務，需要借助自然科學和社會科學等多個領域的知識。在過去幾年，由於缺乏普遍認可且科學的分類方案回答這樣的疑惑，市場從業者採取了務實的方法，構思了一些自願性原則和指引，規定在哪些條件下可以將債券和貸款工具貼上「綠色」、「社會責任」、「可持續發展」或「可持續發展掛鈎」等標籤。在 GSF 領域，貼標債券和貸款可以根據其背後的機制分為兩種：特定收益用途和一般性企業用途。

雖然由於綠色及可持續發展標籤的債券與貸款工具的定義明確且易於識別，本章將重點討論此類金融工具，但應該強調的是，許多其他類型的金融工具同樣可以為環境、社會及／或可持續發展目標作出貢獻。因此，具綠色及可持續發展標籤的金融工具構成了一個金融工具分支，可以申請不同的綠色及可持續發展金融認證。

貼標 GSF 債券的發行量每年都創下新高，但投資者的需求更見日益增長。供需不平衡對一級市場價格持續造成影響，並蔓延至二級市場。本章對超額認購倍數、再發售時與初始定價的利差收緊，及歐元計價債券市場新發行溢價進行實證分析。結果表明，投資者對貼標 GSF 債券的興趣大於類似的傳統債券，而這有利於前者的定價。此外，我們的分析顯示存在「綠色溢價」，即 GSF 債券在二級市場的溢價。雖然這不是一個同質化現象（因可以觀察到正和負的綠色溢價），但綠色溢價長期存在，並往往隨着債券的期限和發行人的信用風險而增加。

隨着 GSF 從小眾走向主流，市場正發生一些演變。個別司法權區正制定相關「分類標準」以正式界定「綠色」或「可持續發展」。這類標準的採用料將會於管理 GSF 貼標工具的市場準則的演變中有所反映。新冠病毒疫情使社會及社會經濟問題成為焦點，從而吸引大眾對社會責任和可持續發展的 GSF 工具的關注，這尤其凸顯出市場上貼標 GSF 債券和貸款在形式上的多元化。雖然按市場上的發行量和未償付金額計，綠色債券仍然是最大的貼標 GSF 工具，但自新冠病毒疫情爆發以來，社會責任和可持續發展債券的份額一直在上升，而且這個趨勢在可預見的將來很可能會持續。而可持續發展掛鈎債券和貸款則提供了一個完全不同的機制，透過吸引對採用特定收益用途機制的綠色、社會責任和可持續發展債券和貸款不感興趣的發行人和借款人，有望大幅擴大 GSF 範圍。與可持續發展掛鈎債券和貸款能在多大程度上擴大 GSF 的吸引力，目前仍是未知數。這些工具因沒有特定收益用途方面的要求，而是關注長期在可持續發展方面的改善，可能尤其適合為碳密集型及／或重污染行業向低碳經濟轉型提供資金。然而，目前尚不清楚「可持續發展掛鈎」是否將能與「轉型」互換稱謂，或者未來會否創造一種全新的「轉型」GSF 工具。

發行人借助 GSF 促進可持續發展的動機

由於氣候變化和可持續發展越來越引人注目，過去幾年，從企業到國家和國際組織等各個層面的相關活動都在增加，目前在不斷努力了解如何使經濟發展更具可持續性，以及向低碳經濟轉型將對金融領域造成甚麼影響。各國正努力探索如何使金融體系與《巴黎協定》[1]保持一致，投資者亦越來越關注其投資組合的碳足跡、氣候風險及影響。這種勢頭已反過來推動綠色及可持續金融（green and sustainable finance，簡稱 GSF）解決方案的供應，其中大部分甚至在十年前還不存在。

中央銀行、金融監管機構和監督者越來越關注金融穩定與氣候轉變的關係，這也激勵金融機構更加關注這些議題。2015 年發生了兩個特別有影響力的事件：《巴黎協定》的簽署和時任英倫銀行行長的馬克·卡尼發表「地平線的悲劇」演講[2]。在此之後，金融業內的氣候和環境行動一直在穩步推進。雖然《巴黎協定》從總體上奠下基礎，但卡尼的演講標誌着環境和氣候方面的考慮首次形成框架在金融界產生共鳴。此後，與理解、衡量和管理氣候相關風險對金融穩定造成的影響有關的方法論研究和發展一日千里，這個快速發展領域的許多最新知識可透過「綠色金融體系網路」（Network for Greening the Financial System，簡稱NGFS）[3] 獲得。NGFS 由中央銀行家、金融監管者和監督者組成，他們共同開展有關綠色金融的分析工作，並制定和分享最佳做法，以「加強金融體系在環境可持續發展大背景下的作用，以管理風險及調動資本進行綠色和低碳投資」[4]。

在這大環境下，越來越多發行人進入市場發行 GSF 工具。部分是熟悉市場的頻繁發行人，但更多的是首次發行人，涉及綠色、社會責任、可持續發展或與可持續發展掛鈎的債券形式（本章將使用簡稱「GSS」代表這些貼標債券形式）。結果，在 2021 年第二季末，貼標GSS 債券工具的個別發行人數量接近 1,300 個（見圖 1）。

1　《巴黎協定》的目標是將本世紀的全球平均氣溫升幅限制在攝氏2度以內，同時努力進一步限制與工業化前水平相比的升幅，最好是攝氏1.5度。（詳見聯合國氣候變化網站上的〈巴黎協定〉網頁）。

2　馬克·卡尼的演講全文（2015年9月29日）可在英倫銀行網站上的〈演講稿〉網頁查閱。

3　又稱「中央銀行與監管機構綠色金融體系網路」（The Network of Central Banks and Supervisors for Greening the Financial System）。

4　資料來源：〈中央銀行與監管機構綠色金融體系網絡創始成員的聯合聲明〉（"Joint statement by the founding members of the Central Banks and Supervisors Network for Greening the Financial System"），可在法蘭西銀行（Banque de France）網站上查閱，2017年12月12日。

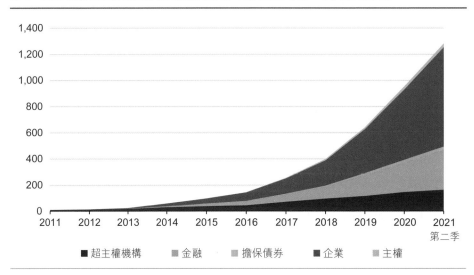

圖 1：GSS 債券工具的個別發行人數量（2011 年至 2021 年第二季）（所有幣種）

■ 超主權機構　■ 金融　■ 擔保債券　■ 企業　■ 主權

資料來源：Natixis 根據 Bloomberg 數據所作的分析。

越來越多實體正在制定綠色及可持續發展戰略，並尋找方式使他們的融資機制符合環境、社會和管治（environment、social、governance，簡稱 ESG）主題及可持續發展。因此，GSF 工具得以蓬勃發展，因為它們提供了一種為環境、社會責任或其他可持續發展主題融資的具體方式。在實踐中，發行人透過發行 GSF 工具獲得資金並享有一些好處，下面將討論這些好處。

形象和傳訊

透過涉足 GSF 市場，發行人／借款人釋出有關其對 ESG 或可持續發展主題作出承諾的明確訊息。若涉及特定收益用途的債券／貸款，表示發行人／借款人會將其獲得的資金用於具有公認環境及／或社會增值的項目和活動；若涉及可持續發展掛鈎債券和貸款所傳遞出的訊息是發行人／借款人致力於長期改善 ESG 領域。使用特定收益用途的形式或與可持續發展掛鈎的形式，通常會為發行人／借款人的聲譽和信譽帶來正面影響，並可能在未來提高其 ESG 評估得分。根據 GSF 融資的性質，發行人／借款人可聲稱對適應或緩解氣候變化作出貢獻、為環境帶來正面影響、為社會進步、經濟賦能／發展或整體可持續發展提供支持。

內部參與

借助 GSF 工具踏上可持續發展之路，長期可促成改善營運／能源效率及／或整體管理的良性循環。例如，透過滿足對發行人／借款人的要求，貼標 GSF 工具有助於其建立或加強內部環境管理系統（例如環境和氣候核算與匯報），或革新公司實踐或採購政策與要求。

監管環境

進入 GSF 市場也為發行人／借款人提供了機會，對未來與氣候變化、能源轉型及整體可持續發展相關的監管與政策轉變／目標／承諾作出預期和配合。例如，為綠色及可持續發展掛鈎的工具提供了機會，讓發行人／借款人與氣候變化和環境相關的國家與國際議程接軌。

投資者要求不同金融工具和經濟活動，須在對環境與可持續發展的實質影響方面提高清晰度。為回應這些訴求，個別司法權區已經開始立法，提供有關 GSF 的官方定義和分類標準，其中最突出的例子，是《歐盟可持續金融分類標準條例》（European Union Taxonomy Regulation，簡稱「歐盟分類標準」）和「中國分類標準」—— 正式名稱為《綠色債券支持項目目錄》。歐盟分類標準是《歐盟永續金融行動計劃》（EU Sustainable Finance Action Plan）的基礎，是對 GSF 更廣泛的立法和監管，其中包括創建以《歐盟綠色債券標準》（EU Green Bond Standard）為基礎的新金融工具「歐盟綠色債券」，以及明確界定哪些零售投資基金可以「綠色」作招徠的「歐盟生態標籤」（EU Ecolabel）。此外，由公共機構組成的多邊論壇「可持續金融國際平台」（International Platform on Sustainable Finance，簡稱 IPSF）亦正努力確保多個司法權區達成一致行動，合力為界定和擴大 GSF 的規模制定監管框架及法律。

投資者和貸款人對 GSF 工具的偏好

上述發展令 GSF 債券和貸款在市場上吸引到越來越多人的興趣。機構投資者和資產管理人越來越關注其投資組合的氣候足跡，以衡量氣候政策及向低碳經濟轉型的能源措施對其潛在的財務影響。買方的許多參與者已經作出量化承諾，增加 GSF 工具在其投資組合中的比重，這推動了市場對這些工具的需求。對於貸款人也是如此，例如，可持續發展掛鈎貸款就非常符合可持續發展需要及貸款人信貸評估政策中的 ESG 標準。有賴於可持續發展掛鈎貸款，貸款人將資本投向致力改善其在可持續發展或 ESG 議程方面表現的借款人，可宣稱自己支持更廣泛的可持續發展或 ESG 議程。一般而言，貼標 GSF 工具可提供更多可用資訊並增加發行人／借款人的問責性，這有助促進金融市場更趨完整，並為投資者提供更全面的資訊，以助他們就 ESG 風險和影響方面對其投資作出評估。

因此，在過去幾年，市場對具有明顯綠色／社會責任／ESG 認證的資產和投資機會的需求不斷增加。貼標 GSF 工具尤其能滿足此需求，因相關債券／貸款的核心原則符合投資者／貸款人對該種工具的期望，包括在符合資格、匯報、透明度和其對環境及／或社會的預期影響方面。特定收益用途的債券形式和可持續發展掛鈎的債券形式均是為廣大固定收益投資者而設。秉持負責任投資策略（如 ESG 整合、同類最佳、主題投資或 ESG 傾向型）的固定收益基金因具前瞻性，可能會認為可持續發展掛鈎債券十分吸引。而有許多特設的GSS 債券基金特別鍾情於特定收益用途債券，這些特設的基金會否考慮將可持續發展掛鈎債券納入其投資組合，會取決於其關鍵績效指標（key performance indicator，簡稱 KPI）和可持續發展表現目標（sustainability performance targets，簡稱 SPT）與基金的相關性。

因此，發行 GSF 債券可使投資者基礎更趨多元化，因發行人可觸及更廣泛的投資者羣體，或吸引此前對其產品不感興趣的各類投資者。

關於以歐元計價之市場的實證見解

一級和二級債券市場均可見以歐元計價之 GSS 債券的供需失衡對其定價的影響。

GSS 債券在一級市場的供需失衡

對以歐元計價之市場的實證數據進行的分析顯示，儘管 GSS 債券的發行量急增，但其需求仍然殷切。這種供需失衡導致 GSS 債券的定價優勢長期存在。我們對 2018 年至 2021 年上半年的市場數據進行的實證分析顯示，相對同類型傳統債券（同一類型的發行人，相近的規模，相近的發行時間）而言，投資者對 GSS 證券[5]的興趣更大，這從兩者超額認購倍數的差異可見一斑。投資者的興趣傾向導致定價差異，表現為發行時利差收窄及新發行溢價（new issuance premium，簡稱 NIP）。

超額認購率

超額認購率顯示投資者在債券發行時對其有多大興趣。雖然債券發行一般都會出現超額認購，但平均而言，GSS 債券的超額認購率更高，表明投資者對 GSS 債券的興趣更大，而這將會對定價造成影響。

---

5 本節使用「證券」而非「金融工具」一詞，是為了明確只限債券（貸款並非證券）。雖然本章的餘下部分談及帶有綠色、社會責任、可持續發展及可持續發展掛鈎債券和貸款工具，但關於一級市場的定價和二級市場的綠色溢價部分只限債券。

如圖 2 所示，GSS 債券和傳統債券的平均季度超額認購率的比較結果顯示，投資者對 GSS 債券的興趣更大。自 2021 年第一季以來，GSS 的 BBB 級公司債超額認購率在各個季度均高於傳統債券。同樣，自 2019 年第二季以來，GSS 高級優先金融債券在各個季度都有更高的超額認購率，自 2020 年第三季以來，GSS 高級非優先金融債券亦出現同樣的趨勢。只有 A 級公司債有細微差別——2019 年第四季至 2020 年第二季，GSS 債券超額認購率平均顯著高於傳統債券；2020 年第三季至 2021 年第一季，GSS 債券和傳統債券認購率相近；而 2021 年第二季 GSS 債券超額認購率較低。

圖 2：以歐元計價的 GSS 債券和傳統債券的超額認購率之比較
（2018 年第一季至 2021 年第二季）

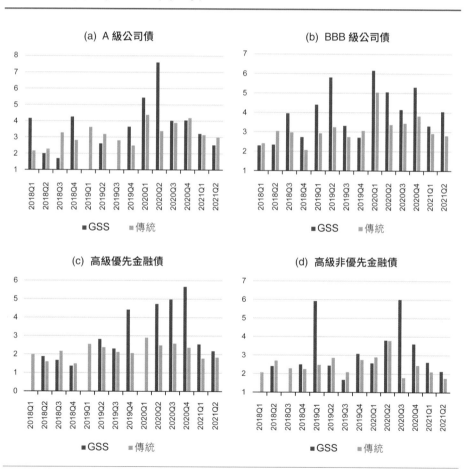

註：「Q1」代表第一季、「Q2」代表第二季、「Q3」代表第三季、「Q4」代表第四季。（適用於以下各圖。）

資料來源：Natixis 根據 Bloomberg 數據所作的分析。

發行時利差收窄

初始指導價與最終定價之間的利差收窄與超額認購率有密切關係。在定價過程中,債券利差會有所收窄。投資者對債券的強勁需求(反映在較高的超額認購率)導致初始指導價和最終定價之間的利差收窄幅度較大。

總括而言,這個指標顯示 GSS 債券相對同類傳統債券具發行定價優勢。由於投資者對 GSS 債券的需求更大,以歐元計價之 GSS BBB 級公司債的平均利差收窄幅度大於在相近時間發行的傳統債券。這現象見諸我們的樣本中除 2018 第二季外的各個季度。2019 年第二季以來 GSS 高級優先金融債各個季度的表現,以及 2020 年第四季以來高級非優先金融債各個季度的表現均出現上述趨勢。只有 A 級公司債有細微差別——GSS 債券的平均利差收窄幅度在某些季度大於傳統債券,而在其餘季度則小於傳統債券。(見圖 3)

圖 3:以歐元計價的 GSS 債券和傳統債券發行時利差收窄幅度之比較
(2018 年第一季至 2021 年第一季)

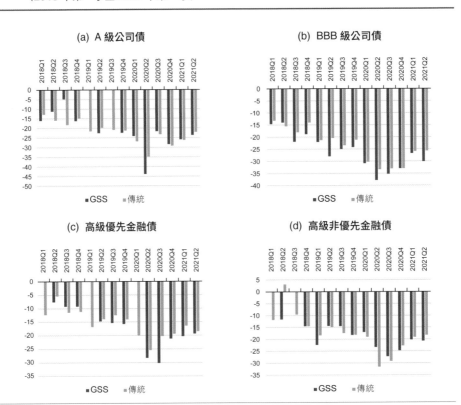

資料來源:Natixis 根據 Bloomberg 數據所作的分析。

新發行溢價（NIP）

NIP 是指相對於新債券定價時在二級市場上交易的同一發行人的其他債券收益率，買方從新發行的債券中得到的額外收益（由賣方支付）。為計算 NIP，我們針對樣本中的每個發行人建立了零波動利差（z-spread[6]）曲線，並在新發行債券的期限上插入了二級曲線。

由於在以歐元計價的債券中投資者偏好 GSS 債券，我們樣本中所有資產類別均表現出發行人的定價優勢，即 GSS 債券的 NIP（有時為負）低於傳統債券。這個趨勢長期存在。此外，許多首次發行或創新型的 GSS 債券的 NIP 不僅顯著低於傳統債券，更甚至為負數。如圖 4 所示，2020 第三季至 2021 第二季，以歐元計價的 GSS BBB 級公司債的平均 NIP 為負數，而傳統債券的平均 NIP 則一直保持正數。此外，在 2021 年第一季，GSS 高級優先和高級非優先金融債的平均 NIP 首次轉為負數，而傳統債券的 NIP 在同一時期保持正數。值得一提的是，自 2020 年第二季以來，儘管 A 級公司債類別下的 GSS 債券和傳統債券的超額認購率及發行時利差收窄幅度均相近，但前者的平均 NIP 仍然較低。

6　Z-spread用於量化市場對債券現金流價值的看法：定義為需要添加到隱含即期收益率曲線，從而使債券的貼現現金流等於其現值（其當前市場價格）的基點價差。我們使用Z-spread，因其不受收益率曲線演變的影響，是衡量信用風險的最佳方法（沒有期限偏差），也是衡量不同債券的相對價值和利差歷史的最佳工具。

圖 4：以歐元計價之 GSS 債券與傳統債券的 NIP 之比較（2018 年第一季至 2021 年第二季）

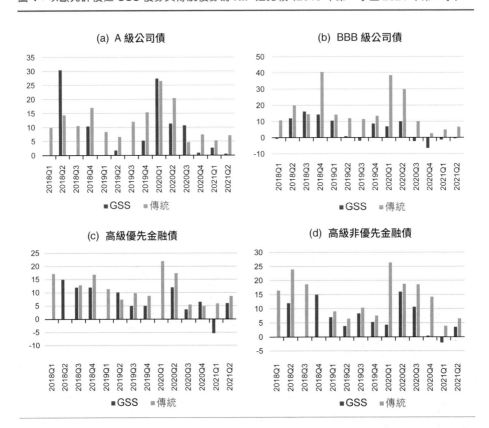

資料來源：Natixis 根據 Bloomberg 數據所作的分析。

二級市場的綠色溢價擴大 [7]

儘管過去幾年 GSS 債券供應暢旺（見圖 1 及圖 10），但對 GSS 債券的投資者需求與其供應之間的不平衡仍然日益加劇，這導致在二級市場，GSS 債券相對傳統債券出現明顯的溢價（所謂的「綠色溢價」），就像於一級市場的一樣（見上文圖 4）。

為了量度綠色溢價，我們需要將某一日期某個發行人在 GSS 市場的產品收益率（或更準確地說是 z-spread），與同一發行人所發行的具有相同清償優先順序、可比期限及流動性的各種工具的收益率（或更準確地說是 z-spread）進行比較。某一 GSS 債券與其同類傳統債券之間的 z-spread 差異是為該 GSS 債券的「綠色溢價」，當投資者接受為 GSS 資產支付溢價時，綠色溢價往往為負值。

在以歐元計價的非金融企業債券市場，GSS 債券與同類傳統債券的比較歷史最長。我們注意到，自 2017 年下半年以來，除 2020 年 3 月歐洲爆發新冠病毒疫情危機的那幾天外，該市場的綠色溢價（對未償還總額約 600 億歐元的 78 隻 GSS 債券進行計算得出）一直為負數。自 2020 年 3 月以後，以歐元計價的公司債券市場的綠色溢價幾乎一直呈負值趨勢（即綠色溢價較大），在 2021 年 8 月初的溢價約為 3.2 個基點。（見圖 5）

7　這一節有關綠色溢價的內容由Natixis實質資產研究主管Thibaut Cuillière撰寫。

資料來源：Thibaut Cuillière（Natixis）根據 Bloomberg 數據所作的分析。

此外，我們還需要考慮綠色溢價是發行人為發行債券（無論是 GSS 債券抑或傳統債券）支付利差的一種方式。事實上，某個發行人的信用風險越高，GSS 債券的溢價就越高，因為對 GSS 債券的需求越大，對風險較高的發行人而言差別就越大（對於這些發行人的債券，無論是傳統抑或 GSS 債券，投資者的需求均會明顯較低）。

如圖 6(a) 所示，自 2020 年 3 月以後，綠色溢價與企業的平均 z-spread 的比率越來越大，而自 2021 年 2 月以後又進入一個加速階段 —— 截至 2021 年 8 月中，非金融企業債發行人的平均綠色溢價與其平均 z-spread 的比率達 9% 至 10%，而於 2021 年初，這個比率為 4% 至 5%，進一步證明對 GSS 資產的強勁需求會影響這些工具的定價。

如圖 6(b) 所示，截至 2021 年 8 月 12 日，以歐元計價的公司債券市場的平均綠色溢價（以基點計）與 z-spread 密切相關。

圖 6：以歐元計價的公司債券的綠色溢價與利差的比率及平均綠色溢價

(a) 綠色溢價與 z-spread 的比率（2018 年 7 月 2 日至 2021 年 8 月 12 日）

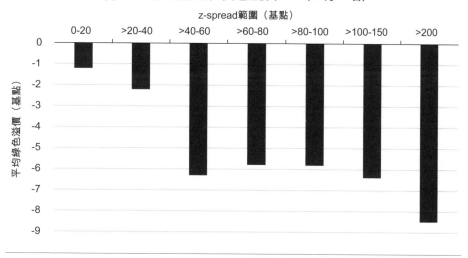

(b) 按利差水平劃分的平均綠色溢價（2021 年 8 月 12 日）

資料來源：Thibaut Cuillière（Natixis）根據 Bloomberg 數據所作的分析。

不僅以歐元計價的公司債券市場的綠色溢價一直在上升，其他債券類別的市場亦如此。在以歐元計價的金融債市場，GSS 債券和傳統債券的定價在 2020 年春季新冠病毒危機爆發前沒有明顯差異（見圖 7）。自 2020 年夏天以來，銀行為滿足其資金需求，更加積極地發行 GSS 債券（尤其是綠色和社會責任債券），而固定收益市場對這些不斷增長的 GSS 債券和傳統債券的定價亦日益分歧。如圖 7 所示，以歐元發行的高級非優先金融債務的平均綠色溢價約為 4 個基點，而這些工具的平均 z-spread 為 45 至 50 個基點（於 2021 年 8 月 12 日）。自 2020 年 9 月以來，這些工具的綠色溢價上升得尤其快速。

圖 7：以歐元計價的高級非優先金融債券的平均綠色溢價之趨勢
（2019 年 8 月 1 日至 2021 年 8 月 12 日）

資料來源：Thibaut Cuillière（Natixis）根據 Bloomberg 數據所作的分析。

以歐元計價的高級優先金融債等其他市場板塊或美元公司債市場的情況亦然。圖 8 顯示了於 2021 年 8 月 12 日，不同市場板塊中以不同貨幣計價的 GSS 債券和傳統債券的平均定價差異：

- 所有市場板塊均錄得明顯的綠色溢價 —— 按 z-spread 計算介乎 2.5 個基點至 6 個基點之間，表明目前 GSS 市場的供需不平衡已經在固定收益市場普遍存在；

- 各個市場板塊的綠色溢價，是基於各自的平均 z-spread 計算得出。與歐元公司債相比，美元公司債的 z-spread 一般較大，其綠色溢價傾向有更大負值。以歐元計價的高級非優先金融債的綠色溢價負值亦大於以歐元計價的高級優先金融債，這證實了我們上述的分析（債務的風險越大，其綠色溢價的絕對值越高，因其通常是基於利差的大小）。

圖 8：按市場板塊和幣種劃分的平均綠色溢價（2021 年 8 月 12 日）

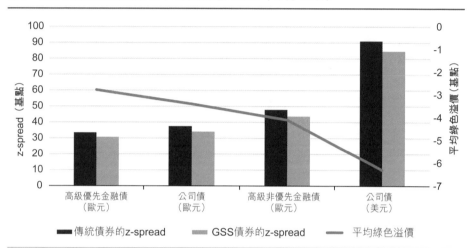

資料來源：Thibaut Cuillière（Natixis）根據 Bloomberg 數據所作的分析。

最後，我們發現綠色溢價取決於 GSS 債券的期限。圖 9 顯示，在公司債券市場，以歐元和美元計價的債券的綠色溢價隨着它們的期限增加而負值越大。這可歸因於兩個因素：(1) 某一發行人本身的平均利差（因綠色溢價與 z-spread 的水平通常成正比）；(2) 採取「買入並持有」策略的投資者更關注期限 7 年以上的債券，在如此長期限內他們的投資組合的綠色化趨勢更明顯。

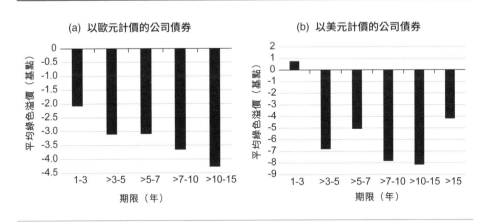

資料來源：Thibaut Cuillière（Natixis）根據 Bloomberg 數據所作的分析。

對以其他貨幣計價的 GSF 金融工具的啟示

在以歐元計價債券的一級市場觀察到的定價表現，可歸因於 GSS 債券的供應和投資者對這些工具需求之間的長期失衡。由於需求仍遠超現有供應，在以歐元計價的市場，新發行的 GSS 債券的超額認購率往往高於同一類型發行人在同一時期發行的傳統債券。此強勁需求反過來導致 GSS 債券具定價優勢，表現為初始指導價與最終定價之間的利差收窄，及發行時出現 NIP。此外，上述供需失衡亦對以歐元計價債券的二級市場造成影響，表現為「綠色溢價」的長期存在。

同樣的情況也適用於以其他貨幣計價的 GSS 債券。例如，若在中國出現類似現時歐洲市場的供需失衡，GSS 債券的人民幣市場或可從一級市場的定價表現和二級市場的「綠色溢價」中受惠。這在很大程度率取決於以人民幣計價的 GSS 債券的供應增長速度，以及人民幣固定收益投資者會否於短時間內對 GSS 債券產生強烈興趣。

GSF 工具的選擇及潛在的挑戰

對於有助於可持續發展及向低碳經濟轉型的項目及經濟活動的融資方面，債務市場可以發揮重要作用。但市場參與者如何得知甚麼是「綠色」或「可持續」？就債務市場而言，答案便是自願性的市場原則和指引，這些原則和指引界定了債券及貸款產品可以被貼上「綠色」、「社會責任」、「可持續發展」或「可持續發展掛鈎」標籤的條件。這些標籤可以被賦予任何符合相關原則和指引的產品，這些原則和指引的制定是為了確保此類產品的真確性，同時有助於提高債務市場的整體透明度。有趣的是，這些標籤是由市場參與者本身所創造，而非由監管者或立法者「強加」。不過，個別司法權區正透過制定所謂的「分類標準」（如上所述），對「綠色」及／或「可持續」經濟活動作出定義。目前管理 GSF 工具的市場原則料將因應這些標準的內容而演變。

所有被貼標的 GSF 債務工具可分為兩種：「特定收益用途」工具及「一般用途」工具。特定收益用途的 GSF 工具是「綠色」、「社會責任」及「可持續發展」債券和貸款。特定收益用途工具使融資用途清晰透明，因為它們要求把收益或同等金額的資金指定給特定的符合要求的項目。貼標為一般用途的 GSF 工具是「可持續發展掛鈎」債券和貸款。它們的收益可以用於任何目的，但發行人／借款人承諾在一段時間內改善其可持續發展相關表現。這些工具的金融特徵將隨着預設的可持續發展目標是否實現而變化。因此，可持續發展掛鈎債券和貸款是前瞻性的金融工具，顯示發行人／借款人所作出的整體承諾。這兩類金融工具在 GSF 範疇內相對較新，這些工具的市場尚處於早期發展階段，而特定收益用途的 GSF 工具市場現在已大致建立起來了。

應該強調的是，並非每個用於環境／社會項目融資和相關支出的債券或貸款均採用正式的綠色／社會責任標籤。有些發行人／借款人只是認為其可持續發展的資格已不言而喻，並不想經歷所需程序為其融資方式取得正式標籤。再者，有些機構幾乎只為符合綠色或社會責任債券／貸款特定收益用途的活動提供資金，但這些機構並沒有把其債券／貸款工具與相關的市場標準保持一致。下面列出的資料是 GSF 債務市場的貼標部分，而非債務市場中用於綠色／社會責任／ESG 主題的全部。

GSS 債券市場正在迅速擴大。正如圖 10 所顯示，單單 2021 年上半年 GSS 債券的發行量便高達 4,200 億歐元，與 2020 年上半年相比增長了 134%。

圖 10：按幣種劃分的 GSS 債券發行量（2013 年至 2021 年上半年）

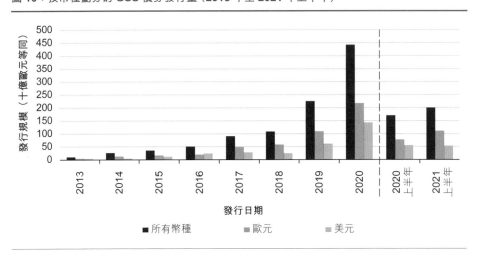

資料來源：Natixis 根據 Bloomberg 數據所作的分析。

截至 2021 年上半年末，GSS 債券的未償還總額達到 1.4 萬億歐元，與 2020 年末的水平相比增加了 40%，GSS 的美元及歐元債券佔了未償還總額的 82%（見圖 11）。

圖 11：按幣種劃分的 GSS 債券未償還金額（2006 年至 2021 年上半年）

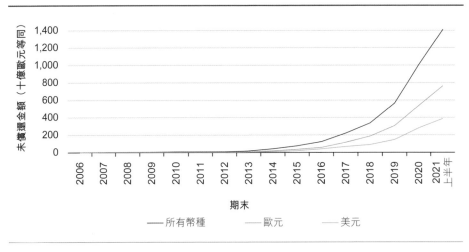

資料來源：Natixis 根據 Bloomberg 數據所作的分析。

特定收益用途的 GSF 工具

任何特定收益用途的金融工具的基本特徵是收益只用於為特定的項目或活動提供資金。就綠色債券和貸款而言，收益被用於具有環境效益的項目。社會責任債券和貸款方面，收益必須分派予具有社會經濟效益的項目。可持續發展債券可謂綠色債券和社會責任債券的混合體，因為其發行的收益會被用於具有環境和社會經濟效益的項目。這並不意味着綠色債券／貸款不會為具有社會經濟共同利益的項目提供資金，亦不意味着採用社會責任債券／貸款融資的項目不會對環境有利。相反，可持續發展債券融資的項目從一開始就有意把環境與社會經濟效益融合起來。

綠色債券與綠色貸款

綠色債券是 GSF 市場上歷史最悠久的貼標債務工具。綠色債券由《綠色債券原則》（Green Bond Principles，簡稱 GBP）[8] 正式定義和規管，是一套廣泛使用的自願性發行指引。GBP 的推出是為了提供指導方針，描述在項目選擇、透明度、信息披露和匯報方面必須進行的事項，用以推出可信的綠色債券。發行人受惠於這套原則，得以知道所有必須採取的關鍵步驟，以儘量減少被指控「漂綠」的風險。投資者受惠於具有明確定義和具備透明環境認證的投資機會，對其投資預計的環境影響有所了解。

哪些項目和經濟活動可以被定義為「綠色」，目前尚具爭議，若干環境可持續活動的目錄及分類標準正在制定當中，以便為這問題提供權威性的詳細答案。GBP 沒有試圖提供一份完備的準則清單，來將各種不同項目和經濟活動附以「綠色」之名（這還需要多年的時間創建）。它是採取務實的方法，建基於五個高層次的環境目標：適應和減緩氣候變化、自然資源保護、生物多樣性保護以及污染預防和控制。基於這些類別，GBP 提供了一份「合格項目」的清單，附以多個例子，這些都載列於表 1 中。該份清單並不意味着已詳盡無遺，因為各種關連性項目或研究與開發等支持性支出，亦有資格獲得綠色債券和貸款融資。

8　GBP由國際資本市場協會（International Capital Market Association，簡稱ICMA）管理，該協會還管理GSF領域內所有規管其他貼標債券工具（即社會責任債券、可持續發展債券和可持續發展掛鈎債券）的自願性市場原則。

表 1：GBP 中列出的綠色項目清單

指示性的合資格類別	例子 / 確述
可再生能源	包括生產、傳輸、設備和產品
能源效益	如在新的和翻新的建築、儲能、區域供熱、智慧電網、電器和產品中
污染防控	包括減少排放、控制溫室氣體、土壤修復、預防廢物、減少廢物、廢物回收和能源 / 排放效率高的廢物變能源
以環境可持續方式管理生物自然資源和土地利用	包括環境可持續的農業、環境可持續的畜牧業；氣候智慧型農場投入（如生物作物保護或滴灌）；環境可持續的漁業和水產養殖業、環境可持續的林業（包括造林和再造林），以及自然景觀的保護或恢復
陸地和水生生物多樣性保護	包括對沿海、海洋和流域環境的保護
清潔交通	如電動、混合動力、公共交通、鐵路、非機動車、多式聯運、清潔能源車輛的基礎設施和減少有害排放等
可持續水資源和廢水管理	包括清潔和 / 或飲用水的可持續基礎設施、廢水處理、可持續城市排水系統和河流治理，以及其他形式的洪水緩解措施
氣候變化適應	包括資訊支援系統，如氣候觀測及預警系統
適應生態效率及 / 或循環經濟的產品、生產技術和過程	如開發及引進環境可持續產品，貼上生態標籤或環境認證，採用資源節約型包裝及分銷方式
綠色建築	符合區域、國家或國際公認的標準或認證的建築

資料來源：《綠色貸款原則》（2021 年），經 ICMA 許可複印。

除了為「合格項目」提供資金外，綠色債券和綠色貸款還必須分別符合 GBP 或《綠色貸款原則》（Green Loan Principles，簡稱 GLP[9]）的四個核心組成部分。這些核心組成部分概述如下。

目前市場上所有貼標特定收益用途的 GSF 工具都受專門的原則（GBP 或 GLP、《社會責任債券原則》或《社會責任貸款原則》）或指引（《可持續發展債券指引》（Sustainability Bond Guidelines））約束，這些原則或指引圍繞四個核心部分：

(1) **募集資金用途**——這是確保特定收益用途工具的可信度及真誠度的關鍵概念。綠色債券 / 貸款的理念是，收益只用於融資「綠色項目」。發行人 / 借款人應明確評估這些項

9　GLP由金融行業制定，建立在GBP的基礎上並參考了GBP。

目的環境效益，並在可行情況下對其進行量化[10]。如果收益被用於現有項目的再融資，應明確說明。如果綠色貸款是以貸款工具的一個或多個分級的形式出現，必須明確指定綠色分級。

(2) **項目評估和遴選的過程** —— 發行人 / 借款人應向投資者 / 貸款人傳達三個要素：

- 發行人 / 借款人的環境可持續性目標；

- 發行人 / 借款人為確定其項目符合合格綠色項目的描述而採用的程序；以及

- 用於確定前一項內容的資格準則，並確定和管理可能與融資項目有關的重大環境或社會風險（如適用）。

(3) **募集資金管理** —— 這方面對於任何特定收益用途產品的透明度和真誠度極為重要。就此，綠色貸款的收益必須記入一個專門的賬戶（這並非一個特別常用的選項）或由借款人追蹤（通常這是首選做法）。同樣，綠色債券籌集的收益（或相當於這些收益的金額）必須由發行人進行追蹤（可以但不一定取把收益記入一個附屬賬戶或轉移至一個附屬組合的形式）。

(4) **匯報** —— 關於特定收益用途的資訊應至少每年更新一次，直到貸款被全部提取或直到債券被全部分派為止。貸款和債券的關鍵區別在於，如果是貸款，資訊只需要提供給參與貸款的機構，而關於債券收益分派的資訊則應包含在發行人的年度報告中。如果由於保密及 / 或競爭原因，及 / 或項目數量眾多而無法提供詳細資訊（綠色項目清單、其描述和預期影響），則至少應以一般方式或以組合方式進行匯報，這同時適用於債券和貸款。當涉及到對融資項目的預期影響的評估時，建議同時使用定性指標和定量措施（取決於其可行性），並披露所採用的基本方法和關鍵假設。

目前市場上有四種不同類型的綠色債券，如表 2 所概述。

10　例如，量化因轉向採用可再生能源而產生的減排量往往明顯易於量化對生物多樣性的影響。

表 2：目前可用的綠色債券類別

債券類別	描述
標準特定收益用途綠色債券	與 GBP 一致的標準追索權債務。
綠色收益債券	與 GBP 一致的無追索權的債務，其中債券的信用風險是針對收入流、費用、稅收等的質押現金流，其收益用於相關或無關的綠色項目。
綠色項目債券	用於單個或多個綠色項目的項目債券，投資者在有或沒有對發行人潛在追索權的情況下直接承擔項目風險，並與 GBP 保持一致。
綠色資產支持證券	由一個或多個具體的綠色項目抵押的債券，包括但不限於擔保債券、資產支持證券、抵押貸款支持證券和其他結構；並與 GBP 保持一致。第一個還款來源一般是資產的現金流。

資料來源：《綠色貸款原則》（2021 年），經 ICMA 許可複印。

就綠色貸款而言，值得注意的是，GLP 已於 2021 年 2 月更新，以考慮到社會議題日益重要：在確定甚麼可以被稱為綠色工具時，社會風險現時是項目評估中需要考慮的一部分。有幾個有趣的觀點專門針對貸款市場，如下所述。

(1) **定期貸款及循環信貸工具（revolving credit facility，簡稱 RCF）**

GLP 旨在適用於各種貸款工具，其中亦包括定期貸款和 RCF。由於定期貸款通常被公司用作購買固定資產，因此對收益用途的識別相對簡單直接。RCF 的情況則比較複雜，因為 RCF 通常不能在開始時提供類似的收益用途識別細節。為了使一個 RCF 被貼上綠色標籤，其收益仍然必須被分派予 GLP 所定義的一些合格類別（就像任何其他綠色貸款一樣）。如果借款人在簽訂貸款時不能指定一個綠色項目，融資協議必須包含可充分識別的合格綠色項目類別，這些項目可由 RCF 的收益來融資。就此，有關各方應共同尋找最佳方式，以表明來自 RCF 的資金確實流向了實現所商定的可持續發展目標。這必須在貸款人和借款人之間就個別個案商議。同樣，貸款人和借款人需要商定在根據 RCF 提取資金時，是否會有任何額外的條件或匯報要求。

(2) **貸款文件應包括的綠色條款**

雖然綠色貸款文件需就個別個案處理，但在起草新文件時，至少有四個考慮因素需要牢記。首先，鑒於其特定收益用途的重要性，「目的條款」或「特定收益用途條款」應明確説明哪些是可作融資的合格綠色項目類別。第二，融資協議書應明確指出與所融資的綠色項目有關的資訊承諾和 / 或契約。第三，任何報告的準確性應該是借款人的義務。第四，每筆交易的融資協議書都應明確甚麼是「綠色違約」，即違反收益使用條款，這將導致從違約時起失去對特定收益用途產品使用綠色標籤的權利。GLP 對這種違約行為（當收益沒有用於綠色項目時）是否應引發違約（以及由此產生的未償還貸款的交叉違約）不持任何立場，這需留待有關各方對每筆貸款作個別考慮。

社會責任債券和貸款

最近在 2021 年 4 月推出的《社會責任貸款原則》（Social Loan Principles，簡稱 SLP）說明了 ESG／GSF 不斷擴大的過程，超越了最初的環境根源，納入了更廣泛的可持續發展主題，包括社會經濟議題。雖然《社會責任債券原則》（Social Bond Principles，簡稱 SBP）於 2017 年首次發佈，但在新冠病毒疫情之前，發行量仍然微不足道。就可以被貼標為「社會責任」的債券／貸款類別而言，之前為綠色債券／貸款案例描述的一切亦適用於「社會責任」標籤。把債券／貸款與 SBP／SLP 達成一致，以貼上「社會責任」標籤，需要遵守 SBP／SLP 的四個核心部分：(1) 募集資金用途；(2) 項目評估和遴選過程；(3) 募集資金管理；以及 (4) 匯報。

對社會議題和其後果以及可能的補救措施的理解不斷變化，而且觀點可能因文化和地理差異而有所不同。考慮到這一點，SBP／SLP 提供了一個被認為有資格為社會責任債券或貸款提供資金、包含廣泛高層次類別的清單（當中，SLP 參考了 SBP）。表 3 所列的清單並非詳盡無遺，而是旨在列出可以用社會責任債券和貸款進行融資／再融資的最常見項目類型。

表 3：社會責任項目的指示性（非詳盡）資格類別

類別	描述
可負擔基本基礎設施	清潔的飲用水、下水道、衛生設施、交通、能源、基本電訊
獲得基本的服務	教育和職業培訓、公共衛生／保健、公共衛生應急能源（包括電力）、融資和金融服務、為特定人羣（及／或在低／中收入國家）服務的其他政府辦公室
可負擔住房	增加可負擔住房及社會住房的數量及／或質量。例如，透過對現有住房的改造和建造新的可負擔社會住房
創造就業，以及旨在防止及／或緩解社會經濟危機引起的失業的方案，包括透過中小型企業融資和小額信貸的潛在影響	專業培訓和再培訓計劃、失業保險計劃及類似的社會經濟緩衝措施
糧食安全及可持續食品系統	在物質、社會和經濟方面獲得安全、營養和充足的食物，滿足飲食需求和要求；有彈性的農業實踐；減少糧食損失和浪費；提高小規模生產者的生產力
社會經濟地位的提高與賦權	公平地獲得和控制資產、服務、資源和機會；公平地參與和融入市場和社會，包括減少收入不平等

資料來源：選取自 SLP（2021），經 ICMA 許可複印。

綠色債券／貸款與社會責任之間的重要區別是社會責任標籤更強調目標人羣，希望他們可從社會責任債券／貸款的收益用途中受惠。社會責任融資的根本目的是協助解決一些社會問題，以取得更佳的社會成果。就此，SBP／SLP 提供了某些人羣可能特別需要社會責任融資的指示性類別。這些類別在表 4 中概述。該清單並非詳盡無遺，社會融資亦可以使整個人口受惠，而非只限於其中特定人羣。

表 4：目標人羣

類別	
• 生活在貧困線以下人士	• 被排斥及／或邊緣化的人口及／或社區
• 殘疾人士	• 移民及／或流離失所者
• 低教育程度人士	• 所得服務不足者（由於缺乏獲得基本商品和服務的高效途徑）
• 失業人士	• 婦女及／或性和性別少數羣體
• 老齡人口及／或弱勢青年	• 其他弱勢羣體，包括受自然災害影響的羣體

資料來源：SBP（2021），經 ICMA 許可複印。

SLP 和 SBP 的聯合使用

SLP 的構想是允許與 SBP 一起使用的可能性，因為 SLP 明確指出，社會責任債券（須與 SBP 的核心內容一致）的發行人可以把債券收益，作為貸款人向其他借款人提供社會責任貸款（須與 SLP 的核心內容一致）。

原始借款人亦可作為貸款人

借款人如政府、發展融資機構或市政當局經常作為其他借款人的貸款人。如果原始借款人借了社會責任貸款，然後若想作為其他借款人的貸款人，只要所有的貸款產品符合 SLP 的核心內容，SLP 便可以用作把每筆貸款定性為社會責任貸款。

可持續發展債券

可持續發展債券是綠色和社會責任債券的混合體。因此，它們具有相同的結構，需要與 GBP 和 SBP 的四個核心部分保持一致，並存在於上述相同的債券類型中（即標準特定收益用途債券、收益債券、項目債券和資產支持債券）。這個標籤是為那些明確結合綠色和社會責任方面的項目而設立的。同樣地，發展金融領域的數個組織發行的債券亦可以歸入此標籤，但它們選擇不這樣做。

一般用途的 GSF 工具

可持續發展掛鈎債券（sustainability-linked bond，簡稱 SLB）和可持續發展掛鈎貸款（sustainability-linked loan，簡稱 SLL）是最近加入 GSF 系列的貼標工具。由於這兩個標籤的正式定義出現的時間較特定收益用途的類別遲得多，部分市場參與者有時把這些產品稱為「KPI 債券 / 貸款」、「ESG 掛鈎債券 / 貸款」，甚至可能是「SDG 掛鈎債券 / 貸款[11]」。此外，更可能有部分使用上述標籤的金融工具，或會符合或不符合被視為 SLB 或 SLL 的標準。要被視為 SLB，債券必須符合下文所述《可持續發展掛鈎債券原則》（Sustainability-linked Bond Principles，簡稱 SLBP[12]）的五個核心組成部分。同樣，一項貸款只有在符合下文所述的《可持續發展掛鈎貸款原則》（Sustainability-linked Loan Principles，簡稱 SLLP[13]）的五個核心組成部分時，才能使用 SLL 標籤。

SLB 和 SLL 旨在透過支持環境及 / 或社會及 / 或管治的長期改善，更廣泛地促進可持續發展。換言之，這些工具旨在激勵發行人 / 借款人在廣泛的環境、社會及管治議題中實現一個或數個範疇績效的改善。

有別於上文討論的所有其他 GSF 工具，SLB 和 SLL 並非特定收益用途的工具。相反，它們是為一般用途作融資工具。SLB 和 SLL 並非透過特定收益用途來確定符合條件的融資類別，而是側重於隨時間過去而改善借款人 / 發行人的可持續發展狀況。因此，這些工具本質上屬前瞻性並基於績效，而特定收益用途債券和貸款則側重於「當時」的融資資格，而沒有考慮到未來的發展。在此意義上，SLB 和 SLL 特別適合傳統上對 GSF 不太感興趣的行業（如石油和天然氣、碳密集型行業）的發行人和借款人，因為他們缺乏符合特定收益用途 GSF 工具的項目，或因他們擔心市場的反彈及「漂綠」的指責。

發行人 / 借款人的可持續性或 ESG 表現的改善是透過可持續發展表現目標（即前述的 SPT）來評估。這些 SPT 從一開始已被設立，發行人 / 借款人在實現這些目標方面的進展（或缺乏進展）由關鍵績效指標（即前述的 KPI）或外部 ESG 評級或兩者的結合來衡量。表 5 概述了常用的 SPT 類別。鑑於與可持續發展有關的主題和問題範圍相當廣泛，潛在的 SPT 組合極大，表中所列的類別和為每個類別所提供的例子純粹是舉例說明；再者，個別行業多數有其獨特的 SPT 和 KPI。考慮到這些概念相對新穎，有理由認為在往後數年的 KPI 篩選、SPT 設定、匯報和評估方法，以及其最佳實踐方面，市場將會越來越成熟。

11　SDG是指聯合國的可持續發展目標（United Nations Sustainable Development Goals）（見聯合國網站上的SDG網頁）。

12　SLBP是由ICMA制定的自願性市場原則。

13　SLLP是由三家市場協會制定的自願性市場原則，這是貸款市場協會（Loan Market Association，簡稱LMA）、銀團貸款和交易協會（Loan Syndications and Trading Association，簡稱LSTA）及亞太貸款市場公會（Asia-Pacific Loan Market Association，簡稱APLMA）。

類別	例子
能源效益	發行人 / 借款人擁有或租賃的建築物及 / 或機器的能源效率等級的提高
溫室氣體排放	與發行人 / 借款人製造或銷售的產品或其生產或製造週期有關的溫室氣體排放的減少
可再生能源	發行人 / 借款人產生或使用的可再生能源數量的增加
水消耗	發行人 / 借款人的節水情況
可負擔住房	發行人 / 借款人開發的可負擔住房單位數量的增加
可持續採購	經核實的可持續原材料 / 供應品使用量的增加
循環經濟	原材料 / 用品的回收率或回收使用量的增加
可持續農業和食物	在採購 / 生產可持續產品及 / 或優質產品方面的改進（使用適當的標籤或認證）
生物多樣性	在保存和保護生物多樣性方面的改進
全球 ESG 評估	借款人的 ESG 評級的提高及 / 或獲得公認的 ESG 認證

資料來源：選取自 SLLP（2021），經 ICMA 許可複印。

可持續發展掛鈎債券和貸款

貼有「可持續發展掛鈎」標籤的債券 / 貸款必須與 SLBP / SLLP 的五個核心組成部分相一致。在 2021 年修訂之前，SLLP 曾經有四個核心組成部分，但這現已與 SLBP 的五個核心組成部分一致（見下文），以免混淆並同時確保對可持續發展掛鈎標籤採取統一方法。

(1) **KPI 的遴選。**如果 SLB 和 SLL 要順利成為一種新資產類別，必須非常審慎地避免選擇毫無意義的 KPI，因為這將損害整個金融工具的可信度，並使發行人容易受到「漂綠」的指責。KPI 將被用以評估發行人 / 借款人可持續性的表現，而這種評估反過來將被用作修改 SLB / SLL 的財務及 / 或結構特徵。因此，KPI 必須與發行人的業務有重大相關性，並有助解決發行人 / 借款人所在行業的 ESG / 可持續發展方面的挑戰。KPI 最終可以在項目層面上進行選擇，儘管在大多數情況下，在發行人 / 貸款人層面上選擇 KPI 更形明顯。表 6 列出了適合構建「可持續發展掛鈎」工具的 KPI 四個主要特徵。

表 6：SLB 與 SLL 的 KPI 的主要考慮因素

- 與發行人 / 借款人的整體業務相關且是核心和重要的，並對發行人 / 借款人目前及 / 或未來的業務具有重要戰略意義；
- 在一致的方法學基礎上可衡量或量化；
- 外部可核查；
- 能夠制定基準，即儘可能使用外部參照物或定義，以便評估 SPT 的目標水平。

資料來源：SLBP（2021），經 ICMA 許可複印。

確保所選的 KPI 在自己的控制之下，乃符合發行人 / 借款人的最佳利益。在此意義上，所選擇的 KPI 若依賴商業上未經證實的技術，將使發行人 / 借款人依賴他們無法控制的技術和政策因素。同樣，選擇使用外部 ESG 評級作為 KPI 亦有風險，因為這種評級若在方法上有所變化可能會對發行人 / 借款人有利或不利。

(2) **校準 SPT** 是構建可持續發展掛鈎工具的重要一環。一旦選擇了追蹤發行人 / 借款人在重大 ESG / 可持續發展議題上的進展的各項 KPI，各項 SPT 就要被校準，以設定這些 KPI 隨着時間過去最終應達到的目標水平。以此，SPT 代表發行人 / 借款人的承諾和雄心。SPT 的目標應該是使 KPI 在「常規業務」的軌道上獲得實質改善，並與發行人 / 借款人的可持續發展策略及整體 ESG 方針保持一致。在可行的前提下，SPT 的設定應基於發行人 / 借款人本身的過往表現（至少過去三年的 KPI）、其同業（所在行業的平均和最佳表現、行業或市場標準）和科學（基於科學的假設、氣候目標[14]、最佳可用技術）。目前，有數個倡議為 SPT 的選擇提供數據和分析，例如「轉型路徑倡議」（Transition Pathway Initiative，簡稱 TPI）[15] 或「科學基礎減碳目標倡議」（Science Based Targets initiative，簡稱 SBTi）[16]。

作為一項規則，SPT 應該富有意義、雄心勃勃並與發行人 / 借款人的核心業務相關，而且適用於為其設定的金融工具生命週期。例如，石油和天然氣公司的 SPT 應該與溫室氣體排放量或強度有關，而非與公司總部所用的再生紙數量有關。

第二方意見可在發行前由外部審查人員闡述，以向投資者提供獨立評估，說明所選 KPI 的相關性、可靠性和穩健性，以及 SPT 是否雄心勃勃且與發行人 / 貸款人有關，以及發行人 / 貸款人實現這些指標的策略是否可信。然而，第二方意見並非強制性的[17]，部分發行人可能傾向於展示 / 發展自己在上述方面的內部專長。在這種情況下，應把相關記錄傳達予投資者 / 貸款人。

---

14 「淨零」碳排放，或者是參照《巴黎協定》。
15 TPI旨在評估企業為轉型至低碳經濟所作的準備，所有相關方法論說明及工具可在TPI網站上查閱。
16 SBTi提供工具以評估企業為符合巴黎協定的目標而須減少碳排放量的速度和規模，相關資訊可在SBTi網站上查閱。
17 SLBP和SLLP都建議使用第二方意見，但金融工具可以貼上SLB或SLL的標籤，而不用經過第二方意見的評估。

雖然在起始時確定的 SPT 提供了透明度,評估其能否實現的方法亦屬簡單,但部分發行人／借款人可能傾向於選擇一些 SPT,其範圍或最終目標值可能在 SLB／SLL 的生命週期內的某個時刻會發生變化,例如,「在選定的 KPI 方面保持在行業前十或前四分之一的水平」。此外,SPT 和 KPI 最終可以作調整,以考慮到發行人的收購合併活動的影響。這種潛在的調整將為每個 SPT 和相關的 KPI 度身訂做,並且必須作出明確説明。

(3) **可持續發展掛鈎的特徵。**有別於特定收益用途 GSF 工具(綠色、社會責任、可持續發展的債券／貸款),可持續發展掛鈎工具的經濟成效可能因「觸發事件」而有所變化。「觸發事件」是指 KPI 在預定的時間範圍內達到或未達到預定 SPT 的情況。就 SLB 而言,這會導致其財務及／或結構特徵的修改。在實務上,息票變化是最常用的特徵,但亦可以考慮其他幾個選項(償還金額、期限、付息日期等)。同樣,對 SLL 而言,若借款人達致／未能達到預先設定的 SPT,SLL 的利潤率將會下降／上升。鑒於整個「可持續發展掛鈎」概念的新穎性,隨着市場創新,與之相關的實踐可能會在未來數年不斷演變。

(4) **匯報。**SLB 的發行人應至少每年公佈有關 KPI 演變的資訊。發行前和發行後的強制性和建議性披露的簡要清單可於線上查閱 SLBP 附錄二 [18]。SLL 方面,由於貸款市場的私人性質,公開報告並非一項要求,借款人可以選擇只與貸款人私下分享相關資訊。

(5) **核查。**就 SLB 和 SLL,兩者都要求至少每年對發行人／借款人在每個 SPT 的表現進行一次獨立的外部核查,直到最後一個 SPT 觸發事件之後為止。對於 SLB 而言,這種 SPT 績效核查須作公開,而 SLL 的借款人可以選擇只與貸款人分享這種資訊。

與 SLB 和 SLL 有關的挑戰

鑒於 SLB 和 SLL 的相對新穎性,當中有數個與這些產品有關的問題。下文將討論其中的部分問題。

(1)「漂綠」／「ESG 漂洗」

SLB 和 SLL 必須有恰當的結構,以避免「漂綠」風險,「漂綠」是指當可持續發展方面的實證被誇大、不準確或以誤導的方式呈現。鑒於可持續發展掛鈎工具的獨特結構,有兩種具體情況可能會出現「漂綠」或「ESG 漂洗」的嫌疑:

---

18 ICMA《可持續發展掛鈎債券原則:自願性流程指引》(*Sustainability-Linked Bond Principles: Voluntary Process Guidelines*),2020年6月。

- 如果 SPT 對發行人／借款人的業務而言不夠雄心勃勃及／或意義不夠重大；以及

- 如果發行人／借款人在 SPT 方面的表現被不適當地監測／評估／披露。

發行人／借款人可以透過遵循 SLBP／SLLP 指引，以及在制定 SPT 和選擇適當的 SPT 績效基準和時間表時，尋求獨立外部機構的幫助來降低這種風險。

(2) 訊息不對稱

談到 SLB 和 SLL 時，另一個值得注意的問題是發行人／借款人與交易的其他各方之間的資訊不對稱。發行人／借款人最熟悉本身的業務，因此在整個目標設定的過程中，他們應該真誠行事並提供準確的資訊。

(3) 為 SLB／SLL 設定 SPT

有幾種可行的方法來選擇 SPT，以及多種相關指標來追蹤其進展。這些方法中並沒有哪一個是「較優越」或「更可信」的。它們只是適合不同的客戶，取決於客戶對 ESG 和可持續性議題的熟悉程度。如果發行人／借款人已經有制定完備的 ESG／可持續發展政策和策略、衡量標準和目標，它們亦可以直接用於 SLB／SLL。相反，剛剛展開 ESG／可持續發展之旅的發行人／借款人，可能更願意依靠外部分析，以獲得專門針對其行業的 ESG 準則及最佳可持續發展的實踐，或者使用根據既定框架報告的現有行業指標。

(4) SLB／SLL 的重要性評估

在某些情況下，確保 SPT 及相關指標的實際相關性或許是一項甚具挑戰性的任務，尤其在 SLB 和 SLL 市場發展的早期階段，因為暫時尚未有市場先例。對重要性作評估可以成為這項任務的實用工具，以確定哪些是對每個經濟活動行業和相關持份者最重要或最具有影響的 ESG 因素。因此，對借款人／發行人所屬行業進行重要性評估，可以確認 SPT 所尋求改善的 ESG 議題確實是相關的。例如，永續會計準則委員會（Sustainability Accounting Standards Board，簡稱 SASB）開發了一個重要性圖譜 [19]，可用於比較各行業在財務上重要的 ESG 議題。數家 ESG 評級機構及諮詢機構亦提供類似服務。

19　見SASB網站上的〈重要性圖譜〉（"Materiality Map"）網頁。

(5) **SLB/SLL 的進取度評估**

同樣，鑒於概念的相對新穎性而導致市場經驗的缺乏，確保 SPT 具足夠的雄心，而不僅僅遵循「常規業務」的軌跡，似乎甚具挑戰性。多個倡議組織在這方面可以提供協助。**TPI** 透過評估企業的碳排放軌跡，以及與氣候相關的議題被納入公司策略目標與決策過程的程度，來評估企業對低碳轉型的準備情況。所有這些評估（按行業和公司）均可在網上公開查閱 [20]。同樣，**SBTi** 提供指導、資源以及對企業溫室氣體減排目標的評估 [21]。對於與可再生能源有關的 SPT，可以諮詢 **RE100**，該倡議集合了致力儘快採用可再生能源作為其電力來源的公司 [22]。

此外，在評估 SPT 的進取度時，應考慮到區域及文化差異。例如，與碳強度或環境保護有關的 SPT，在經濟合作與發展組織（Organisation for Economic Co-operation and Development，簡稱 OECD）國家的背景下可能被認為過於溫和，甚至缺乏雄心，但在發展中國家的背景下可能已是雄心萬丈以及極富影響力。與性別平等或人口統計學等相關的社會議題亦如是。

(6) **SLB / SLL 的具體匯報方式**

鑒於 SLB 與 SLL 的新穎性，目前尚未有全球公認的 SPT 匯報方式。因此，在考慮發行人 / 借款人的性質和所選擇的 SPT 基礎上，須為個別個案選擇適當的匯報方式以監測其實現 SPT 的進展。這方面有幾種可持續性匯報方式可供選擇（詳見上述關於 SLBP 和 SLLP 的部分）。

(7) **結合特定收益用途和可持續發展掛鈎的債券 / 貸款形式**

發行人可以決定把綠色 / 社會責任債券與 SLB 相結合。在這種情況下，SLB 的收益將被指定用於 GPB（或 SBP）認為合格的項目的融資或再融資，而且該債券將與 SLBP 和 GBP（或 SBP）的所有核心組成部分一致。同樣，一項貸款的結構可以設計為既是綠色 / 社會責任貸款亦是 SLB。例如，Verbund 在 2021 年 3 月發行了世界上第一個結合特定收益用途及可持續發展掛鈎機制的債券 [23]。Verbund 的「綠色融資框架」已被設計成與 GBP 和 SLBP 一致 [24]。發行該債券的收益將完全分派予該框架所定義的「綠色」項目，如果 Verbund 不能滿足新安裝的可再生能源生產設施和新安裝的變壓器設施的兩個 SPT[25]，該債券的票息將會上升。然而，截至 2021 年，這樣的交易屬罕見。

---

20 見TPI網站上的〈行業〉（"Sectors"）網頁。
21 見SBTi網站上所載的各項材料和指引。
22 見RE100網站。
23 資料來源：載於Verbund網站上的新聞稿，2021年3月22日。
24 Verbund綠色融資框架(2021年3月)可在其官網上查閱。
25 這些變壓器設施旨在使新安裝的可再生資源的電力能夠輸入高壓電網。

GSF 展望

GSS 債券及貸款市場在自願性市場原則下發展，而監管者與立法者已紛紛介入以創建新的、並有約束力的定義，即甚麼可以被視為「綠色」或「可持續」活動或金融工具的「分類標準」。雖然目的是提高 GSF 工具市場的信譽及可信度，但分類標準的發展亦為發行人帶來挑戰，尤其在資料收集和報告方面。此外，新冠病毒疫情使社會經濟議題成為公眾關注的焦點，並引起投資者的注意，導致多個發行人發行社會責任及可持續發展債券，帶動在 2020 年之前一直以綠色為主的 GSS 債券市場更多元化。可持續發展掛鈎債券和貸款有助擴大 GSF 市場的範圍，因這些工具並不要求將收益撥付特定合資格項目。此外，雖然「轉型」至低碳甚至淨零碳排放經濟的議題越來越重要，但市場尚未對「轉型」GSF 工具作出界定。

正在發展的 GSF 分類標準

雖然最近 GSS 債券的發行令人對市場感到樂觀，但要令全球轉型至低碳經濟，並與 190 多個國家簽署的《巴黎協定》目標一致 —— 把全球溫度上升限制在攝氏 2 度以內，則需要每年投入數萬億美元的綠色資金到各行各業和活動中，而現時我們離這項條件尚遠。儘管公共融資將繼續發揮重要作用，但眼前的挑戰所涉的規模及嚴重性決定了這些「每年數萬億美元的綠色資金」中的絕大部分必須由私營界別提供。

由於投資者正迅速把氣候變化的考量，以及更廣泛的環境與可持續發展議題納入其投資決策過程和投資組合配置當中，私營界別越來越願意參與其中。歐盟和中國等部分司法權區已制定法例，以擴大及進一步發展 GSF。有部分這類的立法工作讓分類標準得以被採用，為哪些經濟活動可被視為「綠色」提供官方定義。如果設計得當，這種分類標準可以提高 GSF 市場的透明和真誠度，從而增強投資者的信心和意願，把更多資金分配予「綠色」或「可持續」項目和經濟活動，同時提高發行人 / 借款人利用 GSF 工具籌集資金的意願。

對發行人而言，有趣的是，歐盟分類標準中減緩和適應氣候變化的部分更包括一些眾所周知的「棕色」或「難以減排」的行業，但這些行業的減碳行動對於向低碳經濟轉型是至關重要的。這些行業主要是鋼鐵、鋁和水泥。雖然以碳足跡衡量，目前這些行業與資格門檻相距甚遠，但這些門檻有可能用於選擇 SPT 軌跡，從而為這些在全球經濟持續減碳行動中發揮關鍵作用的行業釋放與可持續發展掛鈎的融資。

對發行人和投資者而言，每個 GSF 分類標準的關鍵挑戰之一是數據的可得性。例如，歐盟分類標準要求眾多數據點，而這些數據點通常並非由發行人追蹤、收集和披露，這意味着發行人方面的報告需要進行大量工作。投資者方面，歐盟分類標準帶來的數據挑戰將涉及現有數據的匯總及其一致和可比性評估。未來將需要更多的市場數據標準化。

鑒於各司法權區在 GSF 定義及分類標準的一致性極為關鍵，IPSF 作為多邊論壇，已於 2019 年啟動，組織起積極參與制定環境融資政策和激勵措施的公共當局，尤其是財政和經濟部、中央銀行、金融監管機構和監督機構。該平台的目的是促進成員之間關於 GSF 的交流、合作和協調，這些成員加起來代表世界一半人口，佔全球溫室氣體排放量的 55%，佔全球國內生產總值的 55%[26]。雖然 IPSF 的目的並非要建立具約束力的全球 GSF 的各項準則及分類標準並強加於成員，但分享最佳實踐及協調 GSF 分類標準的方法論有可能構建更一致的框架和方法。這會使全球投資者能更好地把資本分配到不同司法權區的 GSF 投資機會，並得以向「每年萬億綠色投資」邁出重要一步。

GSF 工具形式的多元化

2020 年標誌着重要的里程碑，即多種貼標 GSS 債券的發展。雖然在 2019 年年底之前，綠色債券每年都佔 GSS 債券發行額的絕大部分，但 2020 年可見社會責任及可持續發展債券的發行得以真正發展。這主要是由於新冠病毒疫情引發市場對社會經濟議題的關注，因為社會責任及可持續發展債券特別適合把資金引向有助於相關事業的項目。因此，社會責任債券的發行額在 2020 年突破 1,300 億歐元，相當於 2019 年的 7.5 倍，而可持續發展債券的發行量在 2020 年亦達到 1,000 多億歐元，SLB 在同年開始發展，儘管數額偏低。與此同時，綠色債券的發行量相對於 2019 年的水平「僅」增長了 17%，顯示這種債券形式正趨向成熟，故增長速度較慢。

這些結構性趨勢在 2020 年重塑了貼標 GSS 債券市場，並在 2021 年持續。雖然在 2021 年上半年，所有形式的貼標 GSS 債券的供應量及未償還金額都以創紀錄的速度增加，但最急劇的增長來自社會責任債券，說明綠色債券不再是最無可爭議的 GSF 主導工具（見圖 12）。

---

26 資料來源：歐洲委員會網站上的〈可持續金融國際平台〉網頁，2021年7月15日。

圖 12：貼標 GSS 債券按類型劃分的發行額（所有幣種）（2014 年至 2021 年上半年）

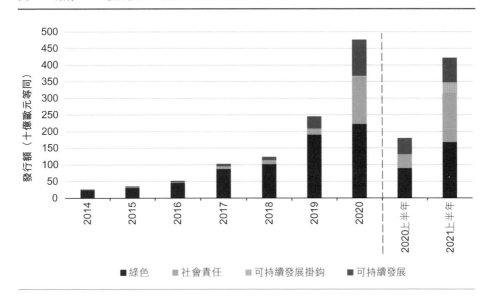

資料來源：Natixis 根據 Bloomberg 數據所作的分析。

截至 2021 年，GSF「轉型」工具尚未有官方貼標。然而，有時當發行人／借款人希望為其減碳行動策略以及向與低碳經濟相容的商業模式轉型尋找資金時，市場上的工具有時會貼上「轉型」主題的標籤。ICMA 的《氣候轉型融資手冊》（*Climate Transition Finance Handbook*）提供指引，建議發行人進行何種類型的披露，以説服投資者相信其轉型策略的公信力。該指南並不針對特定行業，其目的並非為了界定一套特定收益應用類別或一項聲稱符合這種融資方式的經濟活動。因此，「轉型融資」同時開放予特定收益用途以及與可持續發展掛鈎的 GSF 工具，而且適用於碳密集型產業（如水泥、鋼鐵、鋁、石油和天然氣）。

以下列出數個例子説明 GSS 工具如何在可持續發展目標、增長策略和融資策略之間建立聯繫。

綠色房地產投資信託基金（**real estate investment trust**，簡稱 **REIT**）

馬斯達爾綠色房地產投資信託基金（Masdar Green REIT，簡稱 MGR）於 2020 年 12 月 19 日在阿布達比全球市場（Abu Dhabi Global Markets）成立，作為阿布達比金融服務監管局（Financial Services Regulatory Authority）規定的私營 REIT。阿布達比未來能源公司（Abu Dhabi Future Energy Company，或稱「馬斯達爾」）是一家從事可再生能源及可持續城市發展的公司，目前是 MGR 的唯一股東，發展了四項總值 9.49 億迪拉姆（2.58 億美元）的產生收入的資產，納入 MGR 當中。MGR 是阿拉伯聯合酋長國（簡稱「阿聯酋」）的第一個綠色 REIT，用作完全投資馬斯達爾市和阿聯酋境內的可持續的、產生收入的房地產資產[27]。可持續房地產資產組合的基準是「能源與環境設計先鋒」（Leadership in Energy and Environmental Design，簡稱 LEED）和 Estidama[28] 認證，以及一系列可持續績效措施，包括馬斯達爾市的水電消耗、交通、廢物管理、設計和施工。

MGR 正在申請一項綠色融資貸款，目的是支持 MGR 未來的增長及收購目標。該融資正在洽談階段，以符合貸款人的可持續融資承諾和 LMA 的綠色貸款原則，MGR 管理層根據相關的可持續發展措施，對其投資組合中的每項資產的能源效益和績效進行持續的季度追蹤和報告。

綠色可換股債券：NEOEN、EDF 及 Voltalia

NEOEN 是一家專注於太陽能、風能及儲能的獨立可再生能源生產商，於 2020 年 5 月發行了歐洲第一筆綠色可換股債券（1.7 億歐元）[29]。募集資金旨在為可再生能源的生產（太陽能光伏發電及風力發電）和儲能活動提供資金及 / 或再融資。

2020 年 9 月，經常發行綠色債券的法國電力公司（EDF）首次發行面值約為 24 億歐元的綠色高級無擔保債券，可轉換為新股及 / 或可交換為現有股份[30]。該次發行是當時最大宗的綠色可換股債券發行，集資所得用於符合公司綠色債券框架項目的融資及 / 或再融資，這些項目涉及建設可再生能源發電項目、投資現有水電設施，以及投資能源效益和保護生物多樣性。

Voltalia 是一家可再生能源行業的國際企業，於 2021 年 1 月首次發行了價值 2 億歐元的綠色可換股債券[31]，募集資金用於資助及 / 或再融資開發、建設、營運和維護可再生能源工廠（風能、太陽能、生物質能、水能或混合動力）和存儲設施，以及收購在任何可再生能源技術領域非常活躍的公司之多數或少數權益。Voltalia 已開發了一個創新的綠色及可持續發展掛鈎融資框架，結合特定收益用途及一般公司用途的 GSF 主要特點，從而使 Voltalia 未來能夠發行特定收益用途及可持續發展掛鈎債券。

---

27 資料來源：馬斯達爾網站上的新聞稿，2020年1月15日。
28 Estidama是阿拉伯語中的「可持續性」。Estidama認證與綠色建築評級系統有關，用於評估阿布達比的可持續建築發展的實踐。
29 資料來源：NEOEN網站上的新聞稿，2020年5月27日。
30 資料來源：法國電力網站上的新聞稿，2020年9月8日。
31 資料來源：Voltalia網站上的新聞稿，2021年1月6日。

綠色保證金貸款：億萬豪劍橋

加拿大魁北克儲蓄投資集團的房地產子公司億萬豪劍橋（Ivanhoé Cambridge，簡稱 IC）於 2019 年首次透過綠色保證金貸款尋求融資，以改善其可持續發展狀況。該貸款的保證金與四個 KPI 掛鈎：(1) 全球房地產 ESG 基準（Global ESG Benchmark for Real Assets，簡稱 GRESB）的分數；(2) GRESB 的評級；(3) IC 的所有 LEED 金級認證資產（或同等或更高）的價值；以及 (4) 由獨立專家認證其投資組合的碳足跡的減少。

「綠色」首次公開招股（initial public offer，簡稱 IPO）？

本文重點討論被貼標的 GSF 債務工具，因為這些證券定義明確，易於識別。當然，公司亦有其他方法針對環境及 / 或社會目的籌集資金，而毋須使用這些官方貼標，例如，透過發行傳統的債務證券或新股權。確定構成或不構成「綠色股票」的困難，在於缺乏像債券或貸款般普遍被接受的市場原則。相反，有大量數據供應商和 ESG 評級機構使用各種方法為不同的股票「着色」。有趣的情況是：被認為是 GSF 領域中的「純粹參與者」的公司進行 IPO，即「綠色 IPO」。一個案例是，瑞士智慧計量公司 Landis & Gyr Holding 於 2017 年進行的 24 億美元的首次公開招股，該公司把自己定位為「純綠色參與者」來進行資金籌集。另一個例子是 Acciona 的可再生能源業務 Acciona Energia 於 2021 年夏天的上市，該集團旨在籌集資金使其於 2025 年之前將可再生能源產能提高近一倍。

延申討論

GSF 工具日趨流行和多元化，多個司法權區紛紛致力制定相關分類標準，央行、金融監管與監督機構日益關注氣候與環境對金融穩定的影響，這些都顯示 GSF 已成功由「可有可無」的小眾市場發展成為金融體系的主流。

市場正密切關注為減少和預防溫室氣體排放提供資金，以將資本引向減緩氣候變化。然而，正如政府間氣候變化專門委員會（Intergovernmental Panel on Climate Change，簡稱 IPCC）所述，無論全球溫室氣體減排目標成功與否，氣候變化所帶來的若干負面影響已無可避免。這個嚴峻的現實或促使越來越多人關注氣候變化適應問題，因為人們越來越需要對不斷變化的氣候及其影響作出調整。此外，於其他多個重要的環境議題上，GSF 工具亦可以在未來發揮更重要的作用，這些議題包括保護和改善生物多樣性、促進循環經濟及管理水資源和海洋。「地球承載力極限」（Planetary Boundaries）的框架界定了多個重要的環境過程，透過主動管理這些過程，有助於人類社會在地球維持「安全的運作空間」，而 GSF 工具可從「地球承載力極限」的概念及其他科學分析中獲得多少啟示仍有待觀察。

多個司法權區正在制定有關「綠色」及／或「可持續」經濟活動及／或金融工具的分類標準。雖然現有的自願性市場原則料將在日後因應這些標準的內容而作出更新，但這個過程需時較長。與此同時，分類標準能否促使 GSF 市場出現「深綠」的專項市場亦是未知數。再者，若各司法權區設立的相關定義有衝突及資格準則有分歧亦可能在貼標和溝通方面為發行人及投資者帶來挑戰。

可持續發展掛鈎工具正展現它們的潛力，儘管仍處於早期階段，但這些一般用途的工具有望顯著擴大 GSF 的邊界。有關這些工具的一個普遍問題是：就目標（SPT）的進取程度而言，「多少才算足夠？」。例如，是否所有與溫室氣體有關的 SPT 均應以在某個時點實現淨零排放為目標？又或者「轉型」金融日後會否成為可持續發展掛鈎融資市場針對發行人／借款人深度減碳而設的細分領域？

最後，GSF 工具在財務效益方面相對傳統金融工具的吸引力亦是一大問題。以歐元計價的 GSS 債券供求失衡導致 GSS 債券在一級債券市場具定價優勢，並在二級債券市場出現「綠色溢價」。類似的定價機制是否亦會在其他市場出現？

註：本文原稿是英文，另以中文譯本出版。如本文的中文本的字義或詞義與英文本有所出入，概以英文本為準。

Chapter 8

Rating the greenness: ESG in credit ratings and non-credit ESG analysis

S&P Global Ratings

Summary

Timely, transparent, and relevant analytical opinions are essential to the functioning of capital markets and credit opinions, including credit ratings, serve exactly this purpose. This chapter will highlight the analytical approach at S&P Global to reflecting ESG credit factors into credit ratings.

In addition, the strong growth of sustainable debt capital markets is providing opportunities for issuers to secure new sources of funding. To support the functioning of the sustainable debt capital markets, the provision of sustainable financing opinions will be useful in helping companies provide investors with greater insight into how their investments align with sustainability goals.

ESG in credit ratings — How ESG factors can affect credit ratings

Credit ratings help foster the development and smooth functioning of capital markets. They are forward-looking independent analytical opinions on the capacity and willingness of an entity — such as a corporation or municipal government — to meet its financial commitments (to pay back debt and pay interest) in full and on time.

Environmental, Social and Governance (ESG) factors can — and do — influence credit quality, specifically, the capacity and willingness of borrowers to meet financial commitments. They have played a longstanding prominent role in creditworthiness and, thus, in our credit ratings — even before the term ESG was coined more than a decade ago.

What do ESG credit factors in our credit ratings look like?

ESG factors typically incorporate an entity's effect on and impact from the natural and social environment and the quality of its governance; however, not all ESG factors materially influence creditworthiness. Therefore, we define ESG credit factors as those ESG factors that can materially influence the creditworthiness of a rated entity or issue and for which we have sufficient visibility and certainty to include in our credit rating analysis.

Figure 1. The intersection of ESG and credit

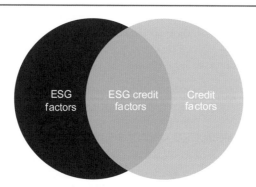

We incorporate ESG credit factors through the application of our sector-specific criteria when we think the ESG credit factors are, or may be, relevant and material to our credit ratings. ESG credit factors can have a positive, neutral or negative impact on creditworthiness, depending on the entity being rated.

For instance, we include the impact of ESG credit factors, such as climate transition risks related to carbon dioxide and other greenhouse gas (GHG) emissions costs, waste and other pollution costs, or health and safety costs, if we deem these material to our analysis of creditworthiness and if we have sufficient visibility on how those factors will evolve or manifest.

Climate transition risk and physical risk-related factors may be among the most significant ESG credit factors that affect the creditworthiness of rated entities. This is primarily because of policymakers' efforts to reduce GHG emissions or to ensure that GHG emissions reflect their full social costs ("climate transition risk") and climate change, which is leading to more frequent and severe extreme weather events ("physical risk"). Nevertheless, as illustrated below there are many relevant ESG credit factors. Examples of social credit factors include health and safety factors which featured prominently since the beginning of the COVID-19 pandemic as a significant number of rating actions reflected a direct health and safety impact.

Figure 2. Examples of ESG credit factors

Environmental Factors	Social Factors	Governance Factors
• Climate transition risks	• Health and safety	• Governance structure
• Physical risks	• Social capital	• Risk management, culture, and oversight
• Natural capital	• Human capital	• Transparency and reporting
• Waste and pollution	• Other social factors	• Other governance factors
• Other environmental factors		

Source: S&P Global Ratings.

The way our analysis reflects ESG credit factors in credit ratings relies on five general principles:

1. Our long-term issuer credit ratings do not have a predetermined time horizon;

2.   The current and potential future influence of ESG credit factors on creditworthiness can differ by industry, geography, and entity;

3.   The direction of and visibility into ESG credit factors may be uncertain and can change rapidly;

4.   The influence of ESG credit factors may change over time, which is reflected in our dynamic credit ratings;

5.   Strong creditworthiness does not necessarily correlate with strong ESG characteristics and vice versa.

Whenever S&P Global Ratings upgrades or downgrades a credit rating, places a credit rating on CreditWatch, or changes a rating outlook, we announce the change and the analytical rationale to all market participants at the same time. The written opinion will include the key drivers of the action. When ESG credit factors are among the key drivers behind the change, it is outlined explicitly and transparently in our publicly available rating reports.

Credit ratings provide timely opinions of creditworthiness to market participants, and will continue to transparently reflect ESG credit factors alongside other credit considerations, where material and relevant to creditworthiness. As the need for understanding the impact of ESG on debt issuers everywhere continues to grow, we continue to implement initiatives to further increase the transparency of how ESG factors can influence creditworthiness.

At times, an entire sector will have its prospects impacted by ESG considerations. In January 2021, we have updated our industry risk assessment for the oil and gas integrated, exploration and production industry to incorporate several increasing and material risks, including the energy transition. This change is an example of current and longer-term ESG risks being factored into our ratings. There is a common misconception that ratings are focused on a short-term horizon of 2-3 years. On the contrary, if we have a sufficiently high degree of visibility about material factors that may crystallise well beyond that period — even a decade out or longer — we would incorporate those factors into our current ratings via our qualitative assessments.

Following the change to our industry risk assessment for the oil and gas industry, we took a series of negative rating actions on global oil majors. These rating actions are among the nearly 2,500 ESG-linked rating actions S&P Global Ratings conducted from the second quarter of 2020 to the first quarter of 2021.

While the downward actions on oil and gas companies are relatively recent, ESG-driven rating actions are not a new phenomenon. For example, in 2009, we lowered the credit rating of a utility company in Europe stating publicly in the report "the downgrade also reflects what we perceive as the company's rising business risk because of its focus on coal-based generation, which is subject to increasingly stringent regulatory and environmental requirements". It was not formally categorised as an ESG-driven rating action then, as the ESG acronym was not in wide use at that point, but it demonstrates how ESG-related risks and opportunities material to creditworthiness have long been incorporated into credit rating analysis.

At S&P Global Ratings, we are committed to providing market participants with further transparency when it comes to incorporating ESG in credit ratings. We intend to start applying ESG Credit Indicators to publicly rated entities. From mid-November to December 2021, we started to publish these indicators for individual companies in the corporate and infrastructure, banking, and insurance sectors, and we will cover other asset classes in 2022. We propose to disclose and systematically explain the degree to which ESG factors are influencing our credit rating analysis, with the aid of a 1-5 scale from positive to very negative for each of: environmental, social, and governance (see Table 1). The proposed ESG Credit Indicators are not a measure of ESG or sustainability performance but they will enhance transparency by indicating our opinion of how material the influence of ESG factors is on various credit rating analytical components in our rating analysis.

Table 1. Planned range of ESG Credit Indicators at S&P Global Ratings

Influence on credit rating analysis	Environmental Credit Indicator	Social Credit Indicator	Governance Credit Indicator
Positive	E-1	S-1	G-1
Neutral	E-2	S-2	G-2
Moderately negative	E-3	S-3	G-3
Negative	E-4	S-4	G-4
Very negative	E-5	S-5	G-5

Source: S&P Global Ratings.

ESG beyond credit ratings: Second-party opinions and ESG evaluations

The sustainable bond market and the latest trends

According to the International Capital Market Association (ICMA):

- Green bonds are use-of-proceed bonds that enable capital-raising and investment for projects with environmental benefits including renewable energy, green buildings, and sustainable agriculture;

- Social bonds raise funds for projects that address or mitigate a specific social issue and/or seek to achieve positive social outcomes, such as improving food security and access to education, health care, and financing, especially but not exclusively for target populations;

- Sustainability bonds target both environmental and social benefits;

- Sustainability-linked bonds and loans are a relatively new class of instruments that provide incentives for issuers and borrowers to set and achieve predetermined sustainability performance targets.

S&P Global Ratings expects issuance of sustainable debt — including green, social and sustainability (GSS) bonds, and sustainability-linked bonds — could exceed US$1 trillion in 2021. This would take cumulative issuance past the US$2 trillion milestone, from US$1.3 trillion as of year-end 2020[1]. Sustainable debt issuance exceeded US$530 billion in 2020, according to Environmental Finance, up a staggering 63% from 2019[2]. Social bonds emerged as the fastest growing segment of the market, growing about 8 times in 2020[3], catapulted by the COVID-19 pandemic and growing concern about social inequities. As issuer attention shifted toward financing pandemic aid and ensuring recession relief measures, green bond issuance slowed in the first half of 2020. However, it rebounded in the second half, reaching a record annual issuance amount of US$270 billion[4] and

---

1   Source: "To mitigate greenwashing concerns, transparency and consistency are key", published on the website of S&P Global Ratings, 23 August 2021.
2   Source: "Sustainable debt markets surge as social and transition financing take root", published on the website of S&P Global Ratings, 27 January 2021.
3   Source: Ibid.
4   Source: ibid.

indicating that issuer and investor appetite for financing climate response and other environmental objectives is strong and accelerating. We believe green-labelled bond issuance could exceed US$400 billion in 2021, as global political and regulatory actions grow, serving as a catalyst for increased sovereign and private issuance.

Sustainable financings opinions in issuing GSS bonds

As a credit rating agency, S&P Global Ratings has been producing credit ratings to companies seeking access to capital markets for decades. But when it comes to accessing the sustainable bond markets, issuers have to demonstrate to investors their green, social or sustainable credentials. After all, how do investors know if a bond is of the green variety?

As bond issuers, entities will create a document known as a bond framework which will detail the company's use of proceeds from the bonds. In the case of a green bond framework, the company is expected to outline the green projects it will finance or refinance with the bonds' proceeds. This is when issuers can obtain framework alignment opinions from external reviewers such as S&P Global Ratings who will assess whether the framework is aligned to market standards. Typically, it would be to the **ICMA's principles and guidelines**, such as the ICMA's Green Bond Principles, Social Bond Principles or Sustainability Bond Guidelines.

These are known as second-party opinions and allow companies to provide investors assurance that their bond framework adheres to market standards. In such a rapidly innovating market, investors are seeking more transparency and a clearer analysis of how exactly their investments support the sustainability agenda. Therefore, although second-party opinions are voluntary, issuers are increasingly looking for informed, independent and respected second-party opinions to satisfy investors' needs.

While investors are keen on framework alignment opinions as a statement of intent that the companies they invest in will promote sustainability through financing, they also demand deeper analysis on the net environmental benefit generated by a green financing. This is what a green transaction evaluation provides. At S&P Global, this is an opinion that reflects our assessment of the relative potential environmental benefits of the use of proceeds over the life of the financed projects, taking into consideration the types of projects financed and their location. It reflects our assessment of the estimated reductions in the costs of expected damages from extreme weather events that projects may achieve.

The environmental impact calculation is done on a net benefit basis, meaning we consider each project's negative and positive environmental impact relative to the regional baseline. For example, the net benefit of a new renewable energy project in a country with a heavy emitting conventional grid would likely be higher than a similar project added to an already carbon-neutral power grid.

A green evaluation is a point-in-time assessment, in part based on an estimate of the expected lifetime net environmental benefit of a project should it perform to industry averages.

Our analysts have developed a detailed analytical approach that underpins the way we assess green transactions. It is freely accessible, aims to increase transparency, and help investors easily compare and benchmark the impact of green financings against each other. Figure 3 highlights part of our process.

Figure 3. Determining the environmental benefits score at S&P Global Ratings

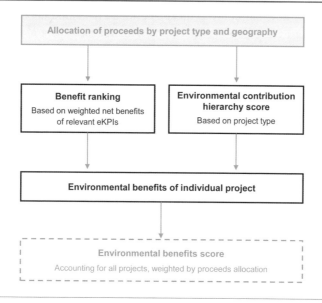

Note: "eKPIs" stand for environmental Key Performance Indicators.

ESG evaluation — a fundamental ESG assessment of an entity

The ESG evaluation is focused on assessing an entity's sustainability performance relative to peers and its preparedness for future disruptions. In this process, we analyse how an entity is exposed to ESG issues along its value chain and its willingness and ability to manage them through future disruptions.

The analysis is carried out in collaboration by our credit analysts with the relevant entity and sector knowledge and members of our sustainable finance team. The analysis draws from discussions with the company's management and engagement from at least one board member.

The ESG evaluation aims to provide a combined view of the ESG profile of the company and its preparedness assessment. First, we establish an ESG Profile for a given entity, which assesses the exposure of the entity's operations to observable ESG risks and opportunities, and how the entity is mitigating these risks and capitalising on these opportunities. Our ESG Profile analysis starts with an assessment of the entity's ESG-related exposure by sector and location. The building blocks of the ESG profile are depicted in Figure 4.

Figure 4. ESG profit building blocks at S&P Global Ratings

Environmental	Social	Governance
• Greenhouse gas emissions	• Workforce and diversity	• Structure and oversight
• Waste and pollution	• Safety management	• Code and values
• Water use	• Customer engagement	• Transparency and reporting
• Land use	• Communities	• Financial and operational risks

Then, the preparedness assessment evaluates the entity's capacity to anticipate and adapt to a variety of long-term plausible disruptions. These disruptions are not limited to environmental and social scenarios, but could also include technological or regulatory changes where relevant, among other factors. This is because, in our opinion, high-quality corporate governance includes the full spectrum of current and potential risks and opportunities an entity faces beyond typical financial planning horizons.

Global harmonisation: The way forward to alleviate "greenwashing" concerns

The mainstreaming of ESG, propelled by legitimate risks and concerns important to market participants, has led to an inevitable and exponential rise in the volume of green claims made by companies in their attempt to demonstrate sustainability credentials to their stakeholder base. However, the sheer volume of ESG marketing and labelling, in combination with non-uniform sustainability commitments and reporting, has made it increasingly difficult for stakeholders to identify which claims are trustworthy and reliable and which are unreliable, or in industry terms, "greenwashed".

In response to the risk of "greenwashing", various standards and taxonomies have emerged that attempt to help standardise the market and mobilise capital toward sustainable objectives. Ultimately, we believe that companies that can substantiate their environmental claims and align financing with a business strategy rooted in long-term ESG goals, will be better fit to withstand potential reputational, financial, and regulatory sustainability-related risks that will evolve over time.

As green taxonomies continue to be developed across the globe, the challenge will be finding a way to maintain global harmonisation. This will be a combined effort of industry organisations, governments, standard setters, consumers, and other stakeholders.

Conclusion

Whether through a credit lens and a sustainability lens, ESG insights are increasingly relevant to market participants' decision making. Whether it is providing further transparency in our credit ratings with our ESG Credit Indicators, or our range of second-party opinions or ESG evaluations, at S&P Global Ratings, we continue to believe transparency matters to the functioning of capital markets.

第8章

評估綠色融資 ——
信用評級中的ESG和
非信用ESG分析

標普全球評級

摘要

及時、透明和相關的分析意見對資本市場的運作至關重要，而包括信用評級在內的信用意見恰恰起到了這個作用。本章將重點介紹標普全球評級的分析方法，及我們如何在信用評級中反映有關「環境、社會、治理」(Environment、Social、Governance，簡稱 ESG) 的信用因素。

此外，可持續債券資本市場的強勁增長為發行人提供了獲得新資金來源的機會。提供有關可持續融資的分析意見將有助企業為投資者提供更多關於其投資如何與可持續發展目標相符的信息，以支持可持續債券資本市場的運作。

信用評級中的 ESG —— ESG 因素如何影響信用評級

信用評級有助於促進資本市場的發展和順利運作。它們是對一個實體 —— 如公司或市政府 —— 按時足額履行其財務承諾（償還債務和支付利息）的能力和意願所作出的前瞻性獨立分析意見。

環境、社會和治理（Environment、Social、Governance，簡稱 ESG）因素有可能（亦實際上）影響信用質量，即借款人履行財務承諾的能力和意願。這些因素在信用狀況中發揮着長期存在及重要的作用，因此在我們的信用評級中也一直同樣重要 —— 儘管 ESG 這個名詞在十多年前才被提出。

標普信用評級中的 ESG 信用因素是怎樣的？

ESG 因素通常包括某一實體施受的自然和社會環境影響，以及其治理質量；然而，並非所有的 ESG 因素都會對信用狀況產生實質影響。因此，我們將 ESG 信用因素定義為那些能夠實質性地影響受評實體或債項信用狀況的 ESG 因素，且這些因素具備足夠水平的可見性和確定性，可被納入我們的信用評級分析之中。

圖 1：ESG 與信用的交集

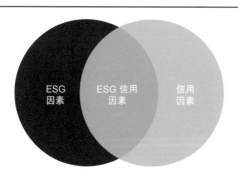

ESG
因素

ESG 信用
因素

信用
因素

當我們認為 ESG 信用因素與我們的信用評級相關且會對其產生實質影響，或具備以上這種可能性時，我們會通過應用我們個別行業專用的方法論將 ESG 信用因素納入考量。ESG 信用因素對信用狀況的影響可能是正面、中性或負面的，這取決於受評實體。

例如，如果我們認為與二氧化碳及其他溫室氣體的排放成本、廢物和其他污染成本、或健康和安全成本有關的氣候轉型風險，會對我們的信用狀況分析有實質影響，且若我們對這些因素將如何演變或顯現有足夠的能見度的話，我們就會考慮這些 ESG 信用因素的影響。

氣候變化風險和物理風險相關的因素也許是影響受評實體信用狀況最重要的 ESG 信用因素，這主要源於政策制定者致力於減少溫室氣體排放或確保排放反映其全部社會成本（是為「氣候變化風險」）及引起更頻繁、更嚴重的極端天氣事件的氣候變化（是為「物理風險」）。然而如下圖所示，多種 ESG 信用因素廣泛存在。與社會相關的信用因素例子包括健康和安全因素，此等因素自 2019 冠狀病毒疫情蔓延以來愈顯突出，其對健康與安全的影響已直接反映在大量評級行動中。

圖 2：ESG 信用因素的例子

環境因素	社會因素	治理因素
• 氣候變化風險	• 健康和安全	• 治理架構
• 物理風險	• 社會資本	• 風險管控、文化與監督
• 自然資本	• 人力資本	• 透明度和匯報
• 廢物和污染	• 其他社會因素	• 其他治理因素
• 其他環境因素		

資料來源：標普全球評級。

我們將 ESG 信用因素反映在我們的信用評級中，是依賴於五個一般性原則：

1. 我們的長期發行人信用評級沒有一個預先確定的時間範圍；

2. ESG 信用因素對當前和未來信用狀況的影響可能會因行業、地域和實體而異；

3. ESG 信用因素的方向和能見度可能存在不確定性，並可能會迅速變化；

4. ESG 信用因素的影響可能會隨着時間流逝而改變，這亦反映在我們動態的信用評級之中；

5. 良好的信用狀況與良好的 ESG 特徵並不一定相關，反之亦然。

標普全球評級在對某一評級進行上調、下調行動，或將其列入信用觀察名單，或改變評級展望時，會同時向所有市場參與者宣佈上述改變及分析理由。這些書面意見會包括該評級行動的主要驅動因素。當 ESG 信用因素亦屬該變化的驅動因素時，我們會在公開的評級報告中對其進行明確及透明的表述。

信用評級為市場參與者提供了及時的、有關信用狀況的分析，並會透明地反映與信用狀況相關且具實質影響的 ESG 信用因素及其他信用考量。隨着市場越來越有需要了解 ESG 對各地債務發行人所產生的影響，我們將繼續實行各種舉措，以進一步提高有關 ESG 因素如何影響信用狀況的透明度。

有時，整個行業的前景會受到 ESG 因素的影響。在 2021 年 1 月，我們更新了對石油和天然氣綜合、勘探和生產行業的行業風險評估，在其中納入幾個不斷增加的重大風險，包括能源轉型。這一變化是當下的和較長期的 ESG 風險被納入我們評級的一個例子。一個普遍存在的誤解是認為評級僅側重於 2-3 年的短期時間範圍。事實上恰恰相反，如果我們認為在這一時期之後 ── 比如十年或更長時間內 ── 一些具有實質影響的因素有足夠高的可見度，我們會通過我們的定性評估將這些因素納入當前的評級之中。

在我們改變了對石油和天然氣行業的風險評估後，我們對全球石油巨頭採取了一系列的負面評級行動。從 2020 年第二季度到 2021 年第一季度，標普全球評級進行了近 2,500 次與 ESG 相關的評級行動。

雖然對石油和天然氣公司的下調評級行動是相對近期的，但由 ESG 驅動的評級行動並非新事物。例如，在 2009 年，我們降低了歐洲一家公用事業公司的信用評級，並在報告中公開表示：「降級反映了我們認為該公司的商業風險在上升，因為它專注於以煤炭為基礎的發電業務，而這一業務受到越來越嚴格的監管和環境要求所影響。」由於當時 ESG 這個名詞並未被廣泛使用，這一行動未被正式歸納為由 ESG 驅動的評級行動，但它表明我們早已將對信用狀況產生實際影響的與 ESG 相關的風險和機會納入信用評級分析之中。

在將 ESG 納入信用評級的過程中，標普全球評級致力於為市場參與者提供更高透明度。我們將對公開受評實體套用 ESG 信用指標（ESG Credit Indicators），並自 2021 年 11 月中旬至 12 月開始針對隸屬工商、基建、銀行和保險行業的公司發佈個體層面的 ESG 信用指標分析，針對其餘資產類別的發佈則將在 2022 年進行。我們建議披露並系統地解釋 ESG 因素對我們信用評級分析的影響程度，並對環境、社會和治理這三項的每一項進行由 1 至 5、從正面到非常負面的評分（見表格 1）。建議中的 ESG 信用指標不是 ESG 或可持續發展績效的衡量標準，但它們將通過表明 ESG 因素如何實質上影響多個信用評級分析要素，來提高透明度。

對信用評級分析的影響	環境指標	社會指標	治理指標
正面	E-1	S-1	G-1
中性	E-2	S-2	G-2
中等負面	E-3	S-3	G-3
負面	E-4	S-4	G-4
非常負面	E-5	S-5	G-5

資料來源：標普全球評級。

信用評級之外的 ESG：第二方意見和 ESG 評估

可持續債券市場及其最新趨勢

據國際資本市場協會（International Capital Market Association，簡稱 ICMA）：

- 綠色債券是由其募集款項用途所定義，為具有環境效益的項目籌集資金和投資，如可再生能源、綠色建築和可持續農業；

- 社會責任債券是為解決或緩解特定社會問題及／或尋求實現積極社會成果的項目籌集資金，如改善糧食安全和獲得教育、醫療保健和融資的機會，着重但不限於目標人羣。

- 可持續發展債券以環境和社會效益為目標。

- 可持續發展掛鈎債券和貸款是一類相對較新的工具，通過為發行人和借款人提供激勵以設定和實現預設的可持續發展績效目標。

標普全球評級預計，包括綠色（Green）、社會責任（Social）和可持續發展（Sustainability）債券（簡稱「GSS 債券」），以及可持續發展掛鈎債券在內的可持續債務的發行總量在 2021 年可能超過 1 萬億美元，這將使其歷史累計發行量從 2020 年年底的 1.3 萬億美元升至超過 2 萬億美元 [1]。據 Environmental Finance 統計，2020 年可持續債務的發行量超過

---

1 資料來源：〈To mitigate greenwashing concerns, transparency and consistency are key〉，載於標普全球評級的網站，2021年8月23日。

5,300 億美元，較 2019 年增長 63%[2]。2019 冠狀病毒疫情及對社會不平等議題日益強烈的關注，使社會責任債券成為該市場增長最快的一部分 —— 在 2020 年增長了約 8 倍[3]。隨着發行人的注意力轉移到疫情援助和針對經濟衰退的救濟措施，綠色債券的發行在 2020 年上半年有所放緩，但在下半年反彈，年度發行量達到了創紀錄的 2,700 億美元[4]，表明發行人和投資者對氣候應對和其他環境目標的融資意欲依舊強勁，並在不斷加速。我們相信，隨着全球政治和監管行動的增多，帶有綠色標籤的債券發行量在 2021 年可能超過 4,000 億美元，成為主權和私營企業發行量增加的催化劑。

GSS 債券發行中的可持續融資意見

作為一家信用評級機構，標普全球評級幾十年來一直為尋求進入資本市場的公司提供信用評級。但當涉及到進入可持續債券市場時，發行人必須向投資者展示其具備綠色、社會責任或可持續的認證。畢竟，投資者如何知道一隻債券是否屬於綠色品種？

作為債券發行人的實體須製作一份被稱為「債券框架」的文件，詳細說明公司對債券收益的用途。在綠色債券框架下，該公司應概述其將會用債券的收益作資助或再融資的綠色項目。這時，發行人可以向標普全球評級等外部審查機構就其框架的符合性獲取意見，這些審查機構將評估該框架是否與市場標準一致。在一般情況下，這須與 ICMA 的原則和指引相一致，如 ICMA 的《綠色債券原則》（Green Bond Principles）、《社會責任債券原則》（Social Bond Principles）或《可持續發展債券指引》（Sustainability Bond Guidelines）。

這些分析被稱為第二方意見，允許公司向投資者保證其債券框架符合市場標準。在這個快速創新的市場中，投資者正在尋求更高的透明度，以及對他們的投資究竟如何支援可持續發展議程的更清晰分析。因此，儘管第二方意見是自願的，但發行人正越來越多地尋找了解市場、獨立的和受尊重的第二方意見，以滿足投資者的需求。

雖然投資者熱衷於將框架符合性意見作為他們所投資的公司將通過融資促進可持續發展的意向聲明，但他們也要求對綠色融資所產生的淨環境效益進行更深入的分析，這正是綠色交易評估所提供的。在標普全球評級，這種意見反映了我們對融資項目的收益用途在項目的生命週期內可能達致的相對環境效益的評估，同時考慮融資項目的類型和地點。它反映了我們對項目能為極端天氣事件會造成的損害預計能降低多少成本所作的評估。

2　資料來源：〈Sustainable debt markets surge as social and transition financing take root〉，載於標普全球評級的網站，
　　2021 年 1 月 27 日。
3　資料來源：同上。
4　資料來源：同上。

環境影響的計算是在淨收益的基礎上進行的,這意味着我們考慮了每個項目相對於區域基線的負面和正面的環境影響。例如,在一個傳統電網排放嚴重的國家,一個新的可再生能源項目的淨效益可能會高於一個存在於已實現碳中和電網內的類似項目。

綠色評估是針對某一時間節點的評估,部分是基於對某一項目的預期終生淨環境效益的估計。

標普全球評級的分析師開發了一套詳細的分析方法,作為我們評估綠色交易的基礎。該分析方法可供免費查閱,並旨在提高透明度,幫助投資者輕鬆比較和衡量各種綠色融資的影響。圖 3 展示了我們的部分流程。

圖 3:標普全球評級如何斷定環境收益評分

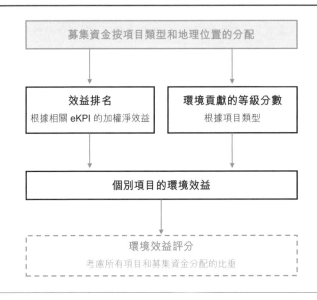

註:"eKPI" 即環境關鍵績效指標。

ESG 評估 —— 對某一實體的 ESG 基本面評估

ESG 評估的重點是放於某一實體相對於同行的可持續性表現,以及它對未來所受影響的準備。在評估過程中,我們分析該實體在其價值鏈中如何受 ESG 議題所影響,以及它在應對未來受影響的過程中應對這些議題的意願和能力。

這種分析是由我們對相關實體有了解和具有相關行業知識的信用分析師，以及可持續金融團隊的成員合作進行的。該分析會參考與公司管理層的討論，以及與至少一名董事會成員的交流所得。

ESG 評估的目的，是提供針對公司的 ESG 概況和其準備情況所作評估的綜合觀點。首先，我們分析某一實體的 ESG 概況，即評估該實體的業務受到可觀察到的 ESG 風險和機會的影響，以及該實體如何減輕這些風險和利用這些機會。ESG 概況分析以評估實體所屬行業和地區的 ESG 相關風險為起點。圖 4 描述了 ESG 概況的構成要素。

圖 4：標普全球評級的 ESG 利潤構建模組

環境	社會	治理
• 溫室氣體排放	• 勞動力和多元化	• 架構和監督
• 廢物和污染	• 安全管理	• 準則和價值
• 用水	• 客戶互動	• 透明度和匯報
• 用地	• 社區	• 財務和營運風險

資料來源：標普全球評級。

之後，我們對該實體在預測和適應各種長期、可能的破壞事件方面的能力進行評估。這些破壞性事件並不局限於環境和社會情景，還可能與技術或監管變化及其他因素相關。在我們看來，高質量的公司治理包括一個實體在典型的財務規劃範圍之外所面臨的全部當前和潛在風險與機會。

全球協調：緩解「漂綠」擔憂的前進之路

對 ESG 實際風險和相關考量對市場參與者有着重要意義，這促進了 ESG 的主流化，也導致了公司在向其利益相關方展示其可持續認證時提出的綠色相關聲明，在數量上不可避免地會呈幾何式增長。但是，ESG 的推廣和貼上標籤的數量之大，加上在可持續發展方面的承諾與匯報的不統一，使得相關方越來越難以鑒別哪些聲稱是可信可靠的，以及哪些是不可靠的 —— 用行業術語來說就是「漂綠」。

為應對「漂綠」的風險，各方面的準則和分類標準應運而生，試圖促進市場的規範化，並調動資本實現可持續發展目標。我們相信，那些能夠證實其環境主張可以付諸實踐，並將其融資與其植根於長期 ESG 目標的商業戰略相結合的公司，將更有能力抵禦與可持續發展相關、並不斷演變的潛在聲譽、財務和監管風險。

在全球各地繼續制定綠色分類標準的過程中，難點是如何保持全球步調一致，並需要行業組織、各國政府、準則制定者、消費者和其他相關方的共同努力。

結語

無論是從信用視角還是可持續發展視角來觀察，在市場參與者的決策過程中，對 ESG 的洞識都越發重要。無論是通過我們的 ESG 信用指標來提高信用評級的透明度，還是參照我們的第二方意見或 ESG 評估，標普全球評級始終相信透明度在資本市場的運作中扮演着重要角色。

註：本文原稿是英文，另以中文譯本出版。如本文的中文本的字義或詞義與英文本有所出入，概以英文本為準。

Chapter 9

ESG indices: A potential driver of ESG product development

Guido GIESE
Executive Director, Research
MSCI

Zoltan NAGY
Executive Director, Research
MSCI

Christine CHARDONNENS
Executive Director, Product
MSCI

Daniel CREMIN
Executive Director, Marketing
MSCI

Summary

The (investment) world is a very different place to what it was in 1990, when the Domini 400 Social Index was launched. This index is generally regarded as the world's first Socially Responsible Index.

With changing times has come a requirement for new approaches to investing that put sustainability at the forefront of investment decision-making. Whereas, historically, sustainable investing once was mainly the preserve of active equity managers — due to the limited number of ESG (environmental, social and governance) indices available — the landscape has changed significantly. Today, thousands of ESG, climate and other sustainable indices exist.

There has been a growing body of empirical research which has demonstrated the value ESG and climate factors can have on the risk and return profile of investments. Consequently, an increasing number of investors are using indices to help inform decisions intended to generate long-term, risk-adjusted returns.

The growth of ESG investing has led to a proliferation of ESG strategies, both active and passive. ESG indices have played a major role in supporting the integration of ESG in institutional portfolios.

In broad terms, ESG indices can be designed to meet common ESG investment approaches by including, re-weighting, or excluding companies based on certain ESG, screening, climate or Sustainable Development Goals (SDGs) criteria. Climate indices can help investors implement climate risk and net-zero carbon strategies across asset classes and portfolios. The indices can select, exclude, or re-weight companies based on their attractiveness in a low-carbon economy. The latest generation of climate indices has evolved to help investors align with the Paris Agreement and support a net-zero investment strategy.

Previous research by MSCI found that companies with high MSCI ESG Ratings were less exposed to systemic risks and, therefore, more resilient to shocks in the MSCI World Index during the study period from end of 2006 until 2017. The COVID-19 outbreak was the first real-world test since the 2008 global financial crisis of the resilience of companies with high MSCI ESG Ratings.

We believe demand for ESG and climate indices will continue to rise, supported by several trends — mainly the growth of sustainable investing, climate change, new regulation and non-regulatory local standards.

The evolution and growth of ESG indices

The dawn of environmental, social and governance (ESG) indexing is commonly associated with the launch of the Domini 400 Social Index (now the MSCI KLD 400 Social Index) in May 1990, which is widely regarded as the world's first socially responsible investing (SRI) index.

The MSCI KLD 400 Social Index is designed to provide investor exposure to companies with high MSCI ESG Ratings while excluding companies incompatible with a common set of value screens: alcohol, tobacco, gambling, civilian firearms, military weapons, nuclear power, adult entertainment and genetically modified organisms (GMOs). The index has closely tracked the performance of the MSCI USA Investable Market Index (IMI) over the last 30 years[1] — a lot has changed since the introduction of the MSCI KLD 400 Social Index.

The world has evolved and continues to rapidly change, requiring new approaches to investing that take long-term sustainability into account. While, historically, sustainable investing was mainly the preserve of active equity managers due to the limited number of ESG indices available, the landscape has changed significantly. A growing body of empirical research has demonstrated the value that ESG and climate factors can have on the risk and return profile of investments. Consequently, an increasing number of investors are using indices to help inform decisions intended to produce long-term, risk-adjusted returns.

Today, thousands of ESG, climate and other sustainable indices exist. According to the Index Industry Association's (IIA) fourth annual benchmark survey, there was a 40% increase in the number of ESG indices over 2020 — the highest year-on-year increase in any major index class. MSCI[2] is the largest provider in terms of assets linked to equity ESG indices[3], with over 1,500 equity and fixed-income ESG and climate indices designed to help institutional investors more effectively benchmark ESG investment performance and manage, measure and report on ESG mandates. These indices are increasingly becoming the cornerstone of asset allocation decision-making for institutional investors

---

1   Source: MSCI. Data as of May 2020. Informational purposes only. Past performance is not indicative of future results.
2   MSCI Equity Indices are products of MSCI Inc. and are administered by MSCI UK Limited. MSCI ESG Research data and information provided by MSCI ESG Research LLC. MSCI ESG Indices and Analytics utilise information from, but are not provided by, MSCI ESG Research LLC.
3   Data based on Refinitiv Universe as of December 2020; only primary listings, and not cross-listings.

including pension funds and endowments as well as among wealth managers and retail investors.

Asset owners adopting ESG indices

In a rapidly changing world, many asset owners are facing one of their biggest challenges for many years. In response, they are transforming their investment processes to reflect today's imperatives, such as ESG investing, innovative technology, ever-shifting regulations and demands for greater transparency. Yet they must do this against the backdrop of an increasingly complex and unstable financial environment.

This backdrop also presents investment opportunities on an unprecedented scale. For asset owners looking to integrate ESG considerations into their investment processes, ESG benchmarks may be essential tools. Investors can use an ESG equity or fixed income policy benchmark, also known as a strategic benchmark, to set a strategic asset allocation, define their reference portfolio, measure performance, and define the eligible universe of investable securities for both their total portfolio and individual allocations.

See Table 1 summarising the growing asset owner adoption of ESG and climate indices in recent years.

Table 1. Examples of asset owner adoption of ESG and climate indices

Year	Asset owner	Adoption of ESG and climate indices/strategies	Covered investment
2014-2016	AMF	ESG policy benchmark	—
	AP4	Low Carbon indices	—
	CalSTRS	Low Carbon Target Index	US$2.5bn
	Taiwan BLF	ESG Factor Mix Index	US$2.4bn
	UK EAPF	Low Carbon Target Index	—

(continued)

Year	Asset owner	Adoption of ESG and climate indices/strategies	Covered investment
2017	GPIF	ESG Index + Japan Empowering Women	—
	Ilmarinen	ESG benchmark indices based on sustainability ratings	—
	New Zealand Super	Custom Low Carbon Index	40% of passive equity portfolio
	Swiss Re	ESG Index + Corporate Sustainability Index	US$130bn active listed equity and credit
	VBV	Low Carbon Target	Approximately US$900m
2018	Brunel Pension Partnership	Low Carbon Target Index	Passive low carbon equities
	London Borough of Tower Hamlets	World Low Carbon Target Index benchmark	Low Carbon Passive Global Equity mandate
	London Borough of Hackney	Low Carbon Target index fund	—
	Migros	Ex China ESG Universal	US$4.5bn
	Ontario Teachers Pension Fund	Ex Tobacco policy benchmark	—
	United Nations Pension Fund	Ex Tobacco Ex Controversial Weapons policy benchmark	—
	Willis Towers Watson	Ex Thermal Coal Adaptive Capped ESG Universal Index	US$750m
2019	Ilmarinen	ETFs linked to ESG Index	US$5bn
	Fonds de solidarité FTQ	Integration of World Low Carbon ESG Screened Index	—

(continued)

Year	Asset owner	Adoption of ESG and climate indices/strategies	Covered investment
2020	Dai-ichi Life	ESG Universal Index	¥400bn foreign equity
	GPIF	ESG Universal Index	Passively investing ¥1 trillion
	Oxford University Endowment Management	Custom World Select Fossil Fuel Screened Index	—
	PenSam	Climate Index	€4.8bn equities portfolio
	PostNL	Sustainable (custom) index	European equity holdings
	Shell Pension (SSPF)	Custom ESG benchmark	22.6% of €30bn portfolio
	Swiss Federal Pension Fund PUBLICA	Custom climate efficient index; based on transition risk and physical risk	Equity portfolio
	Taiwan BLF	Customised Global Aggregate Corporate USD ex Controversial Industry	US$2.3bn
	UC Regents	Ex tobacco ex fossil fuel index	—
2021	Aargauische Pensionskasse	World ex Switzerland Low Carbon Target	Developed market equity
	Dai-ichi Life (AM One)	Climate Paris Aligned Index	—

Source: Information collated by MSCI, based on press releases or other publcly availiable information published from 2014 to May 2021.

Exchange traded products on ESG indices

The landscape of equity and bond exchange traded funds (ETFs) has grown considerably. Globally, ETFs were popular as a vehicle of choice for investors in 2020, with record inflows of more than US$700 billion, putting global assets under management (AUM) in ETFs at US$7 trillion[4].

---

4 Source: Refinitiv/Lipper and MSCI ESG Research LLC, as of 31 December 2020.

ESG ETF strategies also saw record inflows in 2020, driven by demand from investors looking to build sustainable portfolios. This demand is expected to rise in the years ahead[5].

Over the past five years, equity ESG ETFs assets have grown by 24 times since 2015 — from just over US$6 billion to over US$150 billion at the end of 2020. In 2020 alone, ESG ETFs recorded flows in excess of US$75 billion, more than three times the previous year (or approximately 10% of overall ETF flows globally)[6]. Figure 1 illustrates the growth in global ETFs tracking MSCI ESG indices.

Figure 1. Growth in global ETFs tracking MSCI ESG indices (2014 – 2020)

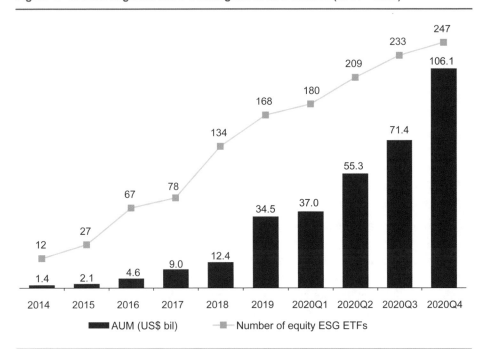

Source: Data based on Refinitiv Universe as of December 2020; only primary listings, and not cross-listings.

---

5   Source: R. Mahmood, "Fund ESG Transparency, Quarterly Report 2021 — Q1 Spotlight: ETFs", MSCI ESG Research LLC, February 2021.
6   Source: Refinitiv/Lipper and MSCI ESG Research LLC, as of 31 December 2020.

As ESG index ETFs continue on an accelerated growth path, investors and market participants alike have begun seeking ESG index exposure in the form of listed derivatives. Whether it be for managing daily cash flows, hedging risk in an ESG portfolio, or outright exposure, the need for ESG index futures and options is a logical development as ESG investing becomes more broadly adopted. In 2018, there was only one ESG index futures contract listed globally[7]. In 2020, there were over 20 different ESG index futures and options contracts traded across seven exchanges, involving five index providers[8].

Exchanges and index providers are currently working with broker dealers and market makers to establish a liquidity system for these contracts so that institutional investors such as asset owners and asset managers are able to comfortably transition from trading standard market-capitalisation index futures to ESG index futures. In 2020, over 2.6 million ESG futures contracts were traded globally[9].

MSCI has an innovative approach to ESG index-linked listed derivatives that offers multi-country, multi-currency ESG exposures, licensing several different ESG index methodologies to multiple exchanges across the world. Open interest across all MSCI ESG index futures has grown from US$170 million at the end of 2019 to over US$600 million at the end of 2020[10].

The drivers of growth in ESG investing

As observed, there are four primary drivers for growth in ESG investments:

- **The world is changing:** Global sustainability challenges — such as flood risk and sea-level rises, privacy and data security, demographic shifts and regulatory pressures — are introducing new risks for investors. As companies face rising complexity globally, the modern investor may seek to re-evaluate traditional investment approaches.

- **A new generation of investors is emerging:** 79% of Asia-Pacific investors said they would increase their ESG investment either significantly or moderately as a response to COVID-19, a higher figure than in the US (78%) and EMEA (Europe, Middle East and Africa) (68%), while 57% of Asia-Pacific institutional investors expect to "completely" or

---

7   This is the futures on OMXS30 ESG Responsible Index, launched by NASDAQ in October 2018.
8   Source: Futures Industry Association (FIA).
9   Source: FIA.
10 Source: MSCI Inc.

"to a large extent" incorporate ESG issues into their investment analysis and decision-making processes by the end of 2021[11].

- **Data and analytics are evolving:** With better data from companies, combined with better ESG research and analytics capabilities, we are seeing more systematic, quantitative, objective and financially relevant approaches to ESG investing.

- **Disclosure and reporting:** Regulation in the European Union (EU) and other markets aims to standardise and harmonise sustainability disclosure and reporting by financial market participants. The EU Sustainable Finance Disclosure Regulation (SFDR) also calls for funds promoted as ESG to be classified depending on certain ESG outcomes. This creates an opportunity for ESG data and index providers to develop frameworks and provide greater transparency to support investors' product-level disclosure requirements.

Types of ESG indices

The growth of ESG investing has led to a proliferation of ESG strategies, both active and passive. This reflects both a more diverse set of investor objectives and improved technical capability to implement more-tailored solutions, as well as the increased breadth and quality of available ESG data.

The integration of ESG into benchmarks enables investors to address their ESG-related investment objectives (see Figure 2), which at a high level can be grouped into three categories: ESG integration, values-based investing, and impact investing.

In the financial industry, benchmarks are used at a strategic level (i.e. as policy benchmarks for defining the eligible investment universe of an investor or helping determine asset allocation), as well as at an implementation level (i.e. as a performance benchmark for actively or passively managed allocations or as a benchmark for financial products). Therefore, integrating ESG into an investor's set of benchmarks is one way to build a consistent framework for the integration of ESG across the entire portfolio.

---

11 Source: *MSCI Investment Insights 2021: Global Institutional Investor Survey,* published on MSCI's website, 27 January 2021.

Figure 2. Objectives in ESG investing

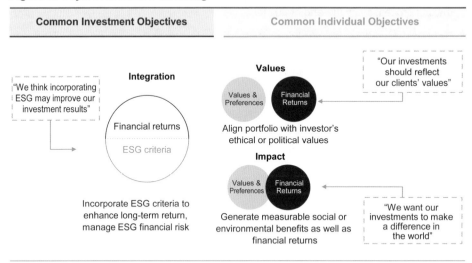

Source: MSCI ESG Research LLC.

Broadly, ESG indices can be designed to meet common ESG investment approaches by including, re-weighting or excluding companies based on certain ESG, screening, climate or Sustainable Development Goals (SDGs) criteria.

At MSCI, we organise our ESG indices into the three categories mentioned above that are aligned to clients' typical objectives (see Figure 3). The indices apply a rules-based approach and all methodologies are publicly available on MSCI's corporate website (msci. com). We calculate these ESG indices for most major regions, countries and currencies:

• **Integration:** These indices target companies that have the highest ESG-rated performance in each sector of the parent index (e.g. MSCI ESG Leaders, MSCI ESG Focus).

• **Values and screens:** These indices screen out companies involved in controversial business activities such as controversial weapons, fossil fuels, tobacco, and civilian firearms etc., and exclude companies involved in controversies (e.g. ex Fossil Fuel indices, ESG Screened indices, SRI indices).

• **Impact:** These indices aim to include companies that generate a measurable benefit to society and the environment (e.g. MSCI Sustainable Impact Indices, MSCI Women's Leadership Indices).

Figure 3. Overview of MSCI ESG and climate indices

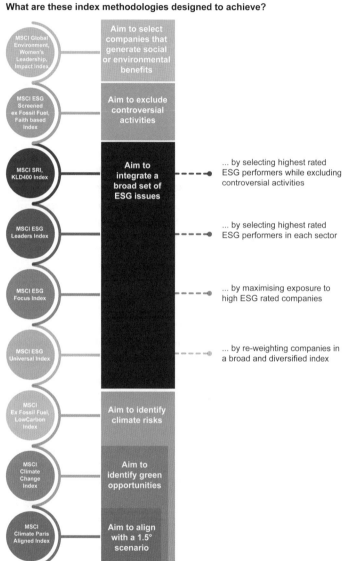

What are these index methodologies designed to achieve?

These indices are designed to support investors seeking to achieve various ESG objectives, such as:

- mitigate ESG or climate related risks and identify opportunities
- align portfolios with individual values or constrains
- have a positive impact on society and the environment

Source: MSCI.

ESG ratings methodology and index construction

There are different approaches and methodologies to building ESG ratings that aim to capture different things. Possible questions to ask when exploring which ESG ratings methodology to use include, for example: Is the ESG rating a measure of the level of disclosure or is it designed to identify the level of exposure to ESG risk? Does it incorporate a wide range of ESG indicators, or is it solely focused on what is most relevant for each sector? Is it an absolute signal, or is it industry-relative? These factors can lead to significant differences in ratings.

At MSCI, for example, ESG ratings aim to serve one specific use case: providing a measure of ESG-related risks and opportunities that might be overlooked by conventional financial analysis. From natural resource scarcity to changing governance standards, from global workforce management to the evolving regulatory landscape, ESG factors can impact the long-term risk and return profile of institutional portfolios. MSCI ESG Ratings are designed to help investors understand ESG risks and opportunities and integrate these factors into their portfolio construction and management processes.

MSCI ESG Research analyses thousands of data points across 35 ESG key issues, focusing on the intersection between a company's core business and the industry issues that can create significant risks and opportunities for the company. Leveraging artificial intelligence (AI), machine learning and natural language processing augmented, we rate companies on an "AAA" to "CCC" scale, according to their exposures to industry-material ESG risks and their ability to manage those risks relative to peers' (industry peers according to the Global Industry Classification Standard (GICS®)[12] sub-industry or sector).

ESG risks and opportunities are posed by large-scale trends (e.g. climate change, resource scarcity, demographic shifts) as well as by the nature of the company's operations. Companies in the same industry generally face the same major risks and opportunities, though their individual exposure can vary.

The MSCI ESG Ratings model seeks to answer five key questions about companies:

1. How do governance structures impede or enable the company to be a long-term steward of capital?

---

12 GICS is the global industry classification standard jointly developed by MSCI and Standard & Poor's.

2.   What are the most significant ESG risks and opportunities faced by a company and its industry?

3.   How exposed is the company to those key risks and/or opportunities?

4.   How well is the company managing key risks and opportunities?

5.   What is the overall picture for the company, and how does it compare to its global industry peers?

A risk is material to an industry when it is likely that companies in a given industry will incur substantial costs in connection with it (e.g. a regulatory ban on a key chemical input requiring reformulation). An opportunity is material to an industry when it is likely that companies in a given industry could capitalise on it for profit (e.g. opportunities in clean technology for the LED lighting industry).

The MSCI ESG Ratings model focuses only on issues that are determined as material for each industry. MSCI identifies material E, S and G-related risks and opportunities for each industry through a quantitative rules-based model that looks at ranges and average values for each industry for externalised impacts such as carbon intensity, water intensity, and injury rates. (See Figure 4 below.)

Figure 4. Relevance of selected key issues across GICS sectors

	CARBON EMISSIONS t CO2e / mil USD sales	WATER STRESS m³ / mil USD sales	PRIVACY & DATA SECURITY Data breaches / USD sales	HEALTH & SAFETY fatalities per million workers
Energy	590	2,704	40	0.26
Materials	818	11,014	5	0.11
Industrials	148	385	26	0.07
Consumer discretionaries	55	779	197	0.03
Consumer staples	81	2,068	12	0.04
Health care	39	472	21	0.02
Financials	6	33	53	0.01
IT	71	854	25	0.01
Telecom	38	63	43	0.02
Utilities	1,746	102,111	11	0.06
Real estate	86	1,424	15	0.07

Note: "t CO2e" stands for tonne of carbon dioxide equivalent.

Source: MSCI ESG Research 2020.

Companies with unusual business models for their industry may face fewer or additional key risks and opportunities. Company-specific exceptions are allowed for companies with diversified business models, those facing controversies, or based on industry rules. Once identified, these key issues are assigned to each industry and company[13].

To arrive at a final ESG Rating, the weighted average of individual Key Issue Scores is normalised relative to ESG Rating Industry peers. After MSCI committee-level approval, each company's Final Industry-Adjusted Score corresponds to a rating between best (AAA) and worst (CCC). MSCI ESG Ratings, produced by MSCI ESG Research, uses a rules-based methodology designed to measure a company's resilience to long-term, industry-material ESG risks.

MSCI ESG Ratings form the foundation of many of the 1,500 MSCI ESG indices. The seven-point ESG Rating scale by sector can be used to exclude, re-weight or optimise standard and custom indices for clients.

Analysis has shown that the outperformance of ESG indices compared to parent indices can be attributed to ESG, when controlling for other factors[14].

Overview of ESG and climate indices

ESG indices

At MSCI, ESG indices are constructed based on a standard market-capitalisation benchmark. Depending on investors' objectives, different ESG indices can be designed using one or more of the following index-methodology components:

1. **Exclusions:** Removing certain industries or companies from the underlying benchmark universe to align the portfolio with investors' values and constraints. As an illustration, all standard MSCI ESG index methodologies discussed below start with an exclusionary screen. It is important to mention that exclusions can follow different investor motivations:

---

13 See more on "ESG industry materiality map", webpage on MSCI's website.
14 Source: Yuliya Plyakha Ferenc, "ESG indexes through the slump and rally of 2020", *Research Insight*, MSCI ESG Research LLC, 19 March 2021.

- Values-based reasons — e.g. divesting from weapons manufacturing or to comply with standards such as the UN Global Compact initiative.

- Constraints — e.g. institutional investors who may face legal restrictions to invest in controversial weapons manufacturers.

- Economic reasons — investors who may want to mitigate certain business risks, such as those who may want to avoid exposure to fossil fuels to mitigate the risk of stranded assets.

It is important to note that the approach to exclusion has evolved, from industrywide exclusions — such as the exclusion of tobacco producers — to company-specific ones, such as the exclusion of companies that have breached the UN Global Compact.

2. **Selection of the best-rated companies:** For example, the MSCI ESG Leaders Index selects the best-rated 50% of companies in terms of free-float market capitalisation, whereas the MSCI SRI Index selects the best 25%. Both indices perform the selection per GICS sector and sub-region to avoid regional and sector biases.

3. **Weight tilt of companies within the benchmark universe:** For example, the MSCI ESG Universal Index tilts the market-cap weights of constituents using a component weighting scheme with a scaling factor between 0.5 and 2.0, with the aim of enhancing exposure to companies that demonstrate both a higher MSCI ESG Rating and a positive ESG trend, while maintaining a broad and diversified investment universe.

4. **Optimisation:** For example, the MSCI ESG Focus Index maximises the index-level ESG score within the benchmark universe, subject to a tracking-error constraint. In addition to this, optimisation also offers the possibility to combine equity-style-factor exposures[15] with ESG exposure.

All MSCI ESG Indices illustrated in this chapter use the MSCI ACWI Index as the underlying universe and then draw on the following MSCI ESG datasets for integrating ESG:

- MSCI ESG scores provide a forward-looking assessment on companies' exposure to financially relevant ESG-related risks and opportunities and their management's capability in managing those risks and opportunities. These MSCI ESG scores are mapped onto MSCI ESG Ratings ranging from CCC to AAA.

---

15 See: Kulkarni, P., M. Alighanbari and S. Doole. (2017) "The MSCI factor ESG target indexes", *MSCI Research Insight*; Giese, G. et al. (2018) "Understanding ESG indexes", *MSCI Product Insight*.

- MSCI controversy scores provide an assessment of controversial events that have been linked to companies and their severity for stakeholders and financial relevance. Scores range between zero (very severe) to ten (no recent incidents).

- MSCI business-involvement screens provide an analysis regarding the percentage of revenue companies derive from certain business activities such as alcohol or tobacco production.

The integration of financially relevant ESG considerations is based on MSCI ESG scores, whereas exclusionary screens/index-eligibility criteria use MSCI controversy scores and MSCI business-involvement screens.

Figure 5 summarises MSCI's standard ESG index series, which are based on the MSCI ACWI Index universe and use one or several of the four ESG integration methodologies described above.

It is interesting to note that all MSCI ESG indices shown in Figure 5 apply some exclusions, with controversial weapons representing the minimum level of exclusions across all indices. This illustrates how, in practice, the achievement of financial objectives through ESG is almost always implemented alongside a reflection of social or reputational considerations.

Figure 5. MSCI ESG index methodologies and their application

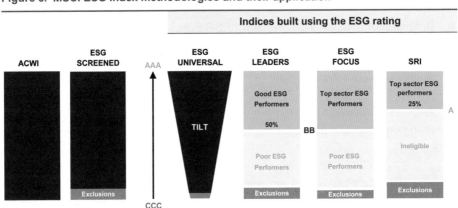

Source: MSCI. All of the above MSCI ESG index methodologies apply certain exclusion screens (based on controversies and business-involvement screens) marked in grey. Light blue indicates companies that are not selected for the index due to low MSCI ESG Ratings.

Climate indices

There has been growing demand from investors for indices which address climate risks and identify opportunities, both globally and in Asia. The launch of the MSCI China Climate Change Index and MSCI China A Climate Change Index reflects that growing interest. These climate indices can help investors implement climate risk and net-zero emissions strategies across asset classes and portfolios (see Figure 6). The indices can select, exclude, or re-weight companies based on their attractiveness in a low-carbon economy. Index methodologies can incorporate annual decarbonisation pathways and take into account corporates' emissions-reduction targets, including science-based targets. These complexities can be captured in rules-based transparent index methodologies, which can be enhanced on a periodic basis to account for new datasets or goals. Passive investors may need such climate benchmarks that reduce or remove carbon intensity/ emissions and increase exposure to climate solutions. Active managers may find it useful to benchmark their strategies to climate indices to compare both the financial performance and the climate risk or footprint, e.g. carbon intensity, or the exposure to providers of low-carbon technologies and renewable energy. See Figure 6 for an illustration of MSCI climate index methodologies.

Figure 6. Overview of different MSCI climate index methodologies

Objectives	MSCI Indices	Low Carbon Transition Score				Climate VaR	
		Fossil Fuels	CO_2 Emissions	Green Opportunities	Company Targets	Physical Risk	1.5°C Alignment*
Reduce Emissions	• Low Carbon • Ex Fossil Fuel	●	●				
Transition to a Low Carbon Economy	• Climate Change	●	●	●	●		
Climate Impact*	• Climate Paris Aligned	●	●	●	●	●	●
Climate Thematic	• Global Environment			●			

* Based on MSCI 1.5°C climate scenario stress test.

Note: Low Carbon Transition Score is designed to identify potential leaders and laggards by measuring companies' exposure to and management of risks and opportunities related to the low carbon transition. Climate Value-at-Risk (VaR) assesses future costs related to climate change and what those future costs could mean towards the current valuation of securities.

Source: MSCI. Climate Data and Metrics, Climate Risk Reporting and Scenario Analysis are provided by MSCI ESG Research LLC. MSCI ESG Indexes and Analytics utilise information from, but are not provided by, MSCI ESG Research LLC. MSCI Indexes and Analytics are products of MSCI Inc. and are administered by MSCI Limited (UK).

The latest generation of climate indices may help investors align with the Paris Agreement[16], Task Force on Climate-related Financial Disclosures (TCFD) recommendations and support a net-zero investment strategy. Some of these include specific constraints to meet or exceed the recommendations of the European regulator, such as "MSCI Climate Transition Benchmark" (CTB) and "EU Paris-Aligned Benchmark" (PAB). For example, the MSCI Climate Paris Aligned Indices are designed to address climate change in a comprehensive manner, targeting risk and opportunities to support stewardship. They exceed the minimum requirements for the EU Paris-Aligned Benchmark and incorporate the recommendations of the TCFD such as physical risk.

Climate indices such as the MSCI Climate Indices can help investors hedge against climate transition risks and direct their investments towards opportunities related to the energy transition to align with the trajectory of the Intergovernmental Panel on Climate Change (IPCC)'s 1.5-degree scenario. In particular, both the Paris-Aligned Benchmark and the Climate Transition Benchmarks include in their construction a self-decarbonisation pathway where the carbon footprint, in the case of MSCI Climate Paris Aligned Indices, is reduced by 10% year-on-year, an important mechanism to help investors achieve their net-zero ambitions.

The MSCI climate index series offering includes equity and fixed-income climate indices, including the MSCI Climate Paris Aligned Fixed Income Indices launched in April 2021.

Another recent development is the expansion of thematic indices, which may help investors capture and capitalise on demographics changes, technological disruptions and changing consumer behaviour as well as support certain ESG objectives. Finally, the rise of customised indices and available data sets offers private investors choices to build sustainability into their portfolios. Demand for personalised approaches in ESG, climate and/or impact investing, will further support the growth of indices.

Financial performance of ESG indices

For illustration purposes, we will look at the longest available performance history for each MSCI ESG index and explore two hypotheses on where the outperformance of these indices during this time period came from and if there was an "ESG effect". Then, in a second step, we will probe the resiliency of these indices with a look at their performance during the COVID-19 pandemic in 2020.

---

16 "The Paris Agreement", webpage on the website of United Nations Framework Convention on Climate Change.

Long-term live track performance

Figure 7 presents the longest available history for MSCI's standard ESG indices at the ACWI level[17].

Figure 7. Live track relative performance of MSCI ACWI ESG index series (31 May 2013 – 26 Feb 2021)

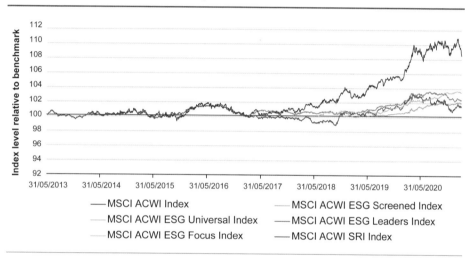

Notes:

(1) Data from 31 May 2013 to 26 February 2021. MSCI ESG Screened is an exclusion-based index that does not incorporate MSCI ESG Ratings; MSCI ESG Universal Index represents an ESG weight-tilt approach; MSCI ESG Leaders is a 50% best-in-class sector approach; MSCI SRI is a 25% best-in-class sector approach; and MSCI ESG Focus is an optimised approach designed to maximise ESG exposure.

(2) The data shows live track performance for each index: MSCI ACWI ESG Leaders has been live since 6 June 2013; MSCI ACWI SRI since 24 March 2014; MSCI ACWI ESG Universal since 8 February 2017; MSCI ACWI ESG Focus since 25 June 2018; and MSCI ESG Screened since 14 December 2018.

Source: "Drivers of ESG return", *MSCI Research Insight*, March 2021.

---

17 The MSCI ACWI Index covers more than 3,000 large- and mid-cap stocks across 23 developed and 27 emerging markets.

Where did this outperformance of ESG indices relative to their benchmark (MSCI ACWI Index) come from? We investigated two possible hypotheses:

1. MSCI ESG Ratings, which are used in the construction of MSCI ESG indices, were exposed to equity style factors that outperformed during this period[18]. ESG (after controlling for equity factors) was a performance factor in its own right.

2. Inflows into ESG investments may have driven up stock prices for high-ESG-rated companies, potentially creating a price bubble.

These two ideas are not mutually exclusive. In practice, outperformance could represent a combination of these two explanations.

We looked at the outperformance of standard MSCI ESG Indices. We start with the first two explanations, in other words, to what extent MSCI ESG Indices' performance can be attributed to other style factors, and whether there is a remaining "ESG effect". We performed a factor attribution using the GEMLT ESG model[19], which includes MSCI ESG Ratings as a factor. Table 2 shows that all standard MSCI ESG indices outperformed during their respective live track periods. This outperformance can be attributed to both existing style factors and (after controlling for all other systematic factors) to the ESG factor. Unintended active industry exposures also contributed to outperformance.

Table 2. Live track active return performance attribution of MSCI ESG indices

	MSCI ACWI ESG Screened	MSCI ACWI ESG Universal	MSCI ACWI ESG Leaders	MSCI ACWI ESG Focus	MSCI ACWI SRI
Total Active	**1.54%**	**1.06%**	**-0.03%**	**2.64%**	**5.06%**
Specific	0.41%	-0.49%	-2.59%	1.33%	0.91%
Industries	0.73%	1.12%	1.27%	0.22%	1.02%
Countries	0.27%	-0.41%	-0.03%	-0.14%	-0.79%
Currencies	0.02%	0.19%	0.07%	0.07%	0.22%
Styles	0.11%	0.66%	1.25%	1.16%	3.70%
• ESG	0.02%	0.58%	0.92%	1.18%	1.58%
• Other styles	0.09%	0.08%	0.33%	-0.02%	2.12%
Start date	31/03/2014	31/12/2018	28/02/2017	30/06/2018	30/06/2013
End date	28/02/2021	28/02/2021	28/02/2021	28/02/2021	28/02/2021

Source: MSCI. All performance figures are annualised.

---

18 For background on this argument, see Kurtz et al. (2011) and Madahavan et al. (2021).
19 GEMLT refers to the MSCI Global Total Market Equity Model for Long-Term Investors.

What accounts for this residual ESG performance effect? Could it have stemmed from rising valuations of high-ESG-rated companies, potentially leading investors into a price bubble?

To answer these questions, we looked at how price-earnings ratios (P/Es) of standard MSCI ESG indices have evolved over time in comparison with the benchmark (see Figure 8). We use P/E as a valuation measure because it allows for an intuitive breakdown of total returns.

**Figure 8. Live track ESG index P/E ratio relative to benchmark over time
(31 May 2013 – 26 Feb 2021)**

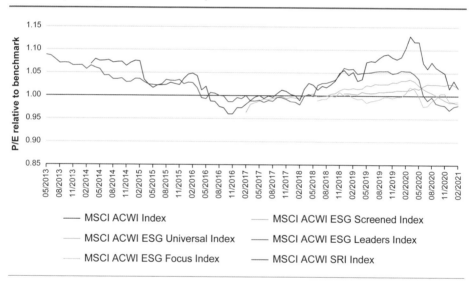

Note: Data from 31 May 2013 to 26 February 2021. Each index is shown with its live track history.
Source: MSCI.

On average, ESG indices showed higher average valuations than the MSCI ACWI Index over time. However, the valuation difference decreased toward the end of the study period. Intuitively, one would expect that ESG indices would have underperformed during the latter part of the period, but, in actuality, the opposite occurred. This means that ESG's outperformance cannot be explained by changes in valuation levels relative to the benchmark.

To probe further into the ESG performance effect, we used a fundamental return decomposition model developed in a previous research study[20]. The model decomposes total equity returns into three components:

Total return = P/E expansion + Growth in earnings + Reinvestment return

where P/E expansion denotes changes in valuation and the Reinvestment return consists of dividend yields.

This model allows us to understand to what extent returns were driven by changes in valuations, earnings growth or dividends.

The model performs a return decomposition in line with the semi-annual rebalancing of the underlying benchmark universe (MSCI ACWI Index). Therefore, we aligned our study period to benchmark rebalancing dates — we used the period from the benchmark rebalancing as of 31 May 2013, until the rebalancing as of 30 November 2020, which is the longest period for which MSCI ESG Ratings are available for MSCI ACWI constituents. We assessed the return decomposition for MSCI ESG indices in line with the semi-annual rebalancing[21]. To compare the performance results of MSCI ESG indices with other factor indices, we also included the corresponding standard MSCI factor indices (value, dividend, quality and momentum indices), as can be seen in Table 3.

---

20 Melas et al. (2019) The model in this study is based on the model proposed by Kushner (2017).

21 We excluded the MSCI ACWI ESG Screened and the MSCI ACWI ESG Focused indices from the analysis, as the former does not use MSCI ESG Ratings and the latter's quarterly rebalancing frequency does not coincide with the semi-annual return decomposition of the model.

Table 3. Active return decomposition of MSCI ESG and factor indices (%)

	P/E expansion	Growth in earnings	Reinvestment return	Active return
MSCI ACWI VALUE WEIGHTED INDEX	6.85	-10.14	0.48	-2.81
MSCI ACWI HIGH DIVIDEND YIELD INDEX	3.16	-7.73	1.59	-2.98
MSCI ACWI QUALITY INDEX	3.45	0.65	-0.35	3.74
MSCI ACWI MOMENTUM INDEX	-3.98	9.07	-0.73	4.36
MSCI ACWI SRI INDEX	-0.96	2.09	0.02	1.16
MSCI ACWI ESG LEADERS INDEX	-1.61	1.79	0.02	0.21
MSCI ACWI ESG UNIVERSAL INDEX	-0.78	1.18	0.03	0.43

Note: Data from 31 May 2013 to 30 November 2020 (last benchmark rebalance).
Source: MSCI.

The main source of active outperformance for all the MSCI ACWI ESG indices was higher earnings growth compared with the MSCI ACWI Index, while the contribution from P/E expansion was below that of the parent index. This means that the outperformance of the MSCI ESG indices during the study period was driven not by increasing valuation levels (suggestive of a price bubble), but rather by higher earnings growth.

The results of our return decomposition for factor indices in Table 3 were in line with the findings in Kushner (2017): The main source of active return of the MSCI ACWI Momentum Index came from earnings growth, while the main source of active return in the MSCI ACWI Value Weighted Index and for the MSCI ACWI Quality Index was P/E expansion. Not surprisingly, the MSCI High Dividend Yield Index was the only index with a strong active-return contribution from reinvestment returns.

To conclude, the outperformance of MSCI ESG indices during their live track periods came from ESG and other style factors. The performance effect attributable to ESG was associated not with increasing valuation levels, but rather with superior earnings growth when compared with the parent index.[22]

---

[22] For further reading on how ESG indices perform in Asia and China, see the Principles for Responsible Investment (PRI), "ESG and alpha: the mainstream argument for ESG integration in China", published on the PRI's website, 18 March 2020, or MSCI Research, "Integrating ESG in emerging markets and Asia", published on MSCI's website, 18 March 2020.

ESG index performance during the COVID-19 pandemic

Previous research by MSCI[23] found that companies with high MSCI ESG Ratings were less exposed to systematic risks and, therefore, more resilient to shocks in the MSCI World Index during the study period from the end of 2006 until 2017. The COVID-19 outbreak was the first real-world test since the 2008 global financial crisis of the resilience of companies with high MSCI ESG Ratings.

Figure 9 shows the relative cumulative performance of standard global MSCI ESG equity indices compared to their MSCI ACWI parent index during 2020 — including the market crash in February and March 2020 and the subsequent market rebounds. It is interesting to note that all MSCI ESG indices outperformed during the market crash and all except the MSCI ACWI ESG Leaders Index maintained a cumulative outperformance gain throughout the year when markets rebounded[24].

---

23 Giese, G., H. D. Varsani and R. Mendiratta, "Foundations of ESG investing in corporate bonds", published on MSCI's website, 11 November 2020.
24 See: Nagy, Z. and G. Giese, "MSCI ESG Indices during the coronavirus crisis", published on MSCI's website, 22 April 2020.

Figure 9. Relative performance of MSCI ESG Indices during 2020

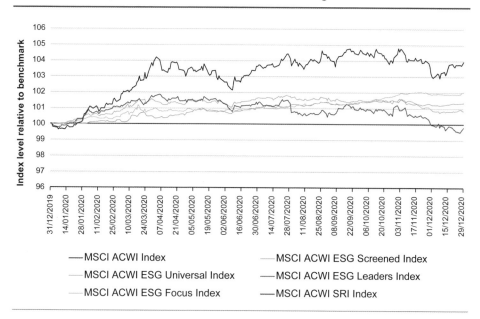

Note: Data from 31 December 2019 to 31 December 2020.
Source: MSCI.

To better understand how these indices performed during the COVID-19 pandemic, we performed a factor attribution, similar to the previous section, to carve out the performance effect associated with MSCI ESG Ratings. Figure 10 shows the performance effect of MSCI ESG indices that is explained by the MSCI ESG Rating throughout the year 2020 (i.e. the performance effect after controlling for other systematic factors). It shows that the MSCI ESG Rating contributed positively to performance for all MSCI ESG indices during 2020.

Figure 10. Active return contribution of MSCI ESG Ratings during 2020

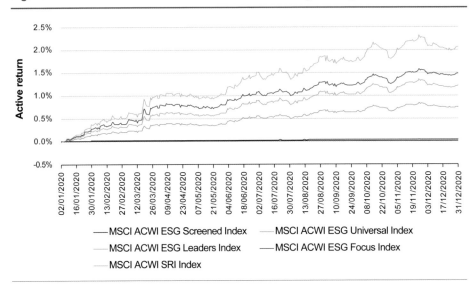

Note: Data from 31 December 2019 to 31 December 2020.
Source: MSCI.

Results by region

We now examine the performance of the same set of ESG indices at a regional level (world and emerging markets) and a sub-regional level (US, Europe and the Pacific) to see how they performed during the coronavirus crisis of 2020. The results can be seen in Figure 11, which shows the performance of the benchmark (x-axis) versus the relative performance to benchmark of the different regional MSCI ESG indices (y-axis). It is noteworthy that all standard MSCI ESG indices outperformed their corresponding benchmarks in all regions during 2020, with only one exception — the MSCI USA ESG Leaders Index, which showed a slight degree of underperformance during 2020.

Figure 11. Relative performance of regional MSCI ESG indices versus benchmark

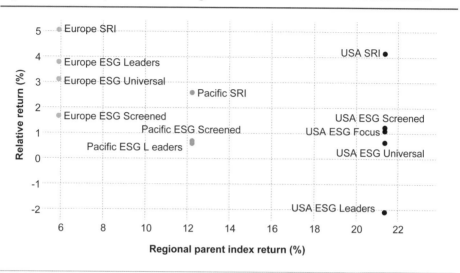

Note: Data from 31 December 2019 to 31 December 2020.

Source: Giese, G. et al. (2018) "Understanding ESG indices", *MSCI Product Insight.*

Outlook for ESG and climate index development

As highlighted in the first section, ESG indices have played a major role in supporting the integration of ESG in institutional portfolios. We believe demand for ESG and climate indices will continue to rise, supported by several trends:

Growth of sustainable investing

Based on data compiled by Morningstar, ESG assets reached US$1.6 trillion as of December 2020. Assets in ESG ETFs are forecast to reach US$1.2 trillion by 2030[25], as institutional, retail and a new generation of investors embrace the trend. The pandemic has reinforced the need to take into account ESG considerations when building portfolios.

---

25 "BlackRock's earth day forecast: $1.2 trillion in global sustainable ETF assets by 2030", Barron's website, 22 April 2020.

Climate change

Climate change is the defining risk of our generation which will reshape the economy and the way capital is allocated. Investors and governments around the world are, respectively, in the process of stress testing their portfolios and economies — assessing the risks and opportunities related to climate change. The TCFD's reporting standards and investor groups such as the Net Zero Asset Owner Alliance or the Institutional Investors Group on Climate Change (IIGCC) are leading and providing guidance on how to measure risks, reduce emissions, and align portfolios with the objectives of the Paris Agreement.

Net-zero targets are a particular type of decarbonisation target in which a company aims to bring its greenhouse gas (GHG) emissions down to zero, on a net basis. The term "net" comes from the fact that in practice most companies cannot operate without emitting at least some GHG into the atmosphere. Hence, there is usually a need to compensate for the remaining unavoidable emissions via carbon offsets or carbon removal.

Regulation and non-regulatory local standards

Increasing voluntary as well as mandatory regulation means awareness of ESG is becoming the new normal. In Asia-Pacific, institutional investors regard regulation as the number one trend for ESG adoption[26]. In this respect, the Stock Exchange of Hong Kong introduced new mandatory ESG disclosure requirements in 2020, new ESG disclosure regulations are expected to be launched in Mainland China in 2021, and the People's Bank of China and the European Union released a common green taxonomy in 2021, following on from the EU Taxonomy Regulation (July 2020) and EU Sustainable Finance Disclosure Regulation (March 2021).

These trends all point towards increasing demand and need for ESG and climate indices for investors to align their ESG and climate policies with their benchmarks and to help incorporate new and often-complex sustainability issues in the investment process, both in passive and active portfolios and across asset classes.

---

26 Source: *MSCI Investment Insights 2021: Global Institutional Investor Survey.*

References

Giese, G., L. E. Lee, D. Melas, Z. Nagy and L. Nishikawa. (2019) "Foundations of ESG investing: How ESG affects equity valuation, risk and performance", *Journal of Portfolio Management*, Volume 45(5), pp.69-83.

Kurtz, L. and D. DiBartolomeo. (2011) "The long-term performance of a social investment universe", *Journal of Investing*, Volume 20(3), pp.95-102.

Kushner, J. (2017) "Two types of factors: A return decomposition for factor portfolios", *Journal of Portfolio Management*, Volume 43(4), pp.17-32.

Madhavan, A., A. Sobczyk and A. Ang. (2021) "Toward ESG alpha: Analyzing ESG exposures through a factor lens", *Financial Analysts Journal*, Volume 77(1), pp.69-88.

Mahmood, R. "Fund ESG transparency: Quarterly Report 2021", *MSCI Research Insight*.

Melas, D., G. Giese, R. Kouzmenko, A. Bhat, N. Kumar, Z. Nagy, and P. Taranenko. (2019) "Selected geographic issues in the global listed equity market", *MSCI Research Insight*, prepared for the Norwegian Ministry of Finance.

第9章

ESG 指數：ESG 產品發展的潛在推手

Guido GIESE
MSCI　研究部執行董事

Zoltan NAGY
MSCI　研究部執行董事

Christine CHARDONNENS
MSCI　產品部執行董事

Daniel CREMIN
MSCI　市場部執行董事

摘要

今天的（投資）世界與 1990 年發佈「Domini 400 社會指數」時的環境已經截然不同，該隻指數一般被視為是世界上首隻社會責任指數。

隨着時代變化，各種新的投資方法需要將可持續發展作為投資決策的首要考慮。然而，由於以往可用的 ESG（即 Environment ─ 環境、Social ─ 社會和 Governance ─ 治理）指數的數量有限，可持續投資主要屬於主動型股票管理人的領域，但是目前情況已有顯著變化。今天，市場充斥着數以千計的 ESG、氣候和其他可持續指數。

越來越多實證研究表明了 ESG 和氣候因素對投資的風險和回報表現能帶來價值。因此，越來越多投資者採用指數來協助制定決策，以期帶來經風險調整後的長期資本回報。

ESG 投資的增長導致主動型和被動型 ESG 策略的激增。在將 ESG 整合至機構投資組合方面，ESG 指數發揮了重要的支持作用。

廣義來説，ESG 指數可以根據特定的 ESG、篩選、氣候或可持續發展目標等準則，將所選的公司納入指數之中，或排除在外，或重新分配權重，以切合常見的 ESG 投資方法。氣候指數有助投資者利用不同資產類別和投資組合來實踐應對氣候風險和淨零排放策略。該等指數可根據各公司在低碳經濟中的吸引力來選擇或排除公司，或重新分配權重。經過不斷演變，最新一代的氣候指數能幫助投資者將其投資策略與《巴黎協定》保持一致，支持實踐淨零排放的投資策略。

MSCI 早前的研究發現，「MSCI ESG 評級」較高的公司面對較小的系統性風險，因此該等公司在 2006 年年底至 2017 年的研究期間，於 MSCI 發達市場指數中有着較強的抗打擊能力。新冠肺炎爆發卻是自 2008 年全球金融危機以來，對 MSCI ESG 評級高的公司在現實世界的抗打擊能力的第一次考驗。

我們相信，在可持續投資的增長、氣候變化、新的監管規則和非監管性地區標準的制定等多種趨勢的支持下，投資者對 ESG 和氣候指數的需求將繼續上升。

ESG 指數的演變和增長

環境、社會和治理（environment、social、governance，簡稱 ESG）指數的首次出現，一般會視為是 1990 年 5 月 Domini 400 社會指數（即現在的 MSCI KLD 400 社會指數）的推出時，該指數被公認為世界上首個社會責任投資（socially responsible investing，簡稱 SRI）指數。

MSCI KLD 400 社會指數旨在為投資者追縱 MSCI ESG 評級高的公司，同時剔除一系列與常見價值觀篩選標準不相容的公司，包括：酒精、煙草、賭博、民用槍械、軍用武器、核能、成人娛樂和基因改造生物等。該指數與 MSCI 美國可投資市場指數（MSCI USA Investable Market Index）在過去 30 年 [1] 的表現非常相近 —— MSCI KLD 400 社會指數自推出以來，見證了很大的變化。

不斷演變且持續快速變化的世界需要考慮長期可持續發展的新投資方法。雖然由於以往可用的 ESG 指數有限，可持續投資主要是主動型股票管理人的專屬領域，但是目前的情況有顯著變化。越來越多實證研究都表明 ESG 和氣候因素對投資的風險和回報表現能帶來價值。因此，越來越多投資者採用指數來協助制定決策，以期帶來經風險調整後的長期資本回報。

今天，市場有數以千計的 ESG、氣候和其他可持續指數。根據指數行業協會（Index Industry Association）第四屆年度基準調查，ESG 指數的數量在 2020 年增加了 40%，是按年增幅最高的主要指數類別。按與股票 ESG 指數相關的資產計算，MSCI[2] 是最大的指數供應商 [3]，擁有超過 1,500 隻股票和固定收益類的 ESG 和氣候指數，旨在協助機構投資者更有效地對標 ESG 投資業績，及對 ESG 委託進行管理、量度和報告。該等指數日漸成為機構投資者（包括養老基金和捐贈基金）、財富管理公司和散戶投資者進行資產配置決策的基石。

1　資料來源：MSCI。數據截至 2020年5月。僅供參考。過往表現並非未來表現的指標。
2　MSCI 股票指數為 MSCI Inc. 的產品，由 MSCI UK Limited 管理。MSCI ESG Research 數據和資訊由 MSCI ESG Research LLC提供。MSCI ESG指數和分析採用的資訊來自 MSCI ESG Research LLC，但並非由該公司提供。
3　數據基於 Refinitiv Universe，截至2020年12月；僅包括主要上市，不包括交叉上市。

採用 ESG 指數的資產擁有者

在瞬息萬變的世界裏，很多資產擁有者正面臨多年以來的一大挑戰。對此，他們正改變投資流程，以反映時下的急務，例如 ESG 投資、創新技術、不斷變化的監管規例及更高透明度的要求。然而，他們必須在金融環境日益複雜和不穩定的背景下作出相關改變。

這種背景亦帶來了規模前所未有的投資機會。對於期望將 ESG 考量整合至投資流程的資產擁有者而言，ESG 基準可能是不可或缺的工具。投資者可以使用 ESG 股票或固定收益政策基準（亦稱為策略基準）以設定策略資產配置、定義參考投資組合、量度業績，及為整體投資組合和個別配置釐定合資格的可投資證券範圍。

表 1 總結了近年資產擁有者越來越多採用 ESG 和氣候指數的現象。

表 1：資產擁有者採用 ESG 和氣候指數的例子

年份	資產擁有者	採用的 ESG 和氣候指數／策略	覆蓋的投資
2014-2016	法國金融市場管理局（AMF）	ESG 政策基準	—
	AP4	低碳指數	—
	加州教師退休金（CalSTRS）	低碳目標指數	25 億美元
	臺灣勞動基金（BLF）	ESG 因子混合指數	24 億美元
	英國環境局養老保險基金（UK EAPF）	低碳目標指數	—
2017	日本政府養老金投資基金（GPIF）	ESG 指數 + 日本女性賦權指數	—
	Ilmarinen	基於可持續發展評級的 ESG 基準指數	—
	紐西蘭退休基金	定制低碳指數	40% 的被動股票投資組合
	瑞士再保險	ESG 指數 + 企業可持續發展指數	1,300 億美元主動型上市股票和債券基金
	VBV	低碳目標	約 9 億美元

（續）

年份	資產擁有者	採用的 ESG 和氣候指數／策略	覆蓋的投資
2018	Brunel Pension Partnership	低碳目標指數	被動低碳股票
	哈姆雷特塔倫敦自治市	世界低碳目標指數基準	低碳被動全球股票委託
	倫敦哈克尼行政區	低碳目標指數基金	—
	Migros	中國除外的 ESG 通用指數	45 億美元
	安大略省教師退休金	剔除煙草的政策基準	—
	聯合國養恤基金	全球（煙草和爭議性武器除外）政策基準	—
	韋萊韜悅	（熱能煤除外）自適應上限 ESG 通用指數	7.5 億美元
2019	Ilmarinen	向 ESG 指數掛鈎 ETF 投資	50 億美元
	Fonds de solidarité FTQ	宣佈整合世界低碳 ESG 篩選指數	—
2020	第一生命保險	ESG 通用指數	4,000 億日圓外國股票
	日本政府養老金投資基金（GPIF）	ESG 通用指數	被動投資 1 萬億日圓
	牛津大學捐贈基金管理	定制世界精選化石燃料篩選指數	—
	PenSam	採用氣候指數	48 億歐元的股票投資組合
	PostNL	可持續（定制）指數	歐洲股票持倉
	蜆殼養老金（SSPF）	定制 ESG 基準	300 億歐元投資組合中的 22.6%
	瑞士聯邦養老基金（Publica）	採用定制氣候效率指數；基於過渡風險和實體風險	股票投資組合
	臺灣勞動基金（BLF）	定制全球綜合企業美元（爭議性行業除外）指數	23 億美元
	加州大學理事會	煙草和化石燃料除外指數	—
2021	Aargauische Pensionskasse	世界（瑞士除外）低碳目標指數	發達市場股票
	第一生命保險（AM One）	巴黎氣候協議一致性指數	

資料來源：MSCI 根據 2014 年至 2021 年 5 月發佈的新聞稿或其他公開可用資訊作整理。

基於 ESG 指數的交易所買賣產品

股票和債券類交易所買賣基金（exchange traded fund，簡稱 ETF）的規模已顯著增長。全球而言，作為投資者可選投資工具的 ETF 在 2020 年廣受歡迎，資金流入超過 7,000 億美元，使 ETF 的全球資產管理規模達到 7 萬億美元[4]。

在投資者對建構可持續投資組合的需求推動下，ESG ETF 策略在 2020 年亦出現創紀錄的資金流入。這種需求預計在未來數年將會持續上升[5]。

過去五年，股票 ESG ETF 的資產自 2015 年以來增長了 24 倍 —— 從略高於 60 億美元增長至 2020 年年底的超過 1,500 億美元。僅在 2020 年，ESG ETF 的資金流入就超過 750 億美元，是前一年的三倍多（約佔全球 ETF 資金流入總額的約 10%）[6]。圖 1 列舉追蹤 MSCI ESG 指數的全球 ETF 增長例子。

圖 1：追蹤 MSCI ESG 指數的全球 ETF 的增長（2014 年至 2020 年）

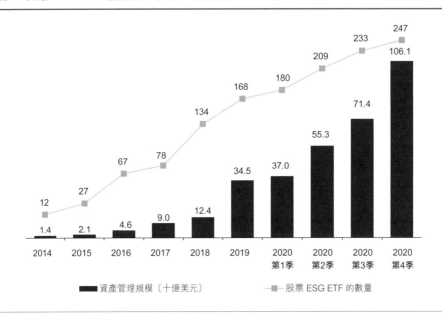

資料來源：數據基於 Refinitiv Universe，截至 2020 年 12 月；僅包括主要上市，不包括交叉上市。

4　資料來源：Refinitiv / 理柏與MSCI ESG Research LLC，截至 2020年12月31日。

5　資料來源：R. Mahmood〈基金ESG透明度，2021 年季度報告 —— 第1季度聚焦：ETF〉（"Fund ESG Transparency, Quarterly Report 2021 — Q1 Spotlight: ETFs"），MSCI ESG Research LLC，2021年2月。

6　資料來源：Refinitiv / 理柏與MSCI ESG Research LLC，截至2020年12月31日。

隨着 ESG 指數 ETF 增長的持續加速，投資者和市場參與者開始尋求上市衍生工具形式的 ESG 指數敞口。隨着 ESG 投資被廣泛採用，無論是為了管理日常現金流、對沖 ESG 投資組合風險，抑或直接敞口，對 ESG 指數期貨和期權產生需求自然是順理成章。在 2018 年，全球僅有一種 ESG 指數期貨合約上市[7]，而在 2020 年，已有超過 20 種不同的 ESG 指數期貨和期權合約在七家交易所交易，涉及五家指數供應商[8]。

交易所和指數供應商目前正與經紀交易商和做市商合作，為該等合約建立流動性體系，以便資產擁有者和資產管理人等機構投資者能夠從標準市值指數期貨的交易輕鬆過渡至 ESG 指數期貨的交易。在 2020 年，全球 ESG 期貨合約交易量超過 260 萬張[9]。

MSCI 對與 ESG 指數掛鈎的上市衍生品採用創新方法，將幾種不同的 ESG 指數方法論授權予全球多個交易所，提供多國、多幣種的 ESG 敞口。所有 MSCI ESG 指數期貨的未平倉合約量已從 2019 年年底的 1.7 億美元增長至 2020 年年底的超過 6 億美元[10]。

ESG 投資增長的驅動因素

如上所述，ESG 投資增長有四個主要驅動因素：

- **世界正在迅速變化**：全球面對的可持續發展挑戰 —— 例如洪水風險和海平面上升、隱私和數據安全、人口結構轉移和監管壓力 —— 正為投資者帶來新的風險。隨着全球的企業面臨日益增加的複雜性，現代投資者可能會重新評估傳統投資方法。

- **新一代投資者正在興起**：79% 的亞太投資者表示，他們將大幅或適度增加 ESG 投資以應對新冠肺炎，這一數字高於美國（78%）和 EMEA（歐洲、中東和非洲；68%），而 57% 的亞太機構投資者預期在 2021 年年底或之前「完全」或「在很大程度上」會把 ESG 議題納入其投資分析和決策流程[11]。

- **數據和分析正在演變**：憑藉更好的公司數據，結合更優越的 ESG 研究和分析能力，我們看到更多的系統化、量化、客觀和與財務相應的 ESG 投資方法面世。

- **披露和報告**：歐盟和其他市場的監管旨在對金融市場參與者就可持續發展的信息披露和報告進行標準化和協調。歐盟《永續金融披露規範》（Sustainable Finance Disclosure

---

7　這是納斯達克於 2018 年 10 月推出的 OMXS30 ESG 責任指數期貨。

8　資料來源：美國期貨業協會（Futures Industry Association，簡稱FIA）。

9　資料來源：FIA。

10　資料來源：MSCI Inc.

11　資料來源：《MSCI 投資洞察2021：全球機構投資者調查》（*MSCI Investment Insights 2021: Global Institutional Investor Survey*），載於MSCI的網站，2021年1月27日。

Regulation）亦呼籲根據某些 ESG 結果對以 ESG 為推廣的基金進行分類。這為 ESG 數據和指數供應商創造機會，開發框架及提供更大透明度以支援投資者在產品層面的披露要求。

ESG 指數的類型

ESG 投資的增長導致主動和被動型 ESG 策略的激增。這反映了投資者目標變得更多元化、在實行定制解決方案方面技術能力有所改善，以及可用 ESG 數據在廣度和質量上有進步。

ESG 與基準的整合使投資者能夠實現其與 ESG 相關的投資目標（見圖 2），該等目標在較高層面可分為三類：ESG 整合、基於價值觀的投資和影響力投資。

在金融行業，基準可用於策略層面（即作為政策基準，以界定投資者的合資格投資範圍，或幫助斷定資產配置）和實施層面（即作為主動或被動型管理配置的業績基準或金融產品的基準）。因此，將 ESG 整合至投資者的一系列基準，是建構一致框架的途徑，達到將 ESG 全面整合至整個投資組合。

圖 2：ESG 投資的目標

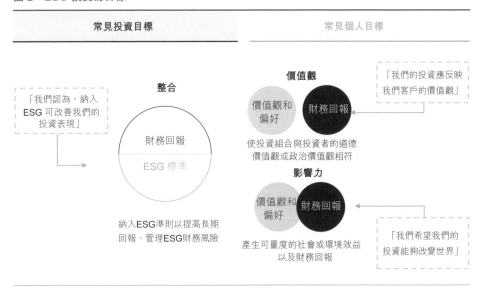

資料來源：MSCI ESG Research LLC。

廣義來說，ESG 指數可以根據特定的 ESG、篩選、氣候或可持續發展目標等準則，將所選的公司納入指數之中，或排除在外，或重新分配權重，以切合常見的 ESG 投資方法。

MSCI 把 ESG 指數分為上述三個類別，皆與客戶典型的目標一致（見圖 3）。該等指數採用基於規則的方法，並且所有方法論均在 MSCI 的企業網站（msci.com）上公佈。我們為大多數主要地區、國家和貨幣計算該三類 ESG 指數：

- **整合**：納入該等指數的公司是母指數（例如 MSCI ESG 領先指數、MSCI ESG 聚焦指數）各個板塊中 ESG 評級表現最高的公司。

- **價值觀和篩選**：該等指數篩走涉及爭議性業務活動的公司，例如爭議性武器、化石燃料、煙草和民用槍械等，並且剔除涉及爭議的公司（例如化石燃料除外指數、ESG 篩選指數、SRI 指數）。

- **影響力**：該等指數旨在納入產生可量度的社會和環境效益的公司（如 MSCI 可持續影響指數、MSCI 女性領導力指數）。

圖 3：MSCI ESG 和氣候指數概覽

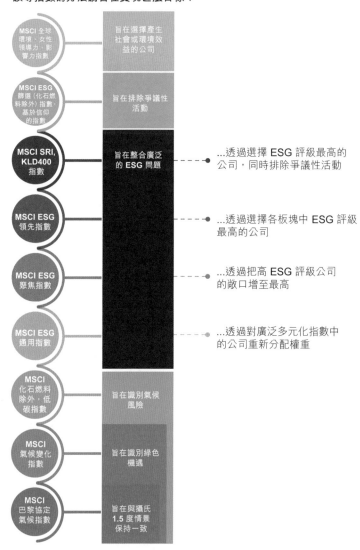

該等指數的方法論旨在實現甚麼目標？

MSCI 全球環境、女性領導力、影響力指數 — 旨在選擇產生社會或環境效益的公司

MSCI ESG 篩選（化石燃料除外）指數，基於信仰的指數 — 旨在排除爭議性活動

MSCI SRI, KLD400 指數 — 旨在整合廣泛的 ESG 問題 ...透過選擇 ESG 評級最高的公司，同時排除爭議性活動

MSCI ESG 領先指數 — ...透過選擇各板塊中 ESG 評級最高的公司

MSCI ESG 聚焦指數 — ...透過把高 ESG 評級公司的敞口增至最高

MSCI ESG 通用指數 — ...透過對廣泛多元化指數中的公司重新分配權重

MSCI 化石燃料除外，低碳指數 — 旨在識別氣候風險

MSCI 氣候變化指數 — 旨在識別綠色機遇

MSCI 巴黎協定氣候指數 — 旨在與攝氏 1.5 度情景保持一致

該等指數旨在支援投資者尋求實現各種 ESG 目標，例如：

- 緩解 ESG 或氣候相關風險和識別機會
- 保持投資組合與個人價值觀或約束因素的一致性
- 對社會和環境產生積極影響

資料來源：MSCI。

ESG 評級方法和指數建構

建構 ESG 評級有不同的做法和方法論，以達致不同的目標。在探索使用哪個 ESG 評級方法論時可能要提出的問題包括：ESG 評級是量度披露水平的指標，還是旨在確定 ESG 風險敞口的水平？它是否包含廣泛的 ESG 指標，還是集中關注各個板塊最相關的指標？它是一個絕對訊號，抑或行業的相對訊號？這些因素都可能導致評級的顯著差異。

舉例來說，MSCI 的 ESG 評級旨在用作一個特定用途：提供傳統財務分析可能忽略的 ESG 相關風險和機會指標。從自然資源稀缺性至不斷變化的治理標準，從全球勞動力管理至不斷演變的監管環境，ESG 因子都會影響機構投資組合的長期風險和回報表現。MSCI ESG 評級旨在協助投資者了解 ESG 風險和機會，並將該等因素整合至其投資組合建構和管理流程之中。

MSCI ESG Research 分析橫跨 35 個 ESG 關鍵議題數以千計的數據點，專注於公司核心業務與能夠為公司造成重大風險或創造重大機會的行業議題之間的交匯點。利用強化的人工智能、機器學習和自然語言處理，我們根據各公司面臨的行業實質性 ESG 風險，以及公司在管理這些風險的能力相對於同業的表現（同業公司的界定是據其所屬全球行業分類標準（GICS®）[12] 子行業或板塊），向各公司授予「AAA」至「CCC」的評級。

ESG 風險和機會源於大規模趨勢（如氣候變化、資源稀缺、人口結構轉移）以及公司的業務性質。相同行業內的公司通常面臨相同的主要風險和機會，但個別風險敞口可能有所不同。

MSCI ESG 評級模型務求解答有關公司的五個關鍵問題：

1. 治理架構如何妨礙或促使該公司成為資本的長期管理者？

2. 公司及其所在行業面臨的最重大 ESG 風險和機會是甚麼？

3. 公司受該等主要風險及 / 或機會所影響的程度有多高？

4. 公司在管理主要風險和機會方面的表現如何？

5. 公司的整體情況如何？與全球同業公司相比如何？

倘若某項風險很可能會令某種行業的公司承擔重大的相關成本（例如關鍵化學原料受到監管禁令而導致需要重製配方），這項風險對該行業而言屬於實質性風險。倘若某一行業的公

12　GICS（Global Industry Classification Standard）是 MSCI 與標準普爾共同制定的全球行業分類標準。

司很可能會從某一機會中投資獲利時（例如清潔技術可為 LED 燈行業帶來的機會），這個機會對該行業而言屬於實質性機會。

MSCI ESG 評級模型僅關注被釐定為具實質性的各行業議題。MSCI 通過基於規則的量化模型釐定各行業的實質性環境、社會和治理的相關風險和機會，該模型着眼於各行業的外部化影響（例如碳強度、水強度和傷害比率）的範圍和平均值。（見圖 4。）

圖 4：各個 GICS 板塊若干關鍵問題的相關性

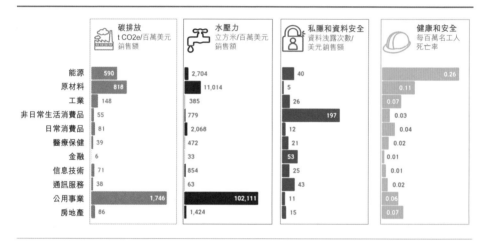

註：「t CO2e」表示噸二氧化碳當量。
資料來源：MSCI ESG Research（2020 年）。

業務模式異於某所在行業的公司可能面臨更少或更多的主要風險和機會，因此對於擁有多元化業務模式、面臨爭議的公司、或基於行業規則，評級模型會允許公司特定的例外情況。在釐定之後，該等主要議題將按每個行業和公司配置 [13]。

為了得出最終的 ESG 評級，個別「主要議題評分」的加權平均值會根據同業公司 ESG 評級進行標準化。經 MSCI 委員會批准後，各公司的最終行業調整評分形成對應最佳（AAA）至最差（CCC）之間的評級。MSCI ESG Research 編製的 MSCI ESG 評級使用基於規則的方法，旨在量度一家公司抵禦長期、對行業具實質性影響的 ESG 風險的抗打擊能力。

13　更多詳情請閱覽 MSCI 網站上的〈ESG industry materiality map〉網頁。

MSCI ESG 評級是 1,500 多個 MSCI ESG 指數的基礎。按板塊劃分的七級 ESG 評級量表可用於為客戶剔除、重新分配權重或優化標準和定制指數。

分析表明，在其他因素不變的情況下，ESG 指數的表現勝於母指數的表現可歸因於各種 ESG 因素[14]。

ESG 和氣候指數概覽

ESG 指數

MSCI 的 ESG 指數的構建是基於標準的市值基準指數。視乎投資者的目標，可使用下列一個或多個指數方法論組成部分以設計不同的 ESG 指數：

1. **排除**：從相關基準指數中剔除某些行業或公司，以使投資組合與投資者的價值觀和限制因素保持一致。例如，下文討論的所有標準 MSCI ESG 指數方法論均從排除性篩選開始。重要的是，可以遵循不同的投資者動機進行排除：

    - 基於價值觀的原因 —— 例如剔除武器製造公司或遵守聯合國全球契約倡議等標準。

    - 限制因素 —— 例如機構投資者可能在投資爭議性武器製造商方面面臨法律限制。

    - 經濟原因 —— 投資者可能希望降低某些業務風險，例如投資者可能刻意避免投資化石燃料以降低擱淺資產的風險。

    值得注意的是，排除方法已經從排除全行業（例如排除煙草生產商）演變至排除特定公司，例如排除違反聯合國全球契約的公司。

2. **選擇評級最佳的公司**：例如，「MSCI ESG 領先指數」選擇按自由流通市值計評級最高的 50% 的公司，而 MSCI SRI 指數選擇評級最佳的 25% 的公司。兩個指數均按 GICS 板塊和子區域進行選擇，以避免側重某些區域或板塊。

3. **基準成份公司的權重傾斜**：例如，「MSCI ESG 通用指數」使用比例因數介於 0.5 和 2.0 的成份權重方案，以實現成份股的市值權重傾斜，目的是對 MSCI ESG 評級高和具正面 ESG 趨勢的公司附以更高權重，同時保持廣泛和多元化的投資領域。

14　資料來源：Yuliya Plyakha Ferenc〈經歷 2020 年暴跌和反彈的 ESG 指數〉（"ESG indexes through the slump and rally of 2020"），《Research Insight》，MSCI ESG Research LLC，2021年3月19日。

4. **最優化**：例如，「MSCI ESG 聚焦指數」在須遵守追蹤誤差的約束情況下，旨在於基準範圍內將指數層面的 ESG 評分最大化。此外，最優化過程亦使股票類型因子敞口 [15] 與 ESG 敞口的結合變得可能。

本章說明的所有 MSCI ESG 指數均使用「MSCI ACWI 指數」作為基準，然後利用以下 MSCI ESG 數據集以整合 ESG 元素：

- 「MSCI ESG 評分」對公司在 ESG 相關風險和機會方面的財務相關敞口以及其管理層對管理該等風險和機會的能力提供前瞻性評估。該等 MSCI ESG 評分會對應從 CCC 至 AAA 的 MSCI ESG 評級。

- 「MSCI 爭議評分」與公司相關的爭議性事件及其對利益相關者影響的嚴重程度和財務相關性提供評估。評分範圍介乎 0（非常嚴重）至 10（近期無事件）之間。

- 「MSCI 業務參與度篩選」對公司從某些業務活動（例如酒精或煙草生產）中獲得的收入比例作分析。

將與財務相關的 ESG 考慮因素作整合乃基於「MSCI ESG 評分」，而排除性篩選或指數資格準則則使用「MSCI 爭議評分」和「MSCI 業務參與度篩選」。

圖 5 總結 MSCI 的標準 ESG 指數系列，該等指數基於 MSCI ACWI 指數，並且使用上文所述的四個 ESG 整合方法中的一個或多個。

值得一提，圖 5 所示的全部 MSCI ESG 指數均採用某些排除條件，而爭議性武器是所有 ESG 指數的最低限度排除項目。這說明在透過 ESG 實現財務目標的實踐過程中，幾乎總會反映社會或聲譽考慮因素。

15　參閱：P. Kulkarni、M. Alighanbari 與 S. Doole（2017 年）〈MSCI 因子 ESG 目標指數〉（"The MSCI factor ESG target indexes"），《MSCI Research Insight》；G. Giese 等（2018 年）〈了解 ESG 指數〉（"Understanding ESG indices"），《MSCI Product Insight》。

圖 5：MSCI ESG 指數方法論及其應用

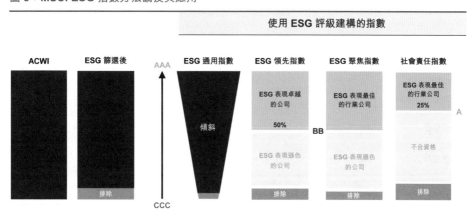

資料來源：MSCI。所有上述 MSCI ESG 指數方法論均採用特定排除篩選（基於爭議性和業務參與度篩選）以灰色標記。淺藍色的部分是因 MSCI ESG 評級較低而未入選指數的公司。

氣候指數

投資者對全球和亞洲應對氣候風險和識別機會之指數的需求不斷增長。「MSCI 中國氣候變化指數」和「MSCI 中國 A 股氣候變化指數」的推出反映這種不斷增長的市場意向。該等氣候指數有助於投資者利用不同資產類別和投資組合來實踐氣候風險和淨零排放策略（見圖 6）。該等指數可根據公司在低碳經濟中的吸引力以選擇和排除公司，或重新分配權重。指數方法論可納入年度脫碳進程，並考慮企業的減排目標，包括基於科學的目標。基於規則而且透明的指數方法論可應對該等複雜性，並且可以定期改進以納入新的數據集或目標。被動型投資者可能需要該等氣候基準指數以減少或消除碳強度／排放，及增加面向氣候解決方案的敞口。主動型基金經理可能會發現，在財務業績以及氣候風險或足跡（例如碳強度，或對低碳技術和可再生能源供應商的敞口）方面將其策略與氣候指數進行基準比較將會很實用。有關 MSCI 氣候指數方法論的說明，見圖 6。

最新一代的氣候指數能幫助投資者將其投資策略與《巴黎協定》[16]，及「氣候相關財務信息披露工作組」（Task Force on Climate-related Financial Disclosures，簡稱 TCFD）的建議保持一致，支持淨零投資策略。其中某些指數包括了設下特定限制以滿足或超越歐洲監管機構建議的要求，如「MSCI 氣候轉型基準」（MSCI Climate Transition Benchmark）和「歐盟巴黎協定基準」（EU Paris-Aligned Benchmark）。例如，「MSCI 巴黎協定氣候指數」旨在全面應對氣候變化，針對風險與機會，並支持管理權的履行。該等指數超越歐盟巴黎協定基準的最低要求，並納入 TCFD 的建議，例如實體風險。

16　參閱聯合國氣候變化框架公約網站上的〈巴黎協定〉網頁。

圖 6：不同 MSCI 氣候指數的方法論概述

目標	MSCI 指數	低碳轉型評分				氣候風險價值	
		化石燃料	二氧化碳排放	綠色機會	公司目標	實體風險	攝氏 1.5 度一致性*
減少排放	• 低碳 • 剔除化石燃料	●	●				
向低碳經濟轉型	• 氣候變化	●	●	●	●		
氣候影響	• 巴黎協定氣候	●	●	●	●	●	●
氣候主題	• 全球環境			●			

* 基於 MSCI 的攝氏 1.5 度氣候情景壓力測試。

註：「低碳轉型評分」旨在量度公司對低碳轉型相關風險和機會的敞口和管理，以識別潛在的領先者和落後者。氣候風險價值（Value-at-Risk）評估與氣候變化相關的未來成本，以及該等未來成本對當前證券估值的影響。

資料來源：MSCI。氣候數據和指標、氣候風險報告及情景分析由 MSCI ESG Research LLC 提供；MSCI ESG 指數和分析採用的資訊來自 MSCI ESG Research LLC，但並非由 MSCI ESG Research LLC 提供。MSCI 指數和分析是 MSCI Inc. 的產品，並且由 MSCI Limited（UK）管理。

氣候指數（例如 MSCI 氣候指數系列）有助於投資者對沖氣候過渡風險，及指引他們攫取與能源過渡相關的投資機會，從而與「政府間氣候變化專門委員會」（Intergovernmental Panel on Climate Change，簡稱 IPCC）的 1.5 度情景軌跡保持一致。具體而言，巴黎協定基準和氣候轉型基準在其建構過程中均包含自我脫碳進程，其中 MSCI 巴黎協定氣候指數的碳足跡逐年減少 10%，這是一個協助投資者實現淨零目標的重要機制。

MSCI 氣候指數系列包括股票和固定收益氣候指數，這包括 2021 年 4 月推出的 MSCI 巴黎協定固定收益氣候指數系列。

最近的另一個發展是主題指數的擴展，可能有助於投資者把握和利用人口結構變化、技術顛覆和不斷變化的消費者行為作投資，並支持達致某些 ESG 目標。最後，定制指數和可用數據集的興起，為私人投資者提供了選擇，把可持續發展納入其投資組合之中。在 ESG、氣候及 / 或影響力投資方面採用個人化方法的需求將進一步推動相關指數的擴展。

ESG 指數的財務表現

為了方便說明，我們將審視各個 MSCI ESG 指數最長的表現歷史，並且探討兩種假設，即該等指數在此段期間的優異表現從何而來，以及是否存在「ESG 效應」。然後，在第二步中，我們將審視 2020 年新冠肺炎疫情期間的表現以探討該等指數的抗打擊能力。

長期實時追蹤表現

圖 7 顯示各 MSCI 標準 ESG 指數在 ACWI 層面的最長歷史表現[17]。

圖 7：MSCI ACWI ESG 指數系列的實時追蹤相對表現（2013 年 5 月 31 日至 2021 年 2 月 26 日）

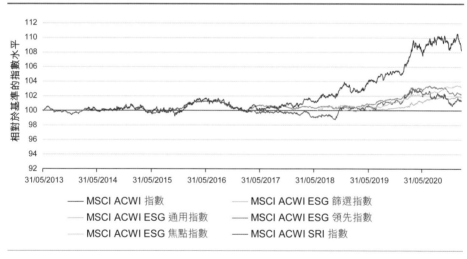

註：

(1) 2013 年 5 月 31 日至 2021 年 2 月 26 日數據。MSCI ESG 篩選指數是一個採用排除篩選法的指數，沒有考慮 MSCI ESG 評級；MSCI ESG 通用指數採用「ESG 權重傾斜」方法；MSCI ESG 領先指數採用「業內最佳的 50%」方法；MSCI SRI 指數採用「業內最佳的 25%」方法；MSCI ESG 聚焦指數採用優化方法，以最大化 ESG 敞口。

(2) 數據顯示各指數的實時追蹤表現：MSCI ACWI ESG 領先指數自 2013 年 6 月 6 日起啟用；MSCI ACWI SRI 指數自 2014 年 3 月 24 日起啟用；MSCI ACWI ESG 通用指數自 2017 年 2 月 8 日起啟用；MSCI ACWI ESG 聚焦指數自 2018 年 6 月 25 日起啟用；MSCI ESG 篩選指數自 2018 年 12 月 14 日起啟用。

資料來源：〈ESG 回報的驅動因素〉（"Drivers of ESG Return"），《MSCI Research Insight》，2021 年 3 月。

17　MSCI ACWI 指數涵蓋 23 個發達市場和 27 個新興市場的 3,000 多隻大中型股票。

ESG 指數相對於基準（MSCI ACWI 指數）的優異表現從何而來？我們研究了兩種可能的假設：

1. 用於建構 MSCI ESG 指數的 MSCI ESG 評級受到在此期間表現優異的股票風格因子所影響[18]。ESG（在剔除股票因子之後）本身就是一個業績因子。

2. 流入 ESG 投資的資金可能推高了 ESG 評級高的公司的股價，從而可能造成價格泡沫。

這兩種想法並不互相矛盾。在實踐中，優異的表現可歸因於這兩種解釋的結合。

我們審視了標準 MSCI ESG 指數的優異表現。我們從前兩種解釋開始，換言之，MSCI ESG 指數的表現在多大程度上可以歸因於其他風格因子，以及是否存在剩餘的「ESG 效應」。我們使用 GEMLT ESG 模型[19]進行了因子歸因分析，其中將 MSCI ESG 評級作為一個因子。表 2 顯示所有標準 MSCI ESG 指數在其各自實時追蹤時段的優異表現。這種優異的表現既可歸因於現有的風格因子，亦可歸因於（在剔除所有其他系統性因子之後）ESG 因子。非預期的主動行業敞口對優異的表現亦有貢獻。

表 2：MSCI ESG 指數實時追蹤表現的主動回報歸因分析

	MSCI ACWI ESG 篩選指數	MSCI ACWI ESG 通用指數	MSCI ACWI ESG 領先指數	MSCI ACWI ESG 聚焦指數	MSCI ACWI SRI 指數
主動敞口總計	**1.54%**	**1.06%**	**-0.03%**	**2.64%**	**5.06%**
特定	0.41%	-0.49%	-2.59%	1.33%	0.91%
行業	0.73%	1.12%	1.27%	0.22%	1.02%
國家	0.27%	-0.41%	-0.03%	-0.14%	-0.79%
貨幣	0.02%	0.19%	0.07%	0.07%	0.22%
風格	0.11%	0.66%	1.25%	1.16%	3.70%
• **ESG**	**0.02%**	**0.58%**	**0.92%**	**1.18%**	**1.58%**
• 其他風格	0.09%	0.08%	0.33%	-0.02%	2.12%
開始日期	31/03/2014	31/12/2018	28/02/2017	30/06/2018	30/06/2013
結束日期	28/02/2021	28/02/2021	28/02/2021	28/02/2021	28/02/2021

資料來源：MSCI。所有業績數據均為年化數字。

甚麼原因導致這種剩餘的 ESG 業績效應？它是否源於 ESG 評級高的公司的估值上升，從而可能導致投資者陷入價格泡沫？

---

18 有關此論點的背景，參閱Kurtz等（2011年）和Madahavan等（2021年）的論文。

19 GEMLT（MSCI Global Total Market Equity Model for Long-Term Investors）是適用於長期投資者的MSCI全球整體市場股票模型。

為了回答這些問題，我們審視了標準 MSCI ESG 指數與基準對比的相對市盈率（P/E）的長期變化（見圖 8）。我們使用市盈率作為估值指標，因為市盈率允許對總回報進行直觀的細分。

圖 8：ESG 指數相對基準的市盈率實時追蹤長期比較（2013 年 5 月 31 日至 2021 年 2 月 26 日）

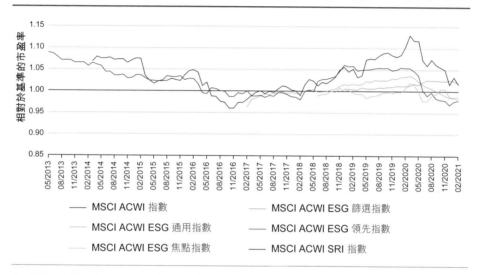

註：2013 年 5 月 31 日至 2021 年 2 月 26 日的數據，為各指數的實時追蹤歷史數據。
資料來源：MSCI。

平均而言，ESG 指數於研究期間內的平均估值高於 MSCI ACWI 指數。然而，估值差異在研究期末段有所減少。人們直覺地會認為 ESG 指數在該期間的後期表現不佳，但實際上，情況恰恰相反。這意味着，ESG 的優異表現無法由相對於基準的估值水平變化來解釋。

為了進一步探討 ESG 對業績的影響，我們使用在之前一項研究[20] 中開發的基本面回報分解模型。該模型將總股票回報分解為三個組成部分：

　　總回報 = 市盈率擴張 + 盈利增長 + 再投資回報

　　其中市盈率擴張表示估值變化，再投資回報包括股息收益率。

該模型使我們能夠了解估值、盈利增長或股息的變化在多大程度上影響回報。

20　Melas等（2019年）。這研究中的模型是基於Kushner（2017 年）提出的模型。

該模型按相關基準（MSCI ACWI 指數）的半年度再平衡來進行回報率分解。於是，我們使研究期與基準再平衡日期保持一致 —— 我們研究的是從 2013 年 5 月 31 日基準再平衡日至 2020 年 11 月 30 日再平衡日的這段期間，這是 MSCI ACWI 指數成份股獲得 MSCI ESG 評級的最長期間。我們對與半年度再平衡期間相一致的 MSCI ESG 指數回報率分解數據作分析[21]。為了將 MSCI ESG 指數與其他因子指數的業績表現相比較，我們又納入了相應的標準 MSCI 因子指數（價值、股息、品質和動量指數），詳見表 3。

表 3：MSCI ESG 指數和因子指數的主動回報分解

	市盈率擴張（%）	盈利增長（%）	再投資回報（%）	主動回報（%）
MSCI ACWI 價值加權指數	6.85	-10.14	0.48	-2.81
MSCI ACWI 高紅利指數	3.16	-7.73	1.59	-2.98
MSCI ACWI 品質指數	3.45	0.65	-0.35	3.74
MSCI ACWI 動量指數	-3.98	9.07	-0.73	4.36
MSCI ACWI SRI 指數	-0.96	2.09	0.02	1.16
MSCI ACWI ESG 領先指數	-1.61	1.79	0.02	0.21
MSCI ACWI ESG 通用指數	-0.78	1.18	0.03	0.43

註：2013 年 5 月 31 日至 2020 年 11 月 30 日（最後一次基準再平衡日期）的數據。
資料來源：MSCI。

與 MSCI ACWI 指數相比，所有 MSCI ACWI ESG 指數表現優異的主要來源是更高的盈利增長，而市盈率擴張的貢獻低於母指數。這意味着，在研究期間，MSCI ESG 指數的優異表現並非由估值水平上升（暗示價格泡沫）所驅動，而是由更高的盈利增長所驅動。

表 3 中的因子指數回報分解結果與 Kushner（2017 年）的發現相一致：MSCI ACWI 動量指數的主動回報主要來源是盈利增長，而 MSCI ACWI 價值加權指數和 MSCI ACWI 品質指數的主動回報的主要來源是市盈率擴張。不出意料的是，MSCI 高紅利指數是從再投資回報中獲得強勁主動回報貢獻的唯一一隻指數。

21　我們在分析中排除 MSCI ACWI ESG 篩選指數和 MSCI ACWI ESG 聚焦指數，因為前者不使用 MSCI ESG 評級，而後者的季度再平衡頻率與該模型使用作回報率分解的半年度期間並不一致。

綜合上述結果，MSCI ESG 指數在實時追蹤時段內的優異表現乃來自 ESG 和其他風格因子。與母指數相比，ESG 帶來的業績影響與估值水平的上升無關，而是與盈利增長顯著相關。[22]

新冠肺炎疫情期間的 ESG 指數表現

MSCI 早前的研究[23] 發現，MSCI ESG 評級高的公司面對較小的系統性風險，因此在 2006 年年底至 2017 年的研究期間，這些公司對於衝擊的抵禦能力勝於 MSCI 世界指數。新冠肺炎爆發卻是自 2008 年全球金融危機以來，對 MSCI ESG 評級高的公司在現實世界的抗打擊能力的第一次考驗。

圖 9 顯示標準的全球 MSCI ESG 股票指數系列與其 MSCI ACWI 母指數於 2020 年的相對表現 —— 包括 2020 年 2 月和 3 月的市場崩盤以及隨後的市場反彈。有趣的是，在市場崩盤期間，所有 MSCI ESG 指數均表現出色，並且除了 MSCI ACWI ESG 領先指數外，所有指數一整年期間在市場反彈時均持續跑贏母指數[24]。

---

22 欲進一步了解亞洲和中國 ESG 指數的表現，請參閱《責任投資原則》(PRI)〈ESG 和超額收益：在中國整合 ESG 的主流論點〉("ESG and alpha: the mainstream argument for ESG integration in China")，載於《PRI》的網站，2020年3月18日；或 MSCI 研究部〈在新興市場和亞洲整合ESG〉("Integrating ESG in emerging markets and Asia")，載於 MSCI 的網站，2020年3月18日。

23 G. Giese、H. D. Varsani 與 R. Mendiratta〈公司債券ESG投資的基礎〉("Foundations of ESG investing in corporate bonds")，載於MSCI的網站，2020年11月11日。

24 參閱 Z. Nagy 與 G. Giese〈新冠肺炎危機期間的MSCI ESG指數〉("MSCI ESG Indices during the coronavirus crisis")，載於MSCI 的網站，2020年4月22日。

圖 9：MSCI ESG 指數於 2020 年的相對表現

註：2019 年 12 月 31 日至 2020 年 12 月 31 日的數據。

資料來源：MSCI。

為了深入了解該等指數在新冠肺炎疫情期間的表現，我們進行了類似於上一節的因子歸因分析，以找出與 MSCI ESG 評級相關的業績影響。圖 10 顯示於 2020 年可由 MSCI ESG 評級解釋的 MSCI ESG 指數的業績影響（即在剔除其他系統性因子之後的業績影響）。這表明 MSCI ESG 評級對 2020 年所有 MSCI ESG 指數的業績均作出了正面貢獻。

圖 10：MSCI ESG 評級於 2020 年的主動回報貢獻

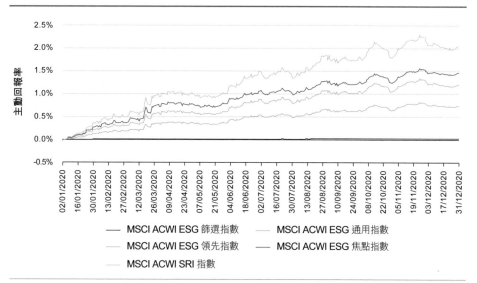

註：2019 年 12 月 31 日至 2020 年 12 月 31 日的數據。

資料來源：MSCI。

各區域的分析結果

我們現在檢視同一組 ESG 指數在區域層面（世界和新興市場）和次區域層面（美國、歐洲和太平洋區）的表現，以了解它們於 2020 年新冠肺炎危機期間的表現。從圖 11 中可以看到相關結果，該圖顯示基準指數（x 軸）的表現與不同的區域性 MSCI ESG 指數（y 軸）相對於基準指數的表現。值得一提的是，所有區域的標準 MSCI ESG 指數的表現於 2020 年皆優於其相應基準指數，只有一個例外，即 MSCI 美國 ESG 領先指數，該指數於 2020 年稍遜於其相應基準指數。

圖 11：區域性 MSCI ESG 指數相對於其基準指數的表現

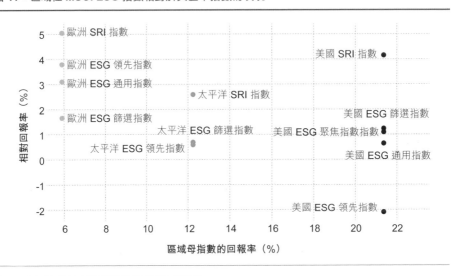

註：2019 年 12 月 31 日至 2020 年 12 月 31 日的數據。

資料來源：G. Giese 等（2018 年）〈了解 ESG 指數〉（" Understanding ESG indices"），《MSCI Product Insight》。

ESG 和氣候指數的發展展望

正如第一部分所述，ESG 指數在支持將 ESG 整合至機構投資組合方面發揮了重要作用。我們認為，在以下數個趨勢的支持下，市場對 ESG 和氣候指數的需求將會持續上升：

可持續投資的增長

根據晨星編製的數據，截至 2020 年 12 月，ESG 資產達到 1.6 萬億美元。隨着機構、散戶與新一代投資者擁抱這個趨勢，預計 ESG ETF 資產到 2030 年將達到 1.2 萬億美元[25]。疫情加強了在建構投資組合過程中須考慮 ESG 因素的必要性。

---

25 〈貝萊德的地球日預測：全球可持續發展ETF的資產到2030年將達到1.2萬億美元〉（" BlackRock's earth day forecast: $1.2 trillion in global sustainable ETF assets by 2030"），載於《巴倫週刊》（Barron）網站，2020年 4月22日。

氣候變化

氣候變化是我們這一代人的決定性風險，它將重塑經濟和資本分配方式。世界各地的投資者對其投資組合以及各地政府對其經濟都正在進行壓力測試，以評估與氣候變化相關的風險和機會。TCFD 的匯報標準和投資者組織（例如「淨零資產所有者聯盟」（Net Zero Asset Owner Alliance）或「機構投資者氣候變化組織」（Institutional Investors Group on Climate Change））正在領導各方量度風險、減少排放，以及使投資組合與巴黎協定的目標保持一致，並且就此提供指引。

淨零排放目標是一種特殊類型的脫碳目標，即公司旨在將其溫室氣體排放淨額降至零。「淨」的用語基於一個事實：實際上大多數公司必定會在某程度上排放溫室氣體，否則無法經營。因此，它們通常需要透過碳抵銷或碳消除來補償餘下不可避免的排放量。

監管規則和非監管性的地區標準

日益增多的自願性和強制性監管意味着 ESG 的意識正成為新常態。在亞太地區，機構投資者採用 ESG 時會將監管視為首要的趨勢[26]。在這方面，香港聯合交易所於 2020 年推出新的強制性 ESG 披露要求，預計中國內地將在 2021 年推出新的 ESG 披露法規，並且繼歐盟可持續金融分類標準條例（2020 年 7 月）和歐盟可持續金融披露條例（2021 年 3 月）之後，中國人民銀行和歐盟已在 2021 年發佈通用綠色分類標準。

這些趨勢表明，投資者對 ESG 和氣候指數的需求會不斷增加，以使其 ESG 和氣候的相關政策與其基準保持一致，並協助他們將嶄新而且複雜的可持續發展議題納入到被動和主動型投資組合，以及跨資產類別的投資流程之中。

26　資料來源：《MSCI Investment Insights 2021: 全球機構投資者調查》。

參考資料

G. Giese、L. E. Lee、D. Melas、Z. Nagy 與 L. Nishikawa（2019 年）〈ESG 投資的基礎：ESG 如何影響股票估值、風險和業績〉（"Foundations of ESG investing: How ESG affects equity valuation, risk and performance"），載於《投資組合管理雜誌》（*Journal of Portfolio Management*），第 45 (5) 卷，69-83 頁。

L. Kurtz 與 D. DiBartolomeo（2011 年）〈社會投資領域的長期表現〉（"The long-term performance of a social investment universe"），載於《投資雜誌》（*Journal of Investing*），第 20 (3) 卷，95-102 頁。

J. Kushner（2017 年）〈兩類因子：因子投資組合的回報分解〉（"Two types of factors: A return decomposition for factor portfolios"），載於《投資組合管理雜誌》（*Journal of Portfolio Management*），第 43 (4) 卷，17-32 頁。

A. Madhavan、A. Sobczyk 與 A. Ang（2021 年）〈創造 ESG 超額收益：透過因子角度分析 ESG 敞口〉（"Toward ESG alpha: Analyzing ESG exposures through a factor lens"），載於《金融分析師雜誌》（*Financial Analysts Journal*），第 77 (1) 卷，69-88 頁。

R. Mahmood〈基金 ESG 透明度：2021 年季度報告〉（"Fund ESG transparency: Quarterly Report 2021"），《MSCI Research Insight》。

D. Melas、G. Giese、R. Kouzmenko、A. Bhat、N. Kumar、Z. Nagy 與 P. Taranenko（2019 年）〈全球上市股票市場的某些地域問題〉（"Selected geographic issues in the global listed equity market"），《MSCI Research Insight》，為挪威財政部編寫。

註：本文原稿是英文，另以中文譯本出版。如本文的中文本的字義或詞義與英文本有所出入，概以英文本為準。